THE
MICHELIN
GUIDE
HONG KONG
MACAU
2015

RESTAURANTS

& HOTELS

米芝蓮指南
香港 澳門 2015
餐廳及酒店

CONTENTS

目錄

香港

■RESTAURANTS 餐廳

■酒店

澳門

■餐廳

■酒店

地圖

DEAR READER

We are delighted to present the 2015 edition of the MICHELIN Guide Hong Kong Macau.

Hong Kong and Macau enjoy a worldwide reputation for the breadth and dynamism of their dining scenes. Our recommendations within these pages bring you the best of virtually every kind of establishment in every price band – all have been selected, first and foremost, for the quality of their cooking. So, whether you want congee for lunch or Cantonese for dinner, a restaurant with a view or one with a private room, you'll find plenty of places from which to choose.

Every one of the establishments in this guide has been selected by our team of local, full-time Michelin inspectors and only the best have made it through! The inspectors are the eyes and ears of our readers; they always pay their own bills and their anonymity is key to ensuring that they receive the same treatment as any other guest.

Our famous Michelin Stars ❀ are awarded to restaurants with exceptional cooking but they are not our only award – look out for the Bib Gourmands ❀. These are places where you can enjoy a carefully prepared but simpler style of cooking for under $300. We're pleased to say we've kept this price limit the same for yet another year and have found many new 'Bibs' for you to try.

As well as restaurants, our independent inspectors have also chosen a selection of the best hotels, ranging from the stylish and intimate to the grand and luxurious. All these hotels underline the region's reputation for the quality of its accommodation.

We are always very interested to hear what you, our readers, think. Your opinions and suggestions matter greatly to us and help shape the guide, so please do get in touch.

You can email us at michelinguide.hongkong-macau@cn.michelin.com

We hope you enjoy all your dining and hotel experiences.

Bon appétit!

親愛的讀者

很高興能為廣大讀者呈獻2015香港澳門米芝蓮指南。

香港和澳門是美食匯聚之都,含蘊豐富的飲食文化在全球享負盛名。本指南內推薦的餐廳種類涵蓋範圍甚廣,從簡單的粥麵店到傳統廣粵菜式,至奢華高檔的食府一應俱全,且全是萬裡挑一的傑出食肆,食物質素無庸置疑。

本指南內推薦的餐廳全部經過本地全職米芝蓮評審員團隊精心挑選,只有最佳的食店才獲推介。為確保經驗到與一般顧客同等的服務待遇,讓評審結果更客觀公正,我們的評審員只會以匿名身份到訪各大食肆。

除了聞名遐邇的米芝蓮星級 ❀ 食肆推介予那些食物質素特佳的食店外,還有車胎人 ⓦ 美食推介。車胎人美食推介推薦的是裝潢簡單、烹調和選料用心卻價格相宜,收費不到HK$300的食店。本年度的車胎人美食推介數量亦作了調整,企能為讀者帶來更多選擇。

與餐廳食肆一樣,米芝蓮評審員團隊在芸芸酒店中挑選了一系列優質酒店,推薦給廣大讀者。從時尚型格到優雅舒適,以致豪華典雅,各個級別和風格的酒店無不包含。指南內的酒店推薦名單充分反映了港澳兩地豐富多彩的優質酒店文化。

我們向來重視讀者的回饋,渴望聆聽閣下的意見。如閣下對本指南有任何意見或提議,歡迎電郵至 michelinguide.hongkong-macau@cn.michelin.com 把您的心聲告訴我們。

祝閣下在香港和澳門擁有愉快的美食和住宿體驗!

Bon appétit!

THE MICHELIN GUIDE'S COMMITMENTS

"This volume was created at the turn of the century and will last at least as long".

This foreword to the very first edition of the MICHELIN Guide, written in 1900, has become famous over the years and the guide has lived up to the prediction. It is read across the world and the key to its popularity is the consistency of its commitment to its readers, which is based on the following promises:

Anonymous inspections:
Our inspectors make regular and anonymous visits to restaurants and hotels to gauge the quality of the products and services offered to an ordinary customer. They settle their own bill and may then introduce themselves and ask for more information about the establishment. Our readers' comments are also a valuable source of information, which we can then follow up with another visit of our own.

Independence:
Our choice of establishments is a completely independent one, made for the benefit of our readers alone. The decisions to be taken are discussed around the table by the inspectors and the editor. Inclusion in the guide is completely free of charge.

Selection and choice:
Our guide offers a selection of the best restaurants and hotels. This is only possible because all the inspectors rigorously apply the same methods.

Annual Updates:
All the practical information, the classifications and awards are revised and updated every single year to give the most reliable information possible.

Consistency:
The criteria for the classifications are the same in every country covered by the MICHELIN Guide.

...And our aim:
To do everything possible to make travel, holidays and eating out a pleasure, as part of Michelin's ongoing commitment to improving travel and mobility.

承諾

「這冊書於世紀交替時創辦，亦將繼續傳承下去。」

這是1900年首冊米芝蓮指南的前言，多年來享負盛名，並如預期般一直傳承下去。指南在世界各地均大受歡迎，關鍵在其秉承一貫宗旨，履行對讀者的承諾。

匿名評審

我們的評審員以匿名方式定期到訪餐廳和酒店，以一般顧客的身份對餐廳和酒店的食品和服務質素作出評估。評審員自行結賬後，在需要時會介紹自己，並會詳細詢問有關餐廳或酒店的資料。讀者的評語和推薦也是寶貴的資訊來源，我們會根據讀者的推薦親身到訪。

獨立性

餐廳的評選完全基於我們獨立的決定，純以讀者利益為依歸。經評審員和編輯一同討論後才作出決定，亦不會向收錄在指南內的餐廳和酒店收取任何費用。

選擇

全賴一眾評審員使用一致的嚴謹評選方法，本指南才能向讀者推介一系列最佳餐廳和酒店。

每年更新

所有實用資訊、分類及評級每年都會修訂和更新，務求為讀者提供最可靠的資料。

一致性

每個國家地區的米芝蓮指南均採用相同的評審和分類準則。

我們的目標

盡全力令旅遊、假期及外出用膳成為一大樂事，實踐米芝蓮一貫優化旅遊和生活的承諾。

ONCE UPON A TIME,
IN THE HEART OF FRANCE...

It all started way back in 1889, in Clermont-Ferrand, when the Michelin brothers founded the Manufacture Française des Pneumatiques Michelin tyre company – this was at a time when driving was considered quite an adventure!

In 1900, fewer than 3,000 cars existed in France. The Michelin brothers hit upon the idea of creating a small guide packed with useful information for the new pioneers of the road, such as where to fill up with petrol or change a tyre, as well as where to eat and sleep. The MICHELIN Guide was born!

The purpose of the guide was obvious: to track down the best hotels and restaurants across the country. To do this, Michelin employed a veritable armada of anonymous professional inspectors to scour every region – something that had never before been attempted!

Over the years, bumpy roads were replaced by smoother highways and the company continued to develop, as indeed did the country's cuisine: cooks became chefs, artisans developed into artists, and traditional dishes were transformed into works of art. All the while, the MICHELIN Guide, by now a faithful travel companion, kept pace with – and encouraged – these changes. The most famous distinction awarded by the guide was created in 1926: the "étoile de bonne table" – the famous star which quickly established itself as the reference in the world of gastronomy!

Bibendum – the famous tyre-clad Michelin Man – continued to widen his reach and by 1911, the guide covered the whole of Europe.

In 2006, the collection crossed the Atlantic, awarding stars to 39 restaurants in New York. In 2007 and 2008, the guide moved on

to San Francisco, Los Angeles and Las Vegas, and in 2011 it was the turn of Chicago to have its own Michelin guide – The Michelin Man had become truly American!

In November 2007, The Michelin Man took his first steps in Asia: in recognition of the excellence of Japanese cuisine, stars rained down on Tokyo, which was gripped by culinary fever! A guide to Kyoto, Kobe, Osaka and Nara followed, with Yokohama andhonan then joining Tokyo.

Hong Kong and Macau arrived in 2009, putting the Red Guide firmly on the map in the Far East. Today the collection covers 24 titles in 24 countries, with over 30 million copies sold in a century. Quite a record!

Meanwhile, the search continues... Looking for a delicious pot-au-feu in a typical Parisian bistro, or a soothing bowl of congee in Hong Kong? The Michelin Man continues to span the globe making new discoveries and selecting the very best the culinary world has to offer!

從前，在法國中部……

這一切始於1889年，米芝蓮兄弟在法國克萊蒙費朗(Clermont-Ferrand)創辦Manufacture Française des Pneumatiques Michelin 輪胎公司 - 當年駕駛汽車仍被視為一大冒險。

在1900年，法國的汽車總數量少於3,000輛。米芝蓮兄弟靈機一觸，想到為道路駕駛的先驅提供含實用資訊的小指南，如補充汽油或更換輪胎，以至用餐和睡覺的好去處。米芝蓮指南就這樣誕生了！

　　　　指南的宗旨非常清晰：搜羅全國各地最好的酒店和餐廳。為達目的，米芝蓮招攬了一整隊神秘專業評審員，走遍全國每一個角落尋找值得推介的酒店和餐廳，這在當時是前所未有的創舉。

多年來，崎嶇不平的道路早已被平順的高速公路所取代，米芝蓮公司持續茁壯成長。同時間，全國各地餐飲業的發展亦一日千里：廚子成為大廚、傳統手藝成為藝術，傳統菜餚亦轉化成為藝術傑作。現今米芝蓮指南已成為廣受信賴的旅遊夥伴，不僅與時並進，更致力推動這些轉變。指南中最著名的是早在1926年面世，並迅即成為美食界權威指標的「星級推介」。

由The Michelin Man「米芝蓮車胎人」Bibendum 為代言人的米芝蓮指南,不斷拓展其版圖,到1911年已覆蓋全歐洲。

2006年,米芝蓮指南系列成功跨越大西洋,授予紐約39家餐廳星級推介。在2007及2008年,米芝蓮指南在三藩市、洛杉磯和

拉斯維加斯出版,2011年已拓展至芝加哥,The Michelin Man「米芝蓮車胎人」Bibendum也正式落戶美國。

2007年11月,The Michelin Man「米芝蓮車胎人」首次踏足亞洲,在東京廣發星級推介,以表揚日本料理的卓越成就,同時亦掀起美食熱潮。其後,旋即推出京都、神戶、大阪及奈良指南,並繼東京之後推出橫濱和湘南指南。

香港和澳門指南亦於2009年推出,令這本以紅色為標誌的指南,在遠東地區的覆蓋範圍更見廣泛。

時至今日,米芝蓮指南系列共計24本,涵蓋24個國家,一個世紀以來,總銷量超過三千萬。這是個令人鼓舞的紀錄!

此時此刻,我們仍然繼續對美食的追尋……是巴黎餐廳的美味雜菜鍋,還是香港令人窩心的粥品?The Michelin Man「米芝蓮車胎人」將會努力不懈,發掘全球美食,為你們挑選最出色的佳餚美饌!

HOW TO USE
THIS RESTAURANT GUIDE
如何使用餐廳指南

Map number / coordinates
地圖號碼 / 座標

New entry in the guide
新增推介

Cuisine type
菜式種類

Name of restaurant
餐廳名稱

Stars for good food
美食星級
☆ to ☆☆☆

Bib Gourmand
(Inspectors' favourite
for good value)
(評審員的推介榜)

Restaurant classification
according to comfort
餐廳 — 以舒適程度分類

Particularly pleasant if in red
紅色代表上佳

	Simple shop 簡單的食店
X	Quite comfortable 頗舒適
XX	Comfortable 舒適
XXX	Very comfortable 十分舒適
XXXX	Top class comfort 高級舒適
XXXXX	Luxury 豪華

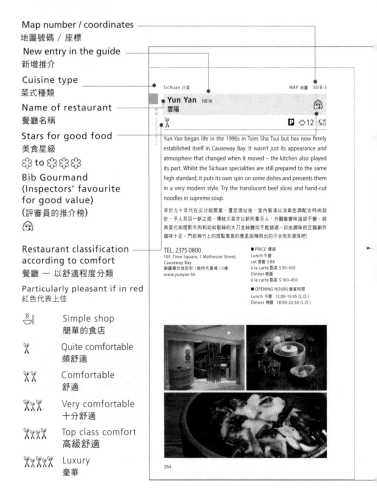

Sichuan 川菜   MAP 地圖 30/B-3

Yun Yan NEW
雲陽

🅿 ⇆12 ℃𝄞

Yun Yan began life in the 1990s in Tsim Sha Tsui but has now firmly established itself in Causeway Bay. It wasn't just its appearance and atmosphere that changed when it moved – the kitchen also played its part. Whilst the Sichuan specialities are still prepared to the same high standard, it puts its own spin on some dishes and presents them in a very modern style. Try the translucent beef slices and hand-cut noodles in supreme soup.

早於九十年代在尖沙咀開業，遷至現址後，室內裝潢以淡素色調配合時尚設計，予人耳目一新之感。傳統川菜亦以新形象示人，外觀雖變味道卻不變。經典菜式如燈影牛肉和幼如髮絲的大刀金絲麵均不能錯過。自由調味的豆腦創作趣味十足。門前湘竹上的斑點寓意的應是因辣而出的汗水而非淚珠吧！

TEL. 2375 0800
10F, Time Square, 1 Matheson Street,
Causeway Bay
銅鑼灣勿地臣街 1 號時代廣場 10 樓
www.yunyan.hk

■ PRICE 價錢
Lunch 午膳
set 套餐 $ 88
à la carte 點菜 $ 90-450
Dinner 晚膳
à la carte 點菜 $ 160-450

● OPENING HOURS 營業時間
Lunch 午膳 12:00-15:45 (L.O.)
Dinner 晚膳 18:00-22:30 (L.O.)

354

Restaurant promoted to a Bib Gourmand or Star
評級有所晉升的餐廳

Cantonese 粵菜   MAP 地圖 25/C-3

Duddell's 🍃 ❀❀

🍴🍴   ⌂12 ©🍴 🍷

Art and food have been inexorably linked since bison first appeared in Palaeolithic cave drawings. Here at Duddell's, art, culture and cuisine all come together over two bright, stylish floors which also host regular exhibitions, screenings and performances. In contrast to the contemporary look of the space, the Cantonese cooking is based on traditional methods, although the kitchen's skill is obvious and the quality of the ingredients palpable.

你或會讚歎鮮黃的長沙發、簡約時尚的硬木傢具和中國水墨畫，竟能如此協調和諧。由名廚主理的美食走的是樸實路線，以頂級材料配合傳統烹調技術與廚師那細緻的功夫製作食物，一點也不花巧。這間位於都爹利街的新餐館除了展現美食與藝術的結合外，亦是一種生活態度。

TEL. 2525 9191
Level 3, Shanghai Tang Mansion,
1 Duddell Street, Central
中環都爹利街 1 號上海灘 3 樓
www.duddells.co

■ PRICE 價錢
Lunch 午膳
set 套餐 $ 350
à la carte 點菜 $ 400-1,500
Dinner 晚膳
set 套餐 $ 980
à la carte 點菜 $ 600-1,500

■ OPENING HOURS 營業時間
Lunch 午膳 12:00-14:30 (L.O.)
Dinner 晚膳 18:00-22:30 (L.O.)

157

Restaurant symbols
餐廳標誌

💲	Cash only	只收現金
♿	Wheelchair access	輪椅適用
☂	Terrace dining	陽台用餐
⋞	Interesting view	上佳景觀
🔑	Valet parking	代客泊車
🅿	Car park	停車場
⌂25	Private room with maximum capacity	私人房間及容納人數
🚃	Counter	櫃枱式
©🍴	Reservations required	需訂座
⊘🍴	Reservations not accepted	不設訂座
🍷	Interesting wine list	供應優良的酒類

13

HOW TO USE
THIS HOTEL GUIDE
如何使用酒店指南

Map number / coordinates
地圖號碼 / 座標

New entry in the guide
新增推介

Name of hotel
酒店名稱

Hotel classification
according to comfort
酒店 — 根據舒適程度分類

Particularly pleasant if in red
紅色代表上佳

	Quite comfortable 頗舒適
	Comfortable 舒適
	Very comfortable 十分舒適
	Top class comfort 高級舒適
	Luxury 豪華

Restaurants
recommended in
MICHELIN Guide
米芝蓮指南內的推薦餐廳

MAP 地圖 26/B-1

The Pottinger NEW
中環 · 石板街

Standing in the middle of Central, and on one of Hong Kong's oldest 'stone slab streets', is this elegant and stylish hotel. Its location is celebrated through its collection of iconic and historic photographs taken by award-winning artist Fan Ho. The 68 bedrooms are contemporary and graceful and boast all the amenities the modern traveller expects.

位於有過百年歷史的砵甸乍街（又名石板街）旁邊，故以此命名。斜斜的石板路見證了中環百多年來的故事，也為酒店增添了一分魅力。接待廳牆小鄒流露着歐陸優雅格調，共有68間客房，面積適中、設備很齊全。位處中環心臟地帶，無論往辦公、飲食、娛樂或乘搭交通工具都非便利，是商務住宿的理想選擇。

TEL. 2308 3188
74 Queen's Road Central, Central
中環皇后大道中 74號
www.thepottinger.com

♦ = $ 2,900-4,100
♦♦ = $ 2,900-4,100
Suites 套房 = $ 5,400-18,000

Rooms 客房 61
Suites 套房 7

RECOMMENDED RESTAURANTS 餐廳推薦
Holytan Grill 葆里湛 ♔♔

Grand Hyatt
君悅

♿ ≼ 🔑 🅿 🚗 🚭 🧑 🏊 🏊 Spa 💪 $

With its striking 22m ceiling and fabulous artwork, the lobby sets the tone – the droplets appear to be falling from a cloud. The contemporary bedrooms are split between two towers. Along with contemporary and luxurious suites, the Grand Club on the top floor provides a dining service where customers can order any kind of cuisine they choose.

君悅酒店是「新濠天地」城市度假村一部份，設有賭場、商場及一系列餐廳與酒店，以水為主題。22米高的天花、藝術品，配合恰似從天上雲層落下的水點打造出格調獨特的酒店大堂。設計時尚的房間分佈於兩棟大樓內。室外庭園Mezza9為顧客提供九種不同餐點。

TEL. 8868 1234
FAX. 8867 1234
City of Dreams, Estrada do Istmo, Cotai
路氹連貫公路新濠天地
www.macau.grand.hyatt.com

RECOMMENDED RESTAURANTS 餐廳推薦
Beijing Kitchen 滿堂彩 ⅩⅩ
Mezza9 ⅩⅩ

🧍 = MOP 1,888-3,888
🧍🧍 = MOP1,888-3,888
Suites 套房 = MOP 2,300-13,000
☕ = MOP 228

Rooms 客房 503
Suites 套房 288

472

Hotel symbols
酒店標誌

♿	Wheelchair access 輪椅適用
≼	Interesting view 上佳景觀
🔑	Valet parking 代客泊車
🅿	Car park 室外停車場
🚗	Garage 室內停車場
🚭	Non smoking rooms 非吸煙房室
🧑	Conference rooms 會議室
🏊 🏊	Outdoor/Indoor swimming pool 室外 / 室內游泳池
Spa	Spa 水療
💪	Exercise room 健身室
$	Casino 娛樂場

Michelin is committed to improving the mobility of travellers

ON EVERY ROAD AND BY EVERY MEANS

Since the company came into being – over a century ago – Michelin has had a single objective: to offer people a better way forward. A technological challenge first, to create increasingly efficient tyres, but also an ongoing commitment to travellers, to help them travel in the best way. This is why Michelin is developing a whole collection of products and services: from maps, atlases, travel guides and auto accessories, to mobile apps, route planners and on-line assistance: Michelin is doing everything it can ~ke travelling more

A tyre...
➡ what is it?

Round, black, supple yet solid, the tyre is to the wheel what the shoe is to the foot. But what is it made of? First and foremost, rubber, but also various textile and/or metallic materials... and then it's filled with air! It is the skilful assembly of all these components that ensures tyres have the qualities they should: grip to the road, shock absorption, in two words: 'comfort' and 'safety'.

1 TREAD
The tread ensures the tyre performs correctly, by dispersing water, providing grip and increasing longevity.

2 CROWN PLIES
This reinforced double or triple belt combines vertical suppleness with transversal rigidity, enabling the tyre to remain flat to the road.

3 SIDEWALLS
These link all the component parts and provide symmetry. They enable the tyre to absorb shock, thus giving a smooth ride.

4 BEADS
The bead wires ensure that the tyre is fixed securely to the wheel to ensure safety.

5 INNER LINER
The inner liner creates an airtight seal between the wheel rim and the tyre.

Michelin
⇒ *innovation in movement*

Created and patented by Michelin in 1946, the belted radial-ply tyre revolutionised the world of tyres. But Michelin did not stop there: over the years other new and original solutions came out, confirming Michelin's position as a leader in research and innovation.

⇒ *the right pressure!*

One of Michelin's priorities is safer mobility. In short, innovating for a better way forward. This is the challenge for researchers, who are working to perfect tyres capable of shorter braking distances and offering the best possible traction to the road. And so, to support motorists, Michelin organises road safety awareness campaigns all over the world: «Fill up with air» initiatives remind everyone that the right tyre pressure is a crucial factor in safety and fuel economy.

The Michelin strategy:
→ *multi-performance tyres*

Michelin is synonymous with safety, fuel saving and the capacity to cover thousands of miles. A MICHELIN tyre is the embodiment of all these things – thanks to our engineers, who work with the very latest technology.

Their challenge: to equip every tyre – whatever the vehicle (car, truck, tractor, bulldozer, plane, motorbike, bicycle or train!) – with the best possible combination of qualities, for optimal overall performance.

Slowing down wear, reducing energy expenditure (and therefore CO_2 emissions), improving safety through enhanced road handling and braking: there are so many qualities in just one tyre – that's Michelin Total Performance.

MICHELIN
Total Performance

Every day, **Michelin** is
working towards
sustainable
mobility

OVER TIME,
WHILE
RESPECTING
THE PLANET

Sustainable mobility
⇒ *is clean mobility... and mobility for everyone*

Sustainable mobility means enabling people to get around in a way that is cleaner, safer, more economical and more accessible to everyone, wherever they might live. Every day, Michelin's 113 000 employees worldwide are innovating:

• by creating tyres and services that meet society's new needs,

• by raising young people's awareness of road safety,

• by inventing new transport solutions that consume less energy and emit less CO_2.

⇒ *Michelin Challenge Bibendum*

Sustainable mobility means allowing the transport of goods and people to continue, while promoting responsible economic, social and societal development. Faced with the increasing scarcity of raw materials and global warming, Michelin is standing up for the environment and public health. Michelin regularly organises 'Michelin Challenge Bibendum', the only event in the world which focuses on sustainable road travel.

ACQUA PANNA
THE FINE DINING WATERS
S.PELLEGRINO

ACQUA PANNA

NATURAL MINERAL WATER

Bottled at the source in Tuscany, Italy.

Thanks to its smooth and velvety taste, Acqua Panna is the ideal complement to the finest meals.

BOTTLED AT THE SOURCE, SAN PELLEGRINO TER

S.PELLEGRI

SPARKLING NATURAL MINERAL W

MINERAL WATER WITH NATURAL CARBONATION (CO_2) ADDED • TOTAL DISSO

NET 33.8 fl. oz. (1 Qt., 1.8 fl. oz.) 1 L

HONG KONG
香港

RESTAURANTS
餐廳

STARRED RESTAURANTS
星級餐廳

Within this selection, we have highlighted a number of restaurants for their particularly good cooking. When awarding one, two or three Michelin Stars there are a number of factors we consider: the quality and compatibility of the ingredients, the technical skill and flair that goes into their preparation, the clarity and combination of flavours, the value for money and above all, the taste. Equally important is the ability to produce excellent cooking not once but time and time again. Our inspectors make as many visits as necessary, so that you can be sure of the quality and consistency.

A two or three star restaurant has to offer something very special that separates it from the rest. Three stars – our highest award – are given to the very best.

Cuisines in any style of restaurant and of any nationality are eligible for a star. The decoration, service and comfort levels have no bearing on the award.

在這系列的選擇裡，我們特意指出菜式上佳的餐廳。給予一、二或三粒米芝蓮星時，我們考慮到以下因素：材料的質素和配搭、烹調技巧和特色、氣味濃度和組合、價錢是否相宜及味道。同樣重要的是能夠持續提供美食。我們的評審員會因應需要而多次到訪，所以讀者可肯定食物品質和一致性。

二或三星餐廳必有獨特之處，比其他餐廳更出眾。最高評級－三星－尸只會給予最好的餐廳。

不論餐廳的風格如何，供應哪個國家的菜式，都可獲星級。餐廳陳設、服務及舒適程度亦不會影響評級。

✿✿✿

Exceptional cuisine, worth a special journey.
出類拔萃的菜餚，值得專程到訪。

One always eats here extremely well, sometimes superbly.
Distinctive dishes are precisely executed, using superlative ingredients.

食客可在這裏享用以最高級的材料和細膩的廚藝烹調的獨特菜式，美味的菜餚，偶爾令人讚不絕口。

Bo Innovation		XxX	Innovative 創新菜	78
L'Atelier de Joël Robuchon		XX	French contemporary 時尚法國菜	167
Lung King Heen 龍景軒		XxxX	Cantonese 粵菜	188
8½ Otto e Mezzo - Bombana		XxxX	Italian 意大利菜	211
Sushi Shikon 志魂		X	Sushi 壽司	254

✿✿

Excellent cuisine, worth a detour.
傑出美食，值得繞道前往。

Skilfully and carefully crafted dishes of outstanding quality.

具烹調技巧且用心製作的菜餚，品質優秀。

Amber		XxxX	French contemporary 時尚法國菜	70
Caprice		XxxxX	French 法國菜	84
Celebrity Cuisine 名人坊		XX	Cantonese 粵菜	86
Duddell's 都爹利會館	⅋	XX	Cantonese 粵菜	113
Pierre		XxxX	French contemporary 時尚法國菜	217
Ryu Gin 天空龍吟		XX	Japanese 日本菜	222
Shang Palace 香宮		XxxX	Cantonese 粵菜	231
Summer Palace 夏宮		XxX	Cantonese 粵菜	247
Sun Tung Lok (Tsim Sha Tsui) 新同樂 (尖沙咀)		XxX	Cantonese 粵菜	250
T'ang Court 唐閣		XxxX	Cantonese 粵菜	259
The Principal	⅋	XxX	Innovative 創新菜	269
Tin Lung Heen 天龍軒		XxxxX	Cantonese 粵菜	278
Wagyu Takumi		XX	Innovative 創新菜	288
Yan Toh Heen 欣圖軒	⅋	XxxX	Cantonese 粵菜	298

A very good restaurant in its category.
同類別中出眾的餐廳。

A place offering cuisine prepared to a consistently high standard.
恆常保持高水準的餐廳。

NEW : New entry in the guide 新增推介
ッ : Restaurant promoted to a Bib Gourmand or Star 評級有所晉升的餐廳

美 食 薈 萃 @ 海 港 城

位處香港的中心,毗鄰維多利亞港,海港城是香港領先的商場,匯集超過四百五十間不同類型的商店、五十多間中外餐廳、三間星級酒店、兩大電影院以及美術館。除了於廣東道的十多個國際頂尖時裝品牌旗艦店和場內多個世界著名品牌外,我們亦有米芝蓮推介餐廳和超過二十間飽覽維港美景餐廳,為大家提供與別不同的一站式時尚購物、美食享受及精彩娛樂體驗。

海港城現誠邀所有「知味」之友於商場內餐廳用餐時拍攝美食,將相片以 **#hcfood** 為主題標籤及於該餐廳簽到,並於Instagram分享。追尋城中「知味」,齊齊品「相」海港城**#hcfood Instagram Menu**。

電話:(852) 2188 8666
網址:www.harbourcity.com.hk
地址:九龍尖沙咀廣東道3-27號

前往方法 Access:
港鐵尖沙咀站A1出口或港鐵尖東站L5出口步行約10分鐘 │ 中環或灣仔乘坐天星小輪至尖沙咀約7分鐘
10-minute walk from MTR Tsim Sha Tsui station (Exit A1) or East Tsim Sha Tsui station (Exit L5) to Harbour City
7-minute ride from Central or Wan Chai Star Ferry Pier to Tsim Sha Tsui Pier

Gourmet Paradise @ Harbour City

Located in the heart of Hong Kong and next to Victoria Harbour, Harbour City is a leading shopping mall in Hong Kong housing over 450 shops of all kinds, more than 50 food & beverage outlets, 3 hotels, 2 cinemas and an art gallery. With more than 10 international fashion flagship stores on Canton Road and many other leading luxury brands, we also have Michelin-recommended restaurants and over 20 harbour view restaurants, ensuring visitors from all over the world enjoy an incredible one-stop shopping, dining and entertainment experience.

Share photos taken at any F&B outlets of Harbour City on Instagram, hashtag **#hcfood** and check-in. Search **#hcfood** to check out our menu on Instagram, kick-start your Taste-FULL Journey @ Harbour City!

Tel : (852) 2188 8666
Website : www.harbourcity.com.hk
Address : 3-27, Canton Road, Tsim Sha Tsui, Kowloon

HARBOUR CITY 海港城
一個海港，只有一個
www.harbourcity.com.hk

BIB GOURMAND RESTAURANTS
車胎人美食推介餐廳

 This symbol indicates our inspectors' favourites for good value. These restaurants offer quality cooking for $300 or less (price of a 3 course meal excluding drinks).

這道標誌表示評審員認為最超值的餐廳:只需300元或以下便可享用優質美食(三道菜式價錢但不包括飲料)。

Restaurant			Cuisine	Page
Ah Chun Shandong Dumpling 阿純山東餃子		🥢	Dumplings 餃子	66
Beef & Liberty	NEW	🗙	American 美國菜	75
Bombay Dreams		🗙🗙	Indian 印度菜	79
Café Hunan (Western District) 書湘門第 (西環)		🗙	Hunanese 湖南菜	81
Café Malacca 馬來一		🗙	Malaysian 馬拉菜	82
Chan Kan Kee Chiu Chow (Sheung Wan) 陳勤記鹵鵝飯店 (上環)		🗙	Chiu Chow 潮州菜	88
Chili Club 辣椒會		🗙	Thai 泰國菜	92
Chuen Cheung Kui (Mong Kok) 泉章居 (旺角)		🗙	Hakkanese 客家菜	96
Congee and Noodle Shop 粥麵館		🥢	Noodles and Congee 粥麵	102
Crystal Jade La Mian Xiao Long Bao (Wan Chai) 翡翠拉麵小籠包 (灣仔)		🗙	Chinese 中菜	103
Din Tai Fung (Causeway Bay) 鼎泰豐 (銅鑼灣)		🗙	Shanghainese 滬菜	107
Din Tai Fung (Tsim Sha Tsui) 鼎泰豐 (尖沙咀)		🗙	Shanghainese 滬菜	108
Dragon Inn 容龍		🗙🗙	Seafood 海鮮	111
From The Yuan 原汁原味	🐷	🥢	Cantonese 粵菜	123
Fu Sing (Causeway Bay) 富聲 (銅鑼灣)		🗙🗙🗙	Cantonese 粵菜	125
Fu Sing (Wan Chai) 富聲 (灣仔)		🗙🗙	Cantonese 粵菜	126

NEW : New entry in the guide 新增推介
🐷 : Restaurant promoted to a Bib Gourmand or Star 評級有所晉升的餐廳

RESTAURANTS BY AREA
餐廳 — 以地區分類

Hong Kong Island 香港島

Admiralty 金鐘

NEW : New entry in the guide 新增推介
ঌ : Restaurant promoted to a Bib Gourmand or Star 評級有所晉升的餐廳

Central 中環

Happy Valley 跑馬地

North Point 北角

Quarry Bay 鰂魚涌

Shugetsu Ramen (Quarry Bay) 麵鮮醬油房周月 (鰂魚涌)		⊕	🍜	Ramen 拉麵	237
Tava			🍴	Turkish 土耳其菜	262
Tulsi (Quarry Bay) 羅勒 (鰂魚涌)			🍴	Indian 印度菜	284

Sheung Wan 上環

Bibo	NEW		🍴🍴	French 法國菜	76
Chan Kan Kee Chiu Chow (Sheung Wan) 陳勤記鹵鵝飯店 (上環)		⊕	🍴	Chiu Chow 潮州菜	88
Lin Heung Kui 蓮香居		⊕	🍜	Cantonese 粵菜	181
Moon Thai (Sheung Wan)			🍴	Thai 泰國菜	196
Noodlemi			🍜	Vietnamese 越南菜	206
Sun Yuen Hing Kee 新園興記		⊕	🍜	Cantonese Roast Meats 燒味	251
Sushi Shikon 志魂		✿✿✿	🍴	Sushi 壽司	254
Tim's Kitchen (Sheung Wan) 桃花源小廚 (上環)			🍴🍴🍴	Cantonese 粵菜	277
Upper Modern Bistro	NEW	✿	🍴🍴	French 法國菜	286
Wagyu Kaiseki Den		✿	🍴🍴🍴	Japanese 日本菜	287

Tai Hang 大坑

Go Ya 五谷	NEW		🍜	Japanese 日本菜	133
IM Teppanyaki & Wine	NEW		🍴🍴	Teppanyaki 鐵板燒	150
No.5 Italian (Tai Hang)	NEW		🍴	Italian 意大利菜	204

Tai Koo Shing 太古城

Grand Cuisine Shanghai Kitchen 君頤上海小廚		🍴	Shanghainese 滬菜	139

Tin Hau 天后

Kam's Kitchen 甘飯館	NEW		🍴	Cantonese 粵菜	156
Shek Kee Kitchen 石記廚房		⊕	🍜	Cantonese 粵菜	235
Sister Wah (Tin Hau) 華姐清湯腩 (天后)		⊕	🍜	Noodles 麵食	239

Diamond Hill 鑽石山

Xiao Wang Beef Noodle (Diamond Hill) 小王牛肉麵 (鑽石山)		Taiwanese 台灣菜	296

Hung Hom 紅磡

Delicious Inn 和味館		Cantonese 粵菜	106
Kazuo Okada 岡田和生		Japanese 日本菜	159
Takeya 竹家		Japanese 日本菜	258
Wing Lai Yuen 詠藜園		Chinese 中菜	292
Yù Lěi 玉蕾		Chinese 中菜	306

Jordan 佐敦

Ho Ho Shanghai 好好上海小館		Shanghainese 滬菜	144
Lo Chiu (Jordan) 老趙 (佐敦)		Vietnamese 越南菜	183
Yau Yuen Siu Tsui 有緣小敍		Shaanxi 陝西菜	300

Kowloon Bay 九龍灣

Lei Garden (Kowloon Bay) 利苑酒家 (九龍灣)		Cantonese 粵菜	174
Siu Shun Village Cuisine (Kowloon Bay) 肇順名滙河鮮專門店 (九龍灣)		Shun Tak 順德菜	240

Kowloon City 九龍城

Gainmore Cuisine 桂寶雞窩米線 NEW		Hotpot 火鍋	130

Kwun Tong 觀塘

Dragon King (Kwun Tong) 龍皇 (觀塘)		Cantonese 粵菜	112
Lei Garden (Kwun Tong) 利苑酒家 (觀塘)		Cantonese 粵菜	175
Lucky Indonesia 好運印尼餐廳		Indonesian 印尼菜	186

Yau Ma Tei 油麻地

New Territories 新界

Sai Kung 西貢

Sai Kung Sing Kee 勝記	✿	✗	Seafood 海鮮	224

Sha Tin 沙田

Fung Lum 楓林小館	⊛	✗✗	Cantonese 粵菜	127
Lei Garden (Sha Tin) 利苑酒家（沙田）	✿	✗✗	Cantonese 粵菜	178
Sha Tin 18 沙田18		✗✗	Chinese 中菜	230

Sham Tseng 深井

Yue Kee 裕記	⊛	✗	Cantonese 粵菜	309

Tseung Kwan O 將軍澳

Jin Cuisine晉薈		✗✗	Shanghainese 滬菜	154
Tze Yuet Heen紫粵軒		✗✗	Cantonese 粵菜	285

Tsuen Wan 荃灣

Nanxiang Steamed Bun (Tsuen Wan) 南翔饅頭店（荃灣）		✗	Shanghainese 滬菜	199
Yin Yue 殷悅 NEW		✗✗	Cantonese 粵菜	304

Tuen Mun 屯門

Dragon Inn 容龍	⊛	✗✗	Seafood 海鮮	111
Yuè (Gold Coast) 粵（黃金海岸）		✗✗	Cantonese 粵菜	307

Yuen Long 元朗

Chiu Chow Rice Roll 潮式腸粉		🍜	Chiu Chow 潮州菜	95
Ho To Tai 好到底	⊛	🍜	Noodles 麵食	146
Tai Wing Wah 大榮華	⊛	✗	Cantonese 粵菜	256

RESTAURANTS BY CUISINE TYPE
餐廳 — 以菜式分類

American 美國菜

Beef & Liberty	NEW	⊕	𝕏	Wan Chai 灣仔	75

Australian 澳洲菜

The Bellbrook	NEW	𝕏	Central 中環	264

British contemporary 時尚英國菜

Aberdeen Street Social	NEW	𝕏	Central 中環	64

Cantonese 粵菜

Above & Beyond 天外天			𝕏𝕏𝕏	Tsim Sha Tsui 尖沙咀	65
Ah Yat Harbour View 阿一海景飯店		❀	𝕏𝕏𝕏	Tsim Sha Tsui 尖沙咀	67
Celebrity Cuisine 名人坊		❀❀	𝕏𝕏	Central 中環	86
Celestial Court 天寶閣			𝕏𝕏𝕏	Tsim Sha Tsui 尖沙咀	87
Che's 車氏粵菜軒			𝕏𝕏	Wan Chai 灣仔	90
Cuisine Cuisine at The Mira 國金軒 (The Mira)			𝕏𝕏𝕏	Tsim Sha Tsui 尖沙咀	104
Delicious Inn 和味館			ㅂ	Hung Hom 紅磡	106
Dragon King (Kwun Tong) 龍皇 (觀塘)			𝕏𝕏	Kwun Tong 觀塘	112
Duddell's 都爹利會館	ꜛ	❀❀	𝕏𝕏	Central 中環	113
Farm House 農圃			𝕏𝕏	Causeway Bay 銅鑼灣	117
Fook Lam Moon (Tsim Sha Tsui) 福臨門 (尖沙咀)			𝕏𝕏𝕏	Tsim Sha Tsui 尖沙咀	120
Fook Lam Moon (Wan Chai) 福臨門 (灣仔)		❀	𝕏𝕏𝕏	Wan Chai 灣仔	121
Forum 富臨飯店	NEW	❀	𝕏𝕏	Causeway Bay 銅鑼灣	122
From The Yuan 原汁原味	ꜛ	⊕	ㅂ	Wan Chai 灣仔	123

NEW : New entry in the guide 新增推介
ꜛ : Restaurant promoted to a Bib Gourmand or Star 評級有所晉升的餐廳

Yuè (North Point) 粤 (北角)		✿	XX	North Point 北角	308
Yue Kee 裕記		⊕	X	Sham Tseng 深井	309
Zaan 饌	NEW		XX	Wan Chai 灣仔	311

Cantonese Roast Meats 燒味

Joi Hing 再興	৩	⊕	ᵘ͜	Wan Chai 灣仔	155
Kam's Roast Goose 甘牌燒鵝	NEW	✿	ᵘ͜	Wan Chai 灣仔	157
Po Kee 波記		⊕	ᵘ͜	Western District 西環	218
Sun Yuen Hing Kee 新園興記		⊕	ᵘ͜	Sheung Wan 上環	251
Yat Lok 一樂燒鵝	৩	✿	ᵘ͜	Central 中環	299

Chinese 中國菜

China Tang 唐人館	NEW		XXX	Central 中環	94
Crystal Jade La Mian Xiao Long Bao (Wan Chai) 翡翠拉麵小籠包 (灣仔)		⊕	X	Wan Chai 灣仔	103
Dong Lai Shun 東來順			XX	Tsim Sha Tsui 尖沙咀	109
Golden Valley 駿景軒		✿	XX	Happy Valley 跑馬地	136
Lei Bistro 利小館			X	Causeway Bay 銅鑼灣	171
Sha Tin 18 沙田18			XX	Sha Tin 沙田	230
Wing Lai Yuen 詠藜園		⊕	X	Hung Hom 紅磡	292
Yù Lěi 玉蕾		✿	XXX	Hung Hom 紅磡	306

Chiu Chow 潮州菜

Chan Kan Kee Chiu Chow (Sheung Wan) 陳勤記鹵鵝飯店 (上環)		⊕	X	Sheung Wan 上環	88
Chiu Chow Rice Roll 潮式腸粉			ᵘ͜	Yuen long 元朗	95
Come-Into Chiu Chow 金燕島			XX	Tsim Sha Tsui 尖沙咀	100

Congee 粥品

Trusty Congee King (Wan Chai) 靠得住 (灣仔)			ᵘ͜	Wan Chai 灣仔	280

Dim Sum 點心

Tim Ho Wan (North Point) 添好運 (北角)	✿	☷	North Point 北角	274
Tim Ho Wan (Sham Shui Po) 添好運 (深水埗)	✿	☷	Sham Shui Po 深水埗	275
Tim Ho Wan (Tai Kwok Tsui) 添好運 (大角咀)	✿	☷	Tai Kwok Tsui 大角咀	276

Dumplings 餃子

Ah Chun Shandong Dumpling 阿純山東餃子	✿	☷	Prince Edward 太子	66
Dumpling Yuan (Central) 餃子園 (中環)		☷	Central 中環	114
Wang Fu (Central) 王府(中環)	✿	☷	Central 中環	289

European 歐陸菜

Hugo's 希戈	✕✕✕	Tsim Sha Tsui 尖沙咀	149

European contemporary 時尚歐陸菜

Café Gray Deluxe		✕✕	Admiralty 金鐘	80
Felix		✕✕	Tsim Sha Tsui 尖沙咀	118
Gold		✕✕✕	Central 中環	134
Mandarin Grill + Bar 文華扒房+酒吧	✿	✕✕✕✕	Central 中環	190
Penthouse	NEW	✕✕	Causeway Bay 銅鑼灣	215
St Betty		✕✕	Central 中環	245
Whisk		✕✕	Tsim Sha Tsui 尖沙咀	291

French 法國菜

Bibo	NEW	✕✕	Sheung Wan 上環	76
Caprice	✿✿	✕✕✕✕✕	Central 中環	84
Cocotte	NEW	✕	Central 中環	99
Gaddi's 吉地士		✕✕✕	Tsim Sha Tsui 尖沙咀	129
La Saison	NEW	✕✕✕	Tsim Sha Tsui 尖沙咀	164
On Lot 10		✕	Central 中環	209

Petrus 珀翠		✗✗✗✗	Admiralty 金鐘	216
Seasons	NEW ❄	✗✗✗	Causeway Bay 銅鑼灣	226
Spoon by Alain Ducasse	❄	✗✗✗✗	Tsim Sha Tsui 尖沙咀	243
Upper Modern Bistro	NEW ❄	✗✗	Sheung Wan 上環	286

French contemporary 時尚法國菜

Akrame	NEW ❄	✗✗	Wan Chai 灣仔	68
Amber	❄❄	✗✗✗	Central 中環	70
Épure	NEW	✗✗	Tsim Sha Tsui 尖沙咀	115
L'Atelier de Joël Robuchon	❄❄❄ ✗✗		Central 中環	167
Pierre	❄❄	✗✗✗	Central 中環	217
Serge et le Phoque	NEW	✗	Wan Chai 灣仔	228

Hakkanese 客家菜

Chuen Cheung Kui (Mong Kok) 泉章居 (旺角)	ⓐ	✗	Mong Kok 旺角	96

Hang Zhou 杭州菜

Hong Zhou 杭州酒家		✗✗	Wan Chai 灣仔	148

Hotpot 火鍋

Gainmore Cuisine 桂寶雞窩米線	NEW ⓐ	🍜	Kowloon City 九龍城	130
King's Garden 東來居	ⓐ	✗	Wan Chai 灣仔	160

Hunanese 湖南菜

Café Hunan (Western District) 書湘門第 (西環)	ⓐ	✗	Western District 西環	81

Indian 印度菜

Bombay Dreams	ⓐ	✗✗	Central 中環	79
Tulsi (North Point) 羅勒 (北角)	ⓐ	✗	North Point 北角	283
Tulsi (Quarry Bay) 羅勒 (鰂魚涌)		✗	Quarry Bay 鰂魚涌	284

Indonesian 印尼菜

Innovative 創新菜

International 國際菜

Italian 意大利菜

Japanese 日本菜

Nishiki 錦	NEW		✗	Tsim Sha Tsui 尖沙咀	203
Ryu Gin 天空龍吟		✿✿	✗✗	Tsim Sha Tsui 尖沙咀	222
Takeya 竹家		✿	🍜	Hung Hom 紅磡	258
Wagyu Kaiseki Den		✿	✗✗✗	Sheung Wan 上環	287
Youka 八日	NEW		✗	Wan Chai 灣仔	305

Japanese contemporary 時尚日本菜

Nobu	✗✗	Tsim Sha Tsui 尖沙咀	205
Zuma	✗✗	Central 中環	313

Korean 韓國菜

Arisu (Tsim Sha Tsui) 阿利水 (尖沙咀)	✗✗	Tsim Sha Tsui 尖沙咀	73
Chang Won 莊園	✗	Tsim Sha Tsui 尖沙咀	89
Sorabol (Causeway Bay) 新羅寶 (銅鑼灣)	✗✗	Causeway Bay 銅鑼灣	242

Malaysian 馬拉菜

Café Malacca 馬來一	✿	✗	Western District 西環	82
Sabah (Wan Chai) 莎巴(灣仔)	✿	✗	Wan Chai 灣仔	223

Mediterranean 地中海菜

Ammo	✗✗	Admiralty 金鐘	71

Middle Eastern 中東菜

Le Souk	✗	Central 中環	170

Ningbo 寧波菜

Wen Ding 文鼎	✗✗	Wan Chai 灣仔	290

Noodles 麵食

Ho To Tai 好到底	✿	🍜	Yuen Long 元朗	146
Kau Kee 九記	✿	🍜	Central 中環	158

Noodles and Congee 粥麵

Pekingese 京菜

Ramen 拉麵

Seafood 海鮮

Shun Tak 順德菜

Siu Shun Village Cuisine (Kowloon Bay)

肇順名匯河鮮專門店（九龍灣）💱	🐨	⅄	Kowloon Bay 九龍灣	240

Sichuan 川菜

Chilli Fagara 麻辣燙		⅄	Central 中環	93
Da Ping Huo 大平伙		⅄	Central 中環	105
Mask of Sichuen & Beijing 面譜京川料理	🐨	⅄	Tsim Sha Tsui 尖沙咀	191
Qi 杞		⅄⅄	Wan Chai 灣仔	219
Yun Yan 雲陽 NEW	🐨	⅄	Causeway Bay 銅鑼灣	310

Spanish 西班牙菜

Catalunya	⅄⅄	Wan Chai 灣仔	85
Fandango	⅄⅄	Tsim Sha Tsui 尖沙咀	116
Fofo by el Willy	⅄	Central 中環	119
Olé	⅄⅄	Central 中環	208

Steakhouse 扒房

BLT Steak	⅄	Tsim Sha Tsui 尖沙咀	77
Grand Hyatt Steakhouse	⅄⅄	Wan Chai 灣仔	140
Holytan Grill 葆里湛 NEW	⅄⅄	Central 中環	147
Steik World Meats	⅄⅄	Tsim Sha Tsui 尖沙咀	246
The Bostonian 美岸海鮮廳	⅄⅄	Tsim Sha Tsui 尖沙咀	266
The Steak House Wine bar + grill ❁	⅄⅄⅄	Tsim Sha Tsui 尖沙咀	271

Sushi 壽司

Sushi Ginza Iwa NEW ❁	⅄	Central 中環	252
Sushi Rozan 鮨魯山	⅄	Wan Chai 灣仔	253
Sushi Shikon 志魂 ❁❁❁	⅄	Sheung Wan 上環	254
Sushi Ta-ke 竹 寿司	⅄	Causeway Bay 銅鑼灣	255
Xuan Sushi 玄鮨	⅄	Central 中環	297

Swiss 瑞士菜

Chesa 瑞樵閣	⅄⅄	Tsim Sha Tsui 尖沙咀	91

The Swiss Chalet
瑞士餐廳   NEW   ✗   Tsim Sha Tsui 尖沙咀   272

Taiwanese 台灣菜

Xiao Wang Beef Noodle (Diamond Hill)
小王牛肉麵 (鑽石山)   🍜   Diamond Hill 鑽石山   296

Teppanyaki 鐵板燒

IM Teppanyaki & Wine   NEW   ✗✗   Tai Hang 大坑   150

Thai 泰國菜

Café Siam   ✗   Central 中環   83

Chili Club 辣椒會   🚇   ✗   Wan Chai 灣仔   92

May's Sawaddee Thailand
旺泰特食   🚇   🍜   Sai Kung 西貢   192

Moon Thai (Sheung Wan)   ✗   Sheung Wan 上環   196

Thai Chiu 泰潮   🚇   🍜   Sham Shui Po 深水埗   263

Turkish 土耳其菜

Tava   ✗   Quarry Bay 鰂魚涌   262

Vegetarian 素食

Kung Tak Lam (Causeway Bay)
功德林 (銅鑼灣)   🚇   ✗✗   Causeway Bay 銅鑼灣   162

Vietnamese 越南菜

An Nam 安南   NEW   ✗✗   Causeway Bay 銅鑼灣   72

Le Soleil   ✗✗   Tsim Sha Tsui 尖沙咀   169

Lo Chiu (Jordan) 老趙 (佐敦)   🍜   Jordan 佐敦   183

Nha Trang (Central) 芽莊 (中環)   ✗   Central 中環   201

Noodlemi   🍜   Sheung Wan 上環   206

The Vietnam Woods 悅木   ✗   Wan Chai 灣仔   273

Xinjiang 新疆菜

Ba Yi 巴依   ✗   Western District 西環   74

RESTAURANTS WITH INTERESTING WINE LISTS
供應優質餐酒的餐廳

NEW : New entry in the guide 新增推介

⤴ : Restaurant promoted to a Bib Gourmand or Star 評級有所晉升的餐廳

RESTAURANTS WITH VIEWS
有景觀的餐廳

NEW : New entry in the guide 新增推介
⟆ : Restaurant promoted to a Bib Gourmand or Star 評級有所晉升的餐廳

Aberdeen Street Social   NEW

✂   🏛 ⛊18 ◑⫴

It's now home to Hong Kong's creative industries but PMQ was originally built back in the '50s as Police married quarters. British chef Jason Atherton occupies two units inside, with a bar on the ground floor and a comfortable restaurant on the second which serves good looking modern dishes. From the private room you can look into the kitchen and admire the skills on show and from the small shop you can buy desserts, bread and chocolate.

原是已婚警察宿舍，獲列為三級歷史建築，保留下來後活化為現在的元創坊。餐廳在靠近荷里活道那邊佔了兩層樓，地下是氣氛輕鬆的酒吧和露天座位，一樓是感覺舒適的餐室及一間能觀看廚房工作的私人房。精心炮製的時尚英國菜外型吸引，食客亦可在地舖的Sweet Social選購自製甜點、麵包和巧克力。

TEL. 2866 0300
PMQ, 35 Aberdeen Street, Central
中環鴨巴甸街 35號
www.aberdeenstreetsocial.hk

■ PRICE 價錢
Lunch 午膳
set 套餐 $ 238-288
à la carte 點菜 $ 480-720
Dinner 晚膳
à la carte 點菜 $ 480-720

■ OPENING HOURS 營業時間
Lunch 午膳   12:00-14:30 (L.O.)
Dinner 晚膳   18:00-22:30 (L.O.)
Weekends & Public Holidays
週末及公眾假期   11:30-15:30 (L.O.)

Above & Beyond
天外天

⫷ 🍷 ⌗30 ☎🍴 ஃ

Designed by Sir Terence Conran, the restaurant of the Hotel Icon (partly run by the education sector and staffed by keen students) is unsurprisingly contemporary and boasts a chic lounge and bar and stunning harbour views. What is unexpected is that this Western-style restaurant serves authentic Cantonese cuisine – dishes like smoked pigeon with Oolong tea leaves, and braised tofu with morels and Chinese mushrooms stand out.

由泰倫斯‧康藍爵士（Sir Terence Conran）設計的唯港薈中菜廳，時尚典雅的酒吧大廳，是其一貫的設計風格，加上醉人的維港景致，叫人讚歎不已。令人驚喜的是，裝潢如此西化的餐廳，卻以提供傳統粵菜為主，如凍頂烏龍茶燻鴿、野生羊肚菌炆腐皮等，都做得十分出色。

TEL. 3400 1318
28F, Hotel Icon, 17 Science Museum Road, East Tsim Sha Tsui
尖東科學館道 17號唯港薈 28樓
www.hotel-icon.com

■ PRICE 價錢
Lunch 午膳
set 套餐 $ 218
à la carte 點菜 $ 300-1,200
Dinner 晚膳
set 套餐 $ 388
à la carte 點菜 $ 300-1,200

■ OPENING HOURS 營業時間
Lunch 午膳   11:00-15:00 (L.O.)
Dinner 晚膳   18:00-22:30 (L.O.)

Ah Chun Shandong Dumpling
阿純山東餃子

Shandong people are famed for their hospitality and when entertaining at home that means serving handmade dumplings. Using fresh ingredients, the owner's wife makes an abundance of authentic dumplings each day in several different varieties; the green onion and mutton dumpling in particular stands out. Other dishes include Shandong roast lamb chop and toffee sweet potatoes. A menu in English is available.

山東人以好客聞名，喜歡在家中以自製餃子招待客人。東主的太太採用新鮮食材，每天親自包製多款不同味道的傳統餃子，其中以京葱羊肉餃最出色。推介菜式包括山東香燒羊排及拔絲地瓜。店內有英文菜牌，便於遊客選擇菜式。

TEL. 2789 9611
60 Lai Chi Kok Road, Prince Edward
太子荔枝角道 60號

■ PRICE 價錢
à la carte 點菜 $ 30-110

■ OPENING HOURS 營業時間
11:00-22:30 (L.O.)

■ ANNUAL AND WEEKLY CLOSING 休息日期
Closed 6 days Lunar New Year and Wednesday
農曆新年休息 6 天及週三休息

Ah Yat Harbour View
阿一海景飯店

🍴🍴🍴   ♿ ⬅ 🪑60 🕐🍽

The first thing you notice as you leave the lift is the photo of owner chef Yeung Koon Yat enjoying his most famous dish – Ah Yat abalone. Ah Yat signature fried rice and stewed oxtail with homemade sauce and red wine casserole are also worth a try. The good value set lunch menu is a great way of experiencing many more of their Cantonese specialities. The contemporary dining room takes full advantage of the wonderful views, as do the smart private rooms.

身處位於iSquare29樓的阿一海景，不光可以欣賞宜人的維港兩岸美景，更能品嘗名廚老闆楊貫一的名菜：阿一鮑魚。此外，不妨試試其他馳名菜如一哥招牌砂窩炒飯及紅酒醬炆牛尾。飯店為客人供應來自波爾多、加洲、新西蘭和澳洲的高級紅酒。店內設有四間私人廂房。

TEL. 2328 0983
29F, iSquare, 63 Nathan Road, Tsim Sha Tsui
尖沙咀彌敦道 63號 iSquare29樓

SPECIALITIES TO PRE-ORDER 預訂食物
Poached sliced fresh sea whelk 白灼響螺盞 ／ Baked chicken filled with abalone matsutake mushroom and morchella mushroom 松茸羊肚菌吉濱鮮鮑魚焗雞 ／ Baked salty chicken 一哥鹽焗雞

■ PRICE 價錢
Lunch 午膳
set 套餐 $ 268
à la carte 點菜 $ 200-1,400
Dinner 晚膳
à la carte 點菜 $ 320-1,400

■ OPENING HOURS 營業時間
Lunch 午膳   12:00-15:30 (L.O.)
Dinner 晚膳   18:00-22:30 (L.O.)

HONG KONG 香港

Akrame NEW

✺

XX

⬭10 ☏⬚

Having conquered Paris, Chef Akrame Benallal has now turned his attention to Hong Kong and has gathered together a strong local team. His eponymous, contemporary French restaurant comes in monochrome and is an understated yet comfortable space. Only set menus are offered, which change every couple of weeks; the emphasis is on seafood and the ingredients are sourced largely from Europe. Sommeliers are on hand to recommend the best wine pairings.

總店設在巴黎的時尚法國菜餐廳，廚師Akrame Benallal 選址船街開設香港分店，室內空間以黑白色作主調，線條簡潔且具時尚魅力。午餐和晚餐均提供以海鮮為主的套餐，大部分食材由法國購入，配合本地時令食材烹調，餐單平均每兩週更新一次。你可讓侍酒師為你調製餐酒，饒有興味。

TEL. 2528 5068
9 Ship Street, Wan Chai
灣仔船街 9號
www.akrame.com.hk

■ PRICE 價錢
Lunch 午膳
set 套餐 $ 280-580
Dinner 晚膳
set 套餐 $ 788-1,398

■ OPENING HOURS 營業時間
Lunch 午膳   12:00-14:30 (L.O.)
Dinner 晚膳   18:30-22:30 (L.O.)

Al Molo

♟ ❮ **P** ◑▮

Modern Italian cuisine by way of New York was brought to Ocean Terminal by celebrated chef Michael White in 2011. This eye-catching restaurant covers an area of 7,000ft^2 and is divided into three distinct dining sections: there's a relaxed spot in front of the pizza ovens; a comfortable middle room with a lively open kitchen and a waterfront terrace overlooking the harbour. Standouts include homemade pasta, polipo and osso buco.

名廚Michael White於2011年將時尚紐約式意大利佳餚引進香港海運大廈。餐廳佔地7,000平方呎，共分為三大區域：薄餅烤爐前方的雅座；設置開放式廚房的中庭及傲視壯麗維港景觀的臨海露台。馳名菜式包括：自製意大利麵，烤八爪魚(polipo)及烤牛膝（osso buco）。

TEL. 2730 7900
Shop G63, GF, Ocean Terminal,
Harbour City, Tsim Sha Tsui
尖沙咀海運大廈海港城地下 G63號舖
www.diningconcepts.com.hk

■ PRICE 價錢
Lunch 午膳
set 套餐 $ 148-238
à la carte 點菜 $ 360-650
Dinner 晚膳
à la carte 點菜 $ 360-650

■ OPENING HOURS 營業時間
12:00-23:00 L.O. 22:30

Amber

✿✿

XXXX   ♿ 🍷 ⟷ 20 ⊘🍴 🎀

The hanging ceiling sculpture, which features over 3,500 copper tubes, is the most striking element of Adam Tihany's bold restaurant design. Service is detailed and courteous yet never overbearing, but it is the adventurous and creative French cuisine, made with superb ingredients, which attracts diners to these plush surroundings. Try Hokkaido sea urchin in a lobster Jell-O or charcoal-grilled Bresse pigeon, and don't miss the chocolate soufflé.

天花懸着由超過3,500條銅管造成的雕像令人神搖目眩, 細心有禮而恰到好處的服務, 令食客感到放心舒適, 然而, 最吸引食客光顧的是選用優質材料製作、大膽與創意兼備的法國菜。推介菜式包括北海道海膽伴龍蝦啫哩及炭燒法國乳鴿, 朱古力疏乎厘亦不能錯過。

TEL. 2132 0066
7F, The Landmark Mandarin Oriental Hotel,
15 Queen's Road, Central
中環皇后大道中 15號置地文華東方酒店 7樓
www.amberhongkong.com

■ PRICE 價錢
Lunch 午膳
set 套餐 $ 548-748
à la carte 點菜 $ 1,200-2,200
Dinner 晚膳
set 套餐 $ 1,788-1,888
à la carte 點菜 $ 1,200-2,200

■ OPENING HOURS 營業時間
Lunch 午膳　12:00-14:30 (L.O.)
Dinner 晚膳　18:30-22:30 (L.O.)

Ammo

🍴🍴

Copper tubes and pipes have been used to great effect to create a striking and quite futuristic looking restaurant, here at the Asia Society Center. The cooking is largely Mediterranean based, with a strong Italian element, but the kitchen also adds some subtle Asian twists. Homemade pasta is something of a speciality – try the burrata cheese ravioli with Peking duck ragout. The name refers to the building's former life as an explosives depot.

Ammo因所處建築物前身是炸藥倉庫而命名。一如其名,吧枱後用銅管堆砌的牆身猶如火球炸開的形態,配上三面落地玻璃牆,風格前衛且予人強烈的空間感。餐館供應的地中海菜混入了意大利與亞洲風味,自製意大利粉是最有特色的食物,首推意大利布袋芝士雲吞伴北京填鴨肉醬。

TEL. 2537 9888
Asia Society, 9 Justice Drive, Admiralty
金鐘正義道 9號亞洲協會香港中心
www.ammo.com.hk

■ PRICE 價錢
Lunch 午膳
set 套餐 $228
à la carte 點菜 $250-500
Dinner 晚膳
à la carte 點菜 $250-500

■ OPENING HOURS 營業時間
Lunch 午膳　12:00-14:30 (L.O.)
Dinner 晚膳　18:00-21:30 (L.O.)

An Nam NEW
安南

☓☓　　　　　　　　　　　　　　　　　P　🍴 14　☎🍴

There is a subtle colonial element to the decoration at this elegant Vietnamese restaurant, thanks to the antique panels, painted walls and tiled flooring. The restaurant offers delicacies from all parts of Vietnam but the dishes that really stand out are those from Huế, the former capital in the middle of the country, such as steamed rice flan and lotus root salad with banana flower. The food is as attractive as it is flavoursome.

到安南用膳是一件賞心樂事：甫踏進餐廳便會為其氣氛和環境吸引。古董越南傢俱、牆飾、懷舊地磚及吊燈，帶着濃濃的殖民地情懷，東西方色彩融合得自然優雅。提供菜式包括越南各地美食及中部城市順化菜式，賣相吸引且味道清新。順化浮萍餅和安南藕藤沙律尤為出色。

TEL. 2787 3922
4F, Lee Gardens One, 33 Hysan Avenue,
Causeway Bay
銅鑼灣希慎道 33號利園一期 4樓
www.annam.com.hk

■ PRICE 價錢
Lunch 午膳
à la carte 點菜　$ 240-680
Dinner 晚膳
à la carte 點菜　$ 240-680

■ OPENING HOURS 營業時間
11:30-24:00 L.O. 23:00

■ ANNUAL AND WEEKLY CLOSING 休息日期
Closed Lunar New Year
農曆新年休息

Arisu (Tsim Sha Tsui)
阿利水 (尖沙咀)

XX   🍽10   🕐

Steam rather than smoke is more likely to fill the air at this bright, contemporary Korean restaurant because hotpot is the popular dish here, with the seafood hotpot being a particular highlight. Other attractively presented dishes include grilled yellow corvine, kimchee and pork pancake; and the noodles are good too. The restaurant is housed within a new building, standing in juxtaposition to its more traditional surroundings.

這家韓國餐廳位於一座新落成大廈內，窗外所見全是舊式樓宇，店內環境卻明亮時尚，以火鍋馳名，在室內常看到火鍋產生的蒸氣，而非燒烤的煙燻。此店以海鮮火鍋最受歡迎，其他招牌菜式包括烤黃花魚和泡菜豬肉煎餅，麵食亦非常美味。

TEL. 2369 8008
3F, H8, 8 Hau Fook Street, Tsim Sha Tsui
尖沙咀厚福街 8 號 H8 3 樓
www.arisuhk.com

■ PRICE 價錢
Lunch 午膳
set 套餐 $ 55-130
à la carte 點菜 $ 170-530
Dinner 晚膳
à la carte 點菜 $ 170-530

■ OPENING HOURS 營業時間
Lunch 午膳   11:00-15:00 (L.O.)
Dinner 晚膳   17:30-22:30 (L.O.)

■ ANNUAL AND WEEKLY CLOSING 休息日期
Closed 2 days Lunar New Year
農曆新年休息 2 天

Ba Yi
巴依

Lamb lovers will be glad they made the effort to find this somewhat out of the way Xinjiang restaurant. The special lamb dishes include traditional stewed lamb, roast leg and mutton skewers, with most of the meat being imported from Xinjiang. The handmade Xinjiang noodles are only available at lunchtime. The interior, dominated by a map of the Silk Route, has been refurbished and is now a little more up-to-date.

食店位置有點偏僻，但嗜羊的食客絕對不會後悔遠道而來。重新裝修後餐廳更富時代氣息，帶有標誌性的巨型絲路圖仍放置在店中央。大部分肉類均由新疆入口，羊肉特式菜包括手抓肉、烤羊腿和羊肉串燒等。三款新疆特色手打麵只於午餐時段供應。

TEL. 2484 9981
43 Water Street, Sai Ying Pun
西營盤水街 43 號

■ PRICE 價錢
Lunch 午膳
à la carte 點菜 $ 38-45
Dinner 晚膳
à la carte 點菜 $ 100-380

■ OPENING HOURS 營業時間
Lunch 午膳　12:00-15:00 L.O.14:30
Dinner 晚膳　18:00-23:00 L.O.22:30

■ ANNUAL AND WEEKLY CLOSING 休息日期
Closed 2 weeks Lunar New Year and Monday
農曆新年休息兩星期及週一休息

Beef & Liberty NEW

This burger specialist uses grass-fed beef from Hereford cattle raised in Cape Grim on Tasmania's west coast. Different cuts are used and the meat is ground twice a day to ensure the burgers are fresh, juicy, and full of flavour – and the homemade sourdough bun proves an ideal companion. The choice also includes a Welsh lamb burger and there's a falafel burger for Veggies. Don't even think about resisting the warm skillet cookie and cream.

鍾情優質漢堡的你，定能在Beef & Liberty得到滿足。選用塔斯曼尼亞格津角，自然生長無激素草飼牛三個不同部位混合而成的牛肉餅，於每天午、晚餐前人手製作，保持了牛肉的鮮味與肉汁，配合特製麵包，滋味無窮。以威爾斯羊肩肉和法拉費素漢堡也十分美味；暖曲奇配奶油更是令人難以抗拒。

TEL. 2811 3009
2F, 23 Wing Fung Street, Wan Chai
灣仔永豐街 23號 2樓
www.beef-liberty.com

■ PRICE 價錢
set 套餐 $ 128-148
à la carte 點菜 $ 160-250

■ OPENING HOURS 營業時間
12:00-22:30 (L.O.)
Weekends and Public Holidays
週末及公眾假期　11:00-22:30 (L.O.)

Bibo NEW

XX   🖵10 ◑🍴 ⚬

It's all about creativity here at Bibo. Descend into the restaurant and you find yourself in a space that's more gallery than restaurant, with works that include street art, paintings and sculpture. This unique and arresting space plays host to French cooking that is not afraid to mix the classical with the more modern. The inexorable link between art and food is also celebrated in the striking way these dishes are presented.

金色滑門後的樓梯通往這間感覺神秘、像藝廊般的餐廳。藝術品、街頭壁畫及雕塑遍佈整間餐廳。菜式結合傳統法國烹調藝術與世界不同地區食材，展現細膩兼充滿時代感的法國風味。或許你的注意力也會隨着其他食客的目光一起遊走於藝術物件之上。

TEL. 2956 3188
163 Hollywood Road, Sheung Wan
上環荷李活道163號
www.bibo.hk

■ PRICE 價錢
Lunch 午膳
set 套餐 $ 238-378
à la carte 點菜 $ 650-1,600
Dinner 晚膳
set 套餐 $ 1,388
à la carte 點菜 $ 650-1,600

■ OPENING HOURS 營業時間
Lunch 午膳 12:00-14:15 (L.O.)
Dinner 晚膳 18:30-22:15 (L.O.)
Weekends & Public Holidays
週末及公眾假期 11:15-14:30 (L.O.)

BLT Steak

In this instance those initials stand for Bistro Laurent Tourondel, a New York celebrity chef. His restaurant specialises in prime beef from the US and Australia, all USDA certified and naturally aged. Choose your cut – perhaps a Porterhouse or a rib-eye – a sauce and sides. There are a few lighter options for those intimidated by a 16oz New York strip. Its terrace overlooking the Star Ferry quay and Victoria Harbour is a 'prime' spot.

BLT供應來自美國及澳洲的頂級牛扒，全部通過美國農產部認證及自然生長。你可選擇喜歡的部分，從大脊骨牛扒到肉眼扒任君選擇，配上自選醬汁及配菜。你亦可選擇輕盈的16安士紐約無骨西冷扒。其平台花園是「搶手」熱點，可觀賞維多利亞港的迷人景色。

TEL. 2730 3508
Shop G62, GF, Ocean Terminal,
Harbour City, Tsim Sha Tsui
尖沙咀海運大廈海港城地下 G62號舖
www.diningconcepts.com.hk

■ PRICE 價錢
Lunch 午膳
set 套餐 $ 138-258
à la carte 點菜 $ 330-800
Dinner 晚膳
à la carte 點菜 $ 330-800

■ OPENING HOURS 營業時間
12:00-22:30 (L.O.)

Bo Innovation

✿ ✿ ✿

🅧🅧🅧

🏠 🚇 ☎🍴 ⅋

Having the open kitchen in a raised position in front of the dining room seems entirely fitting as there's a strong theatrical element to owner-chef Alvin Leung's highly imaginative and innovative cooking. The origins behind each tantalising creation are fully explained and it's clear that this is not creativity for its own sake but a modern interpretation of traditional Chinese flavours; there's no greater example than the 'molecular xiao long bao'.

於食客用膳區的前方較高地方設置開放式廚房，此格局正好配合餐廳老闆兼廚師梁經倫的強烈表演欲及創新煮意。侍應會給客人介紹每道菜的材料和做法。梁經倫熱衷為傳統食譜作全新演繹，務求為食客帶來嶄新的味覺感受，其分子料理小籠包便是絕佳例子。

TEL. 2850 8371
2F, J Residence, 18 Ship Street, Wan Chai
灣仔船街 18號嘉薈軒 2樓
www.boinnovation.com

■ PRICE 價錢
Lunch 午膳
set 套餐 $ 268-780
Dinner 晚膳
set 套餐 $ 1,380-1,880

■ OPENING HOURS 營業時間
Lunch 午膳　12:00-14:00
Dinner 晚膳　19:00-22:00

■ ANNUAL AND WEEKLY CLOSING 休息日期
Closed 3 days Lunar New Year, Saturday lunch, Sunday and Public Holidays
農曆新年 3 天，週六午市，週日及公眾假期休息

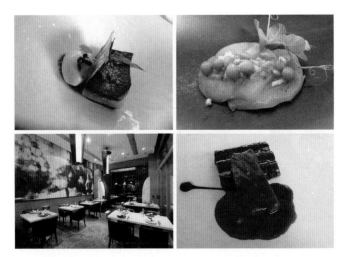

Bombay Dreams

Although most regions of India are represented, the kitchen's strengths lie with dishes from more northerly parts of the country. Lunch sees a well-stocked buffet; at dinner you can experience dishes like spicy prawns with garlic and mustard or spring lamb marinated in yoghurt and spices. The authentic cooking and appealing prices mean that booking is recommended. The pleasantly contemporary room allows for interesting views into the kitchen.

這裏提供印度大部份地區的菜式，當中最出色為印度北部地區之佳餚。午市提供豐富的自助餐，晚市則可一嘗蒜香芥末辣味大蝦，或乳酪香草滷羔羊等美食。食物以正宗方法烹調，而且價錢相宜，建議預先訂座；環境舒適且富現代氣息，用餐時可一窺廚房的工作情況，饒富趣味。

TEL. 2971 0001
4F, 75-77 Wyndham Street, Central
中環雲咸街 75-77號 4樓
www.diningconcepts.com.hk

■ PRICE 價錢
Lunch 午膳
set 套餐 $ 138
à la carte 點菜 $ 160-410
Dinner 晚膳
à la carte 點菜 $ 160-410

■ OPENING HOURS 營業時間
Lunch 午膳　12:00-15:00 (L.O.)
Dinner 晚膳　18:00-23:00 (L.O.)

Café Gray Deluxe

🍴🍴　　　　　　　　← 🗨️ **P** 🪑12 ☎️🍴 🎴

Café Gray Deluxe is a suitably cool restaurant to have on the 49th floor of the fashionable Upper House hotel. It comes with a terrific bar – homage, perhaps, to consulting chef Gary Kunz's New York background – spectacular views and fluent, confident service. The kitchen adds its own twists to mostly European dishes with the likes of pasta fiore; braised short rib of beef with soft grits and Meaux mustard sauce; and Alaskan halibut.

型格餐廳Café Gray Deluxe，位處奕居酒店49樓。充滿活力的酒吧大概與顧問主廚Gray　Kunz的紐約背景有莫大關係。用餐的同時能欣賞維港的超凡美景，服務亦極為周到。廚師在歐陸佳餚中混入獨特的材料變化，如香草汁鮮茄車輪意粉、芥茉汁牛小排及阿拉斯加比目魚等均別具風味。

TEL. 3968 1106
49F, The Upper House Hotel,
Pacific Place, 88 Queensway,
Admiralty
金鐘道 88號太古廣場奕居 49樓
www.cafegrayhk.com

■ PRICE 價錢
Lunch 午膳
set 套餐 $ 385
à la carte 點菜 $ 520-900
Dinner 晚膳
set 套餐 $ 725
à la carte 點菜 $ 550-900

■ OPENING HOURS 營業時間
Lunch 午膳　12:00-14:30 (L.O.)
Dinner 晚膳　18:00-22:30 (L.O.)

湖南菜

MAP 地圖 22/A-1

Café Hunan (Western District)
書湘門第 (西環)

The young Hunanese chef developed his skills while working in his mother's restaurant and has a passion for the dishes of his home town. To ensure authenticity he insists on using ingredients from Hunan, like the different types of chilli and the smoked pickled pork which is supplied directly by the farmer. Try the rich tasting braised pork elbow – it involves 4 complicated stages and around 2 hours of cooking to get the texture just right.

年輕廚師自小在母親的菜館幫忙，入廚經驗豐富。來自湖南的他對家鄉菜充滿熱誠，最怕菜式不辣。此店大部分材料採購自湖南，如向農戶購買的煙燻臘肉及各種辣椒，確保風味正宗。經四個工序以五個小時製作的霸王肘子，味道層次豐富，紅黃二色辣椒蒸煮的鴛鴦魚頭王亦不遑多讓。

TEL. 2803 7177
420-424 Queen's Road West,
Western District
西環皇后大道西 420-424 號

SPECIALITIES TO PRE-ORDER 預訂食物
Steamed fish head with diced red and yellow pepper 鴛鴦魚頭王／Braised pork elbow Hunan style 霸王肘子

■ PRICE 價錢
Lunch 午膳
set 套餐 $ 48   à la carte 點菜 $ 160-350
Dinner 晚膳
à la carte 點菜 $ 160-350

■ OPENING HOURS 營業時間
Lunch 午膳   11:00-15:00 (L.O.)
Dinner 晚膳   18:00-22:30 (L.O.)

■ ANNUAL AND WEEKLY CLOSING 休息日期
Closed 4 days Lunar New Year and Monday 農曆新年休息 4 天及週一休息

HONG KONG 香港

Café Malacca
馬來一

🍴   🖥40   ☎🍴

Located on the second floor of Traders, a Shangri-La hotel, Café Malacca specialises in the cuisines of Malaysia and Singapore. Using recipes and cooking methods garnered from local people during his travels, the head chef prepares classics like assam laksa, satay, and Hainanese chicken rice that taste as good as they look. Regulars beat a path at midday for the generously sized dishes on the lunch menu.

店如其名，馬來一菜館是一家馬來西亞餐廳。主廚曾獲派到馬、星等地取經，並由當地引入一些特別而道地的食材，精心炮製風味正宗的馬來亞菜式，如檳城蝦麵、亞參喇沙、沙爹及海南雞飯等，全部都賣相吸引。多元化的午市套餐非常受歡迎。

TEL. 2213 6613
2F, 508 Queen's Road West,
Western District
西環皇后大道西 508號 2樓

■ PRICE 價錢
Lunch 午膳
set 套餐 $ 128-148
à la carte 點菜 $ 160-300
Dinner 晚膳
à la carte 點菜 $ 160-300

■ OPENING HOURS 營業時間
12:00-22:30 (L.O.)

Café Siam

✂ ❍

For lovers of Thai food, Café Siam has been a reassuring presence in Central for over 15 years, albeit at two different addresses. It now occupies two floors of a building in LKF and keeps its regulars happy with satisfying and aromatic curries, mouth-wateringly fresh salads like Som Tam, hotpots and dishes like spicy stir-fried prawns. Local office workers crowd in at lunchtime for the Pad Thai and Khao Pad.

Café Siam開業十五年，向以正宗風味泰國菜吸引食客。充滿椰香的泰式青咖喱、各式清新可口的沙律，以至香辣刺激的炒蜆都不乏追隨者。各款河粉和炒飯是上班族在午餐時段的最愛。位於蘭桂坊的這家店子佔了兩層樓，室內環境雅致舒適，透出一種閒逸情調，與街道上的繁囂有極大對比。

TEL. 2851 4803
2-3F, 21 D'Aguilar Street, Central
中環德己立街 21號 2-3樓
www.cafesiam.com.hk

■ PRICE 價錢
Lunch 午膳
set 套餐 $ 98-128
à la carte 點菜 $ 130-200
Dinner 晚膳
à la carte 點菜 $ 220-430

■ OPENING HOURS 營業時間
Lunch 午膳 12:00-14:30 (L.O.)
Dinner 晚膳 18:30-23:00 (L.O.)

■ ANNUAL AND WEEKLY CLOSING 休息日期
Closed Sunday lunch 週日午膳休息

Caprice

❀❀

🗭🖤🖤🖤🖤　　　　　　　　　&. ⬱ 🖐️ 🅿️ 💺12 🕐🍴 🐜

Dominating this glamorous room is a raised open kitchen which is framed by a jewelled canopy. From here, the large brigade of chefs produce highly accomplished French dishes such as Challans duck fillet, and langoustine ravioli with sweetbreads; be sure to also sample the impressive selection of cheeses. Along with highly skilled cooking, you can expect great harbour views and charming service – this is a true destination restaurant.

水晶珠簾圍着的開放式廚房華麗且具氣派；陣容鼎盛的廚師團隊精心炮製各款法國佳餚，如螯龍蝦牛仔核雲吞伴黃菌配龍蝦汁、嫩煮法國鴨胸伴燴鴨腿肉薯茸和時令雜菜配蘋果醬等；超水準的特選芝士系列令人一試難忘。精湛的廚藝、迷人的維港景色與一絲不苟的服務，令顧客萬分愜意。

TEL. 3196 8860
6F, Four Seasons Hotel,
8 Finance Street, Central
中環金融街 8號四季酒店平台 6樓
www.fourseasons.com/hongkong

■ PRICE 價錢
Lunch 午膳
set 套餐 $495-560
à la carte 點菜 $1,050-1,550
Dinner 晚膳
set 套餐 $1,990
à la carte 點菜 $1,050-1,550

■ OPENING HOURS 營業時間
Lunch 午膳　12:00-14:30 (L.O.)
Dinner 晚膳　18:00-22:30 (L.O.)

Catalunya

Ｘ Ｘ　　　　　　　　　　　🍽16　◔🍴　𝆓

The clue is there: yes, Catalan cuisine is celebrated here at this comfortable and well run restaurant, found in one of Wan Chai's quieter spots. The chef's inspiration comes from his mother's cooking but to these traditional recipes are added some innovative touches and techniques. The resulting dishes are striking in looks yet still authentic in flavour. Tapas is popular but also try Segovian-style suckling pig, which is cooked for 14 hours.

餐廳在灣仔區較寧靜的一隅，與店內懶洋洋的氣氛很一致。顧名思義這裏主要提供加泰隆尼亞美食。來自當地的廚師，秉承世代相傳的飲食文化，配合優質食材和創新烹飪技術，製作出賣相有創意、味道正宗的小菜。焦店食物是Tapas系列。經十四個小時烹調的烤乳豬皮脆肉嫩，值得一試。

TEL. 2866 7900
GF, Guardian House, 32 Oi Kwan Road,
Wan Chai
灣仔愛群道 32號愛群商業大廈地下
www.catalunya.hk

■ PRICE 價錢
Lunch 午膳
set 套餐 $ 298
à la carte 點菜 $ 400-920
Dinner 晚膳
à la carte 點菜 $ 400-920

■ OPENING HOURS 營業時間
Lunch 午膳　12:00-14:30 (L.O.)
Weekend lunch 週末午膳
12:00-15:00 (L.O.)
Dinner 晚膳　18:00-22:30 (L.O.)

Cantonese 粵菜   MAP 地圖   24/B-2

Celebrity Cuisine
名人坊

🍴🍴   🍽20   ☎🍴

Having just six tables and a host of regulars makes booking ahead vital at this very discreet and colourful restaurant concealed within the Lan Kwai Fong hotel. The Cantonese menu may be quite short but there are usually plenty of specials; highlights of the delicate, sophisticated cuisine include whole superior abalone in oyster sauce; baked chicken with Shaoxing wine and, one of the chef's own creations, 'bird's nest in chicken wing'.

這家隱藏於蘭桂坊酒店內的餐廳，看似不甚出眾但別具魅力，地方雖小卻常客眾多，故此必須提早預約。這裏的廣東菜餐牌頗為精簡，但全是大廚富哥的特選菜式，精美菜餚推介包括富哥頂級鮑魚、花雕焗飛天雞及自創菜式燕窩釀鳳翼。

TEL. 3650 0066
1F, Lan Kwai Fong Hotel, 3 Kau U Fong, Central
中環九如坊 3號蘭桂坊酒店 1樓

■ PRICE 價錢
Lunch 午膳
set 套餐 $ 188-298
à la carte 點菜 $ 160-380
Dinner 晚膳
à la carte 點菜 $ 300-5,000

■ OPENING HOURS 營業時間
Lunch 午膳　12:00-14:30 (L.O.)
Dinner 晚膳　18:00-22:30 (L.O.)

■ ANNUAL AND WEEKLY CLOSING 休息日期
Closed 3 days Lunar New Year
農曆新年休息 3 天

Celestial Court
天寶閣

🏃 ⛳ 🍽100 ◐🍴

Silks and woods adorn this large dining room within the Sheraton Hotel, where service comes courtesy of an experienced team. Despite its size, scores of regulars mean that queuing for a table is sometimes required. A large selection of Cantonese and Chinese specialities includes roasted whole suckling pig, pearl barley, black truffles, glutinous rice with Yunnan ham and deep-fried prawns, spicy termite mushrooms and crispy rice toast.

位於喜來登酒店內的天寶閣，以灰白作主色調、配以絲綢與木材作裝飾。眾多常客令這間面積寬敞的中菜廳偶然也需要排隊輪候入座。餐牌選擇甚多，包括廣東和其他中國地方的佳餚，黑松露薏米燒釀乳豬和飯焦雞瑙菌鳳尾蝦。禮貌周到的服務團隊經驗十分豐富。

TEL. 2732 6991
2F, Sheraton Hotel, 20 Nathan Road,
Tsim Sha Tsui
尖沙咀彌敦道 20號喜來登酒店 2樓
www.sheraton.com/hongkong

SPECIALITIES TO PRE-ORDER 預訂食物
Roasted whole suckling pig, pearl Barley,
black truffles, glutinous rice, Yunnan ham
黑松露薏米燒釀乳豬

■ PRICE 價錢
Lunch 午膳
set 套餐 $ 268
à la carte 點菜 $ 300-800
Dinner 晚膳
set 套餐 $ 638-1,388
à la carte 點菜 $ 300-800

■ OPENING HOURS 營業時間
Lunch 午膳　11:30-14:30 (L.O.)
Dinner 晚膳　18:00-23:00 (L.O.)

Chan Kan Kee Chiu Chow (Sheung Wan)
陳勤記鹵鵝飯店 (上環)

Ms Chan's grandfather set up this family business in 1948 in Sheung Wan; it moved to its current location in 1994 and was completely refurbished in 2010, when the kitchen was also expanded. Chiu Chow goose, cooked in a secret family recipe, remains the main event here, but there are other Chiu Chow specialities on offer such as fried noodle with vinegar and sugar, steamed goby fish with salted lemon, and double-boiled pig's lung and almond soup.

陳小姐的祖父於1948年在上環開創此家族生意，1994年遷至現址，及後於2010年大規模翻新，廚房規模亦加以擴充。家傳秘方炮製的潮州鹵鵝仍然是招牌菜，另外還提供其他潮州特色美食，如潮州糖醋麵、檸檬蒸烏魚和杏汁燉白肺湯等。

TEL. 2858 0033
11 Queen's Road West, Sheung Wan
上環皇后大道西 11 號

■ PRICE 價錢
Lunch 午膳
set 套餐 $ 42-70
à la carte 點菜 $ 75-420
Dinner 晚膳
à la carte 點菜 $ 75-420

■ OPENING HOURS 營業時間
11:00-21:45 (L.O.)

■ ANNUAL AND WEEKLY CLOSING 休息日期
Closed 3 days Lunar New Year
農曆新年休息 3 天

Chang Won
莊園

Put aside the fact that the interior is practical rather than pretty, that you may have to share a table and that it's noisy and smoky, and instead just enjoy the tasty and authentic Korean cooking. Their wide choice of barbecued meats includes venison, pork, lamb, chicken and ox heart, liver and tripe; try the rich and intense beef short ribs or the various noodles, such as the seafood noodle stew or the noodles with black bean sauce.

裝修以實用為主,你或要在嘈雜又煙霧彌漫的環境中跟陌生人拼桌,但來到這裏,就盡情享受美味又傳統的韓式佳餚吧!他們提供多種燒烤肉食,包括鹿肉、豬肉、羊肉、雞肉、牛心、牛肝及牛肚等。此外,濃郁的炆牛肋骨煲及多種麵食,如海鮮火焰麵條或韓式炸醬麵均值得一試。

TEL. 2368 4606
1 Kimberley Street, Tsim Sha Tsui
尖沙咀金巴利街 1 號

■ PRICE 價錢
à la carte 點菜 $ 150-350

■ OPENING HOURS 營業時間
12:00-05:00 (L.O.)

Che's
車氏粵菜軒

✗✗   🍽35 ◐🍴

This unremarkable-looking little restaurant is popular with the local businessmen who come here in their droves for speedy service of the house speciality - crispy pork buns. But there are other reasons to visit: the dim sum at lunch; the extensive menu of classic dishes like crispy chicken or crab and dry scallop soup with bitter melon; simpler offerings such as congee or braised claypot dishes; and the blueberry pudding with which to end.

這家小餐館看似不起眼，但在本地商界人士間卻享負盛名，選擇豐富的經典粵菜如脆皮炸子雞，簡單卻美味的粥品和煲仔菜，還有午市點心，都使一眾食客趣之若鶩。服務快速且有效率，午餐時分往往座無虛席。

TEL. 2528 1123
4F, The Broadway,
54-62 Lockhart Road, Wan Chai
灣仔駱克道 54-62 號博匯大廈 4 樓

■ PRICE 價錢
Lunch 午膳
à la carte 點菜 $ 110-750
Dinner 晚膳
à la carte 點菜 $ 200-750

■ OPENING HOURS 營業時間
Lunch 午膳   11:30-15:00 L.O.14:15
Dinner 晚膳   18:00-22:15 (L.O.)

Chesa
瑞樵閣

XX

For over forty years, the cuisine of Switzerland has found a charming niche here. An imposing wood door leads you into an intimate Swiss-style chalet with wooden objects left, right and centre. Traditional Swiss dishes sit alongside the cheese specialities: fondue Vaudoise (traditional fondue) or raclette du Valais (hot melted cheese with potatoes, pickled onions and gherkins). For dessert: chocolate fondue or Swiss chocolate mousse.

瑞士美食在香港佔一席位超過四十年。氣派莊嚴的木門後是親切的瑞士農舍，四處都有木製的裝飾。傳統瑞士菜式與特選芝士系列互相輝映：沃州芝士火鍋（傳統芝士火鍋）或瓦萊州烤芝士（熱熔的芝士配馬鈴薯、醃洋蔥及青瓜）。至於甜品，巧克力火鍋或瑞士巧克力慕絲是兩大必吃之選！

TEL. 2696 6769
1F, The Peninsula Hotel,
Salisbury Road, Tsim Sha Tsui
尖沙咀梳士巴利道半島酒店 1 樓
www.peninsula.com

■ PRICE 價錢
Lunch 午膳
set 套餐 $ 338
à la carte 點菜 $ 450-850
Dinner 晚膳
à la carte 點菜 $ 450-850

■ OPENING HOURS 營業時間
Lunch 午膳　12:00-14:30 (L.O.)
Dinner 晚膳　18:30-22:30 (L.O.)

Chili Club
辣椒會

It's fair to say that customers aren't attracted to Chili Club by its looks. However, if you're strolling along Lockhart Road in search of sustenance you'll find yourself drawn inexorably into this Thai restaurant by the enticing aromas emanating from it. Proving further than one shouldn't judge by appearance, the kitchen is less preoccupied with presentation and instead focuses on delivering authentic and very satisfying flavours.

每次經過駱克道這幢大廈門前，都會嗅到陣陣香味，有時是混着椰香的泰式咖喱、有時是烤豬沙爹的肉香。推門進去經過曲折的樓梯，是這家開業逾二十年的辣椒會。菜式雖無佳美的外型，卻有正宗而味道層次豐富的泰國風味。室內裝潢亦很簡樸，透過大型玻璃窗能一覽駱克道的繁華景象。

TEL. 2527 2872
1F, 88 Lockhart Road, Wan Chai
灣仔洛克道 88號 1樓

■ PRICE 價錢
Lunch 午膳
à la carte 點菜 $ 100-350
Dinner 晚膳
à la carte 點菜 $ 100-350

■ OPENING HOURS 營業時間
Lunch 午膳   12:00-14:30 (L.O.)
Dinner 晚膳   18:00-22:30 (L.O.)

Chilli Fagara
麻辣燙

Those orange flames in the window represent a warning – chillies are a passion here! The walls come in a suitably rich red colour and a sweet ambience prevails, courtesy of the small team who ensure that all runs smoothly. The heat is turned up as you progress from mild 'natural' dishes through to the likes of red hot chilli prawn – which is only for the very brave. You can even round things off with a chilli chocolate ice cream.

窗上掛滿辣椒，橙色的火焰是預警！濃艷的紅牆意外地營造出親切氣氛，當你從溫和的「普通」菜式吃到辣椒蝦之類的菜餚時，便會渾身發熱！當然，勇氣可加的食客才會一嘗後者。最後以辣椒朱古力雪糕把味覺暫時麻痺。員工人數不多，但和諧的團隊合作，令餐廳運作順暢，更顯溫馨。

TEL. 2893 3330
Shop E, GF, 51A Graham Street, Soho, Central
中環店蘇豪嘉咸街 51A 地下 E 舖
www.chillifagara.com

■ PRICE 價錢
Lunch 午膳
set 套餐 $ 98
Dinner 晚膳
à la carte 點菜 $ 220-400

■ OPENING HOURS 營業時間
Lunch 午膳   11:30-14:30 (L.O.)
Dinner 晚膳   17:00-23:30 L.O.23:00

■ ANNUAL AND WEEKLY CLOSING 休息日期
Closed 3 days Lunar New Year and Monday
農曆新年 3 天及週一休息

HONG KONG 香港

China Tang NEW
唐人館

𝕏𝕏𝕏   P   ⌬24   ◖❢

Conceived and designed by Sir David Tang, this is the sister to the original branch found at The Dorchester hotel in London. The room has been tastefully and attractively decorated with a mix of traditional Chinese art and contemporary Western design, with hand-embroidered wallpaper, mirrors, antique lamps and books. Dishes from Beijing, Sichuan and Canton feature, along with dim sum; don't miss the traditional Beijing roasted duck.

由鄧永鏘爵士構思及設計的唐人館，是繼倫敦首間唐人館後又一傑作。人手刺繡的牆紙、獨特的鏡飾、古董燈以及線裝裝幀中式排版的菜譜－在在流露出一份典雅貴氣，將中式傳統藝術與西方美學結合得天衣無縫。菜單涵蓋粵、京、川等地美食及精製南北點心，其中老北京傳統烤鴨－一鴨三吃－滋味無窮。

TEL. 2522 2148
Shop 411-413, 4F, Landmark Atrium,
15 Queen's Road, Central
中環皇后大道中 15號
置地廣場 4樓 411-413號舖
www.chinatang.hk

SPECIALITIES TO PRE-ORDER 預訂食物
Traditional Beijing roasted duck 松老北京傳統掛爐烤鴨 / Hangzhou Vagabond chicken 火焰杭州富貴雞

■ PRICE 價錢
Lunch 午膳
set 套餐 $638 à la carte 點菜 $220-2,200
Dinner 晚膳
set 套餐 $1,580 à la carte 點菜 $320-2,200

■ OPENING HOURS 營業時間
Lunch 午膳 12:00-14:30 (L.O.)
Dinner 晚膳 18:00-22:30 (L.O.)

■ ANNUAL AND WEEKLY CLOSING 休息日期
Closed 3 days Lunar New Year
農曆新年休息 3 天

Chiu Chow Rice Roll
潮式腸粉

One way of attracting passing customers into your little restaurant is to name it after your speciality. The owner-chef here sells an assortment of Chiu Chow dishes and snacks but it is his rice roll that is the undoubted star of the show. It comes with a variety of toppings that include shrimp, squid or baby oyster with vegetables. You can also ask the owner for Chiu Chow specialities not listed on the menu, such as peach glutinous rice cake.

吸引顧客的最佳方法莫過於以店內著名菜式為餐廳命名。身兼店東的主廚精於製作各式各樣潮式小菜和小吃，當中潮式腸粉為其招牌菜，可以配搭不同餡料，如蝦、魷魚或蠔仔及蔬菜。食客可預訂多款潮州食品如紅桃粿及小米粿等。

TEL. 2418 9638
Shop 5, GF, Kin Fai Building,
69 Fung Cheung Road, Yuen Long
元朗鳳翔路 69號建輝大廈地下 5號舖

■ PRICE 價錢
à la carte 點菜 $30-90

■ OPENING HOURS 營業時間
11:00-22:30 (L.O.)

Chuen Cheung Kui (Mong Kok)
泉章居 (旺角)

Highlights of the menu of this first floor restaurant, which overlooks the street below, are those dishes based largely on traditional Hakkanese recipes, such as chicken baked in salt or stewed pork with preserved vegetables. In the afternoon, the smaller ground floor room is used for the serving of simpler, rice-based dishes. The restaurant has been owned by the same family since the 1960s and relocated to its current location in 2004.

餐館的一樓可看到街景。精選菜式以傳統客家菜為主，為人津津樂道的有鹽焗雞和梅菜扣肉。下層地舖面積較小，在下午時分主要供應烹調工序較簡單的「碟頭飯」。菜館自1960年代起一直由同一家族經營，直至2004年才遷至現址。

TEL. 2396 0672
Lisa House, 33 Nelson Street,
Mong Kok
旺角奶路臣街 33號依利大廈

■ PRICE 價錢
à la carte 點菜 $ 100-330

■ OPENING HOURS 營業時間
11:00-23:15 (L.O.)

■ ANNUAL AND WEEKLY CLOSING 休息日期
Closed 4 days Lunar New Year
農曆新年休息 4 天

Chuen Kee Seafood
全記海鮮菜館

Two family-run restaurants overlook a pleasant harbour to distant islands; choose the one with the rooftop terrace and the quayside plastic seats. An extraordinary range of seafood is available from adjacent fishmongers: cuttlefish, bivalve, crab and lobster, mollusc, shrimps, prawns…Go to the tank, select your meal, and minutes later it appears in front of you: steamed, poached, or wok-fried. Then settle back and watch the boats go by.

這兩家餐廳是家族生意，位置優越，可選擇有陽台的那一家，坐在碼頭邊的膠座椅上觀賞怡人海灣及離島景致。魚缸內的海鮮種類繁多，包括墨魚、貝類、蟹、龍蝦、瀨尿蝦、大蝦小蝦等等，任你隨意挑選。蒸、灼、炒也好，不一會就奉到餐桌上，然後你便可輕鬆地邊品嘗海鮮邊細覽海上景色。

TEL. 2791 1195
53 Hoi Pong Street, Sai Kung
西貢海傍街53號

■ PRICE 價錢
à la carte 點菜 $180-500

■ OPENING HOURS 營業時間
11:00-23:00 L.O. 22:30

CIAK - In The Kitchen NEW

                                                ♿ ⬚6 🚃 ⚇

There are four sections to this casual eatery in the Landmark Atrium which comes courtesy of celebrity chef Umberto Bombana: the kitchen, bakery, charcoal grill, and pasta bar. The decoration is simple yet contemporary and the atmosphere is bustling and busy. The food focuses on the tastes of an Italian home and the produce is available to take away. Afternoon tea is popular, as is brunch which is offered on weekends and public holidays.

此間以地道意大利市集風味作主打的餐廳，設計簡約時尚，置身其中猶如在家中般舒適自在，適合與三五知己共膳閒談。店內分為廚房、麵包店、炭燒食品及意粉吧四個區域，食客可以享受不同烹調風格的意大利家常美食。下午茶套餐格外受歡迎。此外，週末及公眾假期還會供應早午合餐。

TEL. 2522 8869
3F, Landmark Atrium, Shop 327-333,
15 Queen's Road Central
皇后大道中 15 號置地廣場 3 樓
327-333 號舖
www.ciakconcept.com

■ PRICE 價錢
Lunch 午膳
set 套餐 $ 268
à la carte 點菜 $ 250-500
Dinner 晚膳
à la carte 點菜 $ 250-500

■ OPENING HOURS 營業時間
Lunch 午膳　11:30-15:00 (L.O.)
Dinner 晚膳　18:00-23:00 (L.O.)

Cocotte NEW

✕   ©☏️⑪

The French food at this charming little restaurant is presented in a very contemporary style but the dishes are underpinned by traditional combinations of flavours. The cooking skills are accomplished and the seasonal ingredients excellent; dishes are also large enough to satisfy those who like to share. The room has a lively atmosphere and a bright, attractive look, with striking wallpaper, marble-topped tables and green velvet seating.

黑色鐵框玻璃門後是一間空間狹長的餐室。花俏的牆紙、雲石餐桌、橡木地板和綠色絲絨長沙發，創造出亮麗的環境與輕鬆的氣氛。喜歡法國菜的食客定會享受這裏的美食。廚師選用時令食材並以精細的烹調方式製作傳統菜，展現出時尚法國口味。份量較大的分享菜式，適合多人聚會，感覺更親密。

TEL. 2568 8857
9 Shin Hing Street, Central
中環善慶街 9號
www.cocotte.hk

■ PRICE 價錢
Lunch 午膳
set 套餐 $ 168-198
à la carte 點菜 $ 580-1,100
Dinner 晚膳
à la carte 點菜 $ 580-1,100

■ OPENING HOURS 營業時間
Lunch 午膳 12:00-14:30 (L.O.)
Weekends & Public Holidays
週末及公眾假期 11:00-15:00 (L.O.)
Dinner 晚膳 18:00-23:00 (L.O.)

■ ANNUAL AND WEEKLY CLOSING 休息日期
Closed Monday 週一休息

Come-Into Chiu Chow
金燕島

🍴🍴　　　　　　　　　　　　　　　　🛋16　◐🍴

The restaurant may have moved in 2014 but that hasn't stopped all the regulars coming along for their regular fix of Chiu Chow dishes. The team spirit of the staff, many of whom have been working together for over three decades, is clear to see and the restaurant itself has quite a grand feel and comes complete with assorted calligraphy and paintings. The standout Chiu Chow dishes include bird's nest and soyed meat such as goose web and wings.

餐廳在2014年遷至現址，共佔兩層，二樓有多間設備齊全的廂房，一樓的主餐室飾以書畫作品，裝潢甚具中式大宅氣派。　由早年在星光行開業起，此店一直以高級朝州菜馳名，共事已久的員工默契十足，熟客也追隨至今。馳名潮州美食有燕窩菜式和鹵味如鹵水鵝掌翼。

TEL. 2322 0020
1F, Guang Dong Hotel, 18 Prat Avenue, Tsim Sha Tsui
尖沙咀寶勒巷18號粵海酒店1樓
www.come-into.com.hk

■ PRICE 價錢
Lunch 午膳
à la carte 點菜　$ 150-1,000
Dinner 晚膳
à la carte 點菜　$ 250-1,000

■ OPENING HOURS 營業時間
Lunch 午膳　11:00-15:00 (L.O.)
Dinner 晚膳　17:30-22:30 (L.O.)

■ ANNUAL AND WEEKLY CLOSING 休息日期
Closed 3 days Lunar New Year
農曆新年休息3天

Comfort　NEW

Harlan Goldstein's relaxed eatery in LKF celebrates those dishes that can be listed under the heading 'comfort food'. As this notion means different things to different people, he has assembled a menu that includes many of his favourite dishes from all over the world, most of which he's got to know from over thirty years of travelling. The choice is considerable and includes everything from pizzas and tacos to crab cakes, curries and roast chicken.

Harlan Goldstein麾下的餐廳總能帶給食客驚喜!這間位於蘭桂芳的餐廳採用的餐單，是Harlan過去三十多年四處遊歷的結晶。餐單上羅列了他喜愛的世界各地美食，包括意大利薄餅、墨西哥玉米餅、西班牙火腿、美式蟹餅、泰式咖喱，甚至台灣刈包等，應有盡有。一同來用舌尖環遊世界吧!

TEL. 2521 8638
5F, Grand Progress Building, 15-16 Lan Kwai Fong, Central
中環蘭桂坊 15-16號協興大廈 5樓

■ PRICE 價錢
Lunch 午膳
set 套餐 $ 198
à la carte 點菜 $ 250-550
Dinner 晚膳
set 套餐 $ 288
à la carte 點菜 $ 250-550

■ OPENING HOURS 營業時間
Lunch 午膳　12:00-14:30 (L.O.)
Dinner 晚膳　18:00-22:30 (L.O.)

■ ANNUAL AND WEEKLY CLOSING 休息日期
Closed Sunday 週日休息

Congee and Noodle Shop
粥麵館

Just pull up a plastic chair, be willing to share your table with a stranger and simply enjoy traditional congee prepared by a chef with over 30 years' experience. Fresh crab congee and bitter melon and salty spare rib congee are bestsellers, but many of the customers also order congee to accompany a combination of their favourite ingredients, like fish belly and beef. The surroundings may be modest but everyone's here for the congee.

店內裝潢並不講究，然而食客全是為了美味粥品而來。為了品嘗逾三十年經驗老師傅精心炮製的傳統靚粥，客人都不介意坐塑膠椅及跟陌生人拼桌。暢銷粥品有原味蟹皇粥及涼瓜鹹排骨粥，但食客通常會選自己喜愛的配粥材料，如魚腩及牛肉等。

TEL. 2750 0208
2F, Kerry Centre, 683 King's Road,
Quarry Bay
鰂魚涌英皇道 683 號嘉里中心 2 樓

■ PRICE 價錢
à la carte 點菜 $ 25-110

■ OPENING HOURS 營業時間
10:30-20:15 (L.O.)

■ ANNUAL AND WEEKLY CLOSING 休息日期
Closed 3 days Lunar New Year
農曆新年休息 3 天

Crystal Jade La Mian Xiao Long Bao (Wan Chai)
翡翠拉麵小籠包 (灣仔)

🖏24

There's a subtle retro look to this modern diner with its plush, comfy booths and the place positively buzzes with energy. You'll also find contented looks on the faces of its customers and this is largely down to the quality of the Shanghai dumplings and noodles. It also offers home-style dishes, dim sum and decent desserts. Worth trying are sautéed shrimps with tea leaves, pork and vegetable wonton and glutinous dumpling in ginger soup.

餐廳位於商場三樓，裝潢時尚中帶點懷舊味道；巧手精製的上海小籠包與手拉麵食是其鎮店之寶，吸引不少食客，午飯時段更是人聲鼎沸，非常熱鬧。店內還提供多款家常小菜、點心及甜品如龍井蝦仁、菜肉雲吞及酒釀丸子等。

TEL. 2573 8844
Shop 310, 3F, Tai Yau Plaza, Wan Chai
灣仔大有廣場 3 樓 310 號舖
www.crystaljade.com

SPECIALITIES TO PRE-ORDER 預訂食物
Braised whole duck stuffed with glutinous rice 八寶鴨 / Steamed eel 古法蒸河鰻

■ PRICE 價錢
Lunch 午膳
à la carte 點菜 $ 100-200
Dinner 晚膳
à la carte 點菜 $ 100-200

■ OPENING HOURS 營業時間
11:00-22:30 (L.O.)

■ ANNUAL AND WEEKLY CLOSING 休息日期
Closed 2 days Lunar New Year
農曆新年休息 2 天

Cuisine Cuisine at The Mira
國金軒 (The Mira)

♿ ⛽ ⏱24 ❀

When you come across a stylish and contemporary dining room such as this one, with its eye-catching chandeliers, intimate spaces and modern furniture, you can be fairly certain that its Cantonese food will also come with a few modern twists. Along with the dim sum at lunch, try signature dishes like honey-glazed barbecue pork and marinated abalone in Hua Diao. The restaurant is on the 3rd floor of the equally fashionable Mira hotel.

當你踏入這家別具型格又充滿現代感的餐廳：引人注目的吊燈、私人空間和摩登家具，你幾乎可以肯定這裏的廣東美食，也會融入精巧的現代變化。除了午市供應的精美點心外，招牌菜如蜜餞叉燒皇及酒香鮑魚等值得一試。餐廳座落於同樣時尚的The Mira酒店三樓。

TEL. 2315 5222
3F, The Mira Hotel, 118 Nathan Road,
Tsim Sha Tsui
尖沙咀彌敦道 118號 The Mira 3樓
www.themirahotel.com

■ PRICE 價錢
Lunch 午膳
set 套餐 $ 398
à la carte 點菜 $ 200-1,350
Dinner 晚膳
set 套餐 $ 948-1,128
à la carte 點菜 $ 350-1,350

■ OPENING HOURS 營業時間
Lunch 午膳　11:30-14:30 (L.O.)
Dinner 晚膳　18:00-22:30 (L.O.)

Da Ping Huo
大平伙

This charming, hidden restaurant is ideal for those wanting something a little different. It is run by a couple from Sichuan: he is an artist and his wife is a singer. She cooks a nightly 11 course menu (and 6 courses at lunch), using authentic and family-style Sichuan recipes while he welcomes the guests into the modern and elegant restaurant which he created himself. And at the end of the evening, she'll even sing for her customers!

這家獨具魅力的餐廳由一對來自四川的夫婦經營。時尚典雅的餐室由本身是藝術家的男主人親自設計，曾為歌手的太太則主力統籌廚房團隊的運作，為客人烹調正宗四川家常小菜。偶爾，太太會在晚餐時段為客人獻唱一、兩首民謠。

TEL. 2559 1317
LG, Hilltop Plaza, 49 Hollywood Road, Central
中環荷李活道 49 號鴻豐商業中心地下低層
https://dapinghuo.com.hk

■ PRICE 價錢
Lunch 午膳
set 套餐 $ 140-160
Dinner 晚膳
set 套餐 $ 350

■ OPENING HOURS 營業時間
Lunch 午膳   12:00-14:30 (L.O.)
Dinner 晚膳   18:30-23:00 (L.O.)

Delicious Inn
和味館

🍜 ▯▯   🍽30   🕐▯

A large number of locals come to this unremarkable looking restaurant because of its wide selection of reasonably priced Cantonese dishes, assorted seafood and hot casseroles. But Delicious Inn also attracts those with a taste for the exotic, because it is equally known for its more unusual offerings, such as baked fish intestines and donkey casserole, as well as dishes featuring bugs like fried bee pupa with spicy salt or bamboo worm.

很多本地食客會慕名到此外貌平平無奇的餐廳,一嘗其選擇繁多且價錢實惠的廣東菜式、多款海鮮及熱辣辣的煲仔菜。和味館對口味獨特的食客也別具吸引力,因為它供應多款特色美食,如焗魚腸及驢仔煲,及更特別的菜式,如椒鹽皇蜂蛹。

TEL. 2387 1008
6-8 Wing Kwong Street, Hung Hom
紅磡榮光街 6-8號

■ PRICE 價錢
Dinner 晚膳
à la carte 點菜 $ 120-200

■ OPENING HOURS 營業時間
Dinner 晚膳 18:00-02:30 (L.O.)

Din Tai Fung (Causeway Bay)
鼎泰豐 (銅鑼灣)

✄   ⟐ 14 ⊘🍴

Queuing can be a tiresome bind but occasionally the reward for
waiting in line makes it worthwhile. Din Tai Fung's Xiao Long Bao
are so terrific you'll find it hard not to re-order a second basket –
and you can even watch them being made while waiting for a table.
Other standouts are double-boiled chicken soup and braised beef
brisket noodle soup. The place is bigger than the Tsim Sha Tsui
branch and is run with impressive efficiency.

這間位於銅鑼灣的分店不但更摩登，而且佔地更廣，也同樣備受追捧，很多時
都需要輪候入座。菜牌包括上海小菜與點心，小籠包是其重點所在。熱賣菜式
有原盅雞湯與紅燒牛肉湯麵。飯店還為初次光顧的客人提供進食馳名小籠包的
說明，非常周到。

TEL. 3160 8998
Shop G3-G11, GF, 68 Yee Woo Street,
Causeway Bay
銅鑼灣怡和街 68號地下 G3-G11號舖
www.dintaifung.com.hk

■ PRICE 價錢
à la carte 點菜 $ 110-280

■ OPENING HOURS 營業時間
11:30-22:00 (L.O.)

■ ANNUAL AND WEEKLY CLOSING 休息日期
Closed 3 days Lunar New Year
農曆新年休息 3 天

Din Tai Fung (Tsim Sha Tsui)
鼎泰豐 (尖沙咀)

✗   🍽12   ✦🍴

Mr Yang opened up his dumpling shop in Taiwan back in 1958 and focused on delivering service, price and quality; there are now branches in all major Asian cities. Fresh, handmade Shanghai dumplings are their speciality and they are extremely good; the steamed pork ones being especially tasty. Queues are the norm here, but don't worry: a team of 130 smart and efficient staff serve at least 1000 people a day and take it all in their stride.

楊先生在1958年於台灣開辦首家小籠包店，特別注重服務、價格及品質；如今，在所有主要亞洲城市均有分店。新鮮、經人手炮製的上海小籠包是主打，餡料充足，令人食指大動。店前常擠滿排隊輪候的食客，由一百三十名員工組成的服務團隊非常有效率，每天最少服務一千名客人。

TEL. 2730 6928
Shop 130 & Restaurant C,
3F Silvercord, 30 Canton Road,
Tsim Sha Tsui
尖沙咀廣東道 30號新港中心 3樓 C130號舖
www.dintaifung.com.hk

■ PRICE 價錢
à la carte 點菜 $ 110-280

■ OPENING HOURS 營業時間
11:30-22:30 (L.O.)

■ ANNUAL AND WEEKLY CLOSING 休息日期
Closed 3 days Lunar New Year
農曆新年休息 3 天

Dong Lai Shun
東來順

♿ 🖼️ 🍽️24 🕙

The first Dong Lai Shun was founded in 1903 in Peking, and has been successfully transplanted to the basement of the Royal Garden hotel. Its décor is contemporary with distinct Asian nuances, panels and paintings; there's also a water feature which creates a relaxing atmosphere. The mix of Beijing and Huaiyang recipes includes hotpot, Peking duck and 'shuan yang rou': paper thin slices of Mongolian black-headed mutton.

餐廳的裝修揉合了現代和傳統格調；鮮明細緻的亞洲特色，從牆板和壁畫便可略窺一二。這裏的人工噴泉更營造了閒適的氣氛。食物方面，餐廳的北京和淮陽菜共冶一爐，包括火鍋、北京填鴨，以及「涮羊肉」：採用蒙古黑頭白羊的上乘部分，肉質薄如紙，軟如棉。

TEL. 2733 2020
B2F, The Royal Garden Hotel,
69 Mody Road, East Tsim Sha Tsui
尖東麼地道 69 號帝苑酒店地庫 2 樓
www.rghk.com.hk

■ PRICE 價錢
Lunch 午膳
set 套餐 $ 158
à la carte 點菜 $ 220-1,300
Dinner 晚膳
set 套餐 $ 538
à la carte 點菜 $ 220-1,300

■ OPENING HOURS 營業時間
Lunch 午膳　11:30-14:30 (L.O.)
Dinner 晚膳　18:00-22:30 (L.O.)

Dot Cod

✗✗ 20 ☺

A favourite spot for many in Central is Dot Cod, owned by the Hong Kong Cricket Club. The bar gets busy, especially when a match is being shown, but the dining room is a slightly more relaxing spot. It's the seafood that bowls them over here; your waiter will present the daily special on a tray at your table. Fish pie, 'surf and turf' and Blue crab cakes are perennial favourites. Tuesday is 'Lobster night'; Wednesday is 'Oyster night'.

由香港木球會主理、位於地庫,是中環一族經常流連之處。內裏的酒吧在有球賽進行期間特別繁忙,用餐區則相對悠閒。海鮮是這裏一大賣點,侍應會把一大盤當日精選海鮮放在餐桌旁供你點選;魚餡餅、海陸大餐和藍蟹餅是大受歡迎的菜式;逢星期二是龍蝦之夜,星期三則是生蠔之夜。

TEL. 2810 6988
B4, Prince's Building, 10 Charter Road, Central
中環遮打道 10 號太子大廈地庫 B4
www.dotcod.com

■ PRICE 價錢
Lunch 午膳
set 套餐 $ 278-308
à la carte 點菜 $ 480-1,280
Dinner 晚膳
à la carte 點菜 $ 480-1,280

■ OPENING HOURS 營業時間
07:30-22:30 (L.O.)

■ ANNUAL AND WEEKLY CLOSING 休息日期
Closed Sunday and Public Holidays
週日及公眾假期休息

Dragon Inn
容龍

      🅿 ⬭72 🕐

There aren't many locals who haven't heard of Dragon Inn as it's been here in one form or another since 1939. It may have great views to the sea across tropical gardens but it's the seafood most come for – some regulars don't even look at the main menu but just pick from the seafood speciality list. Baked baby lobster with cheese or baked oysters with port are favourites and dim sum is now offered during the day. Ask for a window table.

容龍海鮮酒家在本區可謂無人不曉，不少遊人都喜愛到這裏欣賞一望無際的海景及熱帶花園，受歡迎是意料中事。但最吸引客人的是這裏的海鮮。個別食客完全不看主菜牌，而直接從海鮮單上挑選食物。芝士焗龍蝦與砵酒焗生蠔是必然之選。日間有點心供應。預訂時可選擇靠窗座位。

TEL. 2450 6366
Castle Peak Road, Miles 19, Tuen Mun
屯門青山公路 19 咪

■ PRICE 價錢
à la carte 點菜 $ 150-500

■ OPENING HOURS 營業時間
10:00-22:30 (L.O.)

■ ANNUAL AND WEEKLY CLOSING 休息日期
Closed Lunar New Year 年初一休息

HONG KONG 香港

Dragon King (Kwun Tong)
龍皇 (觀塘)

✗✗　　　　　　　　　　　　　　　&　P　🖥60　◐🍴

Creative Cantonese dishes with a seafood slant are the draw at this contemporary dining room owned by famous local chef Wong Wing Chee. Standout dishes include Australian Tiger Jade abalone double-boiled with herbs, and Mantis prawns steamed in a bamboo basket. From time to time the chefs enter group culinary competitions to aid their cooking skills and creative thinking – the results can be seen in some of the more innovative dishes on the menu.

這家富現代感的中菜館，提供以海鮮為主的創新廣東菜式，東主為香港著名廚師黃永幟。在芸芸美食中，最出眾的有石決明燉老虎鮑和清蒸斑馬富貴蝦。所屬集團會定期舉行廚藝比賽，讓各分店主廚施展實力與創意，同時亦會將配搭新穎的得獎菜式上市供食客品嘗。

TEL. 2955 0668
2F, Yen Sheng Centre,
64 Hoi Yuen Road, Kwun Tong
觀塘開源道 64 號源成中心 2 樓
www.dragonking.com.hk

■ PRICE 價錢
Lunch 午膳
à la carte 點菜 $ 120-650
Dinner 晚膳
à la carte 點菜 $ 150-650

■ OPENING HOURS 營業時間
Lunch 午膳　11:00-15:30 (L.O.)
Dinner 晚膳　18:00-23:00 (L.O.)

Duddell's
都爹利會館

XX 12 📷🍴 ⚘

Art and food have been inexorably linked since bison first appeared in Palaeolithic cave drawings. Here at Duddell's, art, culture and cuisine all come together over two bright, stylish floors which also host regular exhibitions, screenings and performances. In contrast to the contemporary look of the space, the Cantonese cooking is based on traditional methods, although the kitchen's skill is obvious and the quality of the ingredients palpable.

你或會驚歎鮮黃的長沙發、簡約時尚的硬木傢具和中國水墨畫，竟能如此協調和諧。由名廚主理的美食走的是樸實路線，以頂級材料配合傳統烹調技術與廚師那細緻的功夫製作食物，一點也不花巧。這間位於都爹利街的新餐館除了展現美食與藝術的結合外，亦是一種生活態度。

TEL. 2525 9191
Level 3, Shanghai Tang Mansion,
1 Duddell Street, Central
中環都爹利街 1 號上海灘 3 樓
www.duddells.co

■ PRICE 價錢
Lunch 午膳
set 套餐 $ 350
à la carte 點菜 $ 400-1,500
Dinner 晚膳
set 套餐 $ 980
à la carte 點菜 $ 600-1,500

■ OPENING HOURS 營業時間
Lunch 午膳　12:00-14:30 (L.O.)
Dinner 晚膳　18:00-22:30 (L.O.)

HONG KONG 香港

Dumpling Yuan (Central)
餃子園 (中環)

You might wonder why there are only ladies working here – it's because they take their dumplings very seriously and don't consider men to have the required patience or the delicate touch needed to make good dumplings. We recommend the pork with cabbage and the mutton with green onions; but also try bean curd with wild vegetables, and spiced donkey meat with noodles.

你也許會奇怪為何這裏只有女性員工，因為店主非常重視餃子的質素，認為男性不具備做出色餃子必須的條件一足夠耐性與纖細觸覺。推薦鮮肉白菜餃與北蔥羊肉餃。這裏的上海菜也非常出色，特別推介香干馬蘭頭，五香驢肉及炸醬麵。

TEL. 2525 9018
98 Wellington Street, Central
中環威靈頓街 98 號

■ PRICE 價錢
à la carte 點菜 $ 30-100

■ OPENING HOURS 營業時間
11:00-23:00 (L.O.)

■ ANNUAL AND WEEKLY CLOSING 休息日期
Closed 3 days Lunar New Year
農曆新年休息 3 天

Épure NEW

🏠 ≤ **P** 🍽14 ◎🍴 ⚭

If you can avoid the temptations in the patisserie by the entrance you'll find yourself in a very comfortable French restaurant, courtesy of the Dalloyau group. Gold and greens combine with woods to create quite a striking look. The French chef uses his considerable expertise to produce easy-to-eat dishes in an appealing modern style. The food is accompanied by an outstanding wine list, which includes an impressive selection of Burgundy.

印上巴黎舊街道圖的金色大閘，為美食之旅揭開序幕。穿過第二道大門，是長弧形主餐室：綠色、金色與橡木交織出一份奢華時尚。法籍大廚以精湛的烹調功夫，選用法國時令食材，製作細膩味美的菜式。餐酒單內含超過四百款餐酒，當中有不少罕有的布根地垂直年份佳釀。半圓廂座，給你更多私人空間。

TEL. 3185 8338
Shop 403, Level 4,
Ocean Centre Harbour City,
Canton Road,Tsim Sha Tsui
尖沙咀廣東道海港城海洋中心 4樓 403號舖
www.epure.hk

■ PRICE 價錢
Lunch 午膳
set 套餐 $ 398-638
Dinner 晚膳
set 套餐 $ 1,288-1,588
à la carte 點菜 $ 790-1,250

■ OPENING HOURS 營業時間
Lunch 午膳　12:00-14:30 (L.O.)
Dinner 晚膳　18:30-22:00 (L.O.)

Fandango

If ever there was a restaurant ideal for a first date then this is it – for when decoration is as exuberant as this, you're never likely to run out of conversation. Think Castilian hacienda designed by Salvador Dali; and all accompanied by an inimitable live band. The atmosphere is also pretty laid back and the cooking is suitably authentic. Dishes not to be missed are the Iberico ham, the paella and the boquerones.

要選初次約會的理想勝地，非它莫屬。單是充滿活力的裝潢就讓你讚歎不已。試幻想由薩爾瓦多·達利設計的西班牙莊園，配以扣人心弦的現場樂隊演奏，懶洋洋的氣氛加上正宗的西班牙菜餚，是一個何等多姿多彩的畫面!黑毛豬火腿、西班牙海鮮飯和鳳尾魚都不容錯過。

TEL. 2957 8797
9F, The Toy House, 100 Canton Road,
Tsim Sha Tsui
尖沙咀廣東道100號彩星集團9樓

■ PRICE 價錢
Lunch 午膳
set 套餐 $148
à la carte 點菜 $380-950
Dinner 晚膳
à la carte 點菜 $380-950

■ OPENING HOURS 營業時間
Lunch 午膳　12:00-14:30 (L.O.)
Dinner 晚膳　18:00-22:30 (L.O.)

■ ANNUAL AND WEEKLY CLOSING 休息日期
Closed 2 days Lunar New Year
農曆新年休息2天

Farm House
農圃

XX

⊟24 ◎⫯

Set in a sleek business building, this contemporary dining room has private rooms leading off it as well as an eye-catching aquarium running the entire length of one wall. A highlight of the Cantonese menu is the deep-fried chicken wing stuffed with glutinous rice, while other specialities include the baked sea whelk with goose liver, and steamed rice with abalone and dried chicken. Many of the ingredients are also available to buy.

飯店裝潢時尚，進門便可看到數間貴賓房和一個延伸整道牆的巨型水族箱，非常引人注目。農圃的粵菜選用特級新鮮材料炮製而成，著名菜式有古法糯米雞翼、鵝肝焗釀響螺和瑤柱鮑魚雞粒飯。飯店亦出售一些難於家中烹調的食物如鮑魚及海參。

TEL. 2881 1331
1F, 8 Sunning Road, Causeway Bay
銅鑼灣新寧道 8號 1樓
www.farmhouse.com.hk

■ PRICE 價錢
Lunch 午膳
à la carte 點菜 $ 200-900
Dinner 晚膳
à la carte 點菜 $ 200-900

■ OPENING HOURS 營業時間
Lunch 午膳　11:00-15:00 L.O. 14:45
Dinner 晚膳　18:00-00:00 L.O. 22:45

Felix

XX

       ♿ ← ☞♪ ◐‖

The unmistakeable hand of designer Philippe Starck has been at work at the top of The Peninsula, creating a striking restaurant with an ethereal quality. The kitchen matches the surroundings by using modern techniques to create inventive dishes; prices may be as vertiginous as the hotel but there is a reasonably priced early dinner menu. Competing with the theatrical design are some of the best views you'll find in any restaurant in the world.

著名設計師 Philippe Starck 匠心獨運，讓半島酒店的頂樓餐廳盡顯不凡。廚房配合整體環境，運用現代技巧創作新穎精緻的佳餚。餐廳收費大概如酒店的裝潢令人目眩，但亦有提供收費合理的特惠晚餐時段菜單。全球只有少數餐廳能與之匹敵的醉人景色，與舞台般的室內設計完美配合。

TEL. 2696 6778
28F, The Peninsula Hotel,
Salisbury Road, Tsim Sha Tsui
尖沙咀梳士巴利道半島酒店 28樓
www.peninsula.com

■ PRICE 價錢
à la carte 點菜 $ 700-1,400

■ OPENING HOURS 營業時間
Dinner 晚膳 18:00-22:30 (L.O.)

Fofo by el Willy

Fofo means 'chubby' and, judging by the look on the faces of the plump pig and penguin figures dotted around the room, therein lies contentment. For those eating here, three of the authentic Spanish dishes for each person, plus a little rice, should bring equal joy. The appealing tapas range from the popular suckling pig, which is slow-roasted overnight, to fried croquettes of Iberian ham and fried gambas with garlic and chilli. Try the roof terrace for even better views.

Fofo是「圓胖」之意。小豬與企鵝裝飾臉上滿足的表情,與店名非常相配。在這兒,每位食客能享用三道傳統西班牙菜和少許飯,那份滿足,非筆墨能形容。從以慢火通宵烤製的脆皮乳豬,到脆炸伊比利亞火腿丸子和蒜椒炸蝦等,全是令人垂涎的西班牙小菜。可選擇在屋頂露台用餐。

TEL. 2900 2009
20F, M88 2-8 Wellington Street, Central
中環威靈頓街 2-8號 M88 20樓
www.fofo.hk

■ PRICE 價錢
Lunch 午膳
set 套餐 $ 218-285
à la carte 點菜 $ 300-600

Dinner 晚膳
à la carte 點菜 $ 300-650

■ OPENING HOURS 營業時間
Lunch 午膳　12:00-14:30 (L.O.)
Dinner 晚膳　18:00-22:30 (L.O.)

■ ANNUAL AND WEEKLY CLOSING 休息日期
Closed 3 days Lunar New Year and Sunday 農曆新年 3 天及週日休息

HONG KONG 香港

Fook Lam Moon (Tsim Sha Tsui)
福臨門 (尖沙咀)

✗✗✗   ⚐ ☞ ⬭100 ⊙⏲

This Kowloon branch may have fewer corporate customers than the one in Wan Chai but it shares the same principles: fresh ingredients treated with the utmost care. The result is that this refined Cantonese cooking has been attracting a loyal following since the restaurant opened in 1972. Along with their signature crispy chicken are specialities like aged abalone braised with oyster sauce, and braised bird's nest in bamboo fungus.

與灣仔店相比，光顧九龍分店的商務人士可能較少，但兩店都秉承同一宗旨：以新鮮、時令材料精心炮製。這種優良的粵菜烹調方法備受美食愛好者欣賞，難怪自1972年開業迄今吸引不少忠實捧場客。除招牌蠔皇乾鮑外，不妨也嘗嘗當紅炸子雞及官燕釀竹笙卷。

TEL. 2366 0286
53-59 Kimberley Road, Tsim Sha Tsui
尖沙咀金巴利道 53-59號
www.fooklammoon-grp.com

SPECIALITIES TO PRE-ORDER 預訂食物
Barbequed suckling pig (whole) 大紅片皮乳豬全體 / Double-boiled whole chicken stuffed with bird's nest 上湯鳳吞燕

■ PRICE 價錢
Lunch 午膳
à la carte 點菜 $ 200-2,100
Dinner 晚膳
à la carte 點菜 $ 380-2,100

■ OPENING HOURS 營業時間
Lunch 午膳　11:30-14:30 (L.O.)
Dinner 晚膳　18:00-22:30 (L.O.)

■ ANNUAL AND WEEKLY CLOSING 休息日期
Closed 2 days Lunar New Year
農曆新年休息 2 天

Fook Lam Moon (Wan Chai)
福臨門 (灣仔)

☆

🖐 🍴   ♿ ⤴ ⟐150 ◔🍴

Run with considerable passion by the third generation of the same family, Fook Lam Moon is one of the best known restaurants around and attracts many regulars. Decoration of the two large dining rooms is based around a colour scheme of gold, silver and bronze which seems appropriate as there are so many luxury items on the menu. The respect for the ingredients is palpable and signature dishes include baked stuffed crab shell and roast suckling pig.

「福臨門」意指「好運來到你家門」，現由創業家族的第三代經營，是城中最享負盛名的酒家之一，深受一眾食家愛戴。店內的兩個大堂以金、銀、銅色系裝潢，映襯着菜單上的珍饌百味。食材明顯經過精心處理，招牌菜包括釀焗鮮蟹蓋與大紅片皮乳豬。

TEL. 2866 0663
35-45 Johnston Road, Wan Chai
灣仔莊士敦道 35-45號
www.fooklammoon-grp.com

SPECIALITIES TO PRE-ORDER 預訂食物
Barbequed suckling pig (whole) 大紅片皮乳豬全體 / Double-boiled whole chicken stuffed with bird's nest 上湯鳳吞燕

■ PRICE 價錢
Lunch 午膳
à la carte 點菜 $ 300-2,000
Dinner 晚膳
à la carte 點菜 $ 400-2,000

■ OPENING HOURS 營業時間
Lunch 午膳 11:30-14:30 (L.O.)
Dinner 晚膳 18:00-22:30 (L.O.)

■ ANNUAL AND WEEKLY CLOSING 休息日期
Closed 2 days Lunar New Year
農曆新年休息 2 天

Forum NEW
富臨飯店

🍴🍴   💺 🍽48 ☎🍽

Everyone knows the name of Yeung Koon Yat, the owner chef of Forum; indeed, his signature dish of Ah Yat abalone has rapidly acquired iconic status and some have even been known to travel to Hong Kong from overseas just to try his delicacy. The new premises are more comfortable and contemporary than the old address and thankfully all the kitchen team made the move too. As well as abalone, you can try other options like pan-fried star garoupa.

各位對餐廳老闆楊貫一的大名一定不會陌生。多年來他的客由本地食客到世界知名人士，全是他的座上客，其招牌菜阿一鮑魚更是天下聞名。此店搬至現址後，面積更廣、裝潢更豪華兼具時代感。滿有默契的幕後團隊聚首一堂為食客炮製美食。日本乾鮑製作的砂鍋鮑魚和海鮮類如生煎東星斑等均不可錯過。

TEL. 2869 8282
1F, Sino Plaza,
255-257 Gloucester Road,
Causeway Bay
銅鑼灣告士打道 255-257號信和廣場 1樓

■ PRICE 價錢
Lunch 午膳
set 套餐 $ 1,280-1,580
à la carte 點菜 $ 500-5,000
Dinner 晚膳
set 套餐 $ 1,280-1,580
à la carte 點菜 $ 500-5,000

■ OPENING HOURS 營業時間
Lunch 午膳 11:00-14:45 (L.O.)
Sunday lunch 週日午膳
10:30-14:45 (L.O.)
Dinner 晚膳 17:30-22:30 (L.O.)

From The Yuan
原汁原味

You'll find this restaurant, which specialises in healthy, home-style Cantonese dishes along with some Sichuan specialities, on the ground floor of a 1960s building which houses the Mingle Place hotel. The nourishing double-boiled soups are popular and also recommended is the baked chicken in a whole pumpkin and deep-fried fish jaw with garlic. Rustic wooden tables and pictures of old Hong Kong add to the sense of nostalgia.

這家餐廳位於一棟1960年代的唐樓地下,是名樂居精品酒店的所在地。崇尚健康飲食,提供家庭式廣東小菜和滋補燉湯,另有數款四川特色美食。家常小菜午餐頗受上班一族歡迎,晚飯套餐選擇多且價錢實惠。粗糙的木桌和老香港照片為此店添上幾分懷舊氣氛。

TEL. 2891 2018
141 Wan Chai Road, Wan Chai
灣仔灣仔道 141 號
www.minglekitchen.com

■ PRICE 價錢
Lunch 午膳
set 套餐 $ 45-70
à la carte 點菜 $ 130-200
Dinner 晚膳
set 套餐 $ 120-145
à la carte 點菜 $ 130-200

■ OPENING HOURS 營業時間
Lunch 午膳　11:30-15:00 (L.O.)
Dinner 晚膳　18:00-23:00 (L.O.)

■ ANNUAL AND WEEKLY CLOSING 休息日期
Closed 3 days Lunar New Year
農曆新年休息 3 天

Fu Ho (Tsim Sha Tsui)
富豪 (尖沙咀)

XXX   36 ☺Ⅱ

Thanks to its authentic cooking, diners have been coming to this Cantonese restaurant on a hidden floor of the Miramar shopping centre for over a decade. Among the specialities that appeal to these scores of regulars are the signature abalone dishes, the bird's nest with almond cream and the fried rice 'Ah Yung'. The most recent refurbishment gave this comfortable and relaxing restaurant a contemporary and elegant look.

這家粵菜酒家憑着正宗的烹調方式打響名堂，即使位於美麗華商場不太起眼的一層，十多年來依然吸引無數饕客。招牌菜有阿翁鮑魚、杏汁官燕、阿翁炒飯。酒家於近年重新裝修後，不但時尚優雅，更帶來舒適和悠閒感覺。

TEL. 2736 2228
4F, Miramar Shopping Centre,
132 Nathan Road, Tsim Sha Tsui
尖沙咀彌敦道132號美麗華商場4樓

■ PRICE 價錢
Lunch 午膳
set 套餐 $150
à la carte 點菜 $250-2,500
Dinner 晚膳
à la carte 點菜 $250-2,500

■ OPENING HOURS 營業時間
11:00-00:00 L.O. 22:30

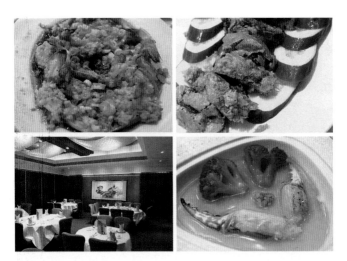

Fu Sing (Causeway Bay)
富聲 (銅鑼灣)

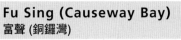

✗✗✗ 　　　　　　　　　　　　　　　🍽32 🕐🍴

With its modern interior, attentive service and accessible location, it is little wonder that this large second Fu Sing restaurant has proved so successful. The dim sum selection is comprehensive and the prices are suitably appealing to allow for much over-ordering. Specialities include steamed crab in Chinese wine and soy sauce chicken in Fu Sing style, but we also recommend the garoupa with preserved vegetables and fish head soup in Shun Tak style.

富現代感的裝潢，細心的服務，加上地點便利，難怪這間富聲第二分店會如此成功。點心選擇多而價錢合理，客人總忍不住多點幾道菜！招牌菜包括富聲花雕蒸蟹和鮑汁豉油雞。甜菜三葱炒斑球及順德無骨魚雲羹同樣值得一試。

TEL. 2504 4228
1F, 68 Yee Wo Street, Causeway Bay
銅鑼灣怡和街 68號 1樓

■ PRICE 價錢
Lunch 午膳
à la carte 點菜 $ 130-600
Dinner 晚膳
à la carte 點菜 $ 200-600

■ OPENING HOURS 營業時間
Lunch 午膳　11:00-15:00 L.O.14:30
Dinner 晚膳　18:00-23:00 L.O.22:30

■ ANNUAL AND WEEKLY CLOSING 休息日期
Closed 2 days Lunar New Year
農曆新年休息 2 天

Fu Sing (Wan Chai)
富聲 (灣仔)

🍴🍴   🍽36 📞🍴

Located in a commercial building in Wan Chai, the dining room of Fu Sing is modern and benefits from having a glass roof. The service team are attentive and the cooking, with its broad repertoire of Cantonese dishes, is undertaken with equal care. Dim sum is recommended, as is fresh garoupa fillet with preserved cabbage, fish head soup in Shun Tak style, soy sauce chicken Fu Sing style, and steamed crab in Chinese wine.

富聲位處時尚大樓之中，升降機可帶你直達這富麗堂皇、佔地寬廣的酒家，採用玻璃天花的餐室設計風格富現代感。侍應服務非常周到，選擇多元化的粵菜餐單，全屬精心炮製之作。除了點心以外，推介菜式包括胡椒豬骨湯、富聲鮑汁豉油雞及花雕蒸蟹。

TEL. 2893 2228
3F, 353 Lockhart Road, Sunshine Plaza,
Wan Chai
灣仔駱克道 353號三湘大廈 3樓

■ PRICE 價錢
Lunch 午膳
à la carte 點菜 $ 130-600
Dinner 晚膳
à la carte 點菜 $ 200-600

■ OPENING HOURS 營業時間
Lunch 午膳　11:00-15:00 (L.O.)
Dinner 晚膳　18:00-23:00 (L.O.)

■ ANNUAL AND WEEKLY CLOSING 休息日期
Closed 2 days Lunar New Year
農曆新年休息 2 天

Fung Lum
楓林小館

😊

✗✗ 　　　　　　　　　　　🗣 ⌖40

Set opposite Tai Wai station and known for its striking façade is the original Fung Lum; the famed replica in Los Angeles was a hit in the 1980s. The recipes remain untarnished to this day, with the seafood being highly recommended, particularly the deep-fried shrimp on toast and the baked crab with black beans; many of the regulars believe that the pigeon is also a must. If ordering several dishes, ask for them to be paced accordingly.

位於大圍火車站對面的楓林小館，門面設計讓人印象深刻，店內裝潢充滿懷舊色彩；仿照這裏的原裝設計—著名的洛杉磯贗品—在一九八零年代曾瘋靡一時。傳統粵菜單依然深受歡迎，海鮮尤其出色，如窩貼蝦球及豉汁焗蟹，乳鴿是常客必吃之選。

TEL. 2692 1175
45-47 Tsuen Nam Road, Tai Wai,
Sha Tin
沙田大圍村南道 45-47號

■ PRICE 價錢
Lunch 午膳
à la carte 點菜 $ 90-500
Dinner 晚膳
à la carte 點菜 $ 150-500

■ OPENING HOURS 營業時間
Lunch 午膳 11:00-15:00 (L.O.)
Dinner 晚膳 17:30-22:30 L.O. 22:00

■ ANNUAL AND WEEKLY CLOSING 休息日期
Closed 4 days Lunar New Year
農曆新年休息 4 天

HONG KONG 香港

Fung Shing (Mong Kok)
鳳城 (旺角)

Owner-chef Mr Tam looks to the region of Shun Tak for inspiration for his tasty Cantonese cooking – must try dishes are stir-fried milk with egg whites and roasted suckling pig. This family business has been going since 1954; they have a second branch in North Point and their story has been published along with assorted recipes. The two-storey restaurant is always busy, so it's well worth booking in advance.

鳳城酒家的歷史與部分食譜已輯錄成書出版。主廚兼老闆譚國景從順德菜中尋找烹調美味廣東菜的靈感，大良炒鮮奶及馳名燒乳豬絕對值得一試。這個由家族經營的生意始於1954年，另外一間店位於北角。位於旺角的這家總店共有兩層。這裏門庭若市，建議預早訂座。

TEL. 2381 5261
1-2F, 749 Nathan Road, Mong Kok
旺角彌敦道 749號 1-2樓

■ PRICE 價錢
Lunch 午膳
à la carte 點菜 $ 140-350
Dinner 晚膳
à la carte 點菜 $ 180-350

■ OPENING HOURS 營業時間
Lunch 午膳　09:00-15:00 (L.O.)
Dinner 晚膳　18:00-22:30 (L.O.)

■ ANNUAL AND WEEKLY CLOSING 休息日期
Closed 4 days Lunar New Year
農曆新年休息 4 天

Gaddi's
吉地士

XXXX 　　　　　　　🍴 ⏱16 📞🍴 🐝

Gaddi's is something of an institution. A private lift whisks you to this 'fine dining' legend, which opened its doors in 1953. Live music and old-style British formality accompany the French cuisine, which is mostly classic but with a light, modern twist – try the Tasting menu. Gaddi's harks back to a bygone age where the act of dining was taken somewhat seriously and, as such, gentlemen are required to wear a jacket.

吉地士可說是城內有名的食府。專用電梯把你帶到這個享譽五十載的優質餐飲傳奇之店。現場音樂和古老英國禮儀配襯着傳統法國菜結合現代元素，Tasting menu值得一試。餐廳保留着昔日的典雅氣派，餐飲的真正意義得到尊重。男士們，謹記帶上一件西裝外套。

TEL. 2696 6763
1F, The Peninsula Hotel,
Salisbury Road, Tsim Sha Tsui
尖沙咀梳士巴利道半島酒店 1 樓
www.peninsula.com

■ PRICE 價錢
Lunch 午膳
set 套餐 $ 520
à la carte 點菜 $ 900-1,500
Dinner 晚膳
set 套餐 $ 1,588-1,888
à la carte 點菜 $ 900-1,500

■ OPENING HOURS 營業時間
Lunch 午膳　12:00-14:30 (L.O.)
Dinner 晚膳　19:00-22:30 (L.O.)

HONG KONG 香港

Gainmore Cuisine NEW
桂寶雞窩米線

⌂10 ☏⑪

It's all about Yunnan Cross Bridge rice noodles at lunch and chicken hotpot for dinner at this simple and clean two storey restaurant. The tasty hotpot uses a secret family recipe supplemented by assorted Chinese herbs and condiments. Lovers of spicier food can opt for the Sichuan hotpot which is available with differing levels of heat. The speciality is the chicken hotpot with abalone. Ask for a seat on the airier ground floor.

白天供應雲南過橋米線，晚上以雞鍋為主。用鐵鍋盛載，以中國香料、香草加自製秘料經數小時熬製而成的醬汁是其靈魂，加上鮮雞，實在是香氣誘人、滋味十足。嗜辣的你，還可選擇不同程度的麻辣味。最特別的首推以古法扣鮑魚作材料的鮑魚雞鍋。餐廳設計簡撲，環境整潔。地舖餐室的空氣較流通。

TEL. 2792 8388
77 Lion Rock Road, Kowloon City
九龍城獅子石道 77號

■ PRICE 價錢
Lunch 午膳
à la carte 點菜 $ 80-130
Dinner 晚膳
à la carte 點菜 $ 130-300

■ OPENING HOURS 營業時間
11:00-23:00 (L.O.)

Giando

The best views may be partially blocked by all the building work happening on the shore, but that hasn't stopped the foodies flocking to this crisply decorated and elegantly understated Italian restaurant. Owner-chef Gianni is at the very heart of the operation: he inspires and leads the kitchen team with his passion for the traditional food culture of Italy and imports many of the excellent quality ingredients directly from home.

主廚兼東主Gianni是餐廳的靈魂人物,他率領其廚師團隊,選用大量意大利進口的高級食材,以簡約的烹調方式和優雅的手法,為食客奉上一道道正宗意式風味的美食,盡顯其忠於傳統的理念。餐室的設計流露著自然的意國情調,一如這兒的美食般雅致,沒有半點造作。

TEL. 2511 8912
1F, The Fleet Arcade,
Fenwick Pier Street, Wan Chai
灣仔分域碼頭街海軍商場 1 樓
www.giandorestaurant.com

■ PRICE 價錢
Lunch 午膳
set 套餐 $ 268
à la carte 點菜 $ 350-700
Dinner 晚膳
à la carte 點菜 $ 350-700

■ OPENING HOURS 營業時間
Lunch 午膳   12:00-14:30 (L.O.)
Dinner 晚膳   18:00-22:30 (L.O.)

Gin Sai
吟彩

Whether your preference is for oden, tempura, sukiyaki, shabu-shabu, sushi, obatayaki or yakitori, you'll find fulfilment here. Indeed, such is the amount of choice on offer, you may be better simply ordering their 'special course'. The Japanese head chef makes very good use of seiro steamers so do try the steamed Wagyu or the Kurobuta pork as they are juicy and delicious. The sake selection is pretty good too!

用「多采多姿」形容吟彩提供的菜式種類實不為過。由日本大廚領導的團隊為你獻上刺身、關東煮、天婦羅、壽喜燒、爐端燒、串燒和涮鍋等美食。特色食物還包括蒸籠蒸，如籠蒸和牛或黑豚肉，肉汁鮮美。花多眼亂，難以取捨？可點選套餐。清酒單內的酒品是精選中的精選。

TEL. 2574 1118
GF, Oak Hill, 32-38 Cross Lane,
Wan Chai
灣仔交加里 32-38號萃峯地下
www.ginsai.com.hk

■ PRICE 價錢
Lunch 午膳
set 套餐 $108-298 à la carte 點菜 $400-1,500
Dinner 晚膳
set 套餐 $580-780 à la carte 點菜 $400-1,500

■ OPENING HOURS 營業時間
Lunch 午膳   12:00-14:15 (L.O.)
Dinner 晚膳   18:00-22:30 (L.O.)

■ ANNUAL AND WEEKLY CLOSING 休息日期
Closed 3 days Lunar New Year and Sunday
農曆新年休息 3 天及週日休息

Go Ya NEW
五谷

10

Owned and operated by the same team as No.5 Italian is this equally cosy yakitori restaurant. The dark colours and wood furnishing add to the intimate atmosphere. The skewers are cooked over traditional Japanese binchotan and the ones certainly worth trying include chicken with cartilage, crispy chicken skin, and high grade beef tongue. Nothing goes with yakitori quite like a beer and here it comes from a small Japanese brewery.

以黑色作主調的餐室內的手繪壁畫，出自五位東主之手，展現別樹一幟的東瀛味道。以備長炭燒烤的美食選擇豐富：雞肉棒、整塊燒烤的脆雞皮及只選用最佳部分的牛舌等是推介之選。店內還供應數款日本小型啤酒廠出品的啤酒，自家浸製果酒如荔枝和菊花酒，必為女士所愛。

TEL. 2504 2000
21 Brown Street, Tai Hang
大坑布朗街21號

■ PRICE 價錢
Dinner 晚膳
à la carte 點菜 $ 200-400

■ OPENING HOURS 營業時間
18:00-23:30 (L.O.)

Gold

Harlan Goldstein is a restaurateur who doesn't do things by halves. For this, his latest venture, he has sought to recreate the chic, yet relaxed atmosphere of a Manhattan brasserie. To go with the look, the kitchen produces 'modern Western cuisine' which means European ingredients with plenty of Italian thrown in, with dishes such as lobster spaghetti and scallop carpaccio with slow-cooked egg and truffle; try the tasting menu.

營辦餐廳經驗豐富的Harlan　Goldstein從來貫徹到底。這間以金色作主調的餐廳重塑了曼哈頓餐館那種時尚又自在的氣氛。菜式以「現代西式烹調」作主打，選用歐洲材料摻合意大利風味，配搭出龍蝦意粉、生帶子薄片配慢煮蛋和松露等精緻菜餚；嘗味套餐可謂精明之選。

TEL. 2869 9986
2F, LFK Tower, 33 Wyndham Street, Central
中環雲咸街 33號 LKF Tower 2樓
www.gold-dining.com

■ PRICE 價錢
Lunch 午膳
set 套餐 $ 288
à la carte 點菜 $ 380-1,030

Dinner 晚膳
set 套餐 $ 880
à la carte 點菜 $ 380-1,030

■ OPENING HOURS 營業時間
Lunch 午膳　12:00-14:30 (L.O.)
Dinner 晚膳　18:30-22:30 (L.O.)

■ ANNUAL AND WEEKLY CLOSING 休息日期
Closed Sunday 週日休息

Golden Leaf
金葉庭

🍴🍴🍴   🖐 🍽12 🕐🍴

The ever popular Golden Leaf restaurant is elegantly dressed with panels, sculptured wood, antique art pieces and chandeliers. It is to this cosy oriental environment that customers come to enjoy the chef's recommendations, such as the barbecued pork glazed with honey, poached prawns with preserved peel and diced vegetables, steamed fresh crab claw with minced ginger and rice wine, and poached chicken with chicken essence.

備受歡迎的金葉庭裝潢高貴典雅，以屏風、木雕、古董藝術品及吊燈裝飾。客人能在舒適且具東方情調的環境下，享受廚師的推介菜式：蜜糖汁叉燒、陳皮頭菜上湯浸鮮蝦、蒸薑米酒鮮蟹鉗或貴妃雞。此外，午市還提供套餐及一系列令人垂涎的點心。

TEL. 2521 3838
5F, Conrad Hotel, Pacific Place,
88 Queensway, Admiralty
金鐘道 88 號太古廣場港麗酒店 5 樓
www.conraddining.com

SPECIALITIES TO PRE-ORDER 預訂食物
Beggar's chicken 杭州富貴雞 / Poached whole pigeon with soya sauce 豉油皇浸乳鴿

■ PRICE 價錢
Lunch 午膳
à la carte 點菜 $ 400-2,000
Dinner 晚膳
à la carte 點菜 $ 400-2,000

■ OPENING HOURS 營業時間
Lunch 午膳　11:30-15:00 (L.O.)
Dinner 晚膳　18:00-23:00 (L.O.)

Golden Valley
駿景軒

✿

The Emperor hotel is a regular haunt of many a famous face and avid race-goer at the celebrated course nearby. The hotel's traditional but fresh looking restaurant serves classic Cantonese and Sichuan cuisines but it is also known for its hotpots, which account for around 80% of its business in the winter months. Deep-fried crispy chicken is a must-have dish, while fish simmered with chilli is another of the kitchen's signature dishes.

備受歡迎的金葉庭裝潢高貴典雅，以屏風、木雕、古董藝術品及吊燈裝飾。客人能在舒適且具東方情調的環境下，享受廚師的推介菜式：蜜糖汁叉燒、陳皮頭菜上湯浸鮮蝦、蒸薑米酒鮮蟹鉗或貴妃雞。此外，午市還提供套餐及一系列令人垂涎的點心。

TEL. 2961 3330
1F, The Emperor Hotel,
1 Wang Tak Street, Happy Valley
跑馬地宏德街 1 號英皇駿景酒店 1 樓
www.emperorhotel.com.hk

■ PRICE 價錢
Lunch 午膳
à la carte 點菜 $ 160-780
Dinner 晚膳
à la carte 點菜 $ 230-780

■ OPENING HOURS 營業時間
Lunch 午膳　11:00-15:30 (L.O.)
Dinner 晚膳　18:00-22:30 (L.O.)

Gonpachi　NEW
權八

🅿 ⏣16 🚃 ☎🍴

HONG KONG 香港

Gonpachi in Tokyo became famous when it was used as the backdrop for a fight scene in Tarantino's 'Kill Bill'. Now there's a branch in Lee Gardens One, where lanterns and wooden architecture add to the Japanese feel. A wide selection of dishes is offered, from high-quality Miyazaki beef to assorted skewers and hand-made soba noodles. There are also over 80 types of sake available, along with a variety of Japanese whiskies and shochu cocktails.

日本甚具名氣的居酒屋落戶利園，古典和風裝潢與傳統日式廂座別有韻味。餐單選擇豐富：高級高崎和牛、炭燒鵝肝、豆味濃郁的手作豆腐，甚至每天以人手打製的蕎麥麵配熱法國鴨肉湯等均十分美味。酒單涵蓋88款清酒及多款酒品如日本威士忌、葡萄酒及燒酌雞尾酒等。

TEL. 2787 3688
4F, Lee Gardens One,
33 Hysan Avenue, Causeway Bay
銅鑼灣希慎道 33號利園一期 4樓
www.gonpachi.com.hk

■ PRICE 價錢
Lunch 午膳
set 套餐 $ 158-388
à la carte 點菜 $ 230-700
Dinner 晚膳
à la carte 點菜 $ 230-700

■ OPENING HOURS 營業時間
Monday - Thursday 週一至週四
11:30-01:00 L.O. 24:00
Friday & Weekends 週五及週末
11:30-02:00 L.O. 01:00

■ ANNUAL AND WEEKLY CLOSING 休息日期
Closed Lunar New Year 農曆新年休息

Good Hope Noodle (Fa Yuen Street)
好旺角麵家 (花園街)

Mong Kok residents will know the name, as Good Hope Noodle has been around for over 40 years – but now they have a more comfortable spot in which to enjoy their favourite dishes. The dining room is neatly furnished with booths, tiles and bright lighting. Food is prepared in the open kitchen, with noodles, congee and snacks served all day. The traditionally prepared noodles are the highlight – it's no wonder they sell a few hundred bowls a day.

好旺角麵家在旺角區開業至今逾四十載，街坊對這名字一定不會陌生。新店以卡座為主，開房式廚房、光潔的牆身、地磚和明亮的燈光，讓顧客在舒適的環境下吃得安心。店家全日供應粥品、粉麵和各式小吃。以傳統方式製作的麵條是其招牌菜，難怪每天售逾數百碗麵食!

TEL. 2384 6898
18 Fa Yuen Street, Mong Kok
旺角花園街 18號

■ PRICE 價錢
à la carte 點菜 $ 45-70

■ OPENING HOURS 營業時間
11:00-00:45 (L.O.)

■ ANNUAL AND WEEKLY CLOSING 休息日期
Closed 3 days Lunar New Year
農曆新年休息 3 天

Grand Cuisine Shanghai Kitchen
君上海小廚

🍴　　　　　　　　　　　　　　　　　　　　　　🍱14

Come at lunch during the week and you'll not only have to queue outside for a while but will probably also find yourself sharing your table. The reason for the popularity of this bright restaurant is the traditional Shanghainese cooking; you can watch the chefs prepare the dim sum and La Mian noodles in the open kitchen. Try the steamed prawn with egg white and yellow wine, boiled mixed meat with white cabbage in casserole, and La Mian with minced meat in spicy sauce.

這家上海菜館供應的小菜全部以傳統上海菜烹調方式製作,非常受食客歡迎,午餐時段,不光要排隊輪候,甚至可能要與其他食客共坐一桌。透過開放式廚房,你可以看見師傅製作點心和拉麵的情形。芙蓉花彫蒸蝦球、什錦砂鍋津白和炸醬拉麵均值得一試。

TEL. 2568 9989
Shop G510-511, Po On Mansion,
Taikoo Shing
太古城寶安閣地下 G510-511號舖

■ PRICE 價錢
Dinner 晚膳
à la carte 點菜 $ 110-450

■ OPENING HOURS 營業時間
11:00-22:30 (L.O.)

HONG KONG 香港

Grand Hyatt Steakhouse

✗✗   🖐️   ⊟32   ⇌   ◐🍴   ஃ

As with most steakhouses around the world, this one comes with a decidedly masculine feel. Accessed via its own elevator, it's divided into three areas; the best spot is the moodily lit bar which has both counter seats and small tables for two by the windows. The prime cuts of beef are sourced from Canada, Nebraska and Japan; be sure to add the chunky chips cooked in duck fat to your order. There are elegant private rooms upstairs.

牛扒屋帶着剛陽味。顧客需乘搭專屬升降機，餐廳分為三區，最佳位置在富情調的酒吧區，設吧枱座位及靠窗的二人桌。廚師深諳烹調肉類的法門，且以來自加拿大、內布拉斯加和日本的特級牛扒作材料。別忘了點鴨油炮製的厚切薯條作配菜。餐廳於上層備有多間設計優雅的私人宴會廳。

TEL. 2584 7722
MF, Grand Hyatt Hotel,
1 Harbour Road, Wan Chai
灣仔港灣道 1 號君悅酒店閣樓
www.hongkong.grand.hyatt.com

■ PRICE 價錢
Dinner 晚膳
à la carte 點菜 $ 700-1,700

■ OPENING HOURS 營業時間
Dinner 晚膳　18:00-22:30 (L.O.)

Grissini

♿ ← 🍴 🅿 🍽28 🕐

Looking for a romantic dinner spot with views to match? Then this smart Italian restaurant with its candlelit tables may just fit the bill. The range of authentic dishes comes from the length and breadth of Italy's regions and there's a good balance struck between tradition and innovation. Specialities include osso bucco and baked sea bass; there's also a decent cheese board. And, as the name suggests, the grissini are rather good too.

假如你嚮往在醉人夜景下享受燭光晚餐，這家時尚餐廳是必然之選。真材實料的菜式涵蓋意大利不同地域的風味，傳統特色與創意兼備。特色菜包括意式牛仔腿、香焗鱸魚及美味芝士拼盤，而作為店名的Grissini長條麵包亦別具水準。

TEL. 2584 7722
2F, Grand Hyatt Hotel,
1 Harbour Road, Wan Chai
灣仔港灣道 1 號君悅酒店 2 樓
www.hongkong.grand.hyatt.com

■ PRICE 價錢
Lunch 午膳
set 套餐 $468 à la carte 點菜 $450-650
Dinner 晚膳
set 套餐 $800 à la carte 點菜 $600-1,000

■ OPENING HOURS 營業時間
Lunch 午膳　12:00-14:30 (L.O.)
Dinner 晚膳　19:00-22:30 (L.O.)

■ ANNUAL AND WEEKLY CLOSING 休息日期
Closed Saturday lunch
週六午膳休息

HONG KONG 香港

Guo Fu Lou
國福樓

✿

XX ♿ 🖐🍷 ⇆16 ◐🍽

Moving from the 31st floor of iSquare TST to the basement of a hotel in Wan Chai may have resulted in more space for the restaurant's celebrity clientele but there's been no change in the quality of the cooking. The chef demonstrates his respect for Cantonese cuisine by adopting traditional cooking methods as well as by using top quality ingredients. Try the baked stuffed crab shell or the fried lobster with black bean chilli sauce.

從尖沙咀iSquare遷至灣仔，國福樓或許不像昔日受關注，然而卻為一眾低調的名人食客帶來方便。環境雖稱不上瑰麗豪華，卻不失優雅舒適，設有多間廂房供私人宴會之用。廚師堅守以頂級食材精心烹調傳統粵菜的宗旨。釀焗鮮蟹蓋及豉椒炒龍蝦球是其得意之作。

TEL. 2861 2060
LG2, The Empire Hotel,
33 Hennessy Road, Wan Chai
灣仔軒尼詩道 33號皇悅酒店 LG2

SPECIALITIES TO PRE-ORDER 預訂食物
Roasted crispy goose 明爐燒鵝 / Deep-fried stuffed crab claw with shrimp paste 百花炸釀蟹鉗 / BBQ suckling pig 大紅袍乳豬 / Traditional baked chicken in rock salt 正宗鹽焗雞

■ PRICE 價錢
Lunch 午膳
à la carte 點菜 $ 150-1,800
Dinner 晚膳
à la carte 點菜 $ 280-1,800

■ OPENING HOURS 營業時間
Lunch 午膳　11:00-15:00 (L.O.)
Dinner 晚膳　18:00-22:30 (L.O.)

■ ANNUAL AND WEEKLY CLOSING 休息日期
Closed 2 days Lunar New Year
農曆新年休息 2 天

Hing Kee
避風塘興記

Originating in Causeway Bay two generations ago, the family moved their business to Tsim Sha Tsui, where they've made a name for themselves with their Boat People style cuisine; further testimony comes from the celebrity signatures lining the walls. Elder sister heads the serving team; younger brother takes charge in the kitchen. They are famous for their stir-fry crabs with black beans and chilli, roast duck and rice noodles in soup and congee.

此店由祖父輩於銅鑼灣開業經營，其後家族將餐廳移往尖沙咀，由家中大姐領導服務團隊、弟弟掌廚，建立了避風塘特色菜，牆上貼滿明星簽名，是此店名聞遐爾的明證。招牌菜包括避風塘炒蟹、燒鴨湯河及艇仔粥。

TEL. 2722 0022
1F, Bowa House, 180 Nathan Road,
Tsim Sha Tsui
尖沙咀彌敦道 180 號寶華商業大廈 1 樓

■ PRICE 價錢
Dinner 晚膳
à la carte 點菜 $ 300-600

■ OPENING HOURS 營業時間
Dinner 晚膳　18:00-04:00 (L.O.)

■ ANNUAL AND WEEKLY CLOSING 休息日期
Closed 2 days Lunar New Year
農曆新年休息 2 天

Ho Ho Shanghai
好好上海小館

To the passer-by, this simple shop on a busy Jordan street looks like any other Shanghainese restaurant. What sets it apart, however, is that its kitchen uses less oil and less corn starch water – with the result that its food comes with a health dividend. The dishes still provide assured flavours – just try the steamed rice with its finely chopped vegetables. Sichuan dishes like beef or prawns in hot chilli sauce are also available.

此店自十多年前開始在佐敦的繁忙街道上營業，平凡的門面與別的滬菜小館沒甚分別，但其少油少獻汁的健康新派上海菜卻是熟客的心頭好。菜飯中的蔬菜全部用人手切成幼粒，吃起上來充滿蔬菜的清香味道。店內亦供應少量川菜，嗜辣者可試試水煮牛肉或蝦球。

TEL. 2369 0086
105 Austin Road, Jordan
佐敦柯士甸道 105 號

■ PRICE 價錢
Lunch 午膳
set 套餐 $40-70　à la carte 點菜 $90-220
Dinner 晚膳
set 套餐 $70　à la carte 點菜 $90-220

■ OPENING HOURS 營業時間
11:00-23:45 (L.O.)

■ ANNUAL AND WEEKLY CLOSING 休息日期
Closed 3 days Lunar New Year
農曆新年休息 3 天

Ho Hung Kee
何洪記

No discussion about Hong Kong's historic noodle shops would be complete without mentioning Ho Hung Kee, which originally opened in Wan Chai in the 1940s and is famed for its springy wonton noodles and fresh, sweet soup. More elements have been added here at its new address – dim sum and some Cantonese dishes are now served too. For the interior, they've adopted a more contemporary, western style aesthetic.

要數香港歷史悠久的麵家，怎少得何洪記？此店自四十年代起在灣仔區營業，多年來其招牌雲吞麵憑着麵條彈牙、湯底鮮甜而口碑載道；其粥品也很出色。遷至現址後的新店，設計加入了不少現代西方元素，華麗而舒適。為滿足食客需求，增加了食物種類，除粥麵外，還供應點心和廣式小菜。

TEL. 2577 6028
Level 12, Hysan Place,
500 Hennessy Road, Causeway Bay
銅鑼灣軒尼詩道 500 號希慎廣場 12 樓

■ PRICE 價錢
à la carte 點菜 $ 80-200

■ OPENING HOURS 營業時間
11:30-22:45 (L.O.)

Ho To Tai
好到底

The atmosphere at this simple, two storey noodle shop is somewhat reminiscent of a bygone era. It's still run by the Chan family, who opened it in 1946. The most popular dishes are the wonton noodles, dried shrimp's roe with noodles, and homemade dumplings stuffed with fish skin. They also have their own noodle factory a few blocks away so as well as enjoying the noodles in the shop you can also buy the un-cooked noodles to take home.

這家麵店於1946年開業，樓高兩層的店舖內是濃濃的懷舊氣氛。蝦子撈麵和特製魚皮水餃向來是此店最受歡迎的食物，還有雲吞，更是非試不可!麵店附近設有製麵工場，店主同時在市區設立多個麵食銷售店，出售自製乾麵。

TEL. 2476 2495
67 Fau Tsoi Street, Yuen Long
元朗阜財街 67號

■ PRICE 價錢
à la carte 點菜 $ 25-65

■ OPENING HOURS 營業時間
08:00-20:00 (L.O.)

■ ANNUAL AND WEEKLY CLOSING 休息日期
Closed 10 days Lunar New Year
農曆新年休息 10 天

Holytan Grill NEW
葆里湛

✗✗   ⊡12 ◖❙|

The impressive piece of kit in the kitchen called a Far Infrared oven is the star of the show at this comfortable and well-dressed hotel restaurant. It is used to great effect to cook high quality Wagyu beef which arrives nicely caramelised on the outside and juicy and tender inside. There are other ingredients given the benefit of the French and Japanese techniques such as imported seafood, but it's really all about the signature steaks.

說起葆里湛西洋料理，焦點自然是其獨一無二的烹調方法。主廚嚴選高級和牛，用其獨家研發的遠紅外線烤爐，以兩段火力反復燒烤三次，再經備長炭烤至香味濃郁。受熱均勻的牛肉，表面焦黃酥脆、內裏嫩滑多汁，啖啖肉香誘人垂涎。室內佈置雅致舒適，好感油然而生。

TEL. 2351 5808
2F, The Pottinger Hotel,
74 Queen's Road Central, Central
中環皇后大道中 74 號石板街酒店 2 樓

■ PRICE 價錢
Dinner 晚膳
set 套餐 $ 1,300-2,000
à la carte 點菜 $ 1,000-2,800

■ OPENING HOURS 營業時間
Dinner 晚膳　18:00-22:30 (L.O.)

■ ANNUAL AND WEEKLY CLOSING 休息日期
Closed Sunday 週日休息

Hong Zhou
杭州酒家

✗✗　　　　　　　　　　　　　　　　　　　　　　　Ⓒ30　◎❙❙

The owner-chef has many of his fresh ingredients delivered from from Hong Zhou directly every afternoon and you certainly can tell when you bite into those delicious fried river prawns with Longjing tea leaves; the braised pork belly is also worth trying. The chef inherited his obvious passion for food and the delicate cuisine of Hong Zhou from his father (who was also a famous chef in town) and strives to keep his cooking authentic.

餐廳主廚兼老闆從同為城中名廚的父親身上遺傳了對食物及杭州美食的熱愛，努力維持正宗烹調方法，堅持每天下午由杭州運來新鮮食材。食材是優是劣，絕對騙不了人。建議嘗嘗鮮美的龍井河蝦仁，東坡肉亦值得一試。

TEL. 2591 1898
1F, Chinachem Johnston Plaza,
178-186 Johnston Road, Wan Chai
灣仔莊士敦道 178-186號
華懋莊士敦廣場 1樓

■ PRICE 價錢
Lunch 午膳
à la carte 點菜　$ 160-740
Dinner 晚膳
à la carte 點菜　$ 160-740

■ OPENING HOURS 營業時間
Lunch 午膳　11:30-14:15 (L.O.)
Dinner 晚膳　17:30-22:15 (L.O.)

■ ANNUAL AND WEEKLY CLOSING 休息日期
Closed 2 days Lunar New Year
農曆新年休息 2 天

Hugo's
希戈

𝐗𝐗𝐗

   🚻 ☝ **P** ⟠12 ☏

The original Hugo's was founded back in 1969 and this new version remains true to its origins by offering the charms of a bygone age. That means there's everything from suits of armour to silver Christofle trolleys being wheeled around the room. The chef and his team prepare traditional European cuisine with pronounced French influences. Expect escargots, lobster bisque, steak au poivre and soufflés, along with grilled meats.

希戈本店創立於1969年，新店延續其懷舊感覺，這意味着店裏的一切 ― 完整的銀鎧甲、Christofle品牌的頭盤餐車，全部原汁原味重現眼前。主廚與他的團隊為客人準備具濃厚法國特色的傳統歐洲菜。你可在這裏找到法國焗田螺、龍蝦湯、法式黑胡椒牛柳、梳乎厘與多款烤肉。

TEL. 3721 7733
Lobby F, Hyatt Regency Tsim Sha Tsui,
18 Hanoi Road, Tsim Sha Tsui
尖沙咀河內道 18號凱悅酒店 -尖沙咀大堂
www.hongkong.tsimshatsui.hyatt.com

■ PRICE 價錢
Lunch 午膳
set 套餐 $ 385-515
à la carte 點菜 $ 650-1,100
Dinner 晚膳
set 套餐 $ 1,090
à la carte 點菜 $ 650-1,100

■ OPENING HOURS 營業時間
Lunch 午膳　12:00-14:30 (L.O.)
Dinner 晚膳　18:30-22:30 (L.O.)

IM Teppanyaki & Wine NEW

Less a meal, more a full multi-sensory experience. Sit at the teppanyaki bar, admire the cooking show and enjoy contemporary Japanese flavours that make great use of prime ingredients like lobster and premium quality Wagyu. You also get to hear all about owner-chef Lawrence Mok's extraordinary triathlon experiences straight from his own mouth while he prepares your food. There is a private room available for small groups.

到這兒光顧的客人，十有八九是慕主廚莫師傅之名而來。坐在鐵板燒桌前，欣賞莫師傅用精湛廚藝為你炮製龍蝦和頂級和牛等美食，確是賞心樂事！莫師傅偶爾會與客人分享其參加鐵人賽的體驗，令你在一頓飯的時間得到多重感觀享受。餐室設計揉合了時尚與和風，小廂房適合私人聚會之用。

TEL. 2570 7088
134 Tung Lo Wan Road, Tai Hang
大坑銅鑼灣道 134號
www.imteppanyaki.com

■ PRICE 價錢
Lunch 午膳
set 套餐 $ 180-320
à la carte 點菜 $ 800-2,200
Dinner 晚膳
set 套餐 $ 880-1,280
à la carte 點菜 $ 800-2,200

■ OPENING HOURS 營業時間
Lunch 午膳　12:00-14:30 (L.O.)
Dinner 晚膳　18:00-22:30 (L.O.)

Inakaya NEW
田舍家

❌❌ ⮜ 🅿 ⟷36 ⇄ ☎️🍴

As it sits on the 101st floor of the ICC, it will come as no surprise to learn that Inakaya provides stunning and unobstructed views of the harbour and Hong Kong Island. Apart from the kaiseki, the robatayaki is the highlight of this stylish Japanese eatery. Much of the produce, which is airfreighted from Japan on a daily basis, is on display – just pick what you fancy and the chefs will prepare it. There are six private rooms for groups.

田舍家進駐環球貿易廣場101樓最佳位置，大部位置都能觀覽維港景色。除了懷石料理，還設有壽司吧及鐵板燒專枱。自成一角的爐端燒也是餐廳焦點所在，一如傳統居酒屋，每天從日本空運到來的新鮮食材鋪滿兩張吧枱，任君挑選，廚師還會即席為你炮製美食。店內有6間廂房，適合各種聚會。

TEL. 2972 2666
101F, International Commerce Centre,
1 Austin Road West, Tsim Sha Tsui
尖沙咀柯士甸道西 1號環球貿易廣場 101樓
www.jcgroup.hk

■ PRICE 價錢
Lunch 午膳
set 套餐 $280-760　à la carte 點菜 $300-800
Dinner 晚膳
set 套餐 $1,480-1,880
à la carte 點菜 $600-1,800

■ OPENING HOURS 營業時間
Lunch 午膳　12:00-14:30 (L.O.)
Dinner 晚膳　18:00-22:30 (L.O.)

■ ANNUAL AND WEEKLY CLOSING 休息日期
Closed Lunar New Year 年初一休息

Island Tang
港島廳

✗✗✗ 　　　　　　　　🍽40 ◐🍴

Sir David Tang's elegant art deco inspired room, with its chandeliers, rich wood panelling and mirrors, is reminiscent of 1940s Hong Kong. The menu offers a range of sophisticated and delicious Cantonese dishes, such as baked crab, sea cucumber with leeks, terrific roasted pigeon leg stuffed with liver sausage and many other classics. As befits the sophisticated surroundings, service is slick, well-organised and professional.

由鄧永鏘爵士設計，靈感源自裝飾藝術的高雅房間配有吊燈、厚木鑲板及鏡子，重現四十年代香港的風采。菜單上提供一系列獨特美味的廣東菜：焗蟹肉、蔥燒遼參到出色的潤腸燒釀鴿腿等。悉心專業的服務與出色的環境相得益彰。

TEL. 2526 8798
Shop 222, The Galleria,
9 Queen's Road, Central
皇后大道中 9號嘉軒廣場 222號舖
www.islandtang.com

■ PRICE 價錢
Lunch 午膳
set 套餐 $338-438 à la carte 點菜 $450-2,400
Dinner 晚膳
à la carte 點菜 $450-2,400

■ OPENING HOURS 營業時間
Lunch 午膳　12:00-14:30 (L.O.)
Dinner 晚膳　18:00-22:30 (L.O.)

■ ANNUAL AND WEEKLY CLOSING 休息日期
Closed 3 days Lunar New Year and Sunday
農曆新年休息 3 天及週日休息

Jardin de Jade
蘇浙滙

𝗫𝗫𝗫   **P** ⇔16 ◐⫼

The first Hong Kong venture from this renowned Shanghai restaurant group is certainly not lacking in grandeur, thanks to its double-height ceiling and striking chandelier. The kitchen naturally focuses on Shanghainese cooking and makes good use of traditional recipes but presents the dishes in a more modern style. High quality ingredients are sourced from the mainland for delicious dishes like steamed reeves shad and braised whole sea cucumber.

作為上海著名餐飲集團落戶香港的首家分店，餐廳的裝潢雅致，特高樓底配上引人注目的吊燈，別具氣派。餐館以時尚包裝演繹傳統上海菜式，味美且外型精緻。集團從內地搜羅優質食材，炮製出多款如清蒸鯽魚及蔥燒大烏參等美食。

TEL. 3528 0228
GF, Sun Hung Kai Centre,
30 Harbour Road, Wan Chai
灣仔港灣道 30號新鴻基中心地下
www.jade388.com

■ PRICE 價錢
à la carte 點菜 $ 200-815

■ OPENING HOURS 營業時間
Lunch 午膳 11:30-15:00 (L.O.)
Dinner 晚膳 17:30-22:30 (L.O.)

SPECIALITIES TO PRE-ORDER 預訂食物
Eight-treasure duck with spicy salt
椒鹽八寶鴨

Jin Cuisine
晉薈

🍴🍴 👆 🍽24 🕐🍴

Located at the Holiday Inn Express but run by the Royal Garden Hotel, Jin Cuisine is a comfortable and contemporary Shanghainese restaurant and one that's brightened considerably by its floor-to-ceiling windows. The various menus offer diners the chance to experience many of the signature dishes which are attractively presented and at times quite innovative, although flavour combinations remain reassuringly familiar.

由帝苑酒店經營管理的晉薈，位於將軍澳鐵路站旁的大樓中，地點便利。餐廳設計時尚中帶點中式元素，佈置簡潔舒適，自然光穿過玻璃窗滲進屋內，為店子帶來了點點生氣。供應的新派滬菜大部分外型小巧精緻。有多款套餐供選擇，適合小家庭。菜式選擇多而價錢合理。

TEL. 2623 2333
2F Holiday Inn Express, Tower 4,
3 Tong Tak Street, Tseung Kwan O,
New Territories
新界將軍澳唐德街 3 號
香港九龍東智選假日酒店 2 樓
www.rghk.com.hk

SPECIALITIES TO PRE-ORDER 預訂食物
Baked beggar's chicken　叫 化 雞 /
Braised deep-fried duck filled with assorted ingredients in brown sauce
紅燒八寶鴨

■ PRICE 價錢
Lunch 午膳
set 套餐 $ 118-498
à la carte 點菜 $ 100-900
Dinner 晚膳
set 套餐 $ 398-498
à la carte 點菜 $ 180-900

■ OPENING HOURS 營業時間
Lunch 午膳　11:00-15:00 (L.O.)
Dinner 晚膳　18:00-23:00 (L.O.)

Joi Hing 😊
再興

The Chow family have had many barbecue shops but this one has been a feature here in Stewart Road since 1975 and is run very capably by the affable Mrs Chow. Her special recipe for the marinade is an integral part of the appeal. Pork, duck and goose are the primary meats, with BBQ pork being highly recommended. There's no menu – just cards stuck on the walls. If barbecue is not your thing then their curry sauce is pretty legendary too.

這家在1975年開業的燒臘店，在區內一直　備受矚目。店家秘製的滷汁深受食客歡迎，叉燒、燒鵝及切雞等配上白飯或瀨粉，是地地道道的美食，令人食指大動。除了堂吃外，還提供外賣燒味，門外經常出現買外賣的人龍。

TEL. 2519 6639
1C Stewart Road, Wan Chai
灣仔史釗域道 1號 C

■ PRICE 價錢
à la carte 點菜 $30-60

■ OPENING HOURS 營業時間
10:00-22:00 (L.O.)

■ ANNUAL AND WEEKLY CLOSING 休息日期
Closed 2 weeks Lunar New Year, Sunday and Public Holidays
農曆新年兩星期、週日及公眾假期休息

HONG KONG 香港

Kam's Kitchen　NEW
甘飯館

This little shop in Tin Hau's residential area is more generalist than its sister operation, Kam's Roast Goose. The small menu is very much geared to the local community and specialises in reassuringly traditional Cantonese dishes. It includes soups, seafood, clay pot dishes and, of course, the family forte - roast meats. There are also dishes, like prawns stuffed with crab's roe, requiring quite a lot of preparation time.

由鏞記甘氏家族第三代夥同共事多年的老伙計，在天后經營這間小菜館。餐牌上只有數十款選項，主打懷舊粵菜。富經驗的經理會向客人介紹特別推介如頗花功夫炮製的四、五十年代菜式禮雲子金龍之類。當然，家族馳名的燒鵝，肉汁豐腴，令人再三回味。餐廳座位不多，建議預先訂座。

TEL. 3568 2832
5 Mercury Street, Tin Hau
天后水星街 5號

■ PRICE 價錢
Lunch 午膳
set 套餐 $ 40-60
à la carte 點菜 $ 150-300
Dinner 晚膳
à la carte 點菜 $ 150-300

■ OPENING HOURS 營業時間
Lunch 午膳　11:30-15:00 (L.O.)
Dinner 晚膳　18:00-22:30 (L.O.)

Kam's Roast Goose　NEW
甘牌燒鵝

The Kam family name is synonymous with their famous roast goose restaurant. This little place is owned by the third generation of the family and he wisely hired his father's former chef to ensure the goose is as crisp and succulent as ever. There's also suckling pig, goose neck and head, and goose blood pudding available. With only 30 seats, don't be surprised to see a queue.

從祖父輩創業至今歷七十多年，甘氏出品的燒鵝早已遠近馳名，現由第三代傳人在灣仔開設全新餐館，承傳父輩廚藝。與父輩共事多年的老師傅以甘氏家傳秘方炮製的燒鵝，掛在窗前令人垂涎欲滴。燒乳豬、鵝頭和鵝紅也非常美味。小店僅有30個座位，故常見輪位或買外賣的人龍。

TEL. 2520 1110
226 Hennessy Road, Wan Chai
灣仔軒尼詩道 226號
www.krg.com.hk

■ PRICE 價錢
Lunch 午膳
set 套餐 $ 60-80
à la carte 點菜 $ 50-150
Dinner 晚膳
à la carte 點菜 $ 50-150

■ OPENING HOURS 營業時間
11:30-21:15 (L.O.)

Kau Kee
九記

You'll probably have to line up in the street first to eat here: Kau Kee has been trading since the 1930s and has consequently built up a huge following which includes some well known faces from show business and politics. It's all very basic and you'll have to share your table but the food is delicious. Beef noodles are the speciality; different cuts of meat with a variety of noodles in a tasty broth or spicy sauce. Try the iced milk tea too.

要在九記用膳，你或許要在街上排隊等候；九記自三零年代開始營業，聚集了大量支持者，包括部分政商名人。其陳設回歸基本，進餐時要和其他人共用餐桌，但食物極具水準。牛腩麵是九記的特色；不同部位的肉塊配以各式粉麵，再加上清湯或辣醬，滋味無窮。奶茶亦值得一試。

TEL. N/A
21 Gough Street, Central
中環歌賦街 21號

■ PRICE 價錢
à la carte 點菜 $30-90

■ OPENING HOURS 營業時間
12:30-22:30 (L.O.)

■ ANNUAL AND WEEKLY CLOSING 休息日期
Closed 10 days Lunar New Year, Sunday and Public Holidays
農曆新年 10 天、週日及公眾假期休息

Kazuo Okada
岡田和生

Harbourfront Landmark is a 25,000 sq.ft restaurant complex offering three distinct operations, one of which is this crisply decorated and elegant Japanese restaurant. Kaiseki is the main attraction and the seasonal ingredients are purchased directly from Japan, having been carefully sourced from all regions of the country. You will also be impressed by the antique crockery collection of over 400 pieces, many of which are more than 200 years old.

座落於海名軒的綜合餐飲場所，設有三家各具特色的餐廳。其中一家是裝潢精緻優雅的日本料理，主打懷石料理；廚師直接從日本十多個地方採購最新鮮的蔬菜、海鮮及肉類，質素無庸置疑，且全是最時令的食材。餐廳擁有四百多件具二、三百年歷史的古董餐具作盛器，令進餐體驗生色不少!

TEL. 3746 2722
5F, Harbourfront Landmark,
11 Wan Hoi Street, Hung Hom
紅磡環海街 11 號海名軒 5 樓
www.KOdining.com

■ PRICE 價錢
Lunch 午膳
set 套餐 $ 480
Dinner 晚膳
set 套餐 $ 1,280-3,500

■ OPENING HOURS 營業時間
Weekends lunch 週末午膳
12:00-15:00 (L.O.)
Dinner 晚膳   18:00-22:30 (L.O.)

■ ANNUAL AND WEEKLY CLOSING 休息日期
Closed Monday 週一休息

King's Garden
東來居

Unlike many hotpot restaurants, the environment here within the King's hotel is both contemporary and intimate. What also stands out is the food, particularly the pork bone soup base which takes more than 14 hours to prepare. Specialities to look out for include flaming king crab soup and chicken soup with coconut. The restaurant uses quality beef and seafood and dumplings are made to order.

有別於一般火鍋店,這間位於王子酒店內的餐廳,環境既親切且有時代感。同樣與別不同的,是這裏的美食及湯底,特別是熬製十四個小時以上的豬骨湯底,另外還有火焰蟹皇湯、椰子雞湯等十數款湯底。餐廳採用上等牛肉和海鮮,餃子更是即點即製。

TEL. 2244 3355
1F, King's Hotel, 303 Jaffe Road,
Wan Chai
灣仔謝斐道303號王子酒店1樓

■ PRICE 價錢
Dinner 晚膳
à la carte 點菜 $ 280-600

■ OPENING HOURS 營業時間
Dinner 晚膳　18:00-00:30 (L.O.)

Kin's Kitchen NEW
留家廚房

✂　　　　　　　　　　　　　　　　　　　🪑36 ◐🍴

When Kin's Kitchen opened in 2004, its natural and authentic Cantonese food quickly attracted a fan base and they remained loyal even when the restaurant moved premises. Its success is largely due to the owner's insistence on using good quality ingredients like organic pork and free-range chicken. His kitchen also tries new cooking methods, like 'sous-vide' for the pigeon in Shaoxing wine sauce. Don't miss the smoked chicken and drunken abalone.

自2004年開業以來，留家廚房一直為食客提供天然且味道純正的傳統粵菜。店東堅持選用優質食材如天然方法飼養的健味豬及絕無激素的本地農場雞等作小菜的材料。烹調方式亦緊貼科技發展，如利用真空低溫烹調法炮製的醉乳鴿。必試菜式包括留家煙燻雞和涼拌醉鮑魚。

TEL. 2571 0913
5F, W Square, 314-324 Hennessy Road, Wan Chai
灣仔軒尼詩道 314-324號 W Square 5樓
www.kinskitchen.com.hk

■ PRICE 價錢
Lunch 午膳
à la carte 點菜 $ 90-400
Dinner 晚膳
à la carte 點菜 $150-400

■ OPENING HOURS 營業時間
Lunch 午膳　12:00-14:30 (L.O.)
Dinner 晚膳　18:00-22:30 (L.O.)

■ ANNUAL AND WEEKLY CLOSING 休息日期
Closed 2 days Lunar New Year
農曆新年休息 2 天

HONG KONG 香港

Kung Tak Lam (Causeway Bay)
功德林 (銅鑼灣)

🍴🍴   🍽30 🕐🍴

As befits a vegetarian restaurant, Kung Tak Lam boasts a fresh, green look. Based on traditional Shanghainese cuisine but with less salt and oil, the dishes are not only healthy and good looking but also deliver some punchy flavours. Don't be alarmed to see words like 'pork' and 'chicken'– they merely show what can be done with soy bean products. Standout dishes include braised vegetarian 'meatball' in casserole and cold noodles.

翠綠配上淺色系的裝潢，予人清新自然的感覺，功德林素食菜館，為食客帶來印象深刻的綠色體驗。店家以傳統上海菜作藍本，配合少鹽少油的烹調方式製作出外型精緻且風味獨特的健康素食。雖然菜單上出現「豬」、「雞」等菜式，但其實全是大豆製品。特別推介菜式有砂鍋獅子頭及上海冷麵。

TEL. 2881 9966
10F, World Trade Centre,
280 Gloucester Road, Causeway Bay
銅鑼灣告士打道 280 號世貿中心 10 樓

■ PRICE 價錢
à la carte 點菜 $ 120-520

■ OPENING HOURS 營業時間
11:00-22:15 (L.O.)

Kwan Kee Bamboo Noodles (Cheung Sha Wan)
坤記竹昇麵 (長沙灣)

His family's successful noodle business in Guangzhou prompted Mr Lee to open his own place in Hong Kong, which he named after his wife. All the noodles here are made using the traditional bamboo method, which may be labour intensive but leaves them tasting great as the noodles are freshly made each day; don't miss the signature dried shrimp roe mix with noodles. A glass wall allows you to watch each step of the noodle making process.

在廣州見證了家族麵食生意的成功後，李先生在香港開設屬於自己的麵店，並以太太的名字命名。這裏的麵條，每天以人手用竹竿打製，新鮮彈牙；主打麵食蝦子撈麵必不可錯過!食客還可以隔着店內小工房的玻璃窗，觀看整個麵條製作過程。

TEL. 3484 9126
1 Wing Lung Street, Cheung Sha Wan
長沙灣永隆街 1 號

■ PRICE 價錢
à la carte 點菜 $ 25-70

■ OPENING HOURS 營業時間
10:00-22:45 (L.O.)

La Saison NEW

XXX

🛏 ☞ ⊕12 ◐〽

Seek sanctuary from the busy streets outside by stepping into a veritable haven of tranquillity. As its name suggests, the focus of this elegant, discreet and comfortable French restaurant is on using the best seasonal ingredients; the French chef does this to great effect to produce carefully crafted dishes with the occasional Asian note. The service team are well-organised and attentive. On a clear day ask for a seat on the garden terrace.

專用電梯將你由大堂送到一個與外面截然不同的環境中:時尚華麗的吊燈、手繪牆壁及高級餐具,流露出一份現代高貴魅力。法國廚師用出色的烹調功夫處理時令食材,混入了亞洲香料的菜式,令你有意想不到的驚喜。喜歡天然感覺的你,還可選擇在開揚優雅的露天花園平台進膳。

TEL. 2789 8000
2F, The Cameron, 33 Cameron Road,
Tsim Sha Tsui
尖沙咀金馬倫道 33號 The Cameron 2樓
www.lasaisonbyjb.com

■ PRICE 價錢
Lunch 午膳
set 套餐 $ 328-368
à la carte 點菜 $ 500-1,200
Dinner 晚膳
set 套餐 $ 1,188
à la carte 點菜 $ 500-1,200

■ OPENING HOURS 營業時間
Lunch 午膳　12:00-14:30 (L.O.)
Dinner 晚膳　18:30-22:30 (L.O.)

L'Altro

✂✂   🍴16 ◔🍴 🎀

This good-looking Italian on the 10th floor of The L Place was created by Philippe Léveillé, from the prestigious Miramonti l'Altro restaurant in Brescia. His style of cuisine combines authentic Italian recipes with French culinary techniques. His signature dishes include spaghetti vongole; Wagyu with Mediterranean herbs; and Sicilian red prawns with chili and tomato foam. Greys and silvers and plenty of glass and marble keep things looking cool.

來自意大利布雷西亞著名食府 Miramonti l'Altro 的大廚 Philippe Léveillé，是這家意大利餐廳背後的靈魂。他的風格結合了傳統意大利食譜和法式烹調技巧。拿手菜式包括琵琶魚、鵝肝及砂鍋野鴨意大利雲吞，意大利雪糕亦不可錯過。餐廳裝潢以灰色及銀色為主調，配以大量玻璃及雲石，別具型格。

TEL. 2555 9100
10F, The L Place,
139 Queen's Road Central
皇后大道中 139號 The L Place 10樓
www.laltro.hk

■ PRICE 價錢
Lunch 午膳
set 套餐 $298-398
à la carte 點菜 $600-900
Dinner 晚膳
set 套餐 $1,280
à la carte 點菜 $600-900

■ OPENING HOURS 營業時間
Lunch 午膳 11:30-14:30 (L.O.)
Dinner 晚膳 18:30-22:30 (L.O.)

HONG KONG 香港

Lan Yuen Chee Koon
蘭苑饎館

The Chan's first place opened back in '84; they moved here in '97 to premises with a proper kitchen and now offer Cantonese claypots, healthy home-style steamed dishes, noodles and deliciously sweet puddings. Fine Chinese furniture is a feature of the small dining room, where Mrs Chan does the cooking and her husband the serving. The set menus at dinner prove particularly popular so be prepared to queue outside.

陳氏夫婦創辦的這家食館，原店在1984年開業，並於1997年遷到有正規廚房的現址；雅致的中式家具是餐廳的特色。廚房由陳太掌舵，供應各種粵式煲仔菜、健康家常蒸煮菜式、麵食和美味糕點。陳先生則負責招呼客人。晚飯時間的套餐特別受歡迎。顧客或需排隊輪候入座。

TEL. 2381 1369
318 Sai Yeung Choi Street,
Prince Edward
太子西洋菜北街 318號

■ PRICE 價錢
set 套餐 $ 80-95
à la carte 點菜 $ 40-80

■ OPENING HOURS 營業時間
12:00-22:00 (L.O.)

■ ANNUAL AND WEEKLY CLOSING 休息日期
Closed 9 days Lunar New Year and Monday
農曆新年休息 9 天及週一休息

L'Atelier de Joël Robuchon

Sit at the counter if you want to be at the centre of the operation, but if perching on a high chair is not for you or you want a little more formality, then Le Jardin is the better choice. The red and black colours marry perfectly, while the highly skilled kitchen uses prime ingredients to produce deceptively simple looking, contemporary dishes that display exquisite depth, balance and flavour. The superb wine list offers around 3,000 labels.

如欲觀賞開放式廚房的運作，建議坐在吧枱旁邊，但若不喜歡高腳椅，或希望正式一點，那麼Le Jardin 也許更佳。紅色與黑色的裝潢配搭得天衣無縫，烹調技巧精湛的廚師選用上等食材，炮製出外觀漂亮吸引的菜式。酒牌包羅超過三千款佳釀。

TEL. 2166 9000
Shop 401, 4F, The Landmark,
15 Queen's Road Central
皇后大道中 15號置地廣場 4樓 401號舖
www.robuchon.hk

■ PRICE 價錢
Lunch 午膳
set 套餐 $ 420-1,980
à la carte 點菜 $ 750-1,400
Dinner 晚膳
set 套餐 $ 830-1,980
à la carte 點菜 $ 750-1,400

■ OPENING HOURS 營業時間
Lunch 午膳 12:00-14:30 (L.O.)
Dinner 晚膳 18:30-22:30 (L.O.)

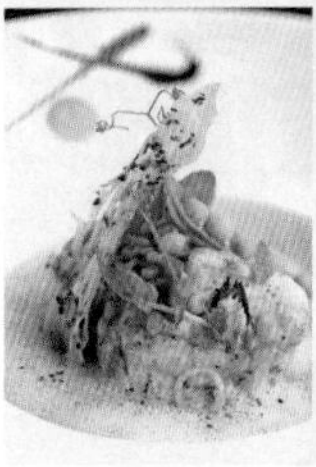

Lau Sum Kee (Fuk Wing Street)
劉森記麵家 (福榮街)

This is one noodle shop that is not afraid of the competition. In a street overflowing with alternatives, Lau Sum Kee (and its sister shop around the corner) are packed with customers buzzing in and out. It is run by the third generation of the family, the noodles are pressed by bamboo and the wontons are freshly made at the shop. Recommendations include wonton noodles, dry prawn roe mix with noodles and pork knuckles mixed with noodles.

這家麵店可謂競爭力強勁!在滿是麵店的街道上,劉森記麵家(及其轉角位的姊妹店)仍然擠滿食客。此家由家族經營的麵店已傳到第三代,全部竹昇麵及雲吞均在店內新鮮人手製造。推薦麵食包括雲吞麵、蝦子撈麵及豬手撈麵。

TEL. 2386 3583
82 Fuk Wing Street, Sham Shui Po
深水埗福榮街82號

■ PRICE 價錢
à la carte 點菜 $30-50

■ OPENING HOURS 營業時間
12:30-22:00 (L.O.)

■ ANNUAL AND WEEKLY CLOSING 休息日期
Closed 3 days Lunar New Year
農曆新年休息3天

Le Soleil

Le Soleil shines a light on Vietnamese cooking, with specialities such as green mango and tripe salad, pork knuckle casserole with tamarind, and Vietnamese-style noodles. The menu also includes dishes boasting a more imprecise provenance, best described as 'Asian fusion'. The restaurant sits on the 3rd floor of the Royal Garden in the shadow of the hotel's atrium. While its decorative style is a little incongruous, it is well run and comfortable.

青芒果牛肚沙律、酸子汁豬手煲和各款越式河粉，Le Soleil 帶你走進越南美食的世界。然而菜牌上的菜式並不局限於傳統越南菜，還有滲入了亞洲風味的越南菜和法式越南菜。店子位於帝苑酒店3樓，能觀賞酒店中庭全景。裝潢清簡得來予人舒適之感。

TEL. 2733 2033
3F, The Royal Garden Hotel,
69 Mody Road, East Tsim Sha Tsui
尖沙咀麼地道 69號帝苑酒店 3樓
www.rghk.com.hk

■ PRICE 價錢
Lunch 午膳
set 套餐 $268   à la carte 點菜 $270-650
Dinner 晚膳
set 套餐 $268   à la carte 點菜 $270-650

■ OPENING HOURS 營業時間
Lunch 午膳   12:00-14:30 (L.O.)
Dinner 晚膳   18:30-22:30 (L.O.)

Le Souk

🍴　　　　　　　　　　　　　　　　　　　　　　　📞🍴

Le Souk brings a little exotic spice to the streets of SoHo and is owned by two friendly and hospitable Egyptian brothers who make time to ensure that everyone is having a good time. Trinkets, jewels and lanterns add plenty of colour to the intimate room, while the kitchen prepares Moroccan and Middle Eastern cuisine with care and attention. Tender and aromatic lamb tagine is a standout dish, as is the roasted fig salad.

由兩位友善好客的埃及兄弟開設的Le Souk 座落於蘇豪，為區內帶來一點獨特的中東味道。餐廳內的空間以色彩繽紛的小飾物、珠寶和燈籠點綴；大廚則在廚房精心烹調摩洛哥和中東美食。嫩滑又香氣洋溢的羊肉煲是出色之作，香燒無花果沙律亦不可錯過。

TEL. 2522 2128
4 Staunton Street, Central
中環士丹頓街 4號

■ PRICE 價錢
Dinner 晚膳
à la carte 點菜 $ 200-400

■ OPENING HOURS 營業時間
Dinner 晚膳　17:00-00:00 (L.O.)

Lei Bistro
利小館

Providing healthy, appealingly priced cooking for everyone is the aim of this very popular restaurant from the Lei Garden group. Influences are northern and southern Chinese but there are also Cantonese dishes, along with some new creations. Specialities include steamed pork dumpling in Shanghai style, a daily Cantonese style soup, and chilled mango with grapefruit and sago. Despite a capacity of 150, it is still advisable to book.

為客人提供健康、價錢大眾化的小菜，正是利苑集團開設這間餐館的概念。菜式來自大江南北，亦有提供新派廣東菜。特式菜包括上海小籠包、粵式老火湯和楊枝金露。雖然餐館可容納一百五 十名客人，但仍建議預先訂座。

TEL. 2602 8283
Shop B217-218, Basement 2, Times Square, 1 Matheson Street, Causeway Bay
銅鑼灣勿地臣街 1 號
時代廣場地庫 2 樓 B217-B218號舖
www.leibistro.com

■ PRICE 價錢
à la carte 點菜 $80-170

■ OPENING HOURS 營業時間
11:00-23:00 L.O.22:15

■ ANNUAL AND WEEKLY CLOSING 休息日期
Closed 3 days Lunar New Year
農曆新年休息 3 天

Lei Garden (Elements)
利苑酒家 （圓方）

  ✗✗   ᕀ ⇌40 ◖❙

The restaurant is located in the blue-tinted 'water' area of this large shopping mall and its décor is more contemporary than some of the other Lei Garden branches. It is composed of a huge dining room, which can be a little noisy when full, and other more intimate rooms. The cooking throughout is reliable Cantonese, with a broad range of interesting seafood preparations as well as some highly unusual double-boiled tonic soups.

這家裝潢華麗優雅的餐館位於大型購物商場中的藍色「水」區，比其他利苑分店更有時代感。這裏設有一個大主廳，滿座的時候可能有點吵，亦可選擇其他更具私人空間的飯廳。菜色是清一色的廣東菜，但以各種方法烹調的海鮮和與別不同的燉湯，使這裏顯得分外出色。

TEL. 2196 8133
Shop 2068-70, 2F, Elements,
1 Austin Road West, Tsim Sha Tsui
尖沙咀柯士甸道西 1 號
圓方 2 樓 2068-70號舖
www.leigarden.com.hk

SPECIALITIES TO PRE-ORDER 預訂食物
Dried abalone in oyster sauce 蠔皇乾鮑 /
Braised whole fish maw 蠔皇香扣原隻繁肚公
/Braised goose web with Kanto spiky sea
cucumber 關東遼參扣玉掌 /Baked chicken
with sea salt in casserole 古仿鹽甑雞

■ PRICE 價錢
Lunch 午膳
à la carte 點菜 $ 160-1,200
Dinner 晚膳
à la carte 點菜 $ 160-1,200

■ OPENING HOURS 營業時間
Lunch 午膳 11:30-14:30 (L.O.)
Dinner 晚膳 18:00-22:30 (L.O.)

■ ANNUAL AND WEEKLY CLOSING 休息日期
Closed 3 days Lunar New Year
農曆新年休息 3 天

Lei Garden (IFC)
利苑酒家 (國際金融中心)

16

Forward planning is advisable here – not only when booking but also when selecting certain roast meat dishes and some of their famous double-boiled soups which require advance notice. The extensive menu features specialist seafood dishes and the lunchtime favourites include shrimp and flaky pastries filled with shredded turnip. All this is served up by an efficient team, in clean, contemporary surroundings.

到這間利苑分店用餐，無論座位，還是食物如燒味或受歡迎的燉湯，均須提早預約。這裏菜式種類繁多，其中以海鮮炮製的佳餚最具特色，而午市時段的美食首推巧製點心如銀蘿千層酥。格局設計富時代氣息，潔淨雅致，服務效率亦十分高。

TEL. 2295 0238
Shop 3008-3011, Podium Level 3,
IFC Mall, 1 Harbour View Street, Central
中環港景街 1號國際金融中心商場第 2期
3樓 3008-3011號舖
www.leigarden.com.hk

SPECIALITIES TO PRE-ORDER 預訂食物
Dried abalone in oyster sauce 蠔皇乾鮑 / Braised whole fish maw 蠔皇香扣原隻鱉肚公 /Braised goose web with Kanto spiky sea cucumber 關東遼參扣玉掌 /Baked chicken with sea salt in casserole 古仿鹽甑雞

■ PRICE 價錢
Lunch 午膳
à la carte 點菜 $ 120-830
Dinner 晚膳
à la carte 點菜 $ 150-830

■ OPENING HOURS 營業時間
Lunch 午膳 11:30-14:30 (L.O.)
Dinner 晚膳 17:30-22:30 (L.O.)

■ ANNUAL AND WEEKLY CLOSING 休息日期
Closed 3 days Lunar New Year
農曆新年休息 3 天

HONG KONG 香港

Lei Garden (Kowloon Bay)
利苑酒家 (九龍灣)

✗✗   ⊡40 ◐⊺⊺

Service is one of the strengths of this Lei Garden, located in a shopping mall near the MTR station. Signature dishes include the 10 different varieties of double-boiled tonic soups (to be ordered in advance), sautéed scallops with macadamia nuts and yellow fungus, and braised boneless spare-ribs with sweet and sour sauce. Those who like to eat lunch early or at pace are rewarded with a discount if they vacate their tables before 12:45pm.

這家利苑分店位於地鐵站附近的商場內，服務周到是其強項。招牌菜包括多款燉湯（須提前預訂）、米網黃耳夏果炒帶子、宮庭醬烤骨。中午12:45前離席有折扣優惠，對於喜歡提早吃午飯或能於短時間內吃畢午飯的顧客而言，確是佳音。

TEL. 2331 3306
Shop Unit F2, Telford Plaza 1,
33 Wai Yip Street, Kowloon Bay
九龍灣偉業街 33 號德褔廣場 F2 號舖
www.leigarden.com.hk

SPECIALITIES TO PRE-ORDER 預訂食物
Dried abalone in oyster sauce 蠔皇乾鮑 /
Braised whole fish maw 蠔皇香扣原隻鱟肚公
/Braised goose web with Kanto spiky sea
cucumber 關東遼參扣玉掌 /Baked chicken
with sea salt in casserole 古仿鹽㷛雞

■ PRICE 價錢
Lunch 午膳
à la carte 點菜 $ 100-750
Dinner 晚膳
à la carte 點菜 $ 120-750

■ OPENING HOURS 營業時間
Lunch 午膳 11:30-15:00 (L.O.)
Dinner 晚膳 18:00-23:00 (L.O.)

■ ANNUAL AND WEEKLY CLOSING 休息日期
Closed 3 days Lunar New Year
農曆新年休息 3 天

Lei Garden (Kwun Tong)
利苑酒家 (觀塘)

XX

⌬20

Avoid the escalators and use the shuttle lift to get to the fifth floor in this confusingly arranged shopping mall. Once there, the set up will seem familiar if you've experienced other Lei Garden branches: dishes are standard Cantonese but are reliably cooked using fresh ingredients. The place is as frantic as the others but has been partitioned into different seating areas by smart trellises. Try not to sit near the entrance as it's noisy.

如欲更易找到和更快到達此酒家，請直接乘搭升降機到5樓。如你曾光顧其他利苑分店，對此店絕不會感到陌生：清一色的廣東菜與可靠的美食及新鮮的材料。當然，這裏同樣擠滿利苑的忠實顧客，簡潔的屏風巧妙地將餐廳分隔成不同用餐區。

TEL. 2365 3238
Level 5, apm, Millennium City 5,
418 Kwun Tong Road
觀塘道 418號創紀之城 第 5期 apm5樓
www.leigarden.com.hk

SPECIALITIES TO PRE-ORDER 預訂食物
Dried abalone in oyster sauce 蠔皇乾鮑 /
Braised fish maw 蠔皇扣繁肚公 /Braised
goose web 遼參扣玉掌 /Baked chicken in
casserole 古仿鹽甑雞

■ PRICE 價錢
Lunch 午膳
à la carte 點菜 $ 100-750
Dinner 晚膳
à la carte 點菜 $ 120-750
■ OPENING HOURS 營業時間
Lunch 午膳　11:30-15:00 (L.O.)
Dinner 晚膳　18:00-23:30 (L.O.)
■ ANNUAL AND WEEKLY CLOSING 休息日期
Closed 3 days Lunar New Year
農曆新年休息 3 天

Lei Garden (Mong Kok)
利苑酒家 (旺角)

✻

✗✗   ⊞30 ☏⅋

This is the original Lei Garden, which opened back in the 1970s; it's still as busy as ever so it's always worth booking ahead. The contemporary restaurant is spread over two floors and the upper space has views out onto the busy street. The long and varied Cantonese menu certainly represents good value; seafood recommendations include Canadian geoduck poached in lobster soup, and steamed Alaska king crab with Hua Diao wine.

由於這家餐廳實在太受歡迎，食客必須預先訂座。這家利苑總店開業於七十年代。富時代感的餐廳共分為兩層，樓上可看到旺角繁華的街景。以廣東菜為主的菜單花樣多變令人目不暇給，絕對物有所值，特別推薦龍蝦湯過橋加拿大象拔蚌或刺生及花雕蒸亞拉斯加蟹。

TEL. 2392 5184
121 Sai Yee Street, Mong Kok
旺角洗衣街 121號
www.leigarden.com.hk

SPECIALITIES TO PRE-ORDER 預訂食物
Dried abalone in oyster sauce 蠔皇乾鮑 /
Braised whole fish maw 蠔皇香扣原隻繁肚公
/Braised goose web with Kanto spiky sea
cucumber 關東遼參扣玉掌 /Baked chicken
with sea salt in casserole 古仿鹽甄雞

■ PRICE 價錢
Lunch 午膳
à la carte 點菜 $ 100-750
Dinner 晚膳
à la carte 點菜 $ 120-750

■ OPENING HOURS 營業時間
Lunch 午膳   11:30-15:00 (L.O.)
Dinner 晚膳   18:00-23:30 (L.O.)

■ ANNUAL AND WEEKLY CLOSING 休息日期
Closed 3 days Lunar New Year
農曆新年休息 3 天

Lei Garden (North Point)
利苑酒家 (北角)

✗✗   🌼

🍽16   ☎🍴

Discreetly tucked away on the first floor of a residential block and overlooking a pleasant courtyard garden is this branch of the popular chain. Things here can certainly get quite frenetic as it accommodates up to 200 people. The lengthy Cantonese menu mirrors what's available at other branches, but particular dishes worth noting here are crispy roasted baby duck, deep-fried lotus root with minced pork and the daily seafood specialities.

這家深受歡迎的連鎖酒家分店，隱藏在住宅大廈一樓。從酒家外望是屋苑的翠綠庭園，寬敞的空間可容納多達二百人，氣氛往往極為熱鬧。這裏的菜單與其他利苑分店大致相同，特別推薦沙溪燒米鴨、家鄉荔芋煎藕餅及每日海鮮精選。

TEL. 2806 0008
1F, Block 9-10, City Garden, North Point
北角城市花園 9-10座 1樓
www.leigarden.com.hk

SPECIALITIES TO PRE-ORDER 預訂食物
Dried abalone in oyster sauce 蠔皇乾鮑 /
Braised whole fish maw 蠔皇香扣原隻繁肚公
/Braised goose web with Kanto spiky sea
cucumber 關東遼參扣玉掌 /Baked chicken
with sea salt in casserole 古仿鹽甑雞

■ PRICE 價錢
Lunch 午膳
à la carte 點菜 $ 100-750
Dinner 晚膳
à la carte 點菜 $ 120-750

■ OPENING HOURS 營業時間
Lunch 午膳　11:30-15:00 L.O.14:30
Dinner 晚膳　18:00-23:30 L.O.22:30

■ ANNUAL AND WEEKLY CLOSING 休息日期
Closed 3 days Lunar New Year
農曆新年休息 3 天

177

Lei Garden (Sha Tin)
利苑酒家 (沙田)

It may have been in town for over 20 years, however, refurbishment has kept this Lei Garden feeling fresh. It is located in New Town Plaza Sha Tin, which means that it can get especially busy at weekends when everyone needs refuelling after a day spent shopping. The menu largely follows the theme of others in the group; always ask for the daily special. Pre-ordering the seasonal double-boiled tonic soup is particularly recommended.

位於沙田新城市廣場的利苑分店已開業超過二十年，憑着精心烹調的正宗粵菜及舒適的室內環境，在區內蠻受食客歡迎，常常座無虛席。細心的服務員會在你致電訂座時提醒你預訂老火湯或時令特色小菜等。

TEL. 2698 9111
6F, Phase I New Town Plaza, Sha Tin
沙田新城市廣場第 1 期 6 樓
www.leigarden.com.hk

SPECIALITIES TO PRE-ORDER 預訂食物
Dried abalone in oyster sauce 蠔皇乾鮑 /
Braised whole fish maw 蠔皇香扣原隻肚公
/Braised goose web with Kanto spiky sea
cucumber 關東遼參扣玉掌 /Baked chicken
with sea salt in casserole 古仿鹽瓶雞

■ PRICE 價錢
Lunch 午膳
à la carte 點菜 $ 100-750
Dinner 晚膳
à la carte 點菜 $ 120-750

■ OPENING HOURS 營業時間
Lunch 午膳 11:30-15:00 L.O. 14:45
Dinner 晚膳 18:00-23:30 L.O. 23:00

■ ANNUAL AND WEEKLY CLOSING 休息日期
Closed 3 days Lunar New Year
農曆新年休息 3 天

Lei Garden (Tsim Sha Tsui)
利苑酒家 (尖沙咀)

🍴🍴　　　　　　　　　　　🛗80　◐🍴

The entrance takes you past an intricately carved wooden wall and a series of large fish tanks into a big, bustling, traditional dining room that's brightly lit and comfortable. There's pagoda detailing on the ceiling, bare red-brick walls and an army of staff in attendance. The varied Cantonese menu reiterates what's on offer at the other Lei Gardens. Classic double-boiled soups and steamed fresh sea fish are highly recommended.

入口處是雕刻精緻的木製牆飾和一列大魚缸，然後是一個燈光明亮、寬敞舒適的餐室；傳統的中式裝潢:天花上是精美寶塔裝飾，牆壁由紅磚砌成，氣氛熱鬧，服務團隊效率超卓。這裏的廣東菜單與其他利苑分店相若。馳名老火湯及清蒸海上鮮不容錯過。

TEL. 2722 1636
B2F, Houston Centre, 63 Mody Road, East Tsim Sha Tsui
尖東麼地道 63 號好時中心地庫 2 樓
www.leigarden.com.hk

SPECIALITIES TO PRE-ORDER 預訂食物
Dried abalone in oyster sauce 蠔皇乾鮑 / Braised whole fish maw 蠔皇香扣原隻繁肚公 / Braised goose web with Kanto spiky sea cucumber 關東遼參扣玉掌 / Baked chicken with sea salt in casserole 古仿鹽甑雞

■ PRICE 價錢
Lunch 午膳
à la carte 點菜 $ 120-830
Dinner 晚膳
à la carte 點菜 $ 150-830

■ OPENING HOURS 營業時間
Lunch 午膳　11:30-14:45 (L.O.)
Dinner 晚膳　18:00-22:45 (L.O.)

■ ANNUAL AND WEEKLY CLOSING 休息日期
Closed 3 days Lunar New Year
農曆新年休息 3 天

HONG KONG 香港

Lei Garden (Wan Chai)
利苑酒家 (灣仔)

XX

P ☐18 ◎î

An inventory of restaurants in Wan Chai wouldn't be complete without a Lei Garden. This branch is bigger than most and boasts a busy, bustling atmosphere, particularly at lunchtime. It follows the group's tried-and-tested formula by offering an extensive menu of dishes with luxurious dishes alongside less elaborate but classic Cantonese specialities. Seafood enthusiasts should consider pre-ordering the Alaskan king crab or Brittany blue lobster.

論灣仔區的出色食肆，當然少不了利苑的份兒。菜單包含珍饈百味與經典粵式小菜，種類繁多，加上巧手精製的點心和便利的地點，難怪總是座無虛席。食客可於訂位時跟店方預訂特別海鮮如亞拉斯加蟹和法國藍龍蝦等。

TEL. 2892 0333
1F, CNT Tower, 338 Hennessy Road,
Wan Chai
灣仔軒尼詩道 338號北海中心 1樓
www.leigarden.com.hk

SPECIALITIES TO PRE-ORDER 預訂食物
Dried abalone in oyster sauce 蠔皇乾鮑 /
Braised whole fish maw 蠔皇香扣原隻鰵肚公
/Braised goose web with Kanto spiky sea
cucumber 關東遼參扣玉掌 /Baked chicken
with sea salt in casserole 古仿鹽焗甁雞

■ PRICE 價錢
Lunch 午膳
à la carte 點菜 $ 120-830
Dinner 晚膳
à la carte 點菜 $ 150-830

■ OPENING HOURS 營業時間
Lunch 午膳　11:30-14:45 (L.O.)
Dinner 晚膳　18:00-22:45 (L.O.)

■ ANNUAL AND WEEKLY CLOSING 休息日期
Closed 3 days Lunar New Year
農曆新年休息 3 天

Lin Heung Kui
蓮香居

This huge two-floor eatery opened in 2009 with the aim of building on the success of the famous Lin Heung Tea House in Wellington Street. It's modest inside but hugely popular and the dim sum trolley is a must, with customers keen to be the first to choose from its extensive offerings. The main menu offers classic Cantonese dishes with specialities such as Lin Heung special duck. The pastry shop below is worth a look on the way out.

佔地甚廣的蓮香居於2009年開幕，樓高兩層，延續威靈頓街蓮香樓的輝煌成績。樸素的內部裝潢掩不住鼎沸的人氣，點心車讓人急不及待從其各式各樣點心中選擇心頭好。菜單上羅列了傳統廣東菜及特色小菜，如蓮香霸王鴨。離開時路經樓下的中式餅店，不妨入內逛逛。

TEL. 2156 9328
2-3F, 40-50 Des Voeux Road West,
Sheung Wan
上環德輔道西 40-50號 2-3樓

■ PRICE 價錢
Lunch 午膳
à la carte 點菜 $ 50-480
Dinner 晚膳
à la carte 點菜 $ 50-480

■ OPENING HOURS 營業時間
06:00-22:30 (L.O.)

Liu Yuan Pavilion
留園雅敘

✗✗   🍽16 ☎🍴

Authentic Shanghainese specialities served in a room where you'll hear plenty of Shanghainese speakers really will make you think you're in Shanghai. Along with dim sum, you shouldn't miss the stir-fried shrimps, Mandarin fish with sweet and sour sauce, braised meatballs with vegetables or braised pig knuckle. A recent renovation has given the restaurant a look of understated elegance; the booths are the prized seats and it's worth pre-booking.

重新裝修後的留園雅敘素淨優雅，靠窗的卡座尤為舒適。開業多年的店子，擁有不少忠心擁躉。有趣的是，店內大部分食客和侍應，都會以上海話交談，當然，大家最關注的，還是這兒的正宗滬菜。不論是清炒蝦仁、松子桂魚、砂窩獅子頭或紅繞元蹄等經小菜，還是點心均值得一試。

TEL. 2804 2000
3F, The Broadway,
54-62 Lockhart Road, Wan Chai
灣仔駱克道 54-62號博匯大廈 3樓

SPECIALITIES TO PRE-ORDER 預訂食物
Steamed Quarry fish with preserved melons 滷香瓜蒸鯽魚 / Smoked pomfret with tea leaves 煙燻倉魚

■ PRICE 價錢
Lunch 午膳
set 套餐 $ 115
à la carte 點菜 $ 180-750
Dinner 晚膳
à la carte 點菜 $ 180-750

■ OPENING HOURS 營業時間
Lunch 午膳　12:00-15:00 L.O.14:30
Dinner 晚膳　18:00-23:00 L.O.22:30

■ ANNUAL AND WEEKLY CLOSING 休息日期
Closed 3 days Lunar New Year
農曆新年休息 3 天

Lo Chiu (Jordan)
老趙 (佐敦)

The Chinese owner had spent several years in Vietnam before arriving in Hong Kong and opening this Vietnamese restaurant back in 1978. He now has two other shops but this is his flagship. Steamed stuffed rice rolls, noodles in beef soup and cold vermicelli with pork, beef or chicken are some of the highlights, but the hotpot curry is also worth trying. The environment is basic but clean and the staff are helpful.

老闆是曾經在越南住過幾年的華僑，回香港後，在1978年開始經營這餐廳，現在已擁有兩家分店，但此店依然是他的旗艦店。越式蒸粉包、牛肉湯河、豬肉、牛肉或雞肉凍檬都是不錯的選擇，椰香咖喱也值得嘗試。餐廳裝修簡單整潔，侍應服務周到。

TEL. 2384 2143
25-27 Man Yuen Street, Jordan
佐敦文苑街 25-27號

■ PRICE 價錢
Lunch 午膳
set 套餐 $30-100   à la carte 點菜 $70-230
Dinner 晚膳
à la carte 點菜 $70-230

■ OPENING HOURS 營業時間
12:00-23:00 (L.O.)

■ ANNUAL AND WEEKLY CLOSING 休息日期
Closed 4 days Lunar New Year
農曆新年休息 4 天

Loaf On
六福菜館

🍴   🛋36   ◐🍽

Spread over three floors and hidden behind a strip of seafood restaurants in Sai Kung is this neat little spot. The daily soup depends on what the owner buys from local fishermen; you can even bring your own fish and have it prepared by the kitchen. Besides seafood, Loaf On also offers simple but flavoursome Cantonese dishes like chilli and garlic bean curd, Loaf On-style chicken, and steamed sea fish with salt. The restaurant will relocate in 2015.

這家佔了三層樓的小菜館,藏身於西貢海鮮餐廳一帶後街。店主每天從當地漁民處搜購最新鮮的食材炮製是日魚湯,你亦可自行攜帶海鮮,交由廚師為你烹調。除了海鮮和魚湯,椒鹽奇脆豆腐和鹽蒸海魚也必須一試,別忘了預訂一客風沙雞。2015年中將會遷址。

TEL. 2792 9966
49 See Cheung Street, Sai Kung
西貢市場街 49號

SPECIALITIES TO PRE-ORDER 預訂食物
Crispy skin chicken 脆皮風沙雞 /Fish soup 西貢地道魚湯 /Minced fish in pumpkin soup 金湯魚蓉羹

■ PRICE 價錢
Lunch 午膳
à la carte 點菜 $ 150-500
Dinner 晚膳
à la carte 點菜 $ 200-500

■ OPENING HOURS 營業時間
11:00-23:00 L.O. 22:30

■ ANNUAL AND WEEKLY CLOSING 休息日期
Closed 3 days Lunar New Year
農曆新年休息 3 天

Lobster Bar and Grill
龍蝦吧

The big seller in this comfortable, clubby room is the seafood platter for two – it includes lobster, oysters, crab, tuna and abalone. Also popular are Maine and Spiny lobsters, the pasta dishes and specialities from the grill which come with a variety of accompaniments and sauces. Live music, a great drinks menu and a busy barman make for a fun, relaxing atmosphere in the evenings; lunch is more of a business affair.

令人垂涎的龍蝦吧海鮮拼盤,讓你一次過品嘗龍蝦、生蠔、阿拉斯加蟹腳、吞拿魚刺身和鮑魚的美味,實在是一大樂事。波士頓龍蝦、各款意大利麵條及提供多種配菜和醬汁伴吃選擇的烤肉菜式也是顧客喜愛的食品。現場樂隊演奏和豐富的餐酒選擇,帶來不一樣的悠閒晚膳。

TEL. 2820 8560
6F, Island Shangri-La Hotel, Pacific Place,
Supreme Court Road, Admiralty
中區法院道太古廣場港島香格里拉酒店 6樓
www.shangri-la.com

■ PRICE 價錢
Lunch 午膳
set 套餐 $458
à la carte 點菜 $540-1,600
Dinner 晚膳
à la carte 點菜 $540-1,600

■ OPENING HOURS 營業時間
Lunch 午膳　12:00-14:30 (L.O.)
Dinner 晚膳　18:30-22:30 (L.O.)

HONG KONG 香港

Lucky Indonesia
好運印尼餐廳

One's first impression of this small dining room, with its wooden furniture and traditional wall hangings, is that it's a little dated, but you'll soon feel as though you have been transported to the Indonesian countryside. The Middle Java cuisine is not unlike the décor – there's no fancy presentation, just authentic and tasty flavours. Satay is charcoal roasted which creates a lovely aroma; also try the Nasi Kuming and Mee Goreng.

細小的用膳區、木製的家具及傳統的掛牆吊飾,室內的裝潢予人點點懷舊感覺,令食客感到自己身處印尼郊區。一如食店的裝潢,此店的食物也不賣弄花巧,只用真材實料炮製出正宗美味的爪哇中部菜式。炭燒沙嗲烤肉帶來特別風味,而印尼黃薑飯和印尼炒麵更不容錯過。

TEL. 2389 3545
46 Tung Ming Street, Kwun Tong
觀塘通明街 46 號

■ PRICE 價錢
à la carte 點菜 $ 40-80

■ OPENING HOURS 營業時間
11:00-21:00 (L.O.)

■ ANNUAL AND WEEKLY CLOSING 休息日期
Closed 3 days Lunar New Year
農曆新年休息 3 天

Luk Yu Tea House
陸羽茶室

✕   🍴6   ◑🍴

Large numbers of both regulars and tourists come to Luk Yu Tea House for the traditionally prepared and flavoursome dim sum, and its three floors fill up quickly. The animated atmosphere and subtle colonial decoration are appealing but no one really stays too long; the serving team in white jackets have seen it all before and go about their work with alacrity. Popular dishes are fried prawns on toast and fried noodles with sliced beef.

陸羽茶室以傳統方法製作的美味點心，不光招來本地常客，更令不少外地遊客慕名而至，所以樓高三層的茶室經常滿座。生氣盎然的環境和帶點殖民地色彩的裝潢別具特色，穿着白色外套的侍應敏捷而專注地工作。除點心外其他菜式，如窩貼蝦及鼓椒牛肉炒麵也值得一試。

TEL. 2523 5464
24-26 Stanley Street, Central
中環士丹利街 24-26號

■ PRICE 價錢
Lunch 午膳
à la carte 點菜 $ 150-300
Dinner 晚膳
à la carte 點菜 $300-400

■ OPENING HOURS 營業時間
07:00-22:00 (L.O.)

■ ANNUAL AND WEEKLY CLOSING 休息日期
Closed 4 days Lunar New Year
農曆新年休息 4 天

Lung King Heen
龍景軒

✿✿ ✿✿ ✿✿

𝄞𝄞𝄞𝄞

♿ ◁ 🖐 🅿 🍽16 🕐🍴 🐾

It's not just Chef Chan Yan Tak's dim sum that's gaining legendary status – every dish is delicately crafted and enticingly presented, and the quality of the ingredients is of the highest order. The delightful serving team describe dishes with care and obvious pride. Translated as 'view of the dragon', the restaurant offers a panorama of the harbour; its interior is smart and uncluttered, with hand-embroidered silk, columns and glass screens.

龍景軒名副其實，坐擁動人心弦的維港全景；餐廳內部時尚整潔，飾以手工刺繡絲綢、圓柱和玻璃屏幕。素負盛名的，絕不僅是美味點心，這裏每一度菜都採用最高級的食材並經過精心雕琢，賣相極其吸引。侍應團隊充滿朝氣，會向客人仔細介紹菜式，讓人感到他們以此餐廳為傲。

TEL. 3196 8880
4F, Four Seasons Hotel,
8 Finance Street, Central
中環金融街 8號四季酒店 4樓
www.fourseasons.com/hongkong

SPECIALITIES TO PRE-ORDER 預訂食物
Roast Peking duck 北京烤鴨

■ PRICE 價錢
Lunch 午膳
set 套餐 $ 520
à la carte 點菜 $ 450-2,000
Dinner 晚膳
set 套餐 $ 1,650
à la carte 點菜 $ 500-2,000

■ OPENING HOURS 營業時間
Lunch 午膳　12:00-14:30 (L.O.)
Dinner 晚膳　18:00-22:30 (L.O.)

Man Wah
文華廳

XXX　　　　⟨ 🍴 🍽14 🕐🍴 🎐

Ceiling lamps resembling birdcages; original, ornate silk paintings; and local rosewood combine to create the striking interior of this Cantonese restaurant on the 25th floor of the Mandarin Oriental hotel. Tsui Yin Ting is their private room for 14 people and is styled on an old Chinese pavilion. The chef's specialities include steamed garoupa with crispy ginger and crabmeat, and roast goose puff with yanmin sauce.

位於文華東方酒店25樓的文華廳裝潢華麗典雅，一盞盞仿鳥籠中式吊燈、牆上古色古香的絲綢畫與紫檀木的運用營造出雅致的古中國情調。裝飾一如中國古時涼亭的聚賢亭廂房能容納十四人。酥薑珊瑚蒸星斑球及仁稔燒鵝酥皆為這兒的名菜。

TEL. 2825 4003
25F, Mandarin Oriental Hotel,
5 Connaught Road, Central
中環干諾道中 5 號文華東方酒店 25 樓
www.mandarinoriental.com/hongkong

■ PRICE 價錢
Lunch 午膳
set 套餐 $ 548-698
à la carte 點菜 $ 500-1,500
Dinner 晚膳
set 套餐 $ 938-1,298
à la carte 點菜 $ 500-1,500

■ OPENING HOURS 營業時間
Lunch 午膳　12:00-14:30 (L.O.)
Dinner 晚膳　18:30-22:30 (L.O.)

Mandarin Grill + Bar
文華扒房+酒吧

❀

Designed by Sir Terence Conran, this is an elegant and luminous restaurant where the emphasis is on comfort and relaxation. If you want to add a little theatre then ask for a seat at the counter to watch the chefs preparing some of the many varieties of oysters that are available here. On the other side, behind a window, the kitchen team specialises in contemporary European cuisine; be sure to leave room for one of their soufflés.

這家典雅明亮的餐廳是著名室內設計師Sir Terence Conran 的作品，注重舒適與優閒。如果你想增添一點娛樂，可預訂吧枱位置，觀賞廚師準備餐廳提供的多種生蠔。選擇餐廳的另一邊，你可透過玻璃窗看到廚房團隊用心準備令人垂涎三尺的歐洲菜；切記預留空間品嘗梳乎厘甜品。

TEL. 2825 4004
1F, Mandarin Oriental Hotel,
5 Connaught Road, Central
中環干諾道中 5號文華東方酒店 1樓
www.mandarinoriental.com/hongkong

■ PRICE 價錢
Lunch 午膳
set 套餐 $608
à la carte 點菜 $1,100-1,500
Dinner 晚膳
set 套餐 $1,788-1,988
à la carte 點菜 $1,100-1,500

■ OPENING HOURS 營業時間
Lunch 午膳　12:00-14:30 (L.O.)
Dinner 晚膳　18:30-22:30 (L.O.)

■ ANNUAL AND WEEKLY CLOSING 休息日期
Closed Saturday lunch
週六午膳休息

Mask of Sichuen & Beijing
面譜京川料理

✂   🚪 **P** ⬚10 ☏🍴

Beijing opera masks hanging from the ceiling add to the atmosphere of this softly lit, contemporary dining room which has intimate booths as well as large tables. The menus offer a comprehensive selection of Sichuan and Pekingese dishes, along with some innovative offerings, like stir-fried shredded potato and mango. Diners can decide on their own level of spiciness and there's also a wide selection of vegetarian dishes available.

懸掛在天花的京劇面譜，為柔和的燈光和富現代感的裝潢增添氣氛；這裏既提供私密的卡座，亦有大型餐桌。餐牌上的菜式種類繁多，既有齊全的川菜選擇，亦有京菜佳餚，更有創新之選，如香芒土豆絲。食客可自選辣度，並有多種素菜供應。

TEL. 2311 9233
Shop 33, GF,
KCR East Tsim Sha Tsui Station,
Tsim Sha Tsui
尖沙咀尖東站地下 33號鋪

■ PRICE 價錢
Lunch 午膳
set 套餐 $ 68
à la carte 點菜 $ 220-500
Dinner 晚膳
à la carte 點菜 $ 220-500

■ OPENING HOURS 營業時間
Lunch 午膳　12:00-15:30 (L.O.)
Dinner 晚膳　17:45-23:30 (L.O.)

HONG KONG 香港

May's Sawaddee Thailand
旺泰特食

On the ground floor of a residential building in the heart of Sai Kung sits this long, narrow, simply decorated but comfortable Thai restaurant. From the hospitable, all-female service team comes an extensive menu of authentic Thai dishes, whose highlights include yellow chicken curry in bread, fried crab with curry, Tom Yum Goong, and fried rice with minced meat and herbs, all made using fresh, good quality ingredients.

這家泰國餐廳位於西貢市中心的住宅大廈地下，店內空間既長且窄，裝修簡約但舒適。全女班的員工服務殷勤，店內提供多款正宗泰國菜，推介有黃咖喱雞配包、咖哩炒蟹、冬蔭功、肉碎香葉炒飯等。週末和假期或需要排隊輪候。

TEL. 2791 0522
24 Man Nin Street, Sai Kung
西貢萬年街 24號

■ PRICE 價錢
Lunch 午膳
à la carte 點菜 $ 55-280
Dinner 晚膳
à la carte 點菜 $ 55-280

■ OPENING HOURS 營業時間
Lunch 午膳　12:00-15:00 (L.O.)
Dinner 晚膳　18:00-22:30 (L.O.)

Megan's Kitchen
美味廚

Can't decide between Cantonese or a hotpot? Or perhaps you'd like both? Megan's Kitchen can help as it offers a grand selection of Cantonese dishes, like steamed minced beef with dried mandarin peel and claypot rice, but is also known for its hotpots, which come with high quality ingredients like seafood or Japanese beef. The dining room has a warm, contemporary feel and there are several well-equipped private rooms.

廣東菜還是火鍋？還是想兩者兼得？美味廚讓你不再苦惱。這兒除了有各式廣東小菜如陳皮蒸手剁牛肉和美味煲仔飯外，火鍋亦同樣聞名，更有海鮮、和牛等高級火鍋配料。大廳設計溫馨時尚，並備有多個設備齊全的私人客房。

TEL. 2866 8305
5F, Lucky Centre,
165-171 Wan Chai Road, Wan Chai
灣仔灣仔道 165-171號樂基中心 5樓
www.meganskitchen.com

■ PRICE 價錢
Lunch 午膳
set 套餐 $ 58-158
à la carte 點菜 $ 120-550
Dinner 晚膳
à la carte 點菜 $ 120-550

■ OPENING HOURS 營業時間
Lunch 午膳　12:00-14:30 (L.O.)
Dinner 晚膳　18:00-23:00 (L.O.)

MIC Kitchen

✧

'Demon chef' Alvin Leung, of Bo Innovation fame, brings his innovative style of cooking to a new building in Kwun Tong. Here at MIC kitchen his team uses creative touches along with superlative cooking skills to mix and match Chinese and Western food – the resulting flavours are bound to surprise you. The interior is relaxed yet contemporary; ask for a seat at the counter if you want to watch the chefs work their magic while you eat.

廚魔Alvin Leung的新餐廳，他繼續發揮無窮創意，配合精湛廚藝和現代化的處理食物方法，揉合中西食材的特點，炮製出令人驚喜兼讚歎的美食。餐廳位於觀塘一棟新建成的大廈內，設計時尚簡約，感覺舒適。建議預訂開放式廚房前的座位，品嘗美食之餘能觀賞廚師的手藝。

TEL. 3758 2239
GF, AIA Kowloon Tower,
100 How Ming Street, Kwun Tong
觀塘巧明街100號友邦九龍大樓地下

■ PRICE 價錢
Lunch 午膳
set 套餐 $ 198-498
à la carte 點菜 $ 450-1,200
Dinner 晚膳
set 套餐 $ 598-898
à la carte 點菜 $ 450-1,200

■ OPENING HOURS 營業時間
Lunch 午膳　11:30-15:00 (L.O.)
Dinner 晚膳　18:30-22:30 (L.O.)

■ ANNUAL AND WEEKLY CLOSING 休息日期
Closed Sunday 週日休息

Ming Court
明閣

✿

🏵 ♿ ᴘ 🅿 ⏲36 ◑ 🍴 ಜಿ

It's not just the expertly prepared Cantonese cooking that attracts diners to Ming Court – many also come here for the great wine list and thoughtfully suggested wine pairings, so expect plenty of expert advice on what wine to order with your garoupa or suckling pig. You also have a choice of dining room: Ming Sun is an elegantly dressed round room with a collection of Ming Dynasty bronzes; Ming Moon is a newer and more spacious room.

明閣吸引顧客之處，除了大廚的精湛粵菜廚藝，更因為此店提供多種餐酒，侍應還會協助顧客揀選適當的佳釀配合龍躉或脆皮乳豬佐吃。顧客還可選擇擺設著青銅器、充滿古風的「明日」或裝潢較現代時髦的「明月」用膳。

TEL. 3552 3300
6F, Langham Place Hotel,
555 Shanghai Street, Mong Kok
旺角上海街 555 號朗豪酒店 6 樓
www.hongkong.langhamplacehotels.com

SPECIALITIES TO PRE-ORDER 預訂食物
Drunken shrimp dumpling 貴妃醉蝦餃

■ PRICE 價錢
Lunch 午膳
set 套餐 $ 398-498
à la carte 點菜 $ 450-1,200
Dinner 晚膳
set 套餐 $ 598-788
à la carte 點菜 $ 450-1,500

■ OPENING HOURS 營業時間
Lunch 午膳　11:00-14:30 (L.O.)
Dinner 晚膳　18:00-22:30 (L.O.)

Moon Thai (Sheung Wan)

✗ 🏠 ⛲14 ◎👤

Secreted on the second floor of the Holiday Inn Express, Moon Thai is led by an experienced Thai chef who insists on using the freshest ingredients. Seafood dishes are the ones that stand out and he is known particularly for his own creation of fried crab with tom yum paste. Get in the mood by beginning your evening with a lemongrass martini. There is also an Indian chef in the kitchen preparing some Indian specialities.

經驗老到的泰籍主廚統領的泰國廚師團隊，以本地新鮮食材與泰國進口香料、菜蔬，炮製正宗高級泰菜，尤擅長以海鮮入餚，主廚獨創的「芭堤雅蟹逅」是代表作。此店還提供小量印度菜如即烘印度酵餅和薄餅，由印裔廚師主理。泰籍調酒師調製的特飲如香茅馬天尼別具風味。

TEL. 2851 1288
2F, Holiday Inn Express,
83 Jervois Road, Sheung Wan
上環蘇豪智選假日酒店 2樓
香港蘇豪智選假日酒店 2樓

■ PRICE 價錢
Lunch 午膳
set 套餐 $ 118-188
à la carte 點菜 $ 210-860
Dinner 晚膳
à la carte 點菜 $ 210-860

■ OPENING HOURS 營業時間
12:00-22:30 (L.O.)

Mott 32 NEW
卅二公館

✗✗ ⛶20 🕐🍴

Mott Street lies at the heart of Manhattan's Chinatown and number 32 was the address of the first Chinese grocery store to open in New York, back in the 19th century. This mix of old NYC and classic Chinese décor adds character to a room which already feels quite secretive as it's in the basement of the Standard Chartered Bank building. Apple wood-roasted Peking duck, and barbecue Spanish Teruel pork with yellow mountain honey are worth trying.

於渣打銀行大廈地庫內的Mott 32，宛如一間隱閉的會所，英文名字源於十九世紀紐約唐人街首家中式辦館的地址。店主花盡心思地揉合舊紐約氣息與中國古典味。為了品嘗粵菜而來的你，不妨試試以蘋果木烤製的北京片皮鴨和蜜汁西班牙黑毛豬叉燒。你還可以隔着玻璃窗觀賞廚師炮製食物的過程。

TEL. 2885 8688
Basement Level,
Standard Chartered Bank Building,
4-4A Des Voeux Road, Central
中環德輔道中 4-4A號渣打銀行中心地庫
www.mott32.com

■ PRICE 價錢
Lunch 午膳
à la carte 點菜 $ 350-2,000
Dinner 晚膳
à la carte 點菜 $ 350-2,000

■ OPENING HOURS 營業時間
Lunch 午膳　12:00-14:30 (L.O.)
Dinner 晚膳　18:00-23:00 (L.O.)

Nanxiang Steamed Bun (Causeway Bay)
南翔饅頭店 (銅鑼灣)

Xiao Long Bao served here are slightly larger than usual and come with a thin, ivory-white wrapper and juicy filling – and is one reason for the popularity of this modern, yet intimate restaurant. The original Nanxiang Steamed Bun shop opened in Shanghai 100 years ago and this is Hong Kong's first branch. It also offers Shanghainese cuisine and dim sum; look out for braised minced pork ball and the seasonal steamed bun with crab roe soup.

南翔饅頭店始於百年前的上海，銅鑼灣店是其在香港首家分店，既時尚又舒適。這裏的小籠包由從上海派駐香港的廚師監督製作，確保味道正宗，且體積較一般小籠包大；象牙色薄嫩麵皮裏，是飽滿香濃的餡料與肉汁。店內亦有提供上海小菜和點心。

TEL. 3690 2088
3F, Causeway Bay Plaza I,
489 Hennessy Road, Causeway Bay
銅鑼灣軒尼詩道 489號銅鑼灣廣場第一期 3樓
www.nanxiang.com.hk

■ PRICE 價錢
Lunch 午膳
set 套餐 $ 58-65
à la carte 點菜 $ 100-150
Dinner 晚膳
à la carte 點菜 $ 100-150

■ OPENING HOURS 營業時間
11:30-23:00 L.O. 22:30

■ ANNUAL AND WEEKLY CLOSING 休息日期
Closed Lunar New Year 年初一休息

Nanxiang Steamed Bun (Tsuen Wan)
南翔饅頭店 (荃灣)

The original shop has been going strong in Shanghai for over 100 years so hopefully Hong Kong's branch should be around for quite some time. It certainly doesn't lack customers, who keep the noise levels up and ensure there's plenty of bustle. Everyone is here for the food, in particular the Xiao Lang Bao with its juicy fillings, but there's also a wide choice of Shanghainese dishes; portion sizes and prices allow for enthusiastic ordering.

在上海屹立超過百年的老店，分店落戶香港後也很受歡迎，顧客絡繹不絕，餐室內有時會頗嘈吵，不失其繁忙感覺。這裏的食客都是為追求美食而來，特別是鮮味多汁的小籠包及選擇繁多的上海菜式。這裏的美食份量恰當，價格相宜，你絕對可以大快朵頤。

TEL. 3692 4078
Shop S22-23, 2F, Luk Yeung Galleria,
22-66 Wai Tsuen Road, Tsuen Wan
荃灣蕙荃路 22-66號綠楊坊 2樓 S22-23號舖
www.nanxiang.com.hk

■ PRICE 價錢
Lunch 午膳
à la carte 點菜 $ 100-150
Dinner 晚膳
à la carte 點菜 $ 100-150

■ OPENING HOURS 營業時間
Lunch 午膳　11:30-16:30 (L.O.)
Dinner 晚膳　18:00-22:30 (L.O.)

■ ANNUAL AND WEEKLY CLOSING 休息日期
Closed Lunar New Year 年初一休息

New Shanghai
新滬坊

🍴14 ⓒ

Glass walls and exquisite Chinese art combine to create a strikingly contemporary interior here on the first floor of the Convention & Exhibition Centre. The menu offers a light, healthy style of Shanghainese cooking and mixes the traditional and the innovative, with dim sum coming from the open kitchen in the middle of the room. Specialities include stir-fried barley with air-dried pork and braised duck stuffed with glutinous rice.

玻璃牆結合精緻的中國藝術，為這家位於香港會議展覽中心一樓的餐廳，營造出極時尚的風格。新滬坊提供以輕盈健康為主、揉合傳統和創新意念的上海菜式，廚師在店中央的開放式廚房內為食客製作各款美味點心。馳名菜式包括豐年藏珍寶和江南八寶鴨。

TEL. 2582 7332
1F, Hong Kong Convention and
Exhibition Centre,
1 Harbour Road, Wan Chai
灣仔港灣道 1 號香港會議展覽中心 1 樓

■ PRICE 價錢
Lunch 午膳
set 套餐 $ 130-170
à la carte 點菜 $ 200-800
Dinner 晚膳
à la carte 點菜 $ 200-800

■ OPENING HOURS 營業時間
Lunch 午膳　12:00-15:00 (L.O.)
Dinner 晚膳　18:30-22:00 (L.O.)

■ ANNUAL AND WEEKLY CLOSING 休息日期
Closed 2 days Lunar New Year
農曆新年休息 2 天

Nha Trang (Central)
芽莊 (中環)

If you're not here bang on midday then you'll probably find yourself queuing as this fun, fast and frantic Vietnamese restaurant really pulls in the crowds. It has a bright, fresh feel, a mix of individual and communal tables and a young service team who are well organised and efficient. The healthy menu ranges from Vietnamese street snacks and salad rolls through to 'broken rice platters' and lemongrass grilled fish, all at affordable prices.

午市時，你若不提早來到，便需要在這家有趣、高效率、極度繁忙的餐廳前排隊。店內裝修明亮而清新，設有小餐桌和可與多人共用的大餐桌，年輕的侍應工作有條理兼具效率。健康菜單從越南街頭小吃與粉卷，到越南碎米飯和香茅燒魚都有，價錢也相當合理。

TEL. 2581 9992
88-90 Wellington Street, Central
中環威靈頓街 88-90號
www.nhatrang.com.hk

■ PRICE 價錢
Lunch 午膳
à la carte 點菜 $ 100-300
Dinner 晚膳
à la carte 點菜 $ 100-300

■ OPENING HOURS 營業時間
Lunch 午膳　12:00-16:15 (L.O.)
Dinner 晚膳　18:00-22:15 (L.O.)

Nicholini's NEW
意寧谷

⚔⚔⚔   ♿ ← 🍷 🛋18 🍽 ⁂

Not only does this Italian restaurant offer great views from its perch on the eighth floor of the Conrad Hotel, but it's also very handsome, thanks to the ornate ceiling, wood panelling and clever lighting. The menu keeps things classical and authentic, with a slight bias towards more northerly parts of Italy. The service is very professional and the wine list is impressive. There are two private rooms and brunch is served on Sundays.

這家風格獨特的意大利餐廳主要供應傳統、地道、正宗的意大利美食。專業細心的服務、醉人的美食、品質淳厚的佳釀，令食客為之動容！淺啡色系的簡約時尚設計，配合別樹一格的桂花葉型燈飾，置身其中，有一份說不出的從容自在。兩間私人廂房，適合十數人聚會。星期天還會供應早午拼餐。

TEL. 2521 3838
8F, Conrad Hotel, Pacific Place,
88 Queensway, Admirality
金鐘道 88 號太古廣場港麗酒店 8 樓
www.conraddining.com

■ PRICE 價錢
Lunch 午膳
à la carte 點菜 $ 825-1,590
Dinner 晚膳
à la carte 點菜 $ 825-1,590

■ OPENING HOURS 營業時間
Lunch 午膳   12:00-15:00 (L.O.)
Dinner 晚膳   18:00-23:00 (L.O.)

■ ANNUAL AND WEEKLY CLOSING 休息日期
Closed Saturday lunch
週末午膳休息

Nishiki NEW
錦

Nishiki is concealed within the Regal Kowloon hotel but is owned and run by its Japanese chef. Tradition runs deep here, as demonstrated by the fact that the decorative style has remained largely unchanged for over 20 years. The atmosphere and the style of food are typical of an izakaya. Chicken meatball and tofu hotpot, BBQ eel and BBQ chicken are the recommendations. Booking is strongly advised – when doing so, ask for seats at the counter.

位於富豪九龍酒店內的這家餐廳，多年來見證着尖沙咀的變遷亦擁有一眾忠實追隨者，內部裝潢由始沒甚大變，很典型的居酒屋格局，氣氛總是熱鬧非常。食客最喜愛這裏的燒烤，如燒鱔、免治雞肉棒，而雞肉丸豆腐鍋亦美味非常。建議預先訂座，開放式廚房邊上的座位能觀賞廚師的技藝，氣氛更佳。

TEL. 2723 8660
Shop 103, 1F Regal Kowloon Hotel,
71 Mody Road, Tsim Sha Tsui
尖沙咀麼地道 71 富豪九龍酒店 1 樓 103 室

■ PRICE 價錢
Lunch 午膳
à la carte 點菜 $ 200-450
Dinner 晚膳
à la carte 點菜 $ 200-450

■ OPENING HOURS 營業時間
Lunch 午膳   12:00-14:00 (L.O.)
Dinner 晚膳   18:00-22:00 (L.O.)

No.5 Italian (Tai Hang)   NEW

Small, cosy and not without a little charm, No. 5 Italian is warmly run by five friends. The menu is equally diminutive with around five choices of starters, pastas and pizzas which are supplemented by a few daily specials on the blackboard. The thin-crust pizzas with homemade tomato sauce are the main attraction, and the owners have christened them after themselves, with names such as Pun's or Franco's. With only 30 seats, it's wise to book.

餐單內只有三十多精選小菜，以脆薄餅底和特製番茄醬作賣點的五款薄餅分別以五位東主的名字命名，風味各異。每日限量供應四款鮮製意粉，當中以海膽扁長條麵配白松露汁最受歡迎。每日精選值得嘗試。座位有限，常常滿座，建議預訂座位。

TEL. 2504 2111
21 Brown Street, Tai Hang
大坑布朗街 21 號

■ PRICE 價錢
Lunch 午膳
à la carte 點菜 $ 250-400
Dinner 晚膳
à la carte 點菜 $ 250-400

■ OPENING HOURS 營業時間
Lunch 午膳   12:00-14:30 (L.O.)
Dinner 晚膳   18:00-23:00 (L.O.)

Nobu

✂✂   ♿ ≺ ✇ ⎋16 🚄 ☏✇ ℨ

This branch of the über-trendy, international Nobu brand boasts an impressive ceiling fashioned from sea urchin spines and images of cherry blossom behind the bar. At lunch, bento boxes are the popular choice. At dinner, Mr Matsuhisa's beguiling blend of Japanese and South American tastes continues to work its magic by featuring sushi and sashimi, good quality seafood and fine salsas.

這家享譽國際的Nobu餐廳分店有着以海膽刺裝飾的天花，讓人印象深刻，背景更配有櫻花美景裝飾。午餐時間最受歡迎的是便當。而晚餐方面，主廚松久信幸融合日本和南美烹調風格，炮製的嶄新口味更是迷人。菜式包括壽司、刺身、優質的海鮮及辛香番茄醬。

TEL. 2313 2340
2F, Intercontinental Hotel,
18 Salisbury Road, Tsim Sha Tsui
尖沙咀梳士巴利道18號洲際酒店2樓

■ PRICE 價錢
Lunch 午膳
set 套餐 $ 338-638
à la carte 點菜 $ 400-1,400
Dinner 晚膳
set 套餐 $ 1,038-1,438
à la carte 點菜 $ 500-1,600

■ OPENING HOURS 營業時間
Lunch 午膳   12:00-14:30 (L.O.)
Dinner 晚膳   18:00-23:00 (L.O.)

Noodlemi

It's easy to miss this little place and that would be a shame if you want fresh, healthy and contemporary-style Vietnamese food. It seats just 24 customers but thanks to some clever design they've managed to use every inch of space available so it never really feels too packed. The lunchtime crowd come mainly for the Vietnamese sandwiches made using French baguettes and the rice vermicelli dishes. All the food is gluten free and MSG free.

若不留心，便會錯過這家小店。店內只有二十四個座位，但特別設計的桌椅善用室內每一寸空間，因此並沒有壓逼感。精選餐單上的是清新健康的新派越式美食，各種用法國麵包做的越式三文治和一系列撈檬粉，頗受區內上班族歡迎。除麵包外，其他食物都不含味精和麩質。

TEL. 2253 1114
2 Bonham Strand, Sheung Wan
上環文咸東街 2號
www.noodle-mi.com

■ PRICE 價錢
à la carte 點菜 $ 50-100

■ OPENING HOURS 營業時間
11:30-21:45 (L.O.)

■ ANNUAL AND WEEKLY CLOSING 休息日期
Closed Public Holidays 公眾假期休息

NUR NEW

❀

✗✗   ⊟8 ◐⏱

Nur means 'light' in Arabic but is also an abbreviation of Chef Nurdin Topham's name. He is a disciple of something called 'nourishing gastronomy' which roughly translates as creating dishes that are tasty, innovative but also healthy and nutritious. The only choice you need to make is to decide which of the two tasting menus you want. The bright, unassuming dining room is dominated by the open kitchen and service is fluent and friendly.

白色系的簡約設計,配合舒適的座椅和露天陽台,給你閒適之感。餐廳名源自阿拉伯文,有「光」之意,也是主廚的名字。主廚依循營養美食學精神,以細膩的廚藝及營養科學的應用,創造出色香味與營養俱備的美食,不光滿足你的味覺,還顧及你的健康。只供應兩款套餐。年輕的服務員態度友善且具效率。

TEL. 2871 9993
3F, Lyndhurst Tower,
1 Lyndhurst Terrace, Central
中環擺花街 1 號廣場 3 樓
www.NUR.hk

■ PRICE 價錢
Dinner 晚膳
set 套餐 $ 788-988

■ OPENING HOURS 營業時間
18:30-21:30 (L.O.)

■ ANNUAL AND WEEKLY CLOSING 休息日期
Closed Sunday 週日休息

Olé

As the name somewhat suggests, both the decorative style and the menu of this Spanish restaurant have an unapologetically traditional look. The tiles, white walls and knick-knacks give it a certain charm and extra colour is provided by a plethora of paintings. The kitchen prepares the classics such as garlic shrimps, seafood paella and squid with ink sauce with aplomb; go for the churros with hot chocolate sauce for dessert.

單看店名就知道，無論裝修還是菜式都會是地地道道的西班牙風味。瓷磚、白牆配以小擺設就是魅力所在，無處不在的掛畫更添幾分色彩。廚房從容地炮製蒜蓉蝦、海鮮炒飯和墨汁墨魚等傳統西班牙菜式。甜品建議一試西班牙小油條配熱朱古力醬。

TEL. 2523 8624
1F, Shun Ho Tower,
24-30 Ice House Street, Central
中環雪廠街 24-30 號順豪大廈 1 樓
www.olespanishrestaurant.com.hk

■ PRICE 價錢
Lunch 午膳
set 套餐 $ 180
à la carte 點菜 $ 400-900
Dinner 晚膳
à la carte 點菜 $ 400-900

■ OPENING HOURS 營業時間
Lunch 午膳 12:00-14:30 (L.O.)
Dinner 晚膳 18:30-23:00 (L.O.)

■ ANNUAL AND WEEKLY CLOSING 休息日期
Closed 4 days Lunar New Year and Sunday
農曆新年 4 天及週日休息

On Lot 10

✗   ⊡20 ◔⏲

It's not quite as small as it looks as there's more space upstairs, but this is still a very intimate French restaurant. What it lacks in size, it makes up for in quality. The keen chef tours the markets daily to compile his good value menu of traditional Gallic home cooking; specialities include whole fish with crushed potatoes and roasted pigeon. Choice is more limited at lunch so dinner is the best time to visit.

這家法國餐廳看似地方細小，但其實樓上別有洞天，上層設有不少座位，是舉辦私人宴會的理想地方。充滿熱情的主廚每天穿梭市場，準備其獨具傳統法國家常菜風格的實惠菜單；店內特色法國菜包括原條野生海魚焗薯蓉、香燒法式乳鴿羔。

TEL. 2155 9210
34 Gough Street, Central
中環歌賦街 34 號

■ PRICE 價錢
Lunch 午膳
set 套餐 $ 118-138
à la carte 點菜 $ 550-850
Dinner 晚膳
à la carte 點菜 $ 550-850

■ OPENING HOURS 營業時間
Lunch 午膳   12:00-14:30 (L.O.)
Dinner 晚膳   18:30-22:30 (L.O.)

■ ANNUAL AND WEEKLY CLOSING 休息日期
Closed Sunday 週日休息

One Harbour Road
港灣壹號

♟♟♟   & ⟨ ⊟ P ⟳22 ⦿⊪

One Harbour Road may be set in a hotel, but its graceful ambience will make you think you're on the terrace of an elegant 1930s Taipan mansion. Split-level dining adds to the airy feel, there are views of the harbour, and the sound of running water softens the bold statement of the huge pillars. Cantonese menus offer a wide variety of well-prepared meat and fish dishes. To see how they're created, consider booking the Chef's Table.

這裏的氣氛，令你仿如置身30年代的優雅大班府第。分層用餐，空間感較大，且能飽覽維港景色。大型蓮花池及潺潺的流水聲，使感覺硬朗的龐大柱子變得柔和。這裏的粵菜包括精心準備、種類繁多的肉類和魚類菜式。如想一睹烹調過程，可考慮預訂「廚師餐桌」。

TEL. 2584 7722
8F, Grand Hyatt Hotel,
1 Harbour Road, Wan Chai
灣仔港灣道一號君悅酒店 8樓
www.hongkong.grand.hyatt.com

■ PRICE 價錢
Lunch 午膳
set 套餐 $ 500-720
à la carte 點菜 $ 450-800
Dinner 晚膳
à la carte 點菜 $ 450-800

■ OPENING HOURS 營業時間
Lunch 午膳　12:00-14:30 (L.O.)
Dinner 晚膳　18:30-22:30 (L.O.)

8 1/2 Otto e Mezzo - Bombana

❀❀❀

⟪⟫ ⟪⟫ 🍴 🍴　　　　　　　⊡30　◔🍴　⌘

Chef-owner Umberto Bombana's bright and bold restaurant takes its name from Fellini's film about the search for inspiration. It is an exquisitely framed and cleverly lit space, with a chic, urbane feel. The Italian cooking is equally appealing: homemade tagliolini; artisanal chitarra with red king prawn; roast turbot with chanterelle mushroom and limoncello soufflé are not to be missed. The 'ageing cellar' for hams and cheeses is an attractive feature and the wine list is predominantly Italian.

費里尼那齣有關尋找靈感的電影，正是這家裝修色彩鮮艷的餐廳命名的來源。餐廳不論裝潢還是照明都帶有都市時尚感。餐廳的意大利菜式同樣精美；自製寬條麵、大蝦手工意粉、鮮菌烤多寶魚及檸檬梳乎厘都是必然之選。火腿與芝士的發酵窖是店內特色，餐酒選擇主要來自意大利 。

TEL. 2537 8859
Shop 202, 2F, Alexandra House,
18 Chater Road, Central
中環遮打道 18號歷山大廈 2樓 202號舖
www.ottoemezzobombana.com

■ PRICE 價錢
Lunch 午膳
set 套餐 $ 470-1,380
à la carte 點菜 $ 800-1,300

Dinner 晚膳
set 套餐 $ 1,380
à la carte 點菜 $ 800-1,300

■ OPENING HOURS 營業時間
Lunch 午膳　12:00-14:30 (L.O.)
Dinner 晚膳　18:30-22:30 (L.O.)

■ ANNUAL AND WEEKLY CLOSING 休息日期
Closed Sunday
週日休息

HONG KONG 香港

Pang's Kitchen
彭慶記

✂️   🕐🍽️

Anyone living in Happy Valley will be familiar with Pang's Kitchen as it has been packing them in since it opened back in 2001. Its reputation is largely down to its Cantonese cuisine which comes in a decidedly homestyle, traditional style, with dishes such as baked fish intestines in a clay pot, whole superior abalone in oyster sauce, and seasonal dishes like snake soup. It is not a huge place so it's worth booking ahead.

跑馬地的街坊必定不會對彭慶記感到陌生，店舖自2001年開業以來一直服務該區。其馳名粵式佳餚主要是家常小菜和傳統菜式，如砵仔焗魚腸、蠔皇原隻吉品鮑，及季節性菜式如太史五蛇羹。由於食店面積不大，食客宜預先訂座。

TEL. 2838 5462
25 Yik Yam Street, Happy Valley
跑馬地奕蔭街 25號

■ PRICE 價錢
Lunch 午膳
set 套餐 $ 60-120
à la carte 點菜 $ 150-850
Dinner 晚膳
à la carte 點菜 $ 150-850

■ OPENING HOURS 營業時間
11:00-22:45 (L.O.)

Peking Garden (Central)
北京樓 (中環)

🍴🍴🍴   🪑48 🍽️

Divided into two large and warmly lit rooms; one more traditionally decorated, the other better suited for bigger family groups. Be sure to time your visit for the noodle-making demonstration, performed by a chef every evening in the restaurant at 8:30pm. The signature dish is, of course, the Peking duck, which is prepared with great care. Also look out for the deep-fried prawns in chilli sauce, and diced steak with walnuts.

餐廳劃分為兩個大廳；一邊風格較為傳統，另一邊則較為適合大家族聚餐。緊記要算準時間，欣賞每晚8時30分的師傅即席拉麵表演。這裏的招牌菜當然是經過精心炮製的北京填鴨。其他值得一試的小菜有宮爆明蝦及琥珀牛柳粒。

TEL. 2526 6456
BF, Alexandra House, 18 Chater Road, Central
中環遮打道 18號歷山大廈地庫
www.maxims.com.hk

■ PRICE 價錢
Lunch 午膳
à la carte 點菜 $ 200-1,000
Dinner 晚膳
à la carte 點菜 $ 200-1,000

■ OPENING HOURS 營業時間
Lunch 午膳　11:30-15:00 L.O.14:45
Dinner 晚膳　18:00-23:30 L.O.22:30

HONG KONG 香港

Peking Garden (Tsim Sha Tsui)
北京樓 (尖沙咀)

🍴　　　　　　　　　　　　　　　　　🍽24

A huge, boisterous Peking restaurant with eight rooms and 500 seats, where the staff are either supervising with calm deliberation, or pushing trolleys and serving. The special dishes are the barbecued Peking duck with pancake, and the braised sea cucumber with spring onion - but look out also for the sauteed prawn in garlic chilli sauce and fried hand-made noodles.

這家偌大且熱鬧的北京樓分為八個部分，可容納五百個座位。員工分工合作，有的沈着地等待候命；有的推着餐車、有的在上菜。招牌菜有北京填鴨、北京葱燒海參、京爆明蝦球等。各款麵食也值得一試。

TEL. 2735 8211
3F, Star House, 3 Salisbury Road,
Tsim Sha Tsui
尖沙咀梳士巴利道 3號星光行 3樓
www.maxims.com.hk

■ PRICE 價錢
Lunch 午膳
set 套餐 $ 150
à la carte 點菜 $ 200-1,000
Dinner 晚膳
à la carte 點菜 $ 200-1,000

■ OPENING HOURS 營業時間
Lunch 午膳　11:30-15:00 L.O.14:45
Dinner 晚膳　17:30-23:30 L.O. 23:00

Penthouse NEW

🍴🍴   🏠 ⟨ 🍽12 🕐🍴

Another restaurant from Harlan Goldstein and this time he's gone for a New York loft-style look with an ersatz industrial feel. The restaurant is perched on the 30th floor – hence the name – and the harbour views are terrific. The menu keeps its influences largely within Europe and there are two main specialities that merit your attention: the homemade pastas and the juicy and tender meats cooked in the Josper grill oven.

Harlan Goldstein的新餐廳。木地板、黑金屬架、水泥磚及鎢絲燈造出紐約風空間。餐廳向海的一面是落地玻璃，維港景色盡收眼底。採自世界各地的食材，以時尚烹調方式與歐陸風格炮製。每日鮮製的手造意粉頗受歡迎；以Josper炭爐烤煮的肉鮮嫩多汁，連骨美國肉眼扒絕不會讓你失望。

TEL. 2970 0828
30F, Soundwin Plaza 2 Midtown,
1-29 Tang Lung Street, Causeway Bay
銅鑼灣登龍街 1-29號金朝陽中心 2期 30樓
www.penthouse-dining.com

■ PRICE 價錢
Lunch 午膳
set 套餐 $258-480
à la carte 點菜 $380-900
Dinner 晚膳
set 套餐 $258-480
à la carte 點菜 $380-900

■ OPENING HOURS 營業時間
Lunch 午膳 12:00-14:30 (L.O.)
Dinner 晚膳 18:00-22:30 (L.O.)

HONG KONG 香港

Petrus
珀翠

XXXXX   ♿ ⟵ 🍷 ⟷20 🕐🍽 🐝

Petrus is firmly in the classical European style, with moulded ceilings, chandeliers, elaborately draped curtains and fine table settings; it also offers great views from its perch on the 56th floor. The service is very professional and at dinner you'll be accompanied by a harpist. All this is matched by very proficient French cooking that relies on a roll-call of top quality ingredients. The wine list has over 20,000 bottles, including Pétrus!

珀翠的經典歐陸格調，充分表現在其雕刻天花、吊燈、高雅的窗簾及排列優雅的餐桌上。餐廳座落於56樓，可飽覽海港美景，其服務專業之餘，晚飯時段更有現場豎琴演奏。這一切配上一流的法式烹調，與新鮮的食材可謂無與倫比。此外，餐酒選擇逾一千二百款，當中包括顯貴的「珀翠」！

TEL. 2820 8590
56F, Island Shangri-La Hotel, Pacific Place,
Supreme Court Road, Admiralty
中區法院道太古廣場
港島香格里拉酒店 56樓
www.shangri-la.com

■ PRICE 價錢
Lunch 午膳
set 套餐 $488
à la carte 點菜 $900-1,400
Dinner 晚膳
set 套餐 $998-1,400
à la carte 點菜 $1,000-1,400

■ OPENING HOURS 營業時間
Lunch 午膳   12:00-14:30 (L.O.)
Dinner 晚膳   18:30-22:30 (L.O.)

Pierre

✿✿

𝄪𝄪𝄪𝄪　　　　　　　　　　♿ ⪡ ☝ ⟡16 ⓞ🍴 ⅋

The top floor of the Mandarin Oriental provides suitably chic surroundings for celebrated French chef Pierre Gagnaire's culinary pyrotechnics. The intricate and innovative dishes and their component parts arrive in a number of vessels, all carefully explained by the charming staff. The views are absolutely terrific and the room itself is stylish, moodily lit and very comfortable. The focus here is on enjoyment with an atmosphere free from pomposity.

文華東方酒店頂樓的環境，與法國名廚Pierre Gagnaire讓人驚歎的美味菜式非常合襯。精緻而創新的菜式與配菜以不同容器盛載着，殷勤細心的侍應會仔細為你講解每道菜式。餐廳景觀迷人，而餐廳本身的裝潢也甚具現代感，配合富情調的燈光，非常舒適。

TEL. 2825 4001
25F, Mandarin Oriental Hotel,
5 Connaught Road, Central
中環干諾道中 5 號文華東方酒店 25 樓
www.mandarinoriental.com/hongkong

■ PRICE 價錢
Lunch 午膳
set 套餐 ＄468-1,588
à la carte 點菜 ＄1,600-1,800

Dinner 晚膳
set 套餐 ＄898-1,588
à la carte 點菜 ＄1,600-1,800

■ OPENING HOURS 營業時間
Lunch 午膳　12:00-14:30 (L.O.)
Dinner 晚膳　19:00-22:30 (L.O.)

■ ANNUAL AND WEEKLY CLOSING 休息日期
Closed Saturday lunch, Sunday and Public Holidays 週六午膳、週日及公眾假期休息

Po Kee
波記

Po Kee is familiar to anyone who's lived in Western District as it's been a feature here for over 40 years and for many local residents a bowl of rice noodles (Lai Fan) with roasted duck leg remains a cherished childhood memory. To prepare his own roast meats, the owner built a factory behind the shop when he moved it to the current address. Regulars know to come before 2pm which is about the time the pork sells out each day.

西環的居民對波記一定不會陌生，此店在區內已有逾四十年歷史，一碗美味的燒鴨腿瀨粉是許多人的童年回憶。遷至現址後，店主在店舖後自設工場，炮製多款燒味。區內居民對店內各款美食了若指掌，燒肉往往在下午二時前售罄，欲試其燒鵝，最好在四時前到達。

TEL. N/A
425 Queen's Road West,
Western District
西環皇后大道西 425號

■ PRICE 價錢
à la carte 點菜 $ 25-80

■ OPENING HOURS 營業時間
11:30-22:30 (L.O.)

■ ANNUAL AND WEEKLY CLOSING 休息日期
Closed Sunday 週日休息

Qi
呇

✗✗   🚇 ⇔10 ◔🍴

The word 'Qi' means 'shining star' and the idea for the name was inspired by the shape of star anise – an important component of Sichuan cooking. This is a hip, moody and atmospherically lit restaurant where the coolness of the look contrasts with the heat of the food. Blacks and reds and opera-inspired paintings help create the striking room while in the kitchen sauces, herbs and chillies from Sichuan are used to prepare hot, spicy dishes.

呇意謂明亮的星星，餐廳以此命名意在比喻四川菜常用的香料八角。室內裝潢別具一格，紅與黑的鮮明對比，昏暗的燈光配上川劇壁畫，時尚中蘊含中式韻味。廚師採用自四川運來的醬汁、香料和辣椒，以傳統烹調方法做出正宗的麻、辣、鮮和香的四川風味，配合不同地區的食材，令人驚喜。

TEL. 2527 7117
2F, J Senses , 60 Johnston Road,
Wan Chai
灣仔莊士敦道 60號 2樓
www.qi-sichuan.hk

SPECIALITIES TO PRE-ORDER 預訂食物
Chili Dungeness crab 霸王辣蟹

■ PRICE 價錢
Lunch 午膳
set 套餐 $ 125-160
à la carte 點菜 $ 200-750
Dinner 晚膳
à la carte 點菜 $ 200-750

■ OPENING HOURS 營業時間
Lunch 午膳　12:00-14:15 (L.O.)
Dinner 晚膳　18:00-22:30 (L.O.)

Ramen Jo
拉麵Jo

There are four kinds of ramen here, along with the seasonal special. The miso ramen is good but those who like a stronger taste should try the spicy ramen with pork char siu. The pork rib soup is cooked over 16 hours and the taste is rich and strong but never thick or greasy. The owner named his shop after his favourite Japanese animated character and he runs it with an energetic team of servers who help create a lively atmosphere.

東主以心愛的漫畫人物名字為店子命名，並與充滿朝氣的服務團隊把這間拉麵店打理得井井有條。餐單內提供四款拉麵及時令推介，花上十六個小時精心熬製的豬骨湯底是此店拉麵的精髓所在，味濃而不膩，再配上特製的麵條和醬汁，令人回味無窮。

TEL. 2885 0638
3 Caroline Hill Road, Causeway Bay
銅鑼灣加路連山道 3號

■ PRICE 價錢
Lunch 午膳
à la carte 點菜 $ 75-95
Dinner 晚膳
à la carte 點菜 $ 75-95

■ OPENING HOURS 營業時間
Lunch 午膳　12:00-14:30 (L.O.)
Dinner 晚膳　18:00-22:00 (L.O.)

Restoran Indonesia 1968
印尼餐廳1968

Having been a fixture in Causeway Bay since 1968, this Indonesian restaurant is now run by the owners' sons. In 2011 they moved it to these more striking surroundings in Central, which are proving a hit with a hip young crowd. It comes divided into two rooms: one side with simple wooden tables, the other more intimate and connected to the bar. Street food specialities include satay cooked over charcoal, Lidah Semur and Ikan Asam.

早於1968年已在銅鑼灣開業的印尼餐廳，現時由東主的兒子接手經營，並於2011年搬到中環，成功吸引年輕食客。餐廳劃分為兩個區域，一邊簡單地放置多張木桌，另一邊則較為舒適，並連接酒吧。店內提供多種印尼街頭食品，包括碳燒沙爹、醬燒牛舌和亞參酸辣魚。

TEL. 2577 9981
5F, The L Place,
139 Queen's Road Central , Central
中環皇后大道中 139號 The L Place 5樓
www.ir1968.com

■ PRICE 價錢
Lunch 午膳
set 套餐 $ 98-158
à la carte 點菜 $ 180-500
Dinner 晚膳
à la carte 點菜 $ 180-500

■ OPENING HOURS 營業時間
12:00-23:30 (L.O.)

HONG KONG 香港

Ryu Gin
天空龍吟

🍴🍴　　　　　　　　　　　　　　♿ ⬅ ⌖12 ◐🍴

Seiji Yamamoto, owner-chef of the celebrated Ryugin in Tokyo, chose Hong Kong and the 101st floor of the ICC tower as the location for his first overseas branch. The only menu is the 10 course kaiseki and it uses high quality ingredients imported from Japan. The food is a mix of traditional flavours, modern influences and personal touches. Wood and silver combine to create an elegant space and the views are spectacular.

東京著名食府龍吟的主廚兼東主山本征治先生，選擇了環球貿易廣場 101樓作首家海外分店的地址，景觀極其壯麗，融合木材與銀色的裝潢，營造出高雅的空間。精緻的十道菜懷石料理採用來自日本的上等食材，並巧妙地融合了傳統與現代風味及創意配搭。

TEL. 2302 0222
101F, International Commerce Centre,
1 Austin Road West, Tsim Sha Tsui
尖沙咀柯士甸道西 1號環球貿易廣場 101樓
www.ryugin.com.hk

■ PRICE 價錢
Dinner 晚膳
set 套餐 $ 1,980

■ OPENING HOURS 營業時間
Dinner 晚膳　18:00-21:30 (L.O.)

■ ANNUAL AND WEEKLY CLOSING 休息日期
Closed 2 days Lunar New Year
農曆新年休息 2 天

Sabah (Wan Chai)
莎巴 (灣仔)

It may have an unremarkable façade, but at least it's easy to find thanks to the huge horizontal neon sign. It's equally modest inside which alerts you to the fact that diners don't come for the interior design but for the authentic Malay specialties. Satay, king prawns with butter and deep-fried egg yolk, beef Rendang and Hainanese chicken rice are some of the highlights. And it's always worth saving room here for the banana fritters.

這家餐廳的外觀也許毫不起眼，但是靠着巨大的霓虹燈招牌，我們可輕易找到它。內部裝潢與外觀一樣平凡，但吸引眾多食客的並不是餐廳的室內設計，而是正宗的馬拉菜。精選菜式包括沙嗲、金絲奶油大蝦、巴東牛肉與海南雞飯。主廚秘方炮製的炸香蕉也十分惹味。

TEL. 2143 6626
98-102 Jaffe Road, Wan Chai
灣仔謝菲道 98-102號

■ PRICE 價錢
Lunch 午膳
set 套餐 $ 75
à la carte 點菜 $ 150-390
Dinner 晚膳
à la carte 點菜 $ 150-390

■ OPENING HOURS 營業時間
11:00-23:00 (L.O.)

■ ANNUAL AND WEEKLY CLOSING 休息日期
Closed 3 days Lunar New Year
農曆新年休息 3 天

HONG KONG 香港

Sai Kung Sing Kee
勝記

⌗36

At first sight, this brightly coloured seafood restaurant may not seem too dissimilar to others in Sai Kung. However, there is something special here and that's the abalone menu. The abalone are prepared in various ways, from deep-fried to steamed; try the stewed abalone in oyster sauce. The building has 12 variously sized dining rooms spread over its three floors, all differently decorated; the most contemporary are on the 1st and 2nd floors.

這棟建築物樓高三層，備有十二個大小不一、裝飾各異的房間，一樓和二樓的餐室裝潢較時尚，驟眼看來，跟西貢其他餐廳並沒兩樣。但是，它真正特別的地方，在於扣鮑魚菜式。這裏提供多種以不同方式烹調的鮑魚菜式，由酥炸到蒸煮式式俱備，特別推介古法扣兩頭鮑魚。

TEL. 2791 9887
39 Sai Kung Tai Street, Sai Kung
西貢西貢大街 39號
www.singkee.ecomm.hk

SPECIALITIES TO PRE-ORDER 預訂食物
Crispy chicken 金 牌 炸 子 雞 / Stewed abalone in oyster sauce 古法扣鮑魚

■ PRICE 價錢
Lunch 午膳
à la carte 點菜 $ 100-950
Dinner 晚膳
à la carte 點菜 $ 180-950

■ OPENING HOURS 營業時間
11:00-22:30 (L.O.)

■ ANNUAL AND WEEKLY CLOSING 休息日期
Closed 2 days Lunar New Year
農曆新年休息 2 天

Sang Kee
生記

Having stood here proudly for over 30 years, Sank Kee is a true symbol of Wan Chai and remains refreshingly impervious to modernisation. The owner insists on buying the seafood herself each day and the Cantonese dishes are prepared using traditional methods. You'll find yourself thinking about their classic dishes like fried snapper, fried minced pork with cuttlefish, and braised fish with bitter melon long after you've sampled them.

現在許多粵菜餐廳都以雷同的裝潢和新派菜單作招徠，令生記這類傳統酒家讓人感到特別親切!開業三十多年，店主一直堅持每天親自採購優質海鮮，以傳統烹調方式製作一道道經典廣東菜：用時令材料炮製的乾煎海臘，家常菜如土魷煎肉餅和涼瓜炆魚等，令人回味無窮。

TEL. 2575 2236
1-2F, Hip Sang Building,
107-115 Hennessy Road, Wan Chai
灣仔軒尼詩道 107-115號協生大廈 1-2樓
www.sangkee.com.hk

■ PRICE 價錢
Lunch 午膳
set 套餐 $ 50-70
à la carte 點菜 $ 100-300
Dinner 晚膳
à la carte 點菜 $ 100-300

■ OPENING HOURS 營業時間
Lunch 午膳　12:00-14:30 (L.O.)
Dinner 晚膳　18:00-22:00 (L.O.)

■ ANNUAL AND WEEKLY CLOSING 休息日期
Closed first Monday of each month
每月第一個週一休息

Seasons　NEW

❊

✗✗✗　　　　　　　　　　　　　　　　　P　🍽12　◐🍴

The elegant Seasons restaurant occupies a huge space within Lee Gardens Two but it's split into four distinct areas, with each one representing one of the four seasons. Traditional French recipes are combined with the young chef's own ideas to create dishes that are full of verve and originality. Go for the Carte Blanche menu – a tasting menu designed for the whole table. The high quality ingredients are, appropriately enough, also very seasonal.

位於利園二期，面積寬敞，餐室分為四個部分，以四季為主題，各具特色與魅力。年輕大廚憑出色技藝與創意，將個人烹調風格應用於法國各地美食內，配合上等時令食材，製作別出心裁的小菜。Carte Blanche套餐是按食客的喜好特別設計的套餐。酒單選擇豐富，有不少由廚師親自引入的特別推介。

TEL. 2505 6228
Shop 308, 3F, Lee Gardens Two,
28 Yun Ping Road, Causeway Bay
銅鑼灣恩平道 28號利園 2期 3樓 308號舖
www.seasonsbyolivier.com

■ PRICE 價錢
Lunch 午膳
set 套餐 $ 288
à la carte 點菜 $ 300-500
Dinner 晚膳
set 套餐 $ 588
à la carte 點菜 $ 600-800

■ OPENING HOURS 營業時間
Lunch 午膳　12:00-14:30 (L.O.)
Dinner 晚膳　18:00-22:30 (L.O.)

Ser Wong Fun
蛇王芬

Regulars flock here for the snake soup and snake banquets in winter. No less than 15 varieties of double-boiled soups and a vast array of seasonal pot dishes are also offered, along with traditional Cantonese dishes and roast meats. The restaurant was established over 70 years ago and is under the stewardship of the fourth generation, so it is little wonder that a book has been published celebrating the family history and their cherished recipes.

七十年前開店的蛇王芬如今由第四代傳人主理，更出版了書籍介紹家族歷史及著名菜式。熟客經常來此品嘗蛇羹，冬天甚至會共享蛇宴。超過十五種老火燉湯任君選擇，此外亦提供一系列煲仔飯、傳統廣東菜式及燒味。

TEL. 2543 1032
30 Cochrane Street, Central
中環閣麟街 30 號

■ PRICE 價錢
à la carte 點菜 $ 120-250

■ OPENING HOURS 營業時間
11:00-22:30 (L.O.)

■ ANNUAL AND WEEKLY CLOSING 休息日期
Closed 4 days Lunar New Year
農曆新年休息 4 天

Serge et le Phoque NEW

🍴

🛋12 📞🍴

Thanks to its large glass façade, discreet sign and understated, faux industrial interior, it's pretty apparent that the refreshingly relaxed Serge and The Seal is unlike many of the city's French restaurants. The appealingly minimalist surroundings contrast somewhat with the cooking, which is detailed and innovative and includes some Japanese influence. The set menus are nicely balanced and are made up of elaborately constructed, diminutive dishes.

小巧精緻的賣相，結合和風口味與創新配搭的烹調方式，讓Serge et le Phoque 的食物有別於一般法國菜館，每道菜式都經過主廚精心設計和鑽研。店內裝潢 與其時尚創新的烹調風格貫徹如一，落地玻璃窗與工業風的陳設，透出不拘一 格的灑脫味道，錯落有致的圓吊燈透着抽象表現主義，不羈中帶點藝術色彩。

TEL. 5465 2000
GF, Shop B2, The Zenith,
3 Wan Chai Road, Wan Chai
灣仔道 3 號尚翹峰地下 B2號舖

■ PRICE 價錢
Dinner 晚膳
set 套餐 $ 650-850

■ OPENING HOURS 營業時間
Dinner 晚膳 18:30-22:00 (L.O.)

Seventh Son
家全七福

🍴🍴　　　　　　　　　　　　　📖 ⟷20 🕐

The owner-chef named his restaurant in honour of his father who taught his seventh son how to cook when he was 14 years old. In the kitchen he insists on using the freshest seasonal ingredients and his technical skills in preparing the traditional Cantonese food are obvious. He uses less seasoning than many, so that his customers can appreciate the true flavour of the food. Barbecued suckling pig and crispy chicken are his specialities.

餐廳名稱含了東主父親的名字，英文名是他在家中的排行輩份，也表示傳承父親廚藝之意。東主自十四歲起隨父習廚，擅長高級功夫粵菜。他堅持用時令食材、以最小的調味料及精細的烹調，帶出食材的真味。大紅片皮乳豬和炸子雞是招牌菜。餐室設計簡潔高雅，服務周到。

TEL. 2892 2888
5-6F, Kwan Chart Tower,
6 Tonnochy Road, Wan Chai
灣仔杜老誌道 6號羣策大廈 5-6樓
www.seventhson.hk

■ PRICE 價錢
Lunch 午膳
à la carte 點菜 $ 200-3,000
Dinner 晚膳
à la carte 點菜 $350-3,000

■ OPENING HOURS 營業時間
Lunch 午膳　　11:30-15:00 (L.O.)
Dinner 晚膳　　18:00-22:30 (L.O.)

■ ANNUAL AND WEEKLY CLOSING 休息日期
Closed 2 days Lunar New Year
農曆新年休息 2 天

Sha Tin 18
沙田18

👨‍🦽 🏯 ← 📖 ⊕36 🚇 ☾🍴

Dongguan and Cantonese specialities, like Houjie fish cakes with Chinese dry sausage and braised spare ribs with soya bean paste, are the draw at this contemporary restaurant. Enthusiastic amateur chefs will appreciate the four separate show kitchens, allowing them the chance to enjoy an insider's view of a culinary team in action. There are private dining rooms as well as a large outside terrace. Have a drink first in the Tin Tin bar.

這家時尚中菜餐廳提供東莞及粵式名菜，如厚街臘味煎魚餅和寮步豆醬炆腩排，令不少食客慕名而來。熱衷烹飪的食客必定欣賞餐廳內4個開放式廚房，讓他們近距離欣賞廚師的精湛廚藝。餐廳亦設有獨立房間和寬敞的露台。食客可於用餐前到毗鄰的天天吧暢飲一番。

TEL. 3723 7932
4F, Hyatt Regency Sha Tin,
18 Chak Cheung Street, University,
Sha Tin
沙田大學站澤祥街18號沙田凱悅酒店4樓
www.hongkong.shatin.hyatt.com

■ PRICE 價錢
Lunch 午膳
set 套餐 $ 255
à la carte 點菜 $ 300-650
Dinner 晚膳
à la carte 點菜 $300-650

■ OPENING HOURS 營業時間
Lunch 午膳　11:30-15:00 (L.O.)
Dinner 晚膳　17:30-22:30 (L.O.)

Shang Palace
香宮

✿✿ ✿✿

👤👤👤👤　　　　　　　　　　♿ 👜 ⌷24 🕐🍴

Antique Chinese window frames, lanterns and Sung style paintings evoke the grandeur of an ancient Chinese palace. Headed by celebrity Chef Mok Kit Keung, Shang Palace offers traditional and authentic Cantonese dishes with a nod to contemporary presentation. The care and attention shown by the service team is exemplary and highlights of the Cantonese menu include braised spare rib with red vinegar, and steamed crab claw and egg white.

經過 2012 年的裝修，私人廂房的位置變了，豪華大廳則保持不變，依然呈現出宋朝的顯赫氣派。其紅色漆牆、古董國畫，以及傳統燈籠，交織出古色古香的感覺。服務團隊仍然是一貫的殷勤周到，烹調精巧的粵菜推介有：醋香排骨及清蒸蛋白鮮蟹鉗。

TEL. 2733 8754
Lower level, Kowloon Shangri-La Hotel,
64 Mody Road, East Tsim Sha Tsui
尖東麼地道 64號九龍香格里拉酒店地庫 1樓
www.shangri-la.com

SPECIALITIES TO PRE-ORDER 預訂食物
Beggar's chicken 富貴雞

■ PRICE 價錢
Lunch 午膳
set 套餐 $ 328-488
à la carte 點菜 $ 250-1,000
Dinner 晚膳
set 套餐 $ 838-1,488
à la carte 點菜 $350-1,000

■ OPENING HOURS 營業時間
Lunch 午膳　12:00-15:00 L.O. 14:45
Dinner 晚膳　18:30-23:00 L.O. 22:45

HONG KONG 香港

Shanghai Garden NEW
紫玉蘭

XX　　　　　　　　　　　　　　🍴15 📞🍴

Local fans of Shanghai Garden needn't have panicked when they heard it was moving because it didn't go far – in fact, it remained in the same building. The new premises are smaller but infinitely better looking. Along with the traditional Shanghainese dishes you can expect some Beijing and Sichuan specialities. Try the juicy pan-fried beef cake and pork dumpling or more traditional offerings like braised sea cucumber with spring onion.

搬遷後的紫玉蘭，仍然在和記大廈內，只換了另一個鋪位。此店提供傳統滬菜及少量京川菜。各款上海涼菜及鹹點最適合午飯享用，美味多汁的牛肉餡餅和鮮肉鍋貼是最佳選擇。晚餐時可按上海人傳統，先嘗點涼菜後再進食熱菜如蔥燒海參和滋味的紅燒八寶鴨。

TEL. 2524 8181
Shop 203, 2F, Hutchison House, 10 Harcourt Road, Admiralty
金鐘夏慤道 10號和記大廈 2樓 203室

■ PRICE 價錢
Lunch 午膳
à la carte 點菜 $ 200-650
Dinner 晚膳
à la carte 點菜 $ 200-650

■ OPENING HOURS 營業時間
Lunch 午膳　11:30-14:45 (L.O.)
Dinner 晚膳　18:00-22:45 (L.O.)

Shanghai Min (One Peking Road)
上海小南國 (北京道一號)

≤ **P** ⊕50 ◑◠

The Xiao Nan Guo group from Shanghai has been in Hong Kong for over 10 years and its aim is to make Shanghainese cooking one of the most popular cuisines internationally. Here at Shanghai Min you can sample both traditional Shanghainese dishes, like wok-fried hairy crabs with rice cakes and stewed pork ball, and more contemporary offerings such as wok-fried Angus beef with shrimps. Ask for a window table to take in the great views.

此店源自上海的滬菜品牌，已登陸香港逾十年，一向致力將本幫菜發展成更貼近國際潮流的新派滬菜。餐單選擇種類繁多，既有傳統菜如毛蟹炒年糕和獅子頭等，亦有新派的牛柳粒炒明蝦球及少量川菜。餐廳裝潢雅致，透過落地玻璃能俯瞰維港美景。

TEL. 2527 8899
10F, One Peking Road, Tsim Sha Tsui
尖沙咀北京道一號 10樓

■ PRICE 價錢
Lunch 午膳
set 套餐 $ 150
à la carte 點菜 $ 350-1,000
Dinner 晚膳
à la carte 點菜 $ 350-1,000

■ OPENING HOURS 營業時間
Lunch 午膳　11:30-15:00 (L.O.)
Dinner 晚膳　17:30-23:00 (L.O.)

She Wong Yee
蛇王二

Their signature snake soup has long been renowned and in winter around 1,200 bowls are served each day. Regulars are quick to occupy one of the few tables for this memorable experience and it is no surprise that the recipe has remained unchanged for years. These days, those regulars come also for the famed barbecued meats and homemade liver sausages; the roast goose and double-boiled soups are good too.

此著名蛇羹集團一向聞名四方，烹調蛇羹的方法多年來不曾改變。此店冬天營業至深夜，平均每天賣出多達一千二百碗蛇羹。熟客光顧時總會急不及待佔坐，享受美味蛇羹。此外，其著名燒味及自製潤腸同樣令食客趨之若鶩，燒鵝及燉湯也值得一試。

TEL. 2831 0163
24 Percival Street, Causeway Bay
銅鑼灣波斯富街 24 號

■ PRICE 價錢
à la carte 點菜 $ 50-160

■ OPENING HOURS 營業時間
11:30-22:45 (L.O.)

■ ANNUAL AND WEEKLY CLOSING 休息日期
Closed 3 days Lunar New Year
農曆新年休息 3 天

Shek Kee Kitchen
石記廚房

🍜 ▮▮　　　　　　　　　　　　　　　　　　🛋8

During the day, the shop sells Cha Chan Tang dishes, but we recommend it for the traditional, home-style Cantonese cooking it serves in the evening. The owner-chef goes to market each day in search of the freshest ingredients and some of his regulars even call him directly to order specific dishes for that night. Specialities are the salt-baked chicken, fried frogs' legs with garlic and chilli, and steamed egg white with crabmeat and asparagus.

在日間，這家餐廳賣的是普通茶餐廳食物，但我們要推介的是其晚間提供的家庭式廣東小菜。大廚兼東主每天會親自往街市選購最新鮮的食材，部分熟客更會直接搖電話給他預訂當晚的菜式。菜單經常更新，確保所用的是最當造的時令食材。

TEL. 2571 3348
GF, 15-17 Ngan Mok Street, Tin Hau
天后銀幕街 17 號地下

■ PRICE 價錢
Lunch 午膳
à la carte 點菜 $ 100-300
Dinner 晚膳
à la carte 點菜 $ 100-300

■ OPENING HOURS 營業時間
Lunch 午膳　07:00-15:00 (L.O.)
Dinner 晚膳　18:00-23:00 (L.O.)

Shugetsu Ramen (Central)
麵鮮醬油房周月(中環)

The queues form early for the ramen here, with many of the customers coming for the Tsukemen ramen, as well as the Abura and special soup ramen. The shop makes its own noodles – which you can have thick or thin – but it is the sauce at the base of the slow-cooked soup that really makes the difference: it's fermented for 18 months in a 100 year old wooden basket and adds richness and depth.

周月與別不同之處，在其以醬油為湯底的神髓：採用有一百四十年歷史的愛媛縣梶田商店特製的醬油，配入沙丁魚粉、鯖魚粉及海帶長時間慢火熬製，味道更醇厚豐富。與日本店一樣，香港店設有製麵房，每天新鮮製造兩款粗幼不同的麵條。除了湯拉麵外，還供應沾麵。

TEL. 2850 6009
5 Gough Street, Central
中環歌賦街 5號
www.shugetsu.com.hk

■ PRICE 價錢
à la carte 點菜 $ 80-100

■ OPENING HOURS 營業時間
11:30-21:00 (L.O.)
Weekends & Public Holidays 週末及公眾假期
12:00-19:00 (L.O.)

Shugetsu Ramen (Quarry Bay)
麵鮮醬油房周月(鰂魚涌)

This was the second branch of Shugetsu to open in Hong Kong. It's the freshly made noodles and the soy sauce base that make them so popular. The broth is prepared with sardines, mackerel and kelp, and soy sauce that is produced by a longstanding factory in Ehime. The popular choice is Tsukemen, for which they use thick noodles to absorb the sauce's taste more easily – you decide how large a portion you want.

這是周月在香港的第二間分店，以鮮製麵條和醬油湯為賣點的拉麵店，湯底用放在百年木桶內經十八個月發酵而成的醬油，加上沙丁魚粉、鯖魚粉及海帶煮成，美味且味道特別。除了湯拉麵外，沾麵也頗受歡迎，選用的麵條較粗但掛湯力強，能盡吸醬汁精華。可選擇麵的份量。

TEL. 2854 9985
30 Hoi Kwong Street, Quarry Bay
鰂魚涌海光街30號
www.shugetsu.com.hk

■ PRICE 價錢
à la carte 點菜 $ 80-100

■ OPENING HOURS 營業時間
11:45-21:15 (L.O.)
Weekends 週末及公眾假期　12:00-19:00 (L.O.)

■ ANNUAL AND WEEKLY CLOSING 休息日期
Closed Public Holidays 公眾假期休息

Sing Kee NEW
星記

🍴 ⟨⟩36 ⟨⟩🍴

Sing Kee stands out from its neighbours thanks to its eye-catching red and yellow sign but its main attraction is its authentic and traditional Cantonese cooking, which is prepared by a kitchen team who came from Sang Kee. The unremarkable interior doesn't matter to the regulars – they're all here for the skilful cooking and, in particular, the day's fresh fish. The pomelo skin dishes and the double-steamed soups are worth pre-ordering.

在酒吧林立的街道不遠處的一幢大廈內，有這間傳統廣東小菜館。鮮黃大紅的招牌非常搶眼，與其供應的菜餚一樣，令人印象深刻，雖沒有華麗包裝，卻憑扎實的烹調功夫和高質素食物贏得食客歡心。廚師每天在市場搜羅最生猛新鮮的海魚；柚皮菜式及燉湯需預訂。

TEL. 2528 9028
3F, The Phoenix, 23 Luard Road,
Wan Chai
灣仔盧押道 23號 The Phoenix 3樓

SPECIALITIES TO PRE-ORDER 預訂食物
Double boiled soup 燉湯

■ PRICE 價錢
Lunch 午膳
à la carte 點菜 $ 150-300
Dinner 晚膳
à la carte 點菜 $ 150-300

■ OPENING HOURS 營業時間
Lunch 午膳　12:00-14:15 (L.O.)
Dinner 晚膳　18:00-22:15 (L.O.)

■ ANNUAL AND WEEKLY CLOSING 休息日期
Closed Sunday lunch 週日午膳休息

Sister Wah (Tin Hau)
華姐清湯腩 (天后)

HONG KONG 香港

With just six round tables, Sister Wah's diminutive dimensions are in direct contrast to the size of its reputation – this is one of the most famous beef brisket noodle shops. This family-run shop is always full and it is easy to see why: there are around 20 items on the menu which include Dan Dan noodles and Drunken chicken, but chief among them is the beef brisket in a clear soup.

只有六張圓桌的華姐清湯腩，規模與其名氣形成鮮明對比 ― 這裏是最馳名的牛腩麵家之一。正因如此，這間家庭式經營的小店經常滿座，餐牌上約有二十種食品，包括擔擔麵和醉雞，但招牌菜當然是清湯牛坑腩。

TEL. 2807 0181
Shop A1, 13 Electric Road, Tin Hau
天后電氣道 13號 A1號鋪

■ PRICE 價錢
à la carte 點菜 $ 25-65

■ OPENING HOURS 營業時間
11:00-23:00 (L.O.)

■ ANNUAL AND WEEKLY CLOSING 休息日期
Closed 6 days Lunar New Year
農曆新年休息 6 天

HONG KONG 香港

Siu Shun Village Cuisine (Kowloon Bay)
肇順名匯河鮮專門店 (九龍灣)

🍴   🍽 32

Imitation bamboo and birdcage lampshades add to the somewhat eccentric decorative style of this restaurant that specialises in Shun Tak cuisine. It's in a shopping mall and is always crowded – so expect noise levels at the lively end of the scale. Customers come for various river fish dishes and specialities like stir-fried freshwater lobster with ginger and shallots, fresh prawns in XO sauce, and fish lips casserole.

這裏的著名菜式包括薑葱龍蝦球、XO醬炒花枝鮮蝦球、瓦罉煎焗魚咀，吸引很多本地食客到此品嘗順德菜及其河鮮菜式。餐廳位於商場內，經常座無虛席，店內鼎沸的人聲足以反映其熱鬧氣氛。仿竹及雀籠燈罩令這裏的裝潢風格更顯特色。

TEL. 2798 9738
7F, MegaBox, 38 Wang Chiu Road, Kowloon Bay
九龍灣宏照道 38號 MegaBox7樓

■ PRICE 價錢
Lunch 午膳
à la carte 點菜 $ 100-550
Dinner 晚膳
à la carte 點菜 $ 140-550

■ OPENING HOURS 營業時間
Lunch 午膳   09:00-16:30 (L.O.)
Dinner 晚膳   18:00-23:30 (L.O.)

■ ANNUAL AND WEEKLY CLOSING 休息日期
Closed 3 days Lunar New Year
農曆新年休息 3 天

Snow Garden
雪園

XX ⊡16 ○⫙

Established in 1992 at this sleek business address and known for its traditional Shanghainese cuisine, this is a restaurant that operates like clockwork and whose staff are warm and attentive. The long-standing chef's specialities are steamed herring and deep-fried chicken skin with four spices; braised sea cucumber with shrimp roe; and yellow fish with sweet and sour sauce. Dishes arrive carefully prepared and bursting with flavour.

餐廳於1992年於此商業區熱點開始營業,以精心烹調的上海菜馳名,人流絡繹不絕,員工態度親切熱誠。清蒸鰣魚、四寶片皮雞、蝦子大烏參及糖醋黃魚都是歷久不衰的廚師精選。每道菜式都經過精心製作,色香味俱全。

TEL. 2881 6837
2F, China Taiping Tower,
8 Sunning Road, Causeway Bay
銅鑼灣新寧道 8號中國太平大廈 2樓
www.snow-garden.com

■ PRICE 價錢
Lunch 午膳
set 套餐 $ 100
à la carte 點菜 $ 250-700
Dinner 晚膳
à la carte 點菜 $ 250-700

■ OPENING HOURS 營業時間
Lunch 午膳　11:30-14:45 (L.O.)
Dinner 晚膳　18:00-22:45 (L.O.)

■ ANNUAL AND WEEKLY CLOSING 休息日期
Closed 3 days Lunar New Year
農曆新年休息 3 天

HONG KONG 香港

Sorabol (Causeway Bay)
新羅寶 (銅鑼灣)

✗✗   ⊞40 ◔❙❙

This branch of the successful restaurant group opened here in 2011. Its aesthetic is based on a traditional and elegant Korean house and uses lotus flower patterned doors, wood carvings and brick walls to good effect. The authentic cuisine is prepared using quality ingredients and includes a special menu of Jeonju dishes, which is the owner's homeland. Beef is the popular choice for barbecuing but do also try the duck.

這個韓國餐廳集團於2011年在銅鑼灣開設此分店，店內裝潢取材自傳統韓國的精緻房舍，採用蓮花圖案的門、木雕和磚牆以塑造最佳的效果。食店選用優質食材製作正宗韓式料理。牛肉是韓式燒烤的最佳選擇，鴨肉及時令特別餐單也值得一試。

TEL. 2881 6823
Shop B, 18F, Lee Theatre Plaza,
99 Percival Street, Causeway Bay
銅鑼灣波斯富街99號利舞臺廣場18樓B號舖
www.sorabol.com.hk

■ PRICE 價錢
Lunch 午膳
set 套餐 $ 68-98
à la carte 點菜 $ 220-670
Dinner 晚膳
à la carte 點菜 $ 220-670

■ OPENING HOURS 營業時間
Lunch 午膳   11:30-14:30 (L.O.)
Dinner 晚膳   17:30-22:30 (L.O.)

■ ANNUAL AND WEEKLY CLOSING 休息日期
Closed Lunar New Year 年初一休息

Spoon by Alain Ducasse

A ceiling lined, appropriately enough, with spoons; an impressive glass cellar holding around 600 wines; stylish surroundings and fantastic views – all characteristics of this fashionable member of Alain Ducasse's global empire. The carefully prepared French cuisine is the ideal match for this environment, with such dishes as steamed duck foie gras with fruit condiment, vol-au-vents with crayfish and chicken; and 'chocolate-hazelnut bliss'.

美妙景觀、時尚雅座、排列着匙羹的天花板,加上擺放了接近600瓶佳釀令人嘆為觀止的玻璃酒櫃,打造成名廚艾倫杜卡斯美食王國的香港分部,為潮流時尚之選。招牌菜包括蒸法國鴨肝伴乾果醬配牛油包及小龍蝦雞肉酥盒;以及朱古力榛子蛋糕。

TEL. 2313 2256
GF, Intercontinental Hotel,
18 Salisbury Road, Tsim Sha Tsui
尖東麼地道 64號九龍香格里拉酒店地庫 1樓
www.hongkong-ic.intercontinental.com

■ PRICE 價錢
Sunday Lunch 週日午膳
set 套餐 $ 888
Dinner 晚膳
set 套餐 $ 1,588
à la carte 點菜 $ 950-1,500

■ OPENING HOURS 營業時間
Sunday Lunch 週日午膳　12:00-14:30
Dinner 晚膳　18:00-23:30 (L.O.)

Spring Moon
嘉麟樓

✗✗✗   ⌂♟ ⌗48 ☏॥

An integral part of The Peninsula hotel is this elegant Cantonese restaurant. Admire the tropical hardwood or the bamboo flower arrangements while sipping tea at the tea bar and then dine in the restaurant or on the more intimate mezzanine floor. Dishes are authentic and flavoursome – the lunch dim sum is very popular. There are 25 different teas available; feel free to ask questions as staff are regularly sent to China for in-depth training.

嘉麟樓是半島酒店不可或缺的部分，裝潢優雅豪華。食客可以邊在「茶檔」茗茶，邊欣賞餐廳內的熱帶硬木和竹花。你可以選擇在餐廳或較隱蔽的私家房內用餐，完善的服務配合美味的傳統菜餚。午餐時段的點心很受歡迎。店內提供二十五種茶，你可以隨意向侍應發問「茗茶」知識。

TEL. 2696 6760
1F, The Peninsula Hotel, Salisbury Road,
Tsim Sha Tsui
尖沙咀梳士巴利道半島酒店 1樓
www.peninsula.com

SPECIALITIES TO PRE-ORDER 預訂食物
Hangzhou beggar's fortune chicken
杭州富貴雞

■ PRICE 價錢
Lunch 午膳
à la carte 點菜 $ 350-950
Dinner 晚膳
à la carte 點菜 $ 500-1,500

■ OPENING HOURS 營業時間
Lunch 午膳   11:30-14:30 (L.O.)
Dinner 晚膳   18:00-22:30 (L.O.)

St Betty

✗✗   👤 ≤ 🍽10 🕐🍴

St Betty and IFC Mall are a good fit as the restaurant is as stylish and well-dressed as many of the neighbouring boutiques. Most of the influences on the menu come from within Europe: pasta dishes are particularly popular, as are steaks from the Josper grill. Weekend brunch is proving a hit and this warm, relaxing restaurant also serves afternoon tea. You can come for the 'Saturday pie' or the traditional Sunday roast. The views are great too.

St Betty跟國際金融中心可算是絕配!時尚型格的設計風格與毗鄰的店子格調統一。此店主打歐洲菜式,以意大利麵條和Josper烤扒最受食客愛戴。週末供應的早午合餐頗吸引,此外還提供下午茶。不妨嘗嘗「週末安格斯牛肉批」 或「週日傳統英式精選」。店內環境不賴 、店外景色幽美。

TEL. 2979 2100
Shop 2075, Podium Level Two, IFC Mall,
8 Finance Street, Central
中環金融街 8號
國際金融中心商場二期 2樓 2075號舖
www.stbetty.com

■ PRICE 價錢
Lunch 午膳
set 套餐 $ 298-368
à la carte 點菜 $ 640-860
Dinner 晚膳
à la carte 點菜 $ 640-860

■ OPENING HOURS 營業時間
Lunch 午膳　11:30-15:00 (L.O.)
Dinner 晚膳　18:00-22:00 (L.O.)

Steik World Meats

XX

🛏30

There may be lobster, oysters, prawns and scallops on the menu but most people come here for the beef. The assorted cuts come mainly from the USA, Australia, the UK and Ireland. The dry-ageing is done in-house and on-view above the part-open kitchen. The restaurant is contemporary yet undoubtedly masculine in its look and its discreet location adds to the clubby feel; ask for one of the booths then enjoy a post-prandial drink on the terrace.

餐牌上不乏龍蝦、蠔、虎蝦和帶子，但大部份客人都是慕牛肉之名而來。這裏的牛扒來自美國、澳洲、蘇格蘭及愛爾蘭，可試試齊集上述四國牛肉的套餐，可配特色杯裝餐酒。半開放式廚房設有dry-ageing（風乾）櫃，既可自行風乾牛肉，又可吸引客人。餐廳設計時尚，充滿陽剛味。

TEL. 2530 0011
Level 3, K11, 18 Hanoi Road,
Tsim Sha Tsui
尖沙咀河內道 18 號 K11 3 樓
www.epicurean.com.hk

■ PRICE 價錢
Lunch 午膳
set 套餐 $216-306
à la carte 點菜 $400-700
Dinner 晚膳
set 套餐 $638-838
à la carte 點菜 $500-800

■ OPENING HOURS 營業時間
Lunch 午膳　12:00-14:30 (L.O.)
Dinner 晚膳　18:00-22:30 (L.O.)

HONG KONG 香港

Summer Palace
夏宮

❀ ❀

🍴🍴🍴   ♿ 📶 🍽14 ☎🍶

They've created a charming environment here in this 5th floor room, with its crystal chandeliers, traditional Chinese screens and well-spaced tables. The Cantonese menu features all the true classics and the kitchen uses carefully chosen ingredients to prepare dishes free from over-elaboration; double boiled soups are a speciality. To drink, there's a varied selection of wines by the glass, assorted Chinese liquors and exquisite teas.

營運者在這位於五樓的空間營造了迷人的環境，配上水晶吊燈、傳統中國屏風及悉心編排的餐桌擺放，為食客營造舒適的用膳空間。粵菜菜譜羅列各款傳統名菜，廚師精心挑選食材，烹調時井井有條，毫不過火，燉湯更是其專長。餐飲方面具杯裝餐酒、中國酒和高級茗茶。

TEL. 2820 8553
5F, Island Shangri-La Hotel, Pacific Place,
Supreme Court Road, Admiralty
中區法院道太古廣場港島香格里拉酒店 5樓
www.shangri-la.com

SPECIALITIES TO PRE-ORDER 預訂食物
Double-boiled soups 燉 湯 /Eight treasure duck 夏 宮 八 寶 鴨 /Beggar's chicken 富貴雞

■ PRICE 價錢
Lunch 午膳
à la carte 點菜 $320-1,400
Dinner 晚膳
à la carte 點菜 $320-1,400

■ OPENING HOURS 營業時間
Lunch 午膳　11:30-14:30 (L.O.)
Dinner 晚膳　18:30-22:30 (L.O.)

Sun Sin (Yau Ma Tei)
新仙清湯腩咖喱專門店(油麻地)

Never mind directions – just follow your nose and those enticing beef aromas will lead you to this small noodle shop in Yau Ma Tei's busiest street. Sun Sin is famous for its well-priced beef brisket in a clear soup and for the curry with its secret recipe. The owner buys high quality beef each morning from a local supplier and it's then cooked for hours. As she sells over three hundred portions each day, don't be surprised when it's all gone.

就算不熟悉這個地區、辨認不到街道，只要跟着香氣走，誘人的牛腩味就會把你帶到這家位於油麻地最繁忙地段的小麵店。此店以價廉物美的清湯腩和秘製咖喱聞名。店主每天早上向本地肉商購入高質素的牛腩，耗數小時烹煮，每天賣出超過三百碗，隨時售罄。

TEL. 2332 6872
37 Portland Street, Yau Ma Tei
油麻地砵蘭街 37號

■ PRICE 價錢
à la carte 點菜 $ 30-130

■ OPENING HOURS 營業時間
11:30-00:00 (L.O.)

Sun Tung Lok (Central) NEW
新同樂 (中環)

XXX   ⌷36 ◐⏣

The original Sun Tung Lok opened in 1969 in Causeway Bay; now fans of its Cantonese cuisine can choose between the branch in Tsim Sha Tsui and this newer one in Central. It's just as comfortable and well run and its private room is ideal for a business meal. Those who come for lunch are rewarded with exquisite handmade dim sum. The signature dishes are roast suckling pig with minced shrimp, and braised prime rib of beef with house gravy.

自1969年創業至今,新同樂的高級粵菜一直備受食客推崇,繼尖沙咀店後,於中環開設了分店。手工精細的點心是午飯聚餐必不能少的美食,馳名菜式如百花脆皮乳豬件和燒汁乾焗牛肋骨,令人回味無窮。裝潢精緻的廂房適合商務宴會。

TEL. 2807 2290
13 Stanley Street, Central
中環士丹利街13號
www.suntunglok.com.hk

■ PRICE 價錢
Lunch 午膳
set 套餐 $ 298
à la carte 點菜 $ 200-5,000
Dinner 晚膳
set 套餐 $ 1,380
à la carte 點菜 $ 400-5,000

■ OPENING HOURS 營業時間
Lunch 午膳   11:00-15:00 (L.O.)
Dinner 晚膳   18:00-22:00 (L.O.)

Sun Tung Lok (Tsim Sha Tsui)
新同樂 (尖沙咀)

❀ ❀

🍴🍴🍴   🗖48 ◐🍽

After 40 years in Happy Valley, Sun Tung Lok is now comfortably ensconced on the fourth floor of the Miramar shopping centre. A contemporary colour palette of grey, brown and beige is used to good effect in this stylish restaurant; ask for one of the three booths for extra privacy. The majority of the menu is Cantonese and dishes include rib of beef with house gravy, stuffed crab shell, and roast suckling pig; the abalone is a must.

在跑馬地駐紮四十年後，新同樂現在於美麗華商場4樓繼續營業。充滿時代感的灰色、咖啡色與米色的巧妙配搭讓店子看起來較摩登。店內設有三個廂座，以滿足需要私人空間的客人。八成菜式是粵菜，包括燒汁乾焗牛肋骨、鮮蘑菇焗釀蟹蓋及燒乳豬件。這裏的鮑魚是必試之選。

TEL. 2152 1417
4F, Miramar Shopping Centre,
132 Nathan Road, Tsim Sha Tsui
尖沙咀彌敦道132號美麗華商場4樓
www.suntunglok.com.hk

■ PRICE 價錢
Lunch 午膳
set 套餐 $ 298
à la carte 點菜 $ 300-5,000
Dinner 晚膳
set 套餐 $ 1,380
à la carte 點菜 $ 300-5,000

■ OPENING HOURS 營業時間
Lunch 午膳　11:30-15:00 (L.O.)
Dinner 晚膳　18:00-22:30 (L.O.)

Sun Yuen Hing Kee
新園興記

Located next to Sheung Wan market, this traditionally styled, simple but well maintained barbecue shop has been run by the same family since the mid-1970s. Over the years they've built up an appreciative following so the small place fills quickly. The appetising looking suckling pigs are not the only draw: roast pork, duck and pigeon all have their followers, as do the soft-boiled chicken, the homemade sausages and the preserved meats.

位於上環街市旁邊，這間格調傳統簡單的燒味店自70年代中一直由同一家族經營。多年來，累積了不少忠實顧客，小小的地方往往座無虛席。這裏受歡迎的不僅是掛在廚房旁邊，賣相令人垂涎欲滴的乳豬，燒肉、烤鴨和乳鴿都各有忠實擁躉。白切雞、臘腸及臘肉亦十分吸引。

TEL. 2541 2207
327-329 Queen's Road Central,
Sheung Wan
上環皇后大道中 327-329號

■ PRICE 價錢
Dinner 晚膳
à la carte 點菜 $ 30-150

■ OPENING HOURS 營業時間
08:00-19:45 (L.O.)

■ ANNUAL AND WEEKLY CLOSING 休息日期
Closed 3 days Lunar New Year
農曆新年休息 3 天

Sushi Ginza Iwa NEW

✂

🛋8 ⏰🍴

There are views of Central through the small windows and the room is authentically uncluttered and calm, but frankly everyone's here for just one thing – sushi. To ensure each customer receives the same experience, the selection process for the ingredients is undertaken with great rigour, with all fish and seafood flown in daily from Tsukiji. And just like the original shop in Tokyo's Ginza district, the sushi is presented on a silver plate.

到達29樓後，要先經過一道木樓梯才能進到這間以日式原木裝潢、非常傳統的餐廳。壽司桌是餐廳焦點。與銀座總店一脈相承的銀色壽司盛器，給你一絲熟悉感覺。店東嚴格限定海產種類和來源地，鮮魚和海產每天由築地運送抵港，確保食客享受到跟總店一樣的味道。

TEL. 2619 0199
30F, Asia Pacific Centre,
8 Wyndham Street, Central
中環雲咸街 8號亞洲太平洋中心 30樓

■ PRICE 價錢
Lunch 午膳
set 套餐 $ 480-1,350
Dinner 晚膳
set 套餐 $ 1,350-3,000

■ OPENING HOURS 營業時間
Lunch 午膳 12:00-14:30 (L.O.)
Dinner 晚膳 18:30-22:30 (L.O.)

Sushi Rozan
鮨魯山

With just 12 seats at its L-shaped counter, this small and elegant Japanese restaurant certainly looks authentic. Only a daily-changing omakase menu is served, which means the chef will decide everything for you, albeit after talking to you about preferences. He then prepares all the dishes in front of you, using top quality produce flown in daily from Japan, such as golden-eye snapper, white sea urchin and Ohmi Wagyu. You can pre-order your lunch a day in advance.

這家優雅傳統的壽司店。小小的店內只有依附着壽司吧枱的十二個座位和一個卡座。這裏只供應廚師套餐，日籍廚師在客人面前炮製食物，餐單和份量會按客人的飲食習慣調整。頂級食材如金目鯛、近江和牛及白海膽等每天由日本即日空運到港。顧客可於一天前預訂午膳。

TEL. 2574 1333
GF Oak Hill, 18 Wood Road, Wan Chai
灣仔活道 18 號萃峯地下
www.ginsai.com.hk

■ PRICE 價錢
Dinner 晚膳
set 套餐 $ 1,580-2,880

■ OPENING HOURS 營業時間
18:00-21:00 (L.O.)

■ ANNUAL AND WEEKLY CLOSING 休息日期
Closed 3 days Lunar New Year and Monday
農曆新年 3 天及週一休息

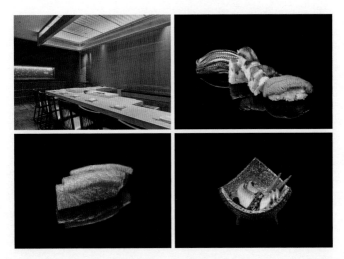

Sushi Shikon
志魂

6

The name may have changed from Sushi Yoshitake to Sushi Shikon but the owner's aim remains the same: he wants his Hong Kong customers to enjoy the same superb quality sushi that he serves in his Tokyo restaurant – thus, the fish arrives daily from Tsukiji market and the rice comes from Niigata. The secret is in the vinegar which "creates harmony between the fish and the rice": it is made from two kinds of sake sediment and aged for four years.

Sushi Yoshitake易名Sushi Shikon後，提供優質食物的宗旨仍然不變，繼續堅持每天由築地漁市場運來鮮魚及選用由新潟運來頂級日本米。這兒的壽司烹調秘訣是以兩種成熟度達四年的清酒糟製造的醋入饌，鮮魚的鮮與米飯的醋香配搭出完美的味道。

TEL. 2643 6800
The Mercer Hotel, 29 Jervois Street,
Sheung Wan
上環蘇杭街 29號尚圜酒店

■ PRICE 價錢
Dinner 晚膳
set 套餐 $ 3,500

■ OPENING HOURS 營業時間
Dinner 晚膳 18:00-20:00, 20:30-22:30

■ ANNUAL AND WEEKLY CLOSING 休息日期
Closed Sunday 週日休息

Sushi Ta-ke
竹寿司

✖️ 🍴   🍽10 🚇 🕐🍴

Sushi Ta-ke presents traditional Edomae sushi using the freshest ingredients. Along with sashimi, it also serves hot dishes like grilled swordfish and Wagyu beef – try too the Japanese pickle salad and boiled golden-eye snapper. The striking and artfully lit interior comes as no surprise when one considers the expertise of the three owners: one is an interior designer, one a lighting designer and the third a restaurateur.

竹寿司的室內設計突出且具藝術氣息，這跟三位東主的背景不無關係：一個室內設計師、一個燈光設計師，一個飲食業專家。餐廳以正宗傳統方式製作的壽司作賣點，魚生均每天由日本空運到港。除壽司外，還供應各款煮物和燒酒。可供選擇的清酒款色也很多。

TEL. 2577 0611
12F, Cubus, 1 Hoi Ping Road,
Causeway Bay
銅鑼灣開平道 1 號 Cubus 12 樓
www.sushitake.com.hk

■ PRICE 價錢
Lunch 午膳
set 套餐 $ 220-400
à la carte 點菜 $ 400-1,550

Dinner 晚膳
set 套餐 $ 1,200-1,500
à la carte 點菜 $ 400-1,550

■ OPENING HOURS 營業時間
Lunch 午膳　12:00-15:00 L.O. 14:30
Dinner 晚膳　18:30-00:00 L.O.22:30

■ ANNUAL AND WEEKLY CLOSING 休息日期
Closed Lunar New Year 年初一休息

HONG KONG 香港

Tai Wing Wah
大榮華

🍴　　　　　　　　　　　　　　　　　　　🍽20

Anyone travelling all the way to Yuen Long (in the north of New Territories) can seek reward for doing so by visiting this restaurant. It's above its own cake shop, which specialises in moon cakes and Chinese sausages, and serves dim sum and 'Walled Village' cuisine, alongside classic Cantonese dishes. Try the roast duck with bean paste and coriander; claypot rice with lard and premium soy sauce; and, above all, the steamed sponge cake.

很多人長途跋涉來到元朗，只有一個原因：光顧大榮華。此酒家除了供應點心外，還提供近百款圍村小菜及經典粤式名菜。香茜燒米鴨及砵仔豬油頭抽撈飯絕對不容錯過，當然少不了奶黃馬拉糕。入口旁的餅店，專門售賣月餅和臘腸，也是大榮華出品的著名食品。

TEL. 2476 9888
2F, 2-6 On Ning Road, Yuen Long
元朗安寧路 2-6號 2樓

■ PRICE 價錢
à la carte 點菜 $ 80-450

■ OPENING HOURS 營業時間
06:30-23:30 (L.O.)

Tai Woo (Causeway Bay)
太湖海鮮城 (銅鑼灣)

XX

🍴24 ◎❚

One of the district's most famous names, Tai Woo moved to these newer, more comfortable surroundings in 2011 and, while the restaurant may be smaller than before, business is better than ever, with over 1,000 customers served every day. What hasn't changed is the quality of the cooking: along with a large menu of Cantonese seafood dishes, such as crunchy shrimp ball and mini lobster casserole, are favourites like sesame chicken baked in salt.

太湖是區內數一數二的馳名酒家，於2011年搬遷到更新更舒適的現址。儘管新店面積較舊店小，生意反而更昌旺，每天服務逾千名食客，全因食物質素維持不變，提供多款廣東海鮮菜式如奇脆明珠伴金龍及招牌菜芝麻鹽焗雞。

TEL. 2893 0822
9F, Causeway Bay Plaza 2,
463-483 Lockhart Road, Causeway Bay
銅鑼灣駱克道 463-483號
銅鑼灣廣場第二期 9樓
www.taiwoorestaurant.com

■ PRICE 價錢
Lunch 午膳
à la carte 點菜 $ 100-600
Dinner 晚膳
à la carte 點菜 $ 200-600

■ OPENING HOURS 營業時間
10:30-02:30 (L.O.)

■ ANNUAL AND WEEKLY CLOSING 休息日期
Closed Lunar New Year 年初一休息

Takeya
竹家

The Japanese owner-chef was originally posted to Hong Kong as an engineer but, having settled here and married a local girl, he switched careers and together they opened this little yakitori shop in Hung Hom. Seating just 15, it's an intimate spot, made warmer with lots of bamboo. There's extensive choice, with seasonal specialities available. Try the special selections of Japanese wine or the high quality homemade umeshu.

日籍店主兼大廚在香港工作多年，其後與太太定居香港並展開新生活，一起經營這間以竹子為主題的串燒小店，小小的店子只有十五個座位卻予人親密溫暖的感覺。店內串燒種類繁多，時有特別食物推介。供應的日本酒較別的店子獨特，尤以自家浸製的梅酒更是不俗。

TEL. 2365 8878
Shop 1, On Wah Building,
31C1 Tak Man Street, Whampoa Estate,
Hung Hom
紅磡黃埔新村德民街 31C1安華樓 1號舖

■ PRICE 價錢
Dinner 晚膳
à la carte 點菜 $150-400

■ OPENING HOURS 營業時間
Dinner 晚膳　18:00-22:30 (L.O.)

■ ANNUAL AND WEEKLY CLOSING 休息日期
Closed 14 days Lunar New Year and
Monday 農曆新年 14 天及週一休息

T'ang Court
唐閣

🌸🌸

XXXX　　　　　　　　　　　　☞ 🅿 ⇔24 ◐¶

Rich silks and contemporary art line the walls of the lavishly furnished main dining room, on the first floor above the hotel's grand lobby. There's also a dramatic staircase leading up to a second floor of tables and exclusive private dining rooms named after famous Tang Dynasty poets. The cooking displays considerable skill; try sautéed prawns with deep-fried taro puffs or crispy, salty chicken. Service is polished and well-structured.

位於酒店大堂樓上的主菜廳，以優質絲緞配合富時代氣息的牆身，裝潢豪華。一道華麗的樓梯連上二樓的餐桌，更設有以唐代著名詩人命名的貴賓廳。菜餚極具水準，荔茸寶盒或脆香芋茸伴蝦球、秘製鹽焗雞均不容錯過。服務也經過精心編排。

TEL. 2132 7898
1F, The Langham Hotel, 8 Peking Road,
Tsim Sha Tsui
尖沙咀北京道 8號朗廷酒店 1樓
www.hongkong.langhamhotels.com

SPECIALITIES TO PRE-ORDER 預訂食物
Baked Blue Point oysters with port wine
砵酒焗美國蠔

■ PRICE 價錢
Lunch 午膳
set 套餐 $ 280
à la carte 點菜 $ 400-1,700
Dinner 晚膳
à la carte 點菜 $ 400-1,700

■ OPENING HOURS 營業時間
Lunch 午膳　12:00-15:00 L.O. 14:30
Dinner 晚膳　18:00-23:00 L.O. 22:30

HONG KONG 香港

Tasty (IFC)
正斗粥麵專家 (國際金融中心)

Over 1,000 customers a day, many of whom work in IFC, crowd into this Tasty, so be prepared to queue and share a table before tucking into the hallmark shrimp wonton or the much-loved beef and rice noodle stir fry. Also recommended from the vast choice is congee with prawns. The interior has been redecorated and is now more contemporary.

這裏每日有逾千名顧客，當中大部分在IFC工作，繁忙時間到訪，便要做好排隊和拼桌的準備。熱門食品包括招牌鮮蝦雲吞麵和極受歡迎的干炒牛河。此外，我們亦向你推介生猛大蝦粥。重新裝修後的餐室更見時尚華麗。

TEL. 2295 0101
Shop 3016, Podium Level 3, IFC Mall,
1 Harbour View Street, Central
中環港景街 1 號國際金融中心商場 3 樓
3016號舖
www.tasty.com.hk

■ PRICE 價錢
à la carte 點菜 $ 90-200
■ OPENING HOURS 營業時間
11:00-22:45 (L.O.)

Tate

❀

⚒ 🍴   ©🍴

HONG KONG 香港

Vicky Lau is the young owner-chef of this contemporary yet also quite intimate restaurant. Her cooking is an eclectic mix of French and Japanese influences and each dish is beautifully presented – a reflection, perhaps, of her previous career as a graphic designer. Two set menus, which change seasonally, are offered; opt for the nine-courses.

年青的劉小姐是這家時尚又親切的餐廳的大廚兼東主。她的烹調風格融合了法國和日本特色，每道菜式都設計得十分精美，與她是前平面設計師的身份不無關係。此店每晚只供應兩款套餐，共計九道菜，並以優質時令食材入饌，因此會隨季節更換餐單。

TEL. 2555 2172
59 Elgin Street, Central
中環伊利近街 59 號

■ PRICE 價錢
Dinner 晚膳
set 套餐 $ 880-1,180

■ OPENING HOURS 營業時間
Dinner 晚膳   18:30-22:00 (L.O.)

■ ANNUAL AND WEEKLY CLOSING 休息日期
Closed Sunday 週日休息

Tava

✕

There's more and more exotic food to be found in Hong Kong these days as increasing numbers of diners demonstrate a willingness to try new tastes. Tava may not be as atmospheric or as characterful as other Middle Eastern restaurants but it is neat and tidy; its menu is extensive and the food is authentic and carefully prepared. It's usually packed for lunch during the week but is more relaxed in the evenings.

因應食客對於嘗試新菜式的需求，近年香港興起了不少提供異國美食的餐廳。「Tava」的裝潢或不如其他中東餐廳般富地方色彩，惟裝修別致整潔，餐單上的食品種類繁多，由廚師悉心烹調的菜餚甚具品質。平日午餐時間往往座無虛席，欲細細品嘗中東菜的食客可選擇於晚上光顧。

TEL. 2856 5155
10 Hoi Kwong Street, Quarry Bay
鰂魚涌海光街 10號

■ PRICE 價錢
Lunch 午膳
set 套餐 $ 60-110
à la carte 點菜 $ 130-260
Dinner 晚膳
à la carte 點菜 $ 130-260

■ OPENING HOURS 營業時間
11:30-22:00 (L.O.)

■ ANNUAL AND WEEKLY CLOSING 休息日期
Closed Sunday and Public Holidays
週日及公眾假期休息

Thai Chiu
泰潮

Hainanese chicken; tom yum kung with seafood; fried egg with herbs and the various different styles of curry are just some of the highlights from an extensive menu prepared by native Thai chefs at this simple little restaurant. It's made up of two modest dining rooms, both decorated in bright green and yellow, with plastic tables and small stools. Simple it may be, but the food is good and the prices are competitive.

海南雞、冬蔭功海鮮湯、香草煎蛋及一系列咖喱只是種類繁多的菜單的一部分，全店食物一律由這家簡樸小餐廳的泰籍廚師主理，味道美味，價錢相宜。餐廳由兩個餐室組成，兩間房都以亮綠及黃色裝潢，配以膠桌和小板凳，感覺樸實自然。

TEL. 2314 3333
101-103 Fuk Wing Street, Sham Shui Po
深水埗福榮街 101-103號

■ PRICE 價錢
set 套餐 $ 40-60
à la carte 點菜 $ 60-190

■ OPENING HOURS 營業時間
11:30-23:00 (L.O.)

■ ANNUAL AND WEEKLY CLOSING 休息日期
Closed 3 days Lunar New Year
農曆新年休息 3 天

HONG KONG 香港

The Bellbrook   NEW

✗   ☏❡

The aromas from the grill in the open kitchen will soon get your taste buds up and running at this self-styled 'Australian urban bistro'. The menu boasts many varied influences and is a reflection of the country's multicultural makeup. Try their version of steak tartare which adds marrow for extra depth or take this opportunity to try classic Aussie tucker like kangaroo or barramundi. As expected, the atmosphere is laid back and friendly.

向街的玻璃窗引入自然光，以木材為主的裝潢與傢俱，加上從開放式廚房傳出的燒烤香味，給人輕鬆隨意之感。食物也是香氣撲人；除了經典的袋鼠肉外，亦要試試澳洲牛肉他他。輕烤過的牛肉夾著牛骨髓，香氣誘人，味佳而不膩；以樹皮包裹烤製的鱸魚，配上澳洲手指青檬，清新味鮮。

TEL. 2530 1600
2F, 75-77 Wyndham Street, Central
中環雲咸街 75-77號 2樓
www.thebellbrook.com

■ PRICE 價錢
Lunch 午膳
set 套餐 $ 148-188
à la carte 點菜 $ 330-600
Dinner 晚膳
à la carte 點菜 $ 330-600

■ OPENING HOURS 營業時間
Lunch 午膳   12:00-14:30 (L.O.)
Dinner 晚膳   18:00-22:30 (L.O.)

The Boss
波士廳

❌❌   🍴14 ◐🍴

The Boss may operate out of a basement location but enthusiastic lighting and a cool colour palette keep things feeling bright and fresh. Top quality Cantonese cooking is the attraction here; the bird's nest with abalone is a very popular dish and seafood lovers will appreciate that they can have their favourite fish cooked the way they like. Try the more innovative dishes like pan-fried Kobe beef and sautéed prawn with wasabi.

乍聽名字，誰會想到這是一家裝潢時尚的粵菜館?具時代感的冷色系與玻璃牆身和鏡子的配搭，非常明亮光潔。菜式方面，提供傳統高級粵菜，鮑魚燕窩是焦點所在。食客亦可從十種烹調方式中擇其一，讓廚師為你炮製心愛的游水海鮮。

TEL. 2155 0552
Basement, Peter Building,
58-62 Queen's Road, Central
皇后大道中 58-62號振邦大廈地庫

■ PRICE 價錢
Lunch 午膳
à la carte 點菜 $ 100-900
Dinner 晚膳
set 套餐 $ 680
à la carte 點菜 $ 200-900

■ OPENING HOURS 營業時間
11:30-22:30 (L.O.)

The Bostonian
美岸海鮮廳

The self-assured Bostonian is a handsome and sophisticated restaurant offering all the things you'd expect from an American restaurant: plenty of hearty salads, lots of lobster, oysters, assorted seafood and, of course, a huge choice of prime beef from the grill. The set lunch with the seafood buffet is particularly popular, as is brunch on a Sunday. It's unlikely anyone has ever left here still feeling hungry.

美岸海鮮廳的高水準美食令人印象深刻，店內供應的菜式完全符合你對美式餐廳的期望：豐富的沙律和大量龍蝦、蠔及各類海鮮，種類多樣的特級烤牛肉當然不會或缺。在這裏進餐，沒人會空肚而回。這裏的半自助海鮮午市套餐及週日早午合餐非常受食客歡迎。

TEL. 2132 7898
BF, The Langham Hotel, 8 Peking Road,
Tsim Sha Tsui
尖沙咀北京道 8號朗廷酒店地庫
www.hongkong.langhamhotels.com

■ PRICE 價錢
Lunch 午膳
set 套餐 $ 378
à la carte 點菜 $ 400-1,000
Dinner 晚膳
à la carte 點菜 $ 400-1,000

■ OPENING HOURS 營業時間
Lunch 午膳   12:00-14:30 (L.O.)
Dinner 晚膳   18:30-23:00 (L.O.)

The Chairman
大班樓

🍴🍴   🛋20   ◐🍽

The Chairman looks to small suppliers and local fishermen for its ingredients and much of the produce used is also organic. Showing respect for the provenance of ingredients, and using them in homemade sauces and flavoursome dishes such as steamed crab with aged Shaoxing, crispy chicken stuffed with shrimp paste and almond sweet soup, has attracted a loyal following. The restaurant is divided into four different sections and service is pleasant and reassuringly experienced.

大班樓的食材來自小型供應商和本地漁民，大部分都是有機材料，且將精挑細選的材料用來製作醬料和烹調美味菜式，如雞油花雕蒸大花蟹、香煎百花雞件配魚露、生磨杏仁菜等，吸引不少忠實擁躉。餐廳分成四個不同用餐區，服務令人賓至如歸。

TEL. 2555 2202
18 Kau U Fong, Central
中環九如坊 18號
www.thechairmangroup.com

■ PRICE 價錢
Lunch 午膳
set 套餐 $ 198-218
à la carte 點菜 $ 300-700
Dinner 晚膳
à la carte 點菜 $ 300-700

■ OPENING HOURS 營業時間
Lunch 午膳 12:00-15:00 L.O. 14:30
Dinner 晚膳 18:00-23:00 L.O. 22:30

■ ANNUAL AND WEEKLY CLOSING 休息日期
Closed 3 days Lunar New Year
農曆新年休息 3 天

The Dragon Palace
龍軒

🍴　　　　　　　　　　　　　　　　　　　　🛋32　◎🍽

Daylight streams through the floor-to-ceiling windows at this contemporary restaurant next to Tin Hau MTR station. What makes the place stand out is the technical skill with which the dishes are prepared and the quality of the handmade dim sum which ensures it's always full at lunchtime. Dishes like deep-fried crispy chicken with glutinous rice and braised eight treasures duck with lotus seeds require cooking processes that are long and complicated.

鄰近天后鐵路站的龍軒，以啡黃色作裝潢主調，設計簡約，自然光通過落地玻璃遍灑一室，時尚舒適。這裏提供的傳統手藝粵菜需花上不少時間與功夫，如工序繁複、需長時間烹調的糯米脆皮雞、八寶蓮子鴨等。此外，這兒的傳統點心亦頗受歡迎。午飯時間往往座無虛席。

TEL. 2508 9318
GF, 31-33 King's Road, Tin Hau
天后英皇道 31-33號地下

■ PRICE 價錢
Lunch 午膳
à la carte 點菜 $70-100
Dinner 晚膳
à la carte 點菜 $150-250

■ OPENING HOURS 營業時間
Lunch 午膳　07:00-15:45 (L.O.)
Dinner 晚膳　18:00-22:45 (L.O.)

The Principal

✿✿

                         HONG KONG 香港

XXX   14 ⚅Ⅱ ⚇

This striking restaurant is elegant and contemporary; its concise menu is not defined by a single country but instead is influenced by the chef's professional experiences in Spain, Denmark and Asia. He uses prime ingredients and a European sensibility to create innovative and delicate dishes, such as black rice with red prawns, and steamed foie gras with Thai consommé. The wine list of over 700 labels is equally international and eclectic.

主廚受各地美食啟發，選用優質食材和新穎烹調方式，再按其在西班牙、丹麥及亞洲工作時積累的烹飪經驗，製作出創意與味道兼備的菜式如紅蝦墨汁飯、泰式清湯配蒸鵝肝等。酒單含超過七百款國際佳釀任君選擇。新穎的室內設計時尚優雅，予人一份清新感覺。

TEL. 2563 3444
9 Star Street, Wan Chai
灣仔星街 9號
www.theprincipal.com.hk

■ PRICE 價錢
Lunch 午膳
set 套餐 $ 290-430
Dinner 晚膳
set 套餐 $ 850-1,180

■ OPENING HOURS 營業時間
Lunch 午膳 12:00-14:00 (L.O.)
Dinner 晚膳 19:00-22:00 (L.O.)

The Square
翠玉軒

✽

✕✕✕　　　　　　　　　　　　　　　　　　🍴48 🕐🍴

To retain the food's natural flavour, the chef insists on using fresh, seasonal produce – he also cooks in a healthy way. Delicacies such as poached spotted garoupa in soya milk broth, and crispy fried boneless chicken stuffed with minced prawn purée are worth a try. Climbing the small staircase up to The Square always adds to the sense of anticipation and this is all the greater these days as the last makeover left the room looking very handsome.

每次踏上往翠玉軒的梯級，內心總會惦念着其美味佳餚和貼心服務，不期然便加快了步伐。這兒的粵菜烹調甚具心思。大廚選用當造食材，加上細膩健康的烹調方式，保留並特出了食材原味。美食包括鮮豆漿浸海星石斑及脆皮江南百花雞等。

TEL. 2525 1163
Shop 401, 4F, Exchange Square Podium, Central
中環交易廣場平臺 4樓 401號舖
www.maxims.com.hk

■ PRICE 價錢
Lunch 午膳
set 套餐 $ 228
à la carte 點菜 $ 180-900
Dinner 晚膳
à la carte 點菜 $ 180-900

■ OPENING HOURS 營業時間
Lunch 午膳　11:00-15:00 (L.O.)
Dinner 晚膳　18:00-22:45 (L.O.)

The Steak House Wine bar + grill

One of the most sophisticated grill rooms in town comes with its own colourful wine bar and an impressive wine list – it's 70% American and includes an impressive number of top Californian wines. The ingredients used here are unimpeachable: beef sourced from Australia, the U.S. and Canada is supplemented by great seafood. You even get to choose your knife from 10 different models. Service is professional but also has personality.

作為城中最著名的扒房之一，它擁有出色的酒吧，及令人眼花繚亂的餐酒名單 — 當中70%產自美國，更包括了許多頂級加州葡萄酒。這裏採用的全是一流食材：來自澳洲、美國與日本的牛肉，配合鮮美的海鮮。你還可以從十種餐刀中挑選最心儀的款式作餐具！服務專業友善。

TEL. 2313 2405
LF, Intercontinental Hotel,
18 Salisbury Road, Tsim Sha Tsui
尖沙咀梳士巴利道18號洲際酒店地庫1樓

■ PRICE 價錢
Weekends lunch 週末午膳
set 套餐 $ 598-798
Dinner 晚膳
à la carte 點菜 $1,000-1,650

■ OPENING HOURS 營業時間
Weekends lunch 週末午膳　12:00-14:30 (L.O.)
Dinner 晚膳　18:00-23:00 (L.O.)

The Swiss Chalet NEW
瑞士餐廳

🍴   ℃🍴

When considering where to eat in Hong Kong, one's thoughts wouldn't necessarily include a Swiss restaurant but step inside and you'll be instantly transported 6,000 miles to an Alpine chalet full of conviviality. The Swiss chef concentrates on the familiar so along with the hearty meat dishes is the famous cheese fondue, made with five different types of cheese together with kirsch. Cheeses are a big deal here, with over 20 varieties on offer.

在香港，可選擇的瑞士餐廳不多，位於赫德道的這家卻值得推介。木傢俱、小窗戶和別的裝飾物，予人置身瑞士小木屋之感。店東兼主廚將家鄉正宗口味帶給食客。牛面沙律、炸牛仔肉和五種芝士混合櫻桃酒而成的芝士火鍋必不可錯過。超過20種瑞士芝士及多款瑞士飲品和餐酒供選擇。

TEL. 2191 9197
12-14 Hart Avenue, Tsim Sha Tsui
尖沙咀赫德道 12-14號

■ PRICE 價錢
Lunch 午膳
set 套餐 $ 185
à la carte 點菜 $ 250-650
Dinner 晚膳
set 套餐 $ 325-495
à la carte 點菜 $ 250-650

■ OPENING HOURS 營業時間
Lunch 午膳　12:00-15:00 (L.O.)
Dinner 晚膳　18:00-22:45 (L.O.)

The Vietnam Woods
悅木

🍴　　　　　　　　　　　　　　　　　　　　🛏8

The latest branch from Lo Chiu is perhaps the most comfortable, with its attractive façade, modern interior, cosy seating and chic, white private room. You'll find all of Lo Chiu's signature Vietnamese dishes on the menu here, along with an extensive selection of appetisers. Deluxe beef noodles in soup is a highlight, with the soup served separately on a small stove. The popular set lunch menu ensures it's particularly busy midday.

作為老趙集團的一員，餐廳外觀吸引，室內裝潢時尚，舒適的雅座和白色主調的獨立廂房。在菜單中會見到所有老趙招牌越南菜及多款餐前特色小吃。悅木牛肉粉是其中一道招牌菜，牛肉與上湯會分開奉上，盛載上湯的小鍋會放在小爐上加熱。午市套餐極受歡迎，因此午市經常座無虛席。

TEL. 2866 0013
Shop 1, York Place, 22 Johnston Road,
Wan Chai
灣仔莊士敦道 22號 York Place1號舖

■ **PRICE 價錢**
Lunch 午膳
set 套餐 $88-108
à la carte 點菜 $90-205
Dinner 晚膳
à la carte 點菜 $90-205

■ OPENING HOURS 營業時間
Lunch 午膳　12:00-15:00 (L.O.)
Dinner 晚膳　18:00-22:30 (L.O.)
Weekends 週末　12:00-22:30 (L.O.)

■ ANNUAL AND WEEKLY CLOSING 休息日期
Closed 4 days Lunar New Year
農曆新年休息 4 天

HONG KONG 香港

Tim Ho Wan (North Point)
添好運 (北角)

The residents of North Point appear mighty glad that Tim Ho Wan finally opened a branch on Hong Kong Island. The soberly furnished dining room is always packed and at peak hours there'll even be a queue outside. The atmosphere is typical of a local tea house and hums with general contentment. There are over twenty different dim sum choices, along with a few desserts, and the menu changes each month.

添好運自從在港島區開設分店以來，一直深受北角區街坊喜愛；裝修雖簡約但客源不絕，每逢繁忙時段更會大排長龍；店內氣氛與一般本地茶樓無異，感覺熱鬧愉快。餐牌上雖只列有二十多款點心及數款甜品，但餐單上的食物款色會每月更新一次。

TEL. 2979 5608
2-8 Wharf Road, North Point
北角和富道 2-8號

■ PRICE 價錢
à la carte 點菜 $30-50

■ OPENING HOURS 營業時間
10:00-21:30 (L.O.)

■ ANNUAL AND WEEKLY CLOSING 休息日期
Closed 3 days Lunar New Year
農曆新年休息 3 天

Tim Ho Wan (Sham Shui Po)
添好運 (深水埗)

🔲 ⌷24 ⊘❗️

The second branch of Tim Ho Wan is able to accommodate a few more customers than the original and is located in a more residential area; but don't be surprised to find a queue of expectant diners outside here too. The 25 different dim sum choices are reasonably priced and carefully prepared. Highlights include steamed shrimp dumpling, baked bun with barbecue pork and steamed beef balls. There are four small private rooms on the first floor.

這家添好運的第二分店，座落於人口稠密的住宅區內，儘管能容納更多人客，但若看到店外等候入座的人龍，你不需要感到意外。供應25款由廚師巧手製作、價錢實惠的點心，不可不試的包括蝦餃、酥皮焗叉燒包和陳皮牛肉球。一樓設有四間小型貴賓房。

TEL. 2788 1226
9-11 Fuk Wing Street, Sham Shui Po
深水埗福榮街 9-11號

■ PRICE 價錢
à la carte 點菜 $30-50

■ OPENING HOURS 營業時間
08:00-21:30 (L.O.)

■ ANNUAL AND WEEKLY CLOSING 休息日期
Closed 3 days Lunar New Year
農曆新年休息 3 天

HONG KONG 香港

Tim Ho Wan (Tai Kwok Tsui) 😊
添好運 (大角咀)

Mention dim sum and many people will instantly think of the bustling Tim Ho Wan shop in Mong Kok. Here, at their new place, the crowds still flock in but the place is more spacious and feels even bigger, thanks to the high ceilings and bright lights. The reason for its popularity is the twenty different kinds of traditional Cantonese dim sum – made by hand with fresh ingredients – and the reasonable prices charged.

想到添好運的美味點心時，便會想起旺角舊店的擁擠。新店位於大角咀一個大型屋苑內，比舊店寬敞，高樓底配搭白色主調的裝潢，舒適明淨。然而，主角還是那二十多款廣式點心。沒有花巧的外型、創新的配搭，有的是傳統手工藝加上新鮮食材，價廉味美，難怪經常座無虛席。

TEL. 2332 2896
Shop G, 72A-B, Olympian City2,
18 Hoi Ting Road, Tai Kwok Tsui
大角咀海庭道 18號奧海城 2期 G72A-B舖

■ PRICE 價錢
à la carte 點菜 $30-50

■ OPENING HOURS 營業時間
10:00-21:30 (L.O.)

■ ANNUAL AND WEEKLY CLOSING 休息日期
Closed 3 days Lunar New Year
農曆新年休息 3 天

Tim's Kitchen (Sheung Wan)
桃花源小廚 (上環)

✗✗✗　　　　　　　　　　　　　　　🍽26　📞🍴

Success lead to Tim's Kitchen moving to these premises in 2010 – it's in the same area as before but, with two floors and a capacity of 100, is much larger; chef-owner Tim's son designed the colourful, modern room. Plenty of choice is offered, including popular specialities like Crystal prawn, pomelo skin and pork stomach, which showcase the kitchen's respect for the ingredients. There are now branches in Shanghai and Macau.

桃花源小廚遷至現址後，樓高兩層，可容納一百人。店主兼廚師黎先生的兒子設計了色彩豐富兼時尚的房間。新店比舊店提供更多粵菜，當然，鎮店菜如玻璃蝦球、柚皮及豬肚仍然羅列在菜單上，每款食品都證明廚房對優質材料的高度重視。業務已擴展至澳門及上海。

TEL. 2543 5919
84-90 Bonham Strand, Sheung Wan
上環文咸東街 84-90號
www.timskitchen.com.hk

SPECIALITIES TO PRE-ORDER 預訂食物
Steamed whole fresh crab claw with winter melon 冬瓜蒸原隻鮮蟹鉗 / Deep-fried whole fresh crab claw with peppercorn salt 椒鹽炸原隻鮮蟹鉗

■ PRICE 價錢
Lunch 午膳
à la carte 點菜 $ 125-300
Dinner 晚膳
à la carte 點菜 $ 250-1,000

■ OPENING HOURS 營業時間
Lunch 午膳　11:30-14:30 (L.O.)
Dinner 晚膳　18:00-22:30 (L.O.)

■ ANNUAL AND WEEKLY CLOSING 休息日期
Closed 4 days Lunar New Year
農曆新年休息 4 天

Tin Lung Heen
天龍軒

✕✕✕✕✕

✿✿✿

♿ ⟨ ⌨ 🍴36 ◐🍴 ⚭

Occupying a large section of the 102nd floor of the Ritz Carlton is this striking Cantonese restaurant, appropriately named 'Dragon in the sky'. Filling such a dramatic space could be daunting but the pleasant staff make it feel more intimate. The menu focuses on traditional, familiar dishes; the chefs, unlike in Tosca next door, are mere shadows glimpsed occasionally through the lattice screens. There are several charming private rooms.

位於香港麗思卡爾頓酒店102樓，這間極具氣派的粵菜餐館以氣勢十足的「天龍」命名。空間感之大幾乎讓人無所適從，但殷勤的服務人員讓你倍感親切。菜單着重傳統菜式。與相鄰的Tosca相反，你只能在屏風後隱約看見大廚的身影。另設有多個精緻的私人包廂。

TEL. 2263 2270
102F, The Ritz Carlton Hotel,
1 Austin Road West, TST
尖沙咀柯士甸道西 1 號
麗思卡爾頓酒店 102 樓
www.ritzcarlton.com/hongkong

■ PRICE 價錢
Lunch 午膳
à la carte 點菜 $450-1,300
Dinner 晚膳
à la carte 點菜 $450-1,300

■ OPENING HOURS 營業時間
Lunch 午膳　12:00-14:30 (L.O.)
Dinner 晚膳　18:00-22:30 (L.O.)

Tosca

✿

𝕏𝕏𝕏𝕏   ⭘ ⟨ ☞ ▢18 ◑⫽ ⚘

It is not just the incomparable views from its lofty location within the Ritz Carlton hotel that set Tosca apart - its striking interior, with its huge Murano glass chandelier and open kitchen, is as dramatic as any production of Puccini's opera. There's a pleasing southern Italian accent to the extensive menu; dishes to look out for include tagliolini with prawns and chilli, and mountain lamb chops with roast potatoes and black olives.

座落於麗思卡爾頓酒店高層位置，能俯瞰全景，但它的獨特之處是富麗堂皇的內部裝修、巨型慕拉諾玻璃吊燈和開放式廚房，加起來比普契尼的歌劇還要扣人心弦。豐富的菜單帶着讓人喜悅的南意情調。推介美食有香辣大蝦意粉及山羊扒伴焗薯黑橄欖。

TEL. 2263 2270
102F, The Ritz Carlton Hotel,
1 Austin Road West, TST
尖沙咀柯士甸道西 1 號麗思卡爾頓酒店 102樓
www.ritzcarlton.com/hongkong

■ PRICE 價錢
Lunch 午膳
set 套餐 $378-480
à la carte 點菜 $500-1,150
Dinner 晚膳
set 套餐 $1,380-2,180
à la carte 點菜 $500-1,150

■ OPENING HOURS 營業時間
Lunch 午膳　12:00-14:30 (L.O.)
Dinner 晚膳　18:00-22:30 (L.O.)

Trusty Congee King (Wan Chai)
靠得住 (灣仔)

The owner, Mr Lam, opened his first shop after his friends were so impressed by his ability to throw together a quick congee meal that they suggested he should start selling it. His was purported to be the first congee shop in Hong Kong to use a fish soup base for congee. These days, his specialities are salted meat rice dumpling and poached fresh fish skin. With a name that includes the words 'trusty' and 'king', how can you go wrong?

「靠得住」的出品一如其名，從不令人失望。店主林先生的巧手粥品備受親友讚賞，因此在2000年他開辦了首間粥店，據說這是全港首家採用魚湯作粥底的粥店。其他招牌食品有鹹肉粽及皇牌魚皮。

TEL. 2882 3268
7 Heard Street, Wan Chai
灣仔克街 7號

■ PRICE 價錢
à la carte 點菜 $30-110

■ OPENING HOURS 營業時間
11:00-22:45 (L.O.)

■ ANNUAL AND WEEKLY CLOSING 休息日期
Closed 2 days Lunar New Year
農曆新年休息 2 天

Tsim Chai Kee (Wellington Street)
沾仔記 (威靈頓街)

This highly regarded, simple noodle shop has been here since 1998 and is easy to spot – just look for the lunchtime queues. The staff are as bright as their aprons; the popular side booths are quickly snapped up; and the regulars know to eat outside peak times when the pace is less frenetic. The attraction is the handmade fish balls, the generously filled wontons and the beef; ordering a three topping noodle is the way to go.

享負盛名的沾仔記於1998年開業，裝修簡單，但依然整潔舒適。待應制服明亮潔淨，切有卡位但經常滿座；熟客會在非繁忙時間光顧，因氣氛較悠閒。著名食品包括自製鮮鯪魚球、餡料豐富的招牌雲吞及鮮牛肉麵；你可以來一碗三拼湯麵，一次過品嘗以上三種美食。

TEL. 2850 6471
98 Wellington Street, Central
中環威靈頓街 98號

■ PRICE 價錢
à la carte 點菜 $25-42

■ OPENING HOURS 營業時間
09:00-22:00 (L.O.)

■ ANNUAL AND WEEKLY CLOSING 休息日期
Closed 4 days Lunar New Year
農曆新年休息 4 天

Tsui Hang Village (Tsim Sha Tsui)
翠亨邨(尖沙咀)

🍴🍴 🅿 🪑60 🕐🍴

Many in Tsim Sha Tsui will recognise the name, as Tsui Hang Village opened in this shopping mall in the 1970s, before moving upstairs in 2011 into more contemporary surroundings. The menu is largely traditional Cantonese, supplemented by the head chef's own creations. Through the large window watch the chefs prepare specialities like braised beef ribs, shredded chicken and honey-glazed barbecued pork – their best seller; the dim sum is also good.

尖沙咀坊眾大都會認識翠亨邨，因為它早在1970年代已經在這個購物商場開業。菜式以傳統粵菜為主，再加上一些大廚自家創作。透過大玻璃窗，你可以看到廚師烹調各式佳餚，如醬燒牛肋排、翠亨邨靚一雞及最暢銷的蜜汁叉燒；這裏的點心也非常出色。

TEL. 2376 2882
5F, Miramar Shopping Centre,
132 Nathan Road, Tsim Sha Tsui
尖沙咀彌敦道132號美麗華商場5樓
www.tsuihangvillage.hk

■ PRICE 價錢
Lunch 午膳
à la carte 點菜 $130-650
Dinner 晚膳
à la carte 點菜 $200-650

■ OPENING HOURS 營業時間
Lunch 午膳　11:30-14:45 (L.O.)
Dinner 晚膳　18:15-23:00 (L.O.)

HONG KONG 香港

Tulsi (North Point)
羅勒 (北角)

The baby sister to Tulsi in Quarry Bay is just by North Point MTR's Exit B4 and comes with tightly packed tables that ensure there's always a warm, convivial atmosphere. You'll find the aromas coming from the compact and clean kitchen will quickly stimulate your appetite; the colourful, tasty Indian dishes made using quality, fresh ingredients ensure you soon feel sated.

Tulsi在北角港鐵站附近開設了這家分店。小小的店子內，牆壁懸着油畫、天花上的吊燈帶有古典味，簡約的設計風格營造出和諧溫馨的氣氛。友善親切的服務和香氣四溢、令人垂涎的亞洲風味美食讓食客賓至如歸。

TEL. 2568 3806
Fairview Court, 5-13 Tsat Tze Mui Road, North Point
北角七姊妹道 7號昌輝閣後座地下
www.tulsi.com.hk

■ PRICE 價錢
Lunch 午膳
set 套餐 $ 72
à la carte 點菜 $ 120-340
Dinner 晚膳
à la carte 點菜 $ 120-340

■ OPENING HOURS 營業時間
Lunch 午膳　11:30-15:00(L.O.)
Dinner 晚膳　18:00-23:00 (L.O.)

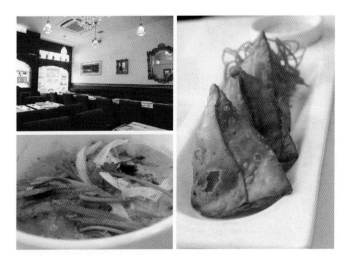

Tulsi (Quarry Bay)
羅勒 (鰂魚涌)

Those in Quarry Bay who are partial to Indian food have but one place to choose. Fortunately that place is Tulsi, a warm and cosy restaurant, opened in 2009, which also represents good value for money. The experienced chef looks to northern India for most of his influences and the specialities include Nawabi chicken and Jheenga Shola. The appealing set lunch explains the full house most weekdays.

鰂魚涌區的老饕想一嘗印度菜，大抵只有一個選擇，它就是於 2009 年開業的 Tulsi，環境舒適親切而且價廉物美。經驗豐富的大廚尤其精於印度北部菜餚，特色菜包括印式帝皇雞和醉酒炭燒蝦。午餐廣受歡迎，平日午市大多數座無虛席。

TEL. 2561 2968
Shop 1, GF, Hoi Kwong Court,
13-15 Hoi Kwong Street, Quarry Bay
鰂魚涌海光街 13-15號海光苑地下 1號舖
www.tulsi.com.hk

■ PRICE 價錢
Lunch 午膳
set 套餐 $ 68
à la carte 點菜 $ 120-260
Dinner 晚膳
à la carte 點菜 $ 120-260

■ OPENING HOURS 營業時間
Lunch 午膳　11:00-14:30(L.O.)
Dinner 晚膳　18:00-22:30 (L.O.)

Tze Yuet Heen
紫粵軒

XX X　　　　　　　　　　　　　　　🛎 ⊙16 ◑

The main restaurant of the Crowne Plaza Kowloon East hotel is this smart Cantonese restaurant. It uses a water theme as the inspiration behind its design and its painted screens and artwork are brought to life by judicious lighting. Over 100 Cantonese dishes are on offer, including plenty of vegetarian options and healthy delicacies, and preparation methods are largely traditional. The set menus are particularly appealing.

紫粵軒提供過百款依照傳統烹調方法炮製的廣東菜，還有一系列美味健康素菜。選擇午、晚市套餐，可一次過品嘗多款廚師推介。裝潢以流水作主題，融入中國傳統繪畫藝術：涓涓流水般的地氈、半透明水墨畫屏風和獨特的天花燈飾等，均顯示出設計者的巧思。

TEL. 3983 0628
2F, Crowne Plaza Kowloon East,
3 Tong Tak Street, Tseung Kwan O
將軍澳唐德街 3 號
香港九龍東皇冠假日酒店 2 樓
www.crowneplaza.com

SPECIALITIES TO PRE-ORDER 預訂食物
Double boiled caterpillar fungus with sea
cucumber 冬蟲夏草燉燎參

■ PRICE 價錢
Lunch 午膳
set 套餐 $ 88
à la carte 點菜 $ 180-700
Dinner 晚膳
à la carte 點菜 $ 180-700

■ OPENING HOURS 營業時間
Lunch 午膳　11:30-14:30 (L.O.)
Dinner 晚膳　18:00-22:30 (L.O.)

Upper Modern Bistro NEW

The owner-chef at this warm, bright and contemporary bistro is Philippe Orrico, who made his name at Hullett House – watch him and his hard-working brigade going about their business in the raised open kitchen. Their creativity is most evident in the starters and the small bites which come with touches of Asian influence; the main courses tend to be more traditionally French in their makeup. There's a great choice of over 30 French cheeses.

落地玻璃牆配以淡灰色裝潢，感覺舒適隨意。開放式廚房設在高了一級的位置，主廚就在當中發揮才華。簡單的菜單上，主菜較傳統，融入了東方色彩的前菜及佐酒小吃則較有創意，當中以偏向日本風味的小吃最為精彩。超過三十款法國芝士必能滿足喜歡芝士的你。

TEL. 2517 0977
6-14 Upper Station Street,
Sheung Wan
上環差館上街 6-14號
www.upper-bistro.com

■ PRICE 價錢
Lunch 午膳
set 套餐 $ 138-400
à la carte 點菜 $ 420-840
Dinner 晚膳
à la carte 點菜 $ 420-840

■ OPENING HOURS 營業時間
12:00-22:30 (L.O.)
Weekends & Public Holidays
週末及公眾假期　11:00-23:00 (L.O.)

Wagyu Kaiseki Den

Don't let the name confuse you - Wagyu beef is not the only ingredient. In fact, it's just one of numerous imported items that appear on the daily changing Kaiseki menu, where some modern touches sit alongside more traditional elements. Seasonality and freshness are fundamental to the passionate Japanese chef here; watch Hiroyuki Saotome and his team perform by reserving at the counter. Expect a comprehensive sake list too.

看店名便知頂級和牛是這兒的主角。主廚對食材要求嚴謹，只用最時令最新鮮的材料。每天更新的懷石餐單，除了和牛外，還包羅多種即日進口的新鮮食材，且傳統與現代兼容的烹調方式炮製。店內提供的清酒從日本各地搜羅而得，選擇豐富。

TEL. 2851 2820
263 Hollywood Road, Sheung Wan
上環荷李活道 263號

■ PRICE 價錢
Dinner 晚膳
set 套餐 $ 1,980

■ OPENING HOURS 營業時間
Dinner 晚膳 19:00-21:30 (L.O.)

■ ANNUAL AND WEEKLY CLOSING 休息日期
Closed 3 days Lunar New Year and Sunday
農曆新年休息 3 天及週日休息

Wagyu Takumi

✿ ✿

✕✕

🗏🍷   🚇   🕐🍴   🎱

There's something appealing about a restaurant that's hidden away: this small, elegant Japanese restaurant is secreted behind wooden doors at the back of a skyscraper. Once you've found it you'll find yourself sitting at one of 12 counter seats arranged around an open kitchen. The Japanese chef uses high quality ingredients and mixes French and Japanese cooking styles to create a daily changing 9-course dinner menu, with Omi Wagyu the speciality.

兩道隱蔽卻又似曾相識的拉門，藏身其後的是這間優雅的小餐廳，全店只有圍着中央開放式廚房的十二個座位。日籍大廚融會法日兩國的烹調技巧和飲食傳統，配上頂級時令食材，炮製出九道菜的法日晚餐，當中的重點菜是炭燒近江和牛。晚餐菜單會每天更新。店內供應的清酒質素非常好。

TEL. 2574 1299
GF, Oak Hill, 16 Wood Road, Wan Chai
灣仔活道 16號萃峯地下
www.ginsai.com.hk

■ PRICE 價錢
Dinner 晚膳
set 套餐 $ 1,880

■ OPENING HOURS 營業時間
Dinner 晚膳   18:00-21:30 (L.O.)

■ ANNUAL AND WEEKLY CLOSING 休息日期
Closed 3 days Lunar New Year
農曆新年休息 3 天

Wang Fu (Central)
王府 (中環)

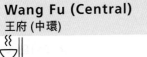

Wang Fu was one of the first shops to open on Wellington Street and its Pekingese dumplings are renowned. Over ten kinds of freshly hand-made dumplings with different fillings are on offer each day. Don't miss the green onion mutton dumpling or the vegetarian dumpling – the tomato and egg dumpling, which is only available after 2pm, is also good. As well as the dumplings and noodles, assorted hot Sichuan dishes are also offered.

王府是威靈頓街最早期開業的水餃店,其北京水餃遠近馳名,供應的餃子款色超過十種,每天均由人手新鮮包製,不可不試的包括羊肉京葱餃和花素餃,西紅柿(番茄)雞蛋餃於二時後才供應。除水餃麵食外,還供應多款京川熱食小菜。

TEL. 2121 8006
65 Wellington Street, Central
中環威靈頓街65號

■ PRICE 價錢
à la carte 點菜 $ 35-55

■ OPENING HOURS 營業時間
11:00-22:30 (L.O.)

■ ANNUAL AND WEEKLY CLOSING 休息日期
Closed 4 days Lunar New Year
農曆新年休息4天

Wen Ding
文鼎

🍴🍴   📬 ⌷18 ☎️🍴

Hong Kong doesn't boast many Ningbo restaurants so try this classic one which is housed in an old three storey building in Wan Chai. The main dining room is on the ground floor with upper floors used for private rooms. Many ingredients are flown in daily from Ningbo, including yellow fish and sea cucumber. The most popular dish is cold marinated crab which is soaked in wine and a secret formula for a week; enjoy it with their homemade sauce.

香港的寧波菜館不多，灣仔卻有這家佔了三層樓、裝潢雅致的寧波酒家。地舖的大廳是主餐室，樓上是私人廂房。為保新鮮，材料如黃魚、活海參均由當地空運抵港。以特製酒汁浸製一星期的文鼎十八斬野生紅膏白蟹最馳名，吃時配上秘製醬汁，令人回味無窮。

TEL. 2520 6268
G-2F, 21-23 Tai Wong Street East,
Wan Chai
灣仔大王東街 21-23號地下及 2樓

■ PRICE 價錢
Lunch 午膳
à la carte 點菜 $ 100-1,400
Dinner 晚膳
à la carte 點菜 $ 200-1,400

■ OPENING HOURS 營業時間
Lunch 午膳　11:00-15:00 (L.O.)
Dinner 晚膳　18:00-22:30 (L.O.)

■ ANNUAL AND WEEKLY CLOSING 休息日期
Closed Lunar New Year 年初一休息

Whisk

☆☆☆　　　　　　　　　　　　 ♿ ➟♨ ⟷24 ◔🍴 ⬡

Contemporary European cooking techniques and the finest seasonal ingredients from around the world are used here at Whisk to create satisfying dishes with appealing combinations of flavours. Try the tagliolini with Bretagne lobster or the crispy suckling pig with braised baby lettuce. There are over 200 wines available; the restaurant has a comfortable, relaxed feel; and you can have drinks on the adjoining terrace.

採用當代歐洲烹調技巧，融合全球時令精選食材的Whisk，創造出多款獨特菜式，為食客的味覺帶來新享受。推介蕃茄香草龍蝦意粉和脆皮乳豬伴燉萵苣。此店提供超過二百款全球精選佳釀，愛酒之士可與良朋在此品酒談心。在露臺享用咖啡亦另有一番風情!

TEL. 2315 5999
5F, The Mira Hotel, 118 Nathan Road, Tsim Sha Tsui
尖沙咀彌敦道 118號 The Mira 5樓
www.themirahotel.com

■ PRICE 價錢
Lunch 午膳
set 套餐 $ 288
à la carte 點菜 $ 550-1,750
Dinner 晚膳
set 套餐 $ 860
à la carte 點菜 $ 550-1,750

■ OPENING HOURS 營業時間
Lunch 午膳　12:00-14:30 (L.O.)
Dinner 晚膳　18:00-22:30 (L.O.)

■ ANNUAL AND WEEKLY CLOSING 休息日期
Closed Monday 週一休息

Wing Lai Yuen
詠藜園

✗   ♿ 🅿 ⇄16 ◔🍴

The film business glitterati used to flock to the original shop in San Po Kong for the authentic Sichuan Dan Dan noodles. A decade ago the Yeung family moved it to its current address in Whampoa Garden, where the Dan Dan noodles are still the main attraction, although these days you can decide whether or not you want them spicy. Along with other Sichuan dishes are a few Shanghainese specialities too.

新蒲崗原舖吸引了無數影星名人，全為了一嘗正宗四川擔擔麵蜂擁而至。十年前，楊氏家族決定把店子遷址到現在的黃埔花園。直至今日擔擔麵仍然是其主打麵食，不過，現在你還可以選擇辣或不辣的湯底。另外，店內同時供應多款川菜和上海美食。

TEL. 2320 6430
Shop 102-105, 1F, Whampoa Plaza,
Site 8, Hung Hom
紅磡黃埔花園第 8 期 1 樓 102-105號舖

■ PRICE 價錢
Lunch 午膳
à la carte 點菜 $60-400
Dinner 晚膳
à la carte 點菜 $60-400

■ OPENING HOURS 營業時間
Lunch 午膳　　11:00-15:30 (L.O.)
Dinner 晚膳　　18:00-22:30 (L.O.)

Wing Wah
永華雲吞麵家

This simple operation has been maintaining high standards for well over 50 years now, the secret being that they do everything from scratch upstairs, making their noodles by hand using bamboo. So proud are they of their skills that there's a photographic display of their craft on the walls. Finest offerings include shrimp wonton and barbecued pork noodle, a coconut milk dessert with honeydew melon and sago and drinks like sweet herbal tea.

這間麵家營運至今逾五十年，一直堅持在店鋪樓上的小工房中，用傳統的竹升法人工打製麵條，店主以高水準的麵條深感自豪，牆上貼滿制麵過程的照片。招牌美食包括鮮蝦雲吞麵及炸醬麵等，亦有令人驚喜的蝦籽柚皮及自家磨制的合桃露。

TEL. 2527 7476
89 Hennessy Road, Wan Chai
灣仔軒尼詩道 89號

■ PRICE 價錢
à la carte 點菜 $40-150

■ OPENING HOURS 營業時間
12:00-02:00 (L.O.)
Sunday 週日   12:00-01:00 (L.O.)

■ ANNUAL AND WEEKLY CLOSING 休息日期
Closed 3 days Lunar New Year
農曆新年休息 3 天

Wonton Master
灃家

Those familiar with the Tasty Group will find the menu and style of food here reassuringly familiar – Cantonese-style congee and noodles, along with dim sum and other Cantonese specialities. It is the springy noodles that pull in the crowds – they're served with soup freshly made to a secret recipe handed down by the Ho family. Creative congee hotpots, made with a water-to-rice ratio of 9 to 1, are offered in winter and are worth trying.

似曾相識的餐單和熟悉的味道，這家餐廳其實是正斗集團一員，以提供廣式粥麵為主，再加點心和多款小菜。沿用家傳秘方烹製的湯底配上新鮮製作、質感彈牙的麵條，令人留下深刻印象。冬季更會供應以九比一米水比例熬煮的粥底火鍋，配合新鮮材料，也值得一試。餐廳設計偏向時尚活潑。

TEL. 3148 9488
Shop 13, L3 APM Millennium City 5,
418 Kwun Tong Road, Kwun Tong
觀塘創紀之城第 5 期 APM商場 3樓 13號舖

■ PRICE 價錢
à la carte 點菜 $40-130

■ OPENING HOURS 營業時間
11:30-22:30 (L.O.)

Wu Kong (Causeway Bay)
滬江 (銅鑼灣)

✗✗   ☕36 ◐❒

The many customers of this Shanghainese restaurant had reason to celebrate its relocation in 2011 to the upper level of Lee Theatre Plaza as it resulted in better views, more space and a nicer environment in which to eat. An experienced kitchen shows its practised hand in specialities such as braised pig's knuckle with brown sauce and honey ham and crispy bean curd in bread. Do try the hairy crab menu in the autumn season.

於2011年搬到利舞臺高層的滬江飯店，為顧客帶來更佳的景觀、更寬敞的空間和更舒適的環境，讓他們更盡情享用美食。廚藝精湛的廚師為顧客炮製多款巧手小菜，如紅燒元蹄和響鈴火腿夾。於秋季期間，肥美的大閘蟹是必吃的時令佳餚。

TEL. 2506 1018
Shop B, 17F, Lee Theatre Plaza,
99 Percival Street, Causeway Bay
銅鑼灣波斯富街 99號利舞臺廣場 17樓 B號舖
www.wukong.com.hk

■ PRICE 價錢
Lunch 午膳
set 套餐 $ 78
à la carte 點菜 $ 155-870
Dinner 晚膳
à la carte 點菜 $ 155-870

■ OPENING HOURS 營業時間
Lunch 午膳　11:45-14:45 (L.O.)
Dinner 晚膳　17:45-22:45 (L.O.)

■ ANNUAL AND WEEKLY CLOSING 休息日期
Closed 3 days Lunar New Year
農曆新年休息 3 天

Xiao Wang Beef Noodle (Diamond Hill)
小王牛肉麵 (鑽石山)

P

This bright and busy outlet comes courtesy of a well-known chain in Taiwan. Their beef noodles use premium quality beef and Chinese herbal soup, which supposedly is a secret recipe handed down from an imperial chef from the Qing dynasty period. They also offer authentic Taiwanese dishes and snacks. For something a little special, ask for their Signature Beef Noodle dish: it uses specific cuts of beef so only ten bowls are made each day.

在鑽石山大型商場內的小王牛肉麵源自台灣，淺棕色主調與紅白磚牆，環境明亮舒適且富時代感。店內焦點是用清宮御廚秘方熬製的中藥湯底及上乘牛肉精心烹調的牛肉麵。此外，還供應台灣地道小菜和小吃。以嫩滑牛胸骨肉烹製的芙蓉牛肉麵，每日只售十碗，值得一試。

TEL. 2324 6628
Shop 373, L3 Hollywood Plaza,
3 Lung Poon Street, Diamond Hill
鑽石山龍蟠街 3號荷里活廣場 3樓 373號舖

■ PRICE 價錢
à la carte 點菜 $ 70-220

■ OPENING HOURS 營業時間
11:30-21:45 (L.O.)

Xuan Sushi
玄鮨

Whilst there are tables in this gracefully decorated and surprisingly spacious dining room, the best place to sit is at the long, wave-shaped counter. From here you can watch the action as the four sushi chefs prepare the omakase menu – they use Niigata rice and two different types of vinegar for the sushi. There are other hot dishes available and many of the ingredients are flown in daily from Japan.

棕色木材與黃銅管的配搭，予人時尚優雅的感覺。壽司吧佔了大部分空間，而大廚就在吧枱後為你準備各款美味壽司。這裏的壽司飯是用新潟米按特定比例加入兩種醋煮成，其餘材料均是每日由日本新鮮運到。坐在櫃枱前享用廚師套餐是最好選擇。此店亦供應燒物及天婦羅等熱食。

TEL. 2537 5555
3F, Parekh House,
61-63 Wyndham Street, Central
中環雲咸街 61-63號巴力大廈 3樓

■ PRICE 價錢
Lunch 午膳
set 套餐 $ 300-500
Dinner 晚膳
à la carte 點菜 $ 1,200-1,600

■ OPENING HOURS 營業時間
Lunch 午膳　12:00-14:30 (L.O.)
Dinner 晚膳　18:00-22:30 (L.O.)

■ ANNUAL AND WEEKLY CLOSING 休息日期
Closed 3 days Lunar New Year and Sunday
農曆新年 3 天及週日休息

Yan Toh Heen
欣圖軒

🌸🌸

Its location on the ground floor of the Intercontinental hotel may be somewhat concealed but it's well worth seeking out this elegant Cantonese restaurant and that's not just because of the lovely views of Hong Kong Island. The authentic, carefully prepared specialities include golden frogs' legs with spicy salt; scallops with minced shrimp and pear; double-boiled fish maw and sea whelk; and wok-fried lobster with crab roe and milk.

這家優雅的粵菜酒家座落於洲際酒店地下，所處位置可能較為隱閉，但十分值得去尋找，而這裏的魅力，絕不止於能夠觀賞香港島的美景，更因其供應多款精心炮製的傳統粵式佳餚，包括：黃金椒鹽田雞腿、龍帶玉梨香、花膠響螺燉湯及龍皇炒鮮奶等。

TEL. 2313 2243
GF, Intercontinental Hotel,
18 Salisbury Road, Tsim Sha Tsui
尖沙咀梳士巴利道18號洲際酒店地下

SPECIALITIES TO PRE-ORDER 預訂食物
Braised fish maw with sea cucumber in oyster jus 蠔皇厚花膠扣遼參 / Barbecued whole suckling pig 金陵脆皮乳豬 / Peking duck 北京片皮鴨 / Hangzhou beggar's fortune chicken 杭州富貴雞

■ PRICE 價錢
Lunch 午膳
set 套餐 $368-628
à la carte 點菜 $350-1,350
Dinner 晚膳
set 套餐 $1,888-3,088
à la carte 點菜 $400-1,450

■ OPENING HOURS 營業時間
Lunch 午膳 12:00-14:30 (L.O.)
Dinner 晚膳 18:00-23:00 (L.O.)

Yat Lok 😋
一樂燒鵝

If you're after delicious roast goose then Yat Lok may fit the bill. This family business has been going since 1957 but moved to its current location in 2011. The owner-chef prepares his roast meats using the family's secret recipe; his barbecue pork is also worth a try. The environment is basic and space is limited – you'll be sharing your table with others – but the owner's wife and her service team help create a pleasant atmosphere.

一樂早於1957年開始營業，其後在2011年遷至現址。每次經過其門前，總會被掛在窗前的燒鵝吸引而垂涎三尺。以家族秘方醃製、經過二十多道工序炮製而成的燒鵝，色香味俱佳，蠻受街坊歡迎，其他食物如脆皮乳豬亦不可錯過。

TEL. 2524 3882
34-38 Stanley Street, Central
中環士丹利街 34-38號

■ PRICE 價錢
à la carte 點菜 $30-360

■ OPENING HOURS 營業時間
09:00-20:30 (L.O.)

■ ANNUAL AND WEEKLY CLOSING 休息日期
Closed 3 days Lunar New Year
農曆新年休息 3 天

Yau Yuen Siu Tsui
有緣小敍

The owner's wife works alone in this shop, serving authentic Shaanxi dishes and snacks from her hometown, like dumplings and baked buns with meat. The most impressive dish is Biang Biang noodles – these long, flat, handmade noodles come with a spicy chilli sauce and are full of flavour. Other specialities include fried mutton with spices, and five-spice donkey meat. This new shop is bigger and more comfortable than their last one.

店東太太為食客烹調其家鄉陝西的正宗小菜及小吃如餃子、肉夾饃等，其中最令人難忘的莫過於Biang　Biang麵。這款由人手製作，麵身寬長的麵食，配辣醬進食，香辣味濃，令人回味再三。其他道地陝西美食還有孜然羊肉與五香驢肉。

TEL. 5300 2682
GF, 36 Man Yuen Street, Jordan
佐敦文苑街 36號地下

■ PRICE 價錢
à la carte 點菜 $30-100

■ OPENING HOURS 營業時間
12:00-22:00 (L.O.)

Yè Shanghai (Admiralty)
夜上海 (金鐘)

XXX   ⟨⟩24   ☏⏐

The attentive staff will guide you through the menu which specialises not only in the cuisine of Shanghai but also in its neighbouring provinces of Jiangsu and Zhejiang – try the deep-fried sweet and sour yellow fish with pine nuts, or fried shredded bean curd with abalone. The large dining room, which is surrounded by jewellery shops and has a bijou chocolate shop at its entrance, is gracefully decorated and boasts floor to ceiling windows.

餐廳外全是名牌鐘錶和珠寶店，入口處設有一家精緻的巧克力店。餐廳內面積寬廣，設有落地玻璃，裝修優雅；素有訓練的侍應樂於為你介紹餐單上款式繁多的菜式；特色美食不光包括上海菜，更有江蘇及浙江菜。建議一試崧子黃魚及鮑魚炒乾絲。

TEL. 2918 9833
Shop 332, 3F, Pacific Place,
88 Queensway, Admiralty
金鐘道 88號太古廣場 3樓 332號舖
www.elite-concepts.com

SPECIALITIES TO PRE-ORDER 預訂食物
Beggar's chicken 富 貴 雞 / Braised duck
with scallion 夏京葱扒大鴨

■ PRICE 價錢
Lunch 午膳
set 套餐 $ 418
à la carte 點菜 $ 230-650
Dinner 晚膳
à la carte 點菜 $ 230-650

■ OPENING HOURS 營業時間
Lunch 午膳　11:30-14:30 (L.O.)
Dinner 晚膳　18:00-22:30 (L.O.)

Yè Shanghai (Tsim Sha Tsui)
夜上海 (尖沙咀)

❀

✕✕✕   ♿ 🚻 ▭80 ◐🍴

Drawing not only on Shanghai but also on the neighbouring provinces of Jiangsu and Zhejiang, the cooking here is subtle and expertly balanced. Specialities include sautéed shredded Mandarin fish, baked stuffed crab shell and Ningbo-style baby ribs glazed with Zhejiang black vinegar. The contemporary décor recalls 1930s Shanghai in its use of dark woods, subdued lighting and semi-private alcoves. This is a busy, sophisticated operation.

這裏的烹調水準專業，技術精湛，不但提供上海菜，還供應江蘇及浙江菜。特色美食包括龍鬚桂魚絲，蟹粉釀蟹蓋及寧波肋骨。餐廳以當代風格設計，採用昏暗的燈光，深色的木材，加上半私家餐桌，散發着三十年代上海的味道。餐廳生氣勃勃，營運順暢，服務非常周到。

TEL. 2376 3322
6F, Marco Polo Hotel, Harbour City,
Canton Road, Tsim Sha Tsui
尖沙咀廣東道海運大廈馬哥孛羅酒店 6樓
www.elite-concepts.com

■ PRICE 價錢
Lunch 午膳
à la carte 點菜 $ 250-630
Dinner 晚膳
à la carte 點菜 $ 250-630

■ OPENING HOURS 營業時間
Lunch 午膳   11:30-15:00 L.O. 14:30
Dinner 晚膳   18:00-23:00 L.O. 22:30

Yee Tung Heen NEW
怡東軒

    📛 **P** 🍴60 📞

The first thing you'll notice is the Chinese ornaments and the second is how well Chinese screens and contemporary lighting go together. This elegant restaurant not only offers traditional Cantonese favourites but also serves specialities of a more creative persuasion. The enthusiastic chef and his team spend much time seeking out the best quality seasonal ingredients, whether that's from local markets or overseas.

踏入怡東酒店內的怡東軒中菜廳，馬上便會讓精緻的中式擺設吸引。往內走，會發現四周的中式屏風與現代天花燈，配搭得十分別致。餐廳供應傳統粵菜，廚師及營運團隊充滿熱誠，專程由本地及世界各地搜羅各種高質素及時令食材，時有創新菜式或特別餐單推出。

TEL. 2837 6790
2F, The Excelsior Hotel,
28 Gloucester Road, Causeway Bay
銅鑼灣告士打道 281號怡東酒店 2樓

■ PRICE 價錢
Lunch 午膳
à la carte 點菜 $ 220-800
Dinner 晚膳
à la carte 點菜 $ 400-800

■ OPENING HOURS 營業時間
Lunch 午膳　12:00-14:30 (L.O.)
Dinner 晚膳　18:00-22:30 (L.O.)

Yin Yue　NEW
殷悅

♿ 🅿 ☏🍴

Yin Yue provides a warm and relaxing space; its large windows letting in lots of light and providing great views of Tsuen Wan from its perch on the top floor of a hotel. The cooking is undertaken by an experienced chef who prepares the attractively presented dishes in a traditional but healthy way, using secret recipes, quality ingredients and a lesser amount of oil. Try suckling pig with dried mullet roe, or stir-fried beef with black truffle.

位於酒店頂樓，以淡色系作裝潢的餐廳，格調輕鬆。兩邊的落地玻璃窗除了引入自然光外，還讓你一覽舊社區的景色。店內粵菜由富數十年經驗大廚主理，結合了健康少油的烹調方式與傳統秘方，再配上世界各地食材和日本美學，型味俱佳。推介菜式有用台灣烏魚子製作的烏金麒麟乳豬和黑松露牛柳粒。

TEL. 2409 3182
30F, Panda Hotel, 3 Tsuen Wah Street,
Tsuen Wan, New Territories
新界荃灣荃華街 3 號悅來酒店 30 樓
www.pandahotel.com.hk

■ PRICE 價錢
Lunch 午膳
à la carte 點菜 $ 150-900
Dinner 晚膳
à la carte 點菜 $ 300-900

■ OPENING HOURS 營業時間
Lunch 午膳　11:00-14:30 (L.O.)
Weekends & Public Holidays
週末及公眾假期　10:00-15:00 (L.O.)
Dinner 晚膳　18:00-22:00 (L.O.)

Youka NEW
八日

The chocolate box façade gives little away but step inside and you'll find yourself in a simple, cosy and contemporary space with a genuine Japanese flavour. Those who are curious to learn more about the cooking process should sit in front of the open kitchen to take advantage of the live cookery show. The chef's unequivocal commitment to using only the best ingredients means that much of the produce is flown in daily from Japan.

餐廳的黑色外牆十分引人注目。室內面積不大，簡單時尚的裝潢隱隱滲出一絲日本韻味。最佳的位置莫過於開放式廚房前的座位，你可以一邊品嘗美食、一邊欣賞廚師出色的廚藝。廚師最着重食材的時令性，因此，美味的和色套餐只選用每天即日由日本運到的新鮮材料炮製。這兒的壽司頗受食客歡迎。

TEL. 2833 5188
35-45 Johnston Road, Wan Chai
灣仔莊士敦道 35-45號
www.youka.hk

■ PRICE 價錢
Lunch 午膳
set 套餐 $ 180-338
à la carte 點菜 $ 250-900
Dinner 晚膳
set 套餐 $ 550-1,280
à la carte 點菜 $ 250-900

■ OPENING HOURS 營業時間
Lunch 午膳 12:00-14:30 (L.O.)
Dinner 晚膳 18:00-22:30 (L.O.)

Yù Lèi
玉蕾

XXX   ← 🍽 ⟷18 ☎🍴

The strikingly decorated Yù Lèi is part of a harbourside restaurant complex, and specialises in Shanghainese cuisine; look out for creatively presented dishes like Drunken Kyu Shu crab, stir-fried sliced abalone with seasonal vegetables, and stir-fried seaweed and water bamboo. At lunch the restaurant also serves Cantonese dim sum and assorted roast meats. The main dining room comes in vivid green and the five private rooms are named after flowers.

裝潢耀目的玉蕾是此區海傍飲食綜合場所的一部份,主要供應上海菜。此店提供的創意菜式包括九州醉蟹、生炒鮮鮑片及苔條茭白。餐廳於午市期間供應廣東點心和燒味併盤;主用餐區以鮮明的綠色為主題,五個私人廂房則以花卉命名。

TEL. 3746 2788
5F, Harbourfront Landmark,
11 Wan Hoi Street, Hung Hom
紅磡環海街 11 號海名軒 5 樓
www.KOdining.com

SPECIALITIES TO PRE-ORDER 預訂食物
Drunken Kyu Shu crab 醉蟹 (10 days 日)

■ PRICE 價錢
Lunch 午膳
set 套餐 $ 398
à la carte 點菜 $ 300-3,500
Dinner 晚膳
à la carte 點菜 $ 300-3,500

■ OPENING HOURS 營業時間
Lunch 午膳   12:00-15:00 (L.O.)
Dinner 晚膳   18:00-22:30 (L.O.)

■ ANNUAL AND WEEKLY CLOSING 休息日期
Closed Monday 週一休息

Yuè (Gold Coast)
粵 (黃金海岸)

🍴 🍽 24 🍷

It's not often one can enjoy Cantonese food surrounded by verdant scenery but here on the ground floor of the Gold Coast hotel that's exactly what you get as this comfortable restaurant looks out onto a delightful garden. The menu includes both traditional and more contemporary dishes and it's worth seeking out the chef's specialities such as barbecued pork and chicken liver with honey, and deep-fried chicken with shrimp paste.

位於黃金海岸酒店的地面層，優雅舒適的室內環境，與大型玻璃窗外的園林景致巧妙地配合起來。選擇豐富的餐單提供傳統懷舊及較創新的粵菜，廚師精選菜式值得一試，如蜜餞金錢雞和星洲蝦醬炸雞件等。邊品嘗美味的廣式點心邊欣賞怡人的園林美景，實在是賞心樂事。

TEL. 2452 8668
LG/F, Gold Coast Hotel,
1 Castle Peak Road, Gold Coast
黃金海岸青山公路 1 號黃金海岸酒店低層
www.goldcoasthotel.com.hk

■ PRICE 價錢
Lunch 午膳
set 套餐 $ 168-238
à la carte 點菜 $ 120-900
Dinner 晚膳
à la carte 點菜 $ 200-900

■ OPENING HOURS 營業時間
Lunch 午膳　11:30-15:30 (L.O.)
Sunday & Public Holidays 週日及公眾假期
09:00-16:00 (L.O.)
Dinner 晚膳　18:30-23:00 (L.O.)

Yuè (North Point)
粵 (北角)

It may seem like nothing more than a mezzanine area of the City Garden hotel but it's well worth coming up here for the Cantonese food. The experienced chef's respect for the traditions of Cantonese cuisine is clearly demonstrated in dishes like double-boiled jus of almonds with fish maw, fried rice with prawns and barbecue pork, and seared garoupa with layered egg white. There are a number of different sized private rooms.

看起來只是城市花園酒店的間層，並不特別，定讓不少人忽略了這間中菜廳，但絕對值得前來一嘗這裏的廣東菜。資深大廚對傳統粵菜的尊重完全反映在各樣菜式上，例如杏汁花膠燉蹄筋、師傅炒飯和雪嶺紅梅映松露等。餐廳設有不同大小的廂房供各類宴會之用。

TEL. 2806 4918
1F, City Garden Hotel,
9 City Garden Road, North Point
北角城市花園道 9號城市花園酒店 1樓
www.citygarden.com.hk

■ PRICE 價錢
Lunch 午膳
à la carte 點菜 $ 220-670
Dinner 晚膳
à la carte 點菜 $ 220-670

■ OPENING HOURS 營業時間
Lunch 午膳 11:30-14:30 (L.O.)
Dinner 晚膳 18:00-22:30 (L.O.)

Yue Kee
裕記

Over 40,000 geese are needed each year to satisfy demand at this large, second-generation family business, which opened back in 1958. The geese are sourced from eight different farms in Mainland China and if contentment is indicated by the amount of noise generated, then clearly these roasted geese are much appreciated by the customers. The restaurant has 50 tables, which are divided between eight simply decorated rooms. It's worth booking ahead.

這家家族經營的餐館於1958年開業，現在由第二代打理。食店每年分別在中國內地八個農場購入超過四萬隻鵝以確保供應充足，店主多年來一直堅持按家傳秘方以炭火烤製燒鵝，味道特佳。店內共有五十桌，分佈於八間房內；若聲浪與滿足程度成正比，這裏的燒鵝肯定非常受歡迎。建議預訂座位。

TEL. 2491 0105
9 Sham Hong Road, Sham Tseng
深井深康路 9號
www.yuekee.com.hk

■ PRICE 價錢
à la carte 點菜 $ 150-550

■ OPENING HOURS 營業時間
11:00-23:00 (L.O.)

■ ANNUAL AND WEEKLY CLOSING 休息日期
Closed 3 days Lunar New Year
農曆新年休息 3 天

Yun Yan NEW
雲陽

Yun Yan began life in the 1990s in Tsim Sha Tsui but has now firmly established itself in Causeway Bay. It wasn't just its appearance and atmosphere that changed when it moved – the kitchen also played its part. Whilst the Sichuan specialities are still prepared to the same high standard, it puts its own spin on some dishes and presents them in a very modern style. Try the translucent beef slices and hand-cut noodles in supreme soup.

早於九十年代在尖沙咀開業，遷至現址後，室內裝潢以淡素色調配合時尚設計，予人耳目一新之感。傳統川菜亦以新形象示人，外觀雖變味道卻不變。經典菜式如燈影牛肉和幼如髮絲的大刀金絲麵均不能錯過。自由調味的豆腦創作趣味十足。門前湘竹上的斑點寓意的應是因辣而出的汗水而非淚珠吧!

TEL. 2375 0800
10F, Time Square, 1 Matheson Street,
Causeway Bay
銅鑼灣勿地臣街 1 號時代廣場 10 樓
www.yunyan.hk

■ PRICE 價錢
Lunch 午膳
set 套餐 $ 88
à la carte 點菜 $ 90-450
Dinner 晚膳
à la carte 點菜 $ 160-450

■ OPENING HOURS 營業時間
Lunch 午膳　12:00-15:45 (L.O.)
Dinner 晚膳　18:00-22:30 (L.O.)

Zaan NEW
饌

🍴🍴　　　　　　　　　　　　　　　　🛋36 ◐🍽

Sitting within the Ozo Wesley hotel is this simply decorated but bright and comfortable Cantonese restaurant. Lunchtimes are popular with local business types when traditional dim sum, handmade daily by the chef, is the order of the day. At night the kitchen takes things up a notch and the main menu includes various healthy and creative Cantonese dishes alongside modern creations which take their influences from across Southeast Asia.

位於遨舍衛蘭軒的饌由酒店營運。光潔明亮的環境、線條簡單帶有時代氣息的裝潢，令人感覺輕鬆舒服。午餐時供應的傳統粵式點心，選擇豐富，且為每日鮮製，適合商務聚餐。主菜單內所見菜式口味新鮮。由具馬來西亞背景的主廚烹調出來的健康新派粵菜，甚具南洋風味。

TEL. 2292 3033
1F, Ozo Wesley Hotel,
22 Hennessy Road, Wan Chai
灣仔軒尼詩道 22 號遨舍衛蘭軒 1 樓
www.ozohotels.com

■ PRICE 價錢
Lunch 午膳
à la carte 點菜 $ 100-350
Dinner 晚膳
à la carte 點菜 $ 150-350

■ OPENING HOURS 營業時間
Lunch 午膳　12:00-14:30 (L.O.)
Dinner 晚膳　18:00-22:30 (L.O.)

HONG KONG 香港

Zhejiang Heen
浙江軒

✗✗ 🍽16 ◐🍴

At what must be one of the easiest restaurants to find – just look for the huge Zhejiang landscape on the outside of the building – you'll find authentic Zhejiang and Shanghainese specialities made from top quality ingredients, such as smoked fish, shrimps with seaweed, and steamed chou tofu. Run by a Zhejiang Fraternity Association, the dining room is spread over two floors and while it may not be particularly lavish, it is comfortable.

要數最容易找的酒家，這家必定榜上有名，因為它的外牆有一大幅浙江風景圖。你可在這裏品嘗到採用上等食材烹調的傳統浙江及上海美食，如長江燻魚、苔條蝦仁及紹興蒸臭豆腐。這裏由香港浙江省同鄉會聯合會經營，樓高兩層，雖然裝修並不豪華，但感覺十分舒適。

TEL. 2877 9011
2-3F, 300-306 Lockhart Road,
Wan Chai
灣仔駱克道 300-306號 2-3樓

SPECIALITIES TO PRE-ORDER 預訂食物
Crispy deep fried chicken with 4 treasures
四寶片皮雞 / Braised duck stuffed with 8
treasures 蟹燒八寶鴨

■ PRICE 價錢
Lunch 午膳
à la carte 點菜 $160-900
Dinner 晚膳
à la carte 點菜 $160-900

■ OPENING HOURS 營業時間
Lunch 午膳　11:00-15:00 (L.O.)
Dinner 晚膳　18:00-23:00 (L.O.)

■ ANNUAL AND WEEKLY CLOSING 休息日期
Closed 3 days Lunar New Year
農曆新年休息 3 天

Zuma

✗✗   ♿ 🏠 ○16 ⇅ ৪৪

A cool cocktail lounge hovers over the dining room, linked by a dramatic spiral staircase, and a DJ plays Tuesday to Saturday – yes, Zuma is as fashionable as ever and is still pulling in the in-crowd. Dishes are prepared in three distinct areas: the open kitchen, the sushi bar and the robata grill, and the kitchen team blend calm precision with dramatic flourish. Over 1,000 wines and 40 types of sake and shochu are also on offer.

餐廳的主餐室樓上,設有型格燒酒吧及酒廊,並以螺旋形樓梯連接。周四至周六有 DJ 在場打碟,散發着時尚氣息,一直是潮流達人的聚腳地。廚房包括三個部分:開放式廚房、壽司吧及爐端燒,廚師廚藝精巧,味道一流。餐廳提供超過一千種葡萄酒及四十種日本酒及燒酒。

TEL. 3657 6388
5-6F, The Landmark,
15 Queen's Road Central
皇后大道中 15號置地廣場 5-6樓
www.zumarestaurant.com

■ PRICE 價錢
Lunch 午膳
set 套餐 $ 350-480
à la carte 點菜 $ 400-1,000
Dinner 晚膳
set 套餐 $970
à la carte 點菜 $ 400-1,000

■ OPENING HOURS 營業時間
Lunch 午膳　11:30-14:30 (L.O.)
Dinner 晚膳　18:00-23:00 (L.O.)

HOTELS
酒店

HOTELS IN ORDER OF COMFORT
酒店 — 以舒適程度分類

City Garden
城市花園

You'll find the City Garden in a largely residential area, a short walk from Fortress Hill MTR. The bedrooms would not necessarily win any design awards but they are fair in both size and price. The Garden Café offers an extensive international buffet; Satay Inn on the basement level provides Asian specialities; and Yuè serves authentic Cantonese dishes.

城市花園酒店座落於寧靜的住宅區內，與炮台山港鐵站只有咫尺，交通網絡非常便利。除了佔盡港島區的優越地勢外，客房空間充裕且收費合理；附屬的綠茵閣餐廳提供豐富的午、晚市自助環球美食，開設在一樓的「粵」中菜廳則提供傳統廣東佳餚。

TEL. 2887 2888
FAX. 28871111
9 City Garden Road, North Point
北角城市花園道 9號
www.citygarden.com.hk

RECOMMENDED RESTAURANTS 餐廳推薦
Yuè 粵 ❀ ✗✗

♦ = $ 880-2,850
♦♦ = $ 880-2,850
Suites 套房 = $1,500-5,800
☕ = $ 178

Rooms 客房　598
Suites 套房　15

Conrad
港麗

  ♿ ☺ **P** ≠ 🏊 🏊 🕶

Sitting above the Pacific Place complex is the Conrad, deftly mixing the traditional with the modern. The vast oval lobby showcases Chinese vases and bronze sculptures. Bedrooms are between the 40th and 61st floors, ensuring sweeping views; suites are particularly spacious and have elegant marble bathrooms. An outdoor swimming pool offers an equally dramatic panorama.

酒店位處集購物娛樂於一身的太古廣場之上。寬闊的橢圓形大堂擺放着中式花瓶及銅像，設計融合了傳統和現代元素，優雅而壯麗；寢室設在40至61樓之間，坐擁遼闊美景，而套房則特別寬敞，設有雲石浴室。室外游泳池讓你飽覽香港全景。

TEL. 2521 3838
FAX. 2521 3888
Pacific Place, 88 Queensway,
Admiralty
金鐘道 88號太古廣場
327-333號舖
www.conradhotels.com

☻ = $ 5,300
☻☻ = $ 5,400
Suites 套房 = $7,700-41,000
⚀ = $ 280

Rooms 客房　467
Suites 套房　46

RECOMMENDED RESTAURANTS 餐廳推薦
Golden Leaf 金葉庭　❉　𝓝𝓝𝓝

Crowne Plaza
皇冠假日

　　　　　　&# < &# ⌐ ⌐

Upper level bedrooms at this modern, corporate-minded hotel have the best outlooks, which include views of the Happy Valley racetrack on the south side. All of the bedrooms are decently sized and come with glass-walled bathrooms and impressive extras such as a wide choice of pillows. On the top floor you'll find Club@28: a chic bar with a terrace.

這家精心設計的時尚酒店，高層客房坐擁最美麗的港島景觀，南邊客房可飽覽跑馬地馬場全景。所有房間都寬敞舒適，浴室牆壁以玻璃砌成，擴闊了視覺上的空間，設施應有盡有，包括不同款色的枕頭。酒店頂層有為時尚人士而設的Club@28 酒吧，還有小型泳池和健身室。

TEL. 3980 3980
FAX. 3980 3900
8 Leighton Road, Causeway Bay
銅鑼灣禮頓道 8號
www.cphongkong.com

♂ = $ 2,300-2,800
♂♂ = $2,300-2,800
Suites 套房 = $ 5,000
☕ = $ 210

Rooms 客房　253
Suites 套房　10

Crowne Plaza Kowloon East
九龍東皇冠假日

A comfortable, well-equipped hotel in a busy commercial district with good transport links. It boasts one of the largest ballrooms around and dining options include a buffet, a Chinese restaurant and an Italian on the roof-top, along with a bar with great views. The contemporary bedrooms are warm and stylish and come with glass-walled bathrooms and a host of extras.

酒店由著名酒店集團管理，座落於將軍澳鐵路站上蓋，交通便捷。客房設計時尚，色調柔和、簡單的線條和善用空間的設計，平實卻不失優雅。大型多用途宴會廳和會議設施是其一大特色。綠草如茵的露天花園可作婚禮場地。酒店頂層的露天酒吧是一個能讓人放鬆心情的好去處。

TEL. 3983 0388
FAX. 3983 0503
3 Tong Tak Street, Tseung Kwan O
將軍澳唐德街 3號
www.crowneplaza.cn

RECOMMENDED RESTAURANTS 餐廳推薦
Tze Yuet Heen 紫粵軒 ✕✕

👤 = $ 1,700-8,100
👥 = $ 1,700-8,100
Suites 套房 = $ 9,100-10,100
🍴 = $ 198

Rooms 客房　354
Suites 套房　5

East
東隅

East is a modern business hotel designed for those who, like the hotel staff, can wear a pair of Converse with their suit. It has an uncluttered lobby, a bright, open plan restaurant serving international cuisine, and a great rooftop terrace bar named 'Sugar', as this was once a sugar factory. Bedrooms are minimalist but well-kept; corner rooms are especially light.

標榜為品味商務酒店。整潔的大堂、時尚的酒吧、提供國際美食的餐廳，加上可觀看迷人維港景色的天台酒吧「Sugar」—— 名字靈感源自酒店前身的糖廠，絕對切合你的需要。客房佈置簡約優雅，以大量玻璃與木材塑造出溫暖感覺與品味。位處轉角的客房景觀尤佳。

TEL. 3968 3968
FAX. 3968 3988
29 Taikoo Shing Road, Island East
港島東太古城道 29 號
327-333 號舖
www.east-hongkong.com

☺ = $ 1,700-3,750
☺☺ = $ 1,800-3,750
Suites 套房 = $3,000-6,200
◻ = $185

Rooms 客房　339
Suites 套房　6

Four Seasons
四季

Four Seasons hotel not only offers some of the most spacious accommodation in Hong Kong but the bedrooms, which have wall-to-wall windows, also feature an impressive array of extras. Choose between a Western style room and one with a more Asian feel; all have large and luxurious bathrooms. The hotel also boasts two bars, two swimming pools and two world class restaurants.

四季酒店與維港毗鄰，景色壯麗，提供香港最寬敞時尚的客房。客房佈置分為現代風格和東方情調兩種，且設有大型豪華浴室。「Blue Bar」專為享受雞尾酒和現場音樂演奏而設。水療設施令人印象難忘，更設有兩個溫度不同的泳池。舒適的環境與高質素服務兩者俱備。

TEL. 3196 8888
FAX. 3196 8899
8 Finance Street, Central
中環金融街 8號
www.fourseasons.com/hongkong

RECOMMENDED RESTAURANTS 餐廳推薦
Caprice ✿✿ ✗✗✗✗
Lung King Heen 龍景軒 ✿✿✿ ✗✗✗✗

👤 = $ 4,900-8,100
👥 = $4,900-8,100
Suites 套房 = $9,800-68,000
☕ = $280

Rooms 客房 339
Suites 套房 54

Gold Coast
黃金海岸

Travel 20 or so minutes from the city centre and you could find yourself relaxing in a hotel on the shoreline surrounded by 10 acres of landscaped garden. Next to the Marina and Yacht Club, the hotel offers extensive recreational facilities and, while the bedrooms are not particularly modern, they are bright, decently proportioned and offer pleasant sea views.

黃金海岸座落於海岸邊，毗鄰泳灘及遊艇會，有多項戶外康樂設施及面積甚廣的園林，與繁囂的市中心有一段距離，是一間理想渡假酒店。客房裝潢稱不上豪華新穎，卻寬敞明亮，且能欣賞怡人海景，部分房間附設露台。酒店的餐飲設施完善，花園旁的「粵」提供美味廣東菜。

TEL. 2452 8888
FAX. 2440 7368
1 Castle Peak Road, Gold Coast
黃金海岸青山公路 1 號
www.goldcoasthotel.com.hk

RECOMMENDED RESTAURANTS 餐廳推薦
Yuè 粵 ✗✗

♦ =	$ 2,400-3,600
♦♦ =	$ 2,400-3,600
Suites 套房 =	$ 5,000-18,000
☐ =	$ 218
Rooms 客房	444
Suites 套房	9

Grand Hyatt
君悅

The hotel, with its striking lobby, has been a fixture here in Wan Chai since 1998 and is perfectly located for the Convention and Exhibition Centre. Most of the bedrooms have recently been refurbished and are now more contemporary. The hotel offers impressive views, a large outdoor pool, and a wide selection of restaurants along with a new champagne bar.

酒店鄰近香港會議展覽中心，維港兩岸景色盡收於眼底。富麗堂皇的大堂早於1998年酒店開業時便已落成，全面修葺後的客房裝潢更時尚。酒店設有多家餐館分別提供中外菜式，還附設了大型室外泳池。

TEL. 2588 1234
FAX. 2802 0677
1 Harbour Road, Wan Chai
灣仔港灣道 1 號
www.hongkong.grand.hyatt.com

RECOMMENDED RESTAURANTS 餐廳推薦
Grand Hyatt Steakhouse ХХ
Grissini ХХХ
One Harbour Road 港灣壹號 ХХХ

🚹 = $5,100-6,900
🚹🚹 = $5,100-6,900
Suites 套房 = $8,500-55,000
☕ = $298

Rooms 客房 536
Suites 套房 13

Harbour Grand Kowloon
九龍海逸君綽

This shimmering glass structure is right on the waterfront and offers superb views across Victoria Harbour. It boasts a spectacularly grand lobby with an impressive white marble staircase and, although the bedrooms are bright, comfortable and well-equipped, they are sober by comparison to other areas. Do visit the dramatic rooftop pool with its glass walls.

這座位於紅磡海濱、閃閃發亮的玻璃建築物與維港相毗鄰，金碧輝煌的大堂設有白色雲石階梯。房間光潔舒適，設備齊全，相比酒店內其他設施或有點樸實。住客可於天台上的玻璃幕牆泳池內盡情暢泳及享用頂樓健身中心設施及蒸氣浴。

TEL. 2621 3188
FAX. 2621 3311
20 Tak Fung Street, Whampoa Garden,
Hung Hom
紅磡黃埔花園德豐街 20號
www.harbourgrand.com/kowloon

👤 = $ 2,900-3,700
👥 = $3,100-5,800
Suites 套房 = $6,800-35,000
☕ = $218

Rooms 客房　506
Suites 套房　48

Harbour Plaza 8 Degrees
8度海逸

An eight degree incline is this tall and contemporary hotel's unique selling point, from the lobby ceiling and walls to the glasses in the restaurant. Bedrooms may be quite compact but they are thoughtfully laid out and come in warm hues; the higher the floor, the brighter the room. The hotel should benefit from the huge development project that's upgrading this area.

這家酒店的最大特色是，從大堂天花到牆身以至餐廳玻璃都傾斜了八度。以暖色系裝潢的睡房，面積雖然不算寬敞，但絕對經過精心佈置。層數愈高，房間愈光亮開揚。泳池雖然四面被牆圍繞，但環境依然清幽宜人。

TEL. 2126 1988
FAX. 2126 1900
199 Kowloon City Road, To Kwa Wan
土瓜灣九龍城道 199號
www.harbour-plaza.com/hp8d

👤 = $ 2,200-3,400
👥 = $ 2,200-3,400
Suites 套房 = $ 4,000-5,000
☕ = $ 145

Rooms 客房　678
Suites 套房　24

Harbour Plaza North Point
北角海逸

Those doing business in North Point or Quarry Bay will find this hotel a useful address. It's spread over 32 floors and everything feels contemporary, right from the moment you enter the lobby with its unusual water feature. Bedrooms are a fair size and well soundproofed. There are also 180 serviced suites available for long-stay clients (a minimum of one month).

樓高32層的北角海逸酒店地點便利,對在北角或鰂魚涌洽談商務的人士來說,是短暫停留的好住處。大堂水池的設計盡顯時尚氣派。客房寬敞而寧靜:大部分房間只有淋浴設備,如需泡浴,須於訂房時提出。酒店另設有180間為長期住客而設的服務式套房,租期最短為一個月。

TEL. 2187 8888
FAX. 2187 8899
665 King's Road, North Point
北角英皇道665號
www.harbour-plaza.com

 = $ 2,150-3,500
 = $2,150-3,500
Suites 套房 = $ 3,950-6,950
 = $ 148

Rooms 客房 489

Hyatt Regency Sha Tin
沙田凱悅

Just a minute's walk from University Station is this 26 floor hotel, whose large, well-equipped bedrooms have either harbour or mountain views. It makes clever use of neutral colours and natural materials like stone and wood to create a soothing ambience. It's business-orientated during the week; the impressive leisure facilities appeal to families at weekends.

沙田凱悅於2009年開幕,從港鐵大學站前往僅需步行兩分鐘。酒店設計充滿時代感,巧妙運用中性色彩及天然物料如石材及木材製造出柔和融洽的感覺。酒店平日以接待商務旅客為主,到週末則以出色的休閒設施吸引家庭顧客。

TEL. 3723 1234
FAX. 3723 1235
18 Chak Cheung Street, University, Sha Tin
沙田大學站澤祥街18號
www.hongkong.shatin.hyatt.com

RECOMMENDED RESTAURANTS 餐廳推薦
Sha Tin 18 沙田18 ✗✗

👤 = $ 1,200-3,900
👥 = $1,200-3,900
Suites 套房 = $ 4,500-21,300
☕ = $ 218

Rooms 客房 434
Suites 套房 133

329

Hyatt Regency Tsim Sha Tsui
尖沙咀凱悅

Occupying floors 3-24 of the impressive K11 skyscraper means that bedrooms here at the Hyatt Regency benefit from impressive views of the city or harbour. The rooms are decorated in a crisp, modern style; anyone choosing the Regency Club level has access to a private lounge. There are dining options galore and an impressive selection of whiskies in the Chin Chin Bar.

尖沙咀凱悅佔據K11摩天大樓的3至24層，並與K11購物藝術館相連，酒店房間能看到城市的繁華景色，或是醉人的維港景致。房間風格清新時尚，選擇嘉賓軒樓層的住客更可享受專用酒廊服務。酒店提供多種餐飲選擇，「請請吧」內的威士忌種類之多更是令人歎為觀止。

TEL. 2311 1234
FAX. 3721 1235
18 Hanoi Road, Tsim Sha Tsui
尖沙咀河內道18號
www.hongkong.tsimshatsui.hyatt.com

RECOMMENDED RESTAURANTS 餐廳推薦
Hugo's 希戈 ✗✗✗

🛉 = $2,500
🛉🛉 = $4,200
Suites 套房 = $4,200-22,000
☕ = $228

Rooms 客房　348
Suites 套房　33

Icon
唯港薈

♿ ≼ ⌂ ⚑ 🏊 ♨ Spa 👟

Rocco Yim, Sir Terence Conran and William Lim were among the celebrated designers brought together to create this chic hotel, which is owned and run by the Hong Kong Polytechnic University. Its style credentials are clear, from the works by local artists to the modern staircase and 'vertical garden'. Market is a buffet restaurant; formal dining in Above and Beyond.

著名設計師嚴迅奇、泰倫斯・康藍爵士和林偉而等攜手打造出這間由香港理工大學營運、最新最潮的酒店。它的設計風格鮮明,可欣賞本地藝術家的精彩作品,亦有令人驚歎的現代化樓梯和垂直花園。「The Market」是廣受歡迎的自助餐廳,「天外天」則供應傳統粵菜。

TEL. 3400 1000
FAX. 3400 1001
17 Science Museum Road,
East Tsim Sha Tsui
尖東科學館道 17號
www.hotel-icon.com

RECOMMENDED RESTAURANTS 餐廳推薦
Above & Beyond 天外天 ✗✗✗

🧍 = $ 2,400-4,100
🧍🧍 = $ 2,400-4,100
Suites 套房 = $ 3,500-6,500
☕ = $ 218

Rooms 客房　236
Suites 套房　26

Indigo NEW
英迪格

Bordering Tai Yuen Street and its market, so ideally placed for discovering old Hong Kong, Indigo is also a good choice for those who've come to shop – there's even a shopping bag placed in every room! For others, there's always the rooftop bar and infinity pool. The bedrooms come with floor-to-ceiling windows and boast some cute design touches.

這幢外觀獨特的建築物座落於灣仔商業區及住宅區交界，不光擁有完善的交通網絡，更與有濃厚地區色彩的市集毗鄰，讓你深入了解本區生活脈搏。全部房間設有落地玻璃窗，傢俱擺設均經過精心設計，設施亦十分齊全，文具、購物袋一應俱全。天台玻璃底泳池，前臨山巒，感覺開揚，是放鬆身心的好地方。

TEL. 3926 3888
FAX. 3926 3926
246 Queen's Road East, Wan Chai
灣仔皇后大道東 246號
www.hotelindigo.com/hongkong

= $ 1,800-2,800
= $1,800-2,800
Suites 套房 = $ 3,200-5,800
= $ 180

Rooms 客房　132
Suites 套房　6

Intercontinental
洲際

It may be unremarkable from the outside, but this hotel is decidedly impressive once you're in the lobby with its magnificent harbour views. All bedrooms are well-equipped, with spacious marble bathrooms. Relax in either the swimming pool or spa pool, or enjoy a massage in an outside cabana. Options for dining are excellent (see separate entries) and service is exemplary.

踏入富麗堂皇的酒店大堂,望着一流海景,絕對令你印象深刻。客房非常寬敞,淺色調的設計予人寧靜感覺,更設有寬闊的雲石浴室。你可以在優雅的游泳池或水療池鬆弛身心;戶外的池邊小室內有按摩服務。酒店內的餐飲服務非常出色,服務水準一流。

TEL. 2721 1211
FAX. 2739 4546
18 Salisbury Road, Tsim Sha Tsui
尖沙咀梳士巴利道 18號
327-333號舖
www.intercontinental.com

♦ = $7,000
♦♦ = $10,500
Suites 套房 = $12,500-98,000
⊊ = $320

Rooms 客房 478
Suites 套房 25

RECOMMENDED RESTAURANTS 餐廳推薦
Nobu ✗✗
Spoon by Alain Ducasse ❀ ✗✗✗
The Steak House Wine bar + grill ❀ ✗✗
Yan Toh Heen 欣圖軒 ❀❀ ✗✗✗

Intercontinental Grand Stanford
海景嘉福

After a comprehensive renovation programme, this 18-storey waterfront hotel, which opened back in 1981, is looking much more contemporary in style. The service is good and the bedrooms are a decent size – just be sure to ask for one with a harbour view. There are plenty of dining options and the heated outdoor swimming pool on the roof is nicely secluded.

這幢龐大的臨海建築物樓高18層，建於1981年並剛完成全面翻新工程。翻新後的寢室雅致時尚，因此訂房時謹記要選擇一間有海景並且經過翻新的房間。酒店頂層設有健身室及戶外溫水泳池。酒店內有數間食店供住客選擇。

TEL. 2721 5161
FAX. 2732 2233
70 Mody Road, East Tsim Sha Tsui
尖東麼地道70號
327-333號舖
www.hongkong.intercontinental.com

👤 = $ 1,800-4,500
👥 = $1,800-4,500
Suites 套房 = $4,800-15,000
☕ = $248

Rooms 客房　556
Suites 套房　23

Island Shangri-La
港島香格里拉

A vast, intricate Chinese silk painting towers over the glamorous atrium and rises up all of 16 storeys; more sparkle is provided by the dazzling array of chandeliers placed around the hotel. The bedrooms are thoughtfully laid out and comfortable; those rooms on the Horizon Club (52nd to 55th floor) are especially sumptuous and have access to a super rooftop terrace.

延伸至16樓的世上最大幅的中國絲綢畫，筆工細膩、構圖錯綜複雜，散發着迷人魅力，加上金光閃爍的吊燈，營造出五光十色的中庭，令人目眩神馳。樓上是華麗典雅的客房，尤以52至55樓豪華閣樓層的房間為甚，此樓層的住客可使用專屬會客廳和美不勝收的天台庭園。

TEL. 2877 3838
FAX. 2521 8742
Pacific Place, Supreme Court Road,
Admiralty
中區法院道太古廣場
www.shangri-la.com

RECOMMENDED RESTAURANTS 餐廳推薦
Lobster Bar and Grill 龍蝦吧 ХХ
Petrus 珀翠 ХХХХХ
Summer Palace 夏宮 ❀❀ ХХХ

♦ = $ 4,600-6,000
♦♦ = $4,950-6,350
Suites 套房 = $10,400-31,600
☕ = $298

Rooms 客房 531
Suites 套房 34

JW Marriott
萬豪

Boasting 602 rooms spread over 35 storeys, this business hotel also offers a number of executive floors which have their own discreet lounge and meeting rooms. The bedrooms are functional but up-to-date and there's a pleasant outdoor pool and a well-equipped fitness centre. Dining options include Cantonese and seafood, along with a wine bar and tea room.

以商務住客為主的萬豪酒店樓高三十五層，客房數量達602間。位於頂樓的一列行政套房，附有素雅的休息室和會議室。房間設計富現代感且十分實用。戶外游泳池環境清幽、健身中心設備齊全，還網羅了各地餐飲美食，廣東菜、海鮮、酒吧、茶室等不同類別的餐室任君選擇。

TEL. 2810 8366
FAX. 2845 0737
Pacific Place, 88 Queensway, Admiralty
金鐘道 88號太古廣場
www.jwmarriotthongkong.com

♟ = $ 3,800-6,100
♟♟ = $3,800-6,400
Suites 套房 = $5,800-40,000
☕ = $275

Rooms 客房 577
Suites 套房 25

Kowloon Shangri-La
九龍香格里拉

The first thing to strike you will be the size and grandeur of the lobby, with its marble, sparkling chandeliers and tiered water fountain – it is certainly one of the most impressive aspects of this business-orientated hotel. The enthusiastic staff are another great strength. The bedrooms are larger than many of its competitors and come with a subtle Asian theme.

不僅是氣派宏偉的雲石酒店大堂，還是閃爍的吊燈與三層噴泉水池，都令你對這家以商務為主的酒店留下極深刻印象。全部客房都經過重新粉飾，跟其他同級酒店比較更見寬敞，服務水準更是無庸置疑。最佳的客房採用亞洲風情為主題作裝潢。

TEL. 2721 2111
FAX. 2723 8686
64 Mody Road, East Tsim Sha Tsui
尖東麼地道 64 號
www.shangri-la.com

RECOMMENDED RESTAURANTS 餐廳推薦
Shang Palace 香宮 ❀❀ ✕✕✕✕

♦ = $2,400
♦♦ = $3,600
Suites 套房 = $4,380-22,480
☕ = $255

Rooms 客房　645
Suites 套房　43

Lan Kwai Fong
蘭桂坊

A hotel which feels part of the local area and mixes Chinese and contemporary furniture, neutral tones and dark wood veneers to create a relaxing environment. Try to secure one of the deluxe corner bedrooms or a suite with a balcony if you want more space; those higher than the 21st floor have the harbour views. Celebrity Cuisine offers accomplished Cantonese food.

融合了中國傳統與現代品味的傢俱，中性色調及深色木間隔，營造出舒適環境。如果你需要更寬敞的空間，建議預訂轉角位置的豪華客房或附設露台的套房。21樓以上的房間可飽覽維港景色。客人可借用房間內的流動電話，方便在外與朋友聯絡。

TEL. 3650 0000
FAX. 3650 0088
3 Kau U Fong, Central
中環九如坊 3號
www.lankwaifonghotel.com.hk

RECOMMENDED RESTAURANTS 餐廳推薦
Celebrity Cuisine 名人坊 ✿✿ ✗✗

👤 = $ 1,200-4,000
👥 = $ 1,200-4,000
Suites 套房 = $ 3,000-7,000
☕ = $ 165

Rooms 客房   157
Suites 套房   5

Langham Place
朗豪

Chinese modern art is showcased at this 42-storey glass tower – there are over 1,500 paintings, sculptures and installations spread around the hotel, which is located in a vibrant and bustling neighbourhood. Bedrooms come in a sober yet contemporary style, there's a pool on the roof and guests can choose from a wide selection of restaurants and bars.

酒店座落於行人如鯽的旺角中心地帶，琉璃塔般的大樓高42層，不僅有科技發燒友夢寐以求的電子產品，還有超過1,500 幅畫作、雕塑與裝置藝術品分佈於整棟大樓內，是一個中國現代美術展覽館。客房的設計含蓄而時髦，天台設有游泳池，並有多間餐廳供客人選擇。

TEL. 3552 3388
FAX. 3552 3322
555 Shanghai Street, Mong Kok
旺角上海街555號
www.hongkong.langhamplacehotels.com

RECOMMENDED RESTAURANTS 餐廳推薦
Ming Court 明閣 ❀ ☽☽☽

🛉 = $ 2,100-3,700
🛉🛉 = $2,100-3,700
Suites 套房 = $3,300-11,000
☕ = $218

Rooms 客房　625
Suites 套房　40

Lanson Place

             ♿ ↲ 🛌 🛏

This discreet and stylish boutique hotel comes with an air of calm exclusivity and an attractive European-influenced aesthetic. The cool lounge and bar allows the hotel to feel more intimate than the number of bedrooms would suggest. Those rooms come with small kitchenettes and have a clean and bright feel. The hotel is ideally located for those going to HK stadium.

擁有歐洲風格的典雅外觀，Lanson Place能稱為一間時尚精品酒店。古典與現代設計交織出酒店的獨特氣派，室內的藝術作品，營造溫暖寧靜的感覺。客房雅致明亮，設有大型窗戶，多家客房能眺望香港大球場。休閒舒適的休息室與酒吧也是入住期間值得蹓躂的地方。

TEL. 3477 6888
FAX. 3477 6999
133 Leighton Road, Causeway Bay
銅鑼灣禮頓道133號
www.lansonplace.com

🧍 = $ 1,800-4,000
🧍🧍 = $ 1,800-4,000
Suites 套房 = $ 4,800-10,500
☕ = $ 220

Rooms 客房　188
Suites 套房　6

LKF
蘭桂坊

LKF styles itself in the 'boutique' class and the wining and dining happens on the higher floors: Slash, on the 29th, is an intimate lounge bar and leads up to their restaurant and roof terrace. Contemporary bedrooms have been thoughtfully designed and come with espresso machines to give you a high, and comfortable beds with goose down pillows to bring you back down.

LKF屬於精品級酒店之列。酒店的樞紐安置在較高樓層：29樓的「Slash」是舒適時尚的酒廊；沿級而上便是酒店附設的餐廳及屋頂平台，客人可在此遠眺迷人景色。寬敞及時尚的客房設有蒸餾咖啡機，你可以邊呷着咖啡，邊靠着睡床上的鵝絨枕頭，享受一刻悠閒與安寧。

TEL. 3518 9688
FAX. 3518 9699
33 Wyndham Street, Lan Kwai Fong, Central
中環蘭桂坊雲咸街33號
www.hotel-LKF.com.hk

= $8,000-15,000
= $8,000-15,000
Suites 套房 = $18,000
= $200

Rooms 客房 86
Suites 套房 9

HONG KONG 香港

Mandarin Oriental
文華東方

Having celebrated its 50th birthday in 2013, this iconic hotel continues to update itself while remaining true to its heritage. Bedrooms may not be the largest but are charmingly decorated and are split between Tai Pan-style (woods and browns) and brighter Veranda-style. The spa is a spiritual haven and the dining and bar options are many and varied.

開業超過五十年，營運者在保留其優良傳統之餘，還致力提升其質素。和其他酒店相比，其客房並非最大，但無論是典雅的大班風格或陽台房間的裝潢均非常精緻，附設的水療設施令你如置身伊甸園；酒店還為客人提供多元化餐飲選擇。

TEL. 2522 0111
FAX. 2810 6190
5 Connaught Road, Central
中環干諾道中 5號
www.mandarinoriental.com/hongkong

RECOMMENDED RESTAURANTS 餐廳推薦
Mandarin Grill + Bar 文華扒房 + 酒吧 ❀ ✗✗✗✗
Man Wah 文華廳 ❀ ✗✗✗
Pierre ❀❀ ✗✗✗✗

♦ = $ 5,300-7,400
♦♦ = $5,300-7,400
Suites 套房 = $8,000-65,000
☐ = $288

Rooms 客房 430
Suites 套房 71

Metropark (Causeway Bay)
銅鑼灣維景

This 31-storey tower near Victoria is a popular choice for business travellers. Its bedrooms are not that large so it's worth booking one of the executive rooms, many of which have harbour views. The rooftop swimming pool is small but appealing and the views from the fitness centre help you deal with the pain of exercise. Café du Parc offers all-day buffet dining.

酒店大樓樓高三十一層，鄰近維多利亞公園，為商務旅客提供舒適環境及娛樂設施。這兒大部分房間的面積較小，因此選擇面積較大的行政套房絕對物有所值，而大部分房間可看到無敵海景。小型天台游泳池配備水底音樂，設計別出心裁。附設的「繽紛維苑餐廳」全日均有自助餐供應。

TEL. 2600 1000
FAX. 2600 1111
148 Tung Lo Wan Road, Causeway Bay
銅鑼灣道 148號
www.metroparkhotel.com

♦ = $ 2,500-5,900
♦♦ = $2,500-5,900
Suites 套房 = $ 6,900
☕ = $ 130

Rooms 客房 243
Suites 套房 23

HONG KONG 香港

New World Millennium
千禧新世界

The former Nikko hotel is now run by a different management company but little else has changed here. The hotel is known for its comprehensive banqueting and conference rooms and its impressive number of restaurants providing a wide range of different cuisines. The smart bedrooms come with up-to-the-minute comforts. The harbour-front location adds to the appeal.

日航酒店易名後，酒店完善的宴會及會議設施仍然保留，四間提供不同菜式的餐廳仍然為賓客提供多種選擇，令他們樂在其中；優越的海濱地段及設計現代化的智能客房，為顧客帶來舒適享受，上述種種條件均足以令它躋身國際級酒店之列。

TEL. 2739 1111
FAX. 2311 3122
72 Mody Road, East Tsim Sha Tsui
尖東麼地道72號
www.hotelnikko.com.hk

👤 = $ 2,700-3,700
👥 = $2,700-3,700
Suites 套房 = $ 8,500-16,500
☕ = $ 270

Rooms 客房 445
Suites 套房 18

Ozo Wesley NEW
遨舍衛蘭軒

                                          🦽 🚭 🏋️

You'll find Ozo Wesley sitting pretty between Wan Chai and Admiralty so it's ideally placed whether you're in town for business or just in the mood for shopping and dining. All of the guest rooms are crisply decorated in a bright, fresh and contemporary style and the effective soundproofing ensures a decent night's sleep however busy it is outside.

位於金鐘與灣仔交界，距金鐘的商業金融區只有數分鐘路程，附近的小街道滿佈食店，位置便利，適合商業旅客。大堂設計具時代感。251間客房，均以素色系配搭簡單時尚裝潢，舒適的感覺令你身心放鬆。全部房間都設有大玻璃窗和隔音設備，讓你既能欣賞灣仔的繁華景象又能享受片刻寧靜。

TEL. 2292 3000
FAX. 2292 3001
22 Hennessy Road, Wan Chai
灣仔軒尼詩道 22號
www.ozohotels.com

🧍 = $ 1,200-4,800
🧍🧍 = $ 1,200-4,800
☕ = $ 145

Rooms 客房　235

RECOMMENDED RESTAURANTS 餐廳推薦
Zaan 饌 ✕✕

Panorama
麗景

It will come as no great surprise to learn that the views from this well located hotel are rather impressive. The 324 bedrooms are divided into various categories that include Silver, Gold, Club Harbour and Suites. All benefit from having large windows but book a corner suite and you can even enjoy the terrific harbour vista from the bathtub!

麗景共有324間客房，按最新穎的意念，設計出三種房間類型：銀賓客房、黃金客房和尊貴海景客房。層數愈高，景觀愈發動人心弦。酒店最佳的客房位於角位，客人可以一邊享受泡浴，一邊欣賞迷人的維港美景。設於38樓的「AVA餐廳」佈置時尚，各式各樣的歐陸佳餚任君品嘗。

TEL. 3550 0388
FAX. 3550 0288
8A Hart Avenue, Tsim Sha Tsui
尖沙咀赫德道 8A號
www.hotelpanorama.com.hk

♦ = $ 3,000-6,000
♦♦ = $3,000-6,000
Suites 套房 = $ 10,000-12,000
☕ = $ 198

Rooms 客房 312
Suites 套房 12

Royal Plaza
帝京

A comprehensive renovation has left the Royal Plaza looking stylish and contemporary. A new bar was created which provides striking views of Lion Rock, and the bedrooms, which were already a good size, now come with plenty of mod cons. The hotel is ideally placed in the heart of Kowloon and is surrounded by many of Hong Kong's traditional markets.

全新裝修的帝京酒店，時尚而富格調。新開設的「Lion Rock酒吧」，讓你飽覽獅子山美景。原本已稱得上寬敞的客房內，增設了不少現代化設備。酒店座落於繁盛的九龍中心位置，附近是最具本土氣息的街道市集。

TEL. 2928 8822
FAX. 2606 0088
193 Prince Edward Road West,
Mong Kok
旺角太子道西 193號
www.royalplaza.com.hk

👤 = $ 3,000-4,600
👥 = $ 3,400-5,200
Suites 套房 = $ 6,600-7,600
☕ = $ 148

Rooms 客房 659
Suites 套房 34

HONG KONG 香港

Sheraton
喜來登

One of Hong Kong's biggest hotels is a short walk from the Star Ferry Pier so you can expect some great views of Victoria Harbour. These can be best appreciated from the health club's rooftop pool, over a plate of oysters in the wine bar, or from a swish executive room on the 16th or 17th floor. The hotel also has a cigar room, a wine shop and an international café.

位於九龍半島的喜來登是香港最大的酒店之一，只需短短的步行距離便到達天星碼頭。客人可盡覽維多利亞港景色，最佳位置包括健身俱樂部的天台游泳池、16樓及17樓的高級面海行政套房，在「蠔酒吧」吃蠔時亦可欣賞美景。較為樸實但非常舒適的有「雪茄廊」、「酒舖」和「國際咖啡廳」。

TEL. 2369 1111
FAX. 2739 8707
20 Nathan Road, Tsim Sha Tsui
尖沙咀彌敦道 20號
www.sheraton.com/hongkong

RECOMMENDED RESTAURANTS 餐廳推薦
Celestial Court 天寶閣 ✗✗✗

👤 = $ 2,000
👥 = $ 4,000
Suites 套房 = $3,500-13,500
☕ = $ 245

Rooms 客房　691
Suites 套房　91

The Fleming
芬名

An attractive, contemporary lobby draws you into this centrally located Wan Chai hotel. Bedrooms offer decent dimensions for such an urban environment, with standard rooms measuring 20 square metres. The hotel also acknowledges its varied clientele by offering 'Her Space' or 'His Space' rooms with differing amenities. The diminutive Cubix serves international cuisine.

酒店位於灣仔心臟地帶，充滿時尚氣息的大堂極具吸引力。其標準客房面積達20平方米，在擁擠的市區環境中，為你提供充裕的私人空間。為照顧不同客人需要，店內設有「男士」及「女士」專用客房，備有各具特色的用品。精巧的餐廳「Cubix」供應多國美食。

TEL. 3607 2288
FAX. 3607 2299
41 Fleming Road, Wan Chai
灣仔菲林明道 41號
www.thefleming.com

♦ = $ 1,100-4,280
♦♦ = $1,100-4,280
☕ = $ 158

Rooms 客房 66

The Landmark Mandarin Oriental
置地文華東方

From the personal airport pick-up to the endless spa choices, this is the hotel for those after a little pampering. Not only are the comfortable, smartly designed bedrooms big on luxury and size but they also come with stylish bathrooms attached; these feature either sunken or circular baths. MO is the cool ground floor bar for all-day dining or night time cocktails.

從專人機場接送服務到設備完善的水療設備，置地文華東方讓你盡享尊貴服務。令人讚歎的不光是設計型格獨特、面積達450至600呎的寬敞客房，還有房內豪華時尚的浴室設備，包括巨型下沈式或圓形浴缸。位於地下的「MO Bar」是解決一日三餐和品嘗雞尾酒的好去處。

TEL. 2132 0188
FAX. 2132 0199
15 Queen's Road, Central
中環皇后大道中 15號
www.mandarinoriental.com/landmark

RECOMMENDED RESTAURANTS 餐廳推薦
Amber ✿✿ ✗✗✗✗

👤 = $ 5,600-8,000
👥 = $ 5,600-8,000
Suites 套房 = $ 16,800
☕ = $ 288

Rooms 客房 100
Suites 套房 13

The Langham
朗廷

Once inside the hushed surroundings of this elegant hotel, the clamour of Peking Road feels like a distant memory. Its striking lobby, furnished in a classical European style, features some impressive contemporary art and sculptures. Bedrooms are quite traditional in style and comfortable. The charm of the hotel is underpinned by modern facilities and attentive service.

進入這棟優雅建築物，讓你立刻忘卻北京道熙來攘往的煩囂。大堂以傳統歐洲風格裝潢，配上當代藝術品及雕塑作點綴，奢華奪目。豪華客房融合了古典歐陸情調和當代中國風格兩種風味迥異的元素。迷人之處，盡見於其現代設施及細心服務。

TEL. 2375 1133
FAX. 2375 6611
8 Peking Road, Tsim Sha Tsui
尖沙咀北京道 8號
www.hongkong.langhamhotels.com

RECOMMENDED RESTAURANTS 餐廳推薦
T'ang Court 唐閣 ✿✿ XXXX
The Bostonian 美岸海鮮廳 XX

† = $4,100-5,400
†† = $4,100-5,400
Suites 套房 = $5,900-9,800
☕ = $238

Rooms 客房 464
Suites 套房 25

The Mercer
尚圜

Those who need the convenience of a Central location but also want a little space should consider The Mercer. The narrow 31 storey building just has 15 standard bedrooms but 40 one-bedroom suites. Ubiquitous beige tones add to the up-to-date feel and rooms come with large writing desks and a host of free extras which include the minibar and local phone calls.

如果你既愛中環的便利，又需要較多私人空間，尚圜酒店絕對適合你。建築外型修長，樓高31層，只有15間標準客房，卻有達40間單人睡房套間。統一的米白色調營造出時尚感覺，房間設有大型書桌和附送多項免費服務，包括免費本地電話服務和迷你酒吧。

TEL. 2922 9900
FAX. 2922 9920
29 Jervois Street, Sheung Wan
上環蘇杭街 29號
www.themercer.com.hk

RECOMMENDED RESTAURANTS 餐廳推薦
Sushi Shikon 志魂 ✿✿✿ 🍴

👤 = $ 1,980-4,000
👥 = $1,980-4,000
Suites 套房 = $ 3,000-6,000

Rooms 客房　15
Suites 套房　40

The Mira

♿ 🛎 🚗 🚭 🧖 🏔 🧖‍♀️ 🏊

Give every room an Arne Jacobsen 'Egg chair'; add a cool, urban aesthetic and all the hi-tech extras you'll ever need and you have The Mira – a stylish, vibrant and modern hotel. What the rooms may lack in size, they more than make up for in design and it's worth asking for one facing Kowloon Park. Bathrooms are equally impressive and suites even more spectacular.

型格、現代的設計，再加上高科技產品，你得到的就是The Mira－一家極為時尚、充滿活力的摩登酒店。房間面積略小，但出色的設計可彌補不足，浴室非常現代化；套房裝潢豪華。訂房時不妨要求面向九龍公園的客房。舒適豪華的水療設施值得一讚。

TEL. 2368 1111
FAX. 2369 1788
118 Nathan Road, Tsim Sha Tsui
尖沙咀彌敦道 118號
www.themirahotel.com

RECOMMENDED RESTAURANTS 餐廳推薦
Cuisine Cuisine at The Mira 國金軒　✗✗✗
Whisk　✗✗

🚶 = $3,600
🚶🚶 = $4,500
Suites 套房 = $7,000-48,000
☕ = $228

Rooms 客房　446
Suites 套房　46

The Peninsula
半島

2013 saw the grande dame of Hong Kong hotels celebrate her 85th birthday, just as the refurbishment of the bedrooms was completed – they now come with a contemporary elegance and clever touch-pad technology. The iconic lobby remains the place for afternoon tea; the spa boasts a Roman-style pool; and a host of dining choices range from the modern to the traditional.

酒店內部修葺已於2013年年初竣工，剛好趕及慶祝酒店開業85週年。經重新粉飾後的客房更時尚雅致，房內設備全部透過高科技觸控屏操作。作為酒店標誌的大堂保留原來樣式，供顧客享用下午茶；羅馬式泳池仍然是一貫的迷人；新派菜和傳統菜餐館一應俱全。

TEL. 2920 2888
FAX. 2722 4170
Salisbury Road, Tsim Sha Tsui
尖沙咀梳士巴利道
www.peninsula.com

RECOMMENDED RESTAURANTS 餐廳推薦
Chesa 瑞樵閣　XX
Felix　XX
Gaddi's 吉地士　XXXX
Spring Moon 嘉麟樓　XXX

♟ = $ 5,880-8,580
♟♟ = $5,880-8,580
Suites 套房 = $10,800-128,000
◸ = $310

Rooms 客房　243
Suites 套房　54

The Pottinger NEW
中環・石板街

     占 ⅄

Standing in the middle of Central, and on one of Hong Kong's oldest 'stone slab streets', is this elegant and stylish hotel. Its location is celebrated through its collection of iconic and historic photographs taken by award-winning artist Fan Ho. The 68 bedrooms are contemporary and graceful and boast all the amenities the modern traveller expects.

位於有過百年歷史的砵甸乍街(又名石板街)旁邊,故以此命名。斜斜的石板路見證了中環百多年來的故事,也為酒店增添了一分魅力。接待廳雖小卻流露着歐陸優雅格調,共有68間客房,面積適中、設備齊全。位處中環心臟地帶,無論往辦公、飲食、娛樂或乘搭交通工具都非常便利,是商務住宿的理想選擇。

TEL. 2308 3188
74 Queen's Road Central, Central
中環皇后大道中 74號
www.thepottinger.com

RECOMMENDED RESTAURANTS 餐廳推薦
Holytan Grill 葉里湛 ✗✗

� = $2,900-4,100
♟♟ = $2,900-4,100
Suites 套房 = $5,400-18,000

Rooms 客房　61
Suites 套房　7

The Ritz Carlton
麗思卡爾頓

The highest hotel in the world occupies the top 16 floors of Hong Kong's tallest building; to witness first-hand just how high this feels, head up to the cool Ozone bar on the 118th floor – it even comes with an outside terrace! Bedrooms are large and elegant and the suites are equipped with telescopes so guests can keep an eye on what's happening down on earth.

這家全球最高酒店佔據了香港最高建築物最頂的16層樓，部分人置身其中可能會感到暈眩。其位於118層的「Ozone 酒吧」設有戶外露台，而游泳池也設於海拔490米高處。酒店客房空間佳大、裝潢高雅，套房中還設有望遠鏡，讓住客居高臨下俯瞰香港景色。

TEL. 2263 2263
FAX. 2263 2260
International Commerce Centre,
1 Austin Road West, Tsim Sha Tsui
尖沙咀柯士甸道西 1 號環球貿易廣場
www.ritzcarlton.com/hongkong

♦ = $ 7,200-9,900
♦♦ = $ 7,200-9,900
Suites 套房 = $ 13,000-120,000
☕ = $288

Rooms 客房   262
Suites 套房   50

RECOMMENDED RESTAURANTS 餐廳推薦
Tin Lung Heen 天龍軒 ✿✿ 𝕏𝕏𝕏𝕏
Tosca ✿ 𝕏𝕏𝕏𝕏

356

The Royal Garden
帝苑

The Royal Garden is a hotel that seems to exude class. One of its most notable features is its 110 foot atrium – guestrooms are accessed through corridors which overlook it. Those bedrooms are decorated to a good standard and come with an impressive array of modern facilities. Guests also have an impressive number of restaurants from which to choose.

帝苑酒店是一間與別不同的酒店，110呎高以繁茂的枝葉裝潢的中庭更是其最大特色，不論住宿在哪一個樓層，沿走廊進入客房時都能俯視庭內景況。客房設計具水準，且附有大量現代化設備。酒店內還設有多家不同種類的餐館，中外菜式應有盡有。

TEL. 2721 5215
FAX. 2369 9976
69 Mody Road, East Tsim Sha Tsui
尖東麼地道69號
www.rghk.com.hk

♂ = $4,000-6,000
♂♂ = $4,000-6,000
Suites 套房 = $8,800-12,800
☕ = $288

Rooms 客房　372
Suites 套房　48

RECOMMENDED RESTAURANTS 餐廳推薦
Dong Lai Shun 東來順　✕✕
Le Soleil　✕✕

HONG KONG 香港

The Upper House
奕居

♿ ⟨ 🅿 ♿ ♿

This discreet and stylish hotel is on the wish-list of fashionistas everywhere. The clever use of art, sculpture and natural materials makes one feel one is in a private house, albeit one with a pervading sense of calm and luxury. Bedrooms are airy and uncluttered, with concealed hi-tech extras. The large bathrooms have great 'traveller's bags' and good views.

奕居早已成為潮流人士趨之若鶩的住宿熱點。這裏是一家經過精心設計，細緻豪華的時尚酒店。藝術品、雕塑和天然物料帶來非凡效果，瀰漫着平和氣息，營造出私人居所的感覺。房間開揚而秩序井然，隱藏着不少高科技用品。大型浴室提供高級沐浴用品，更可觀賞美妙景色。

TEL. 2918 1838
FAX. 3968 1200
Pacific Place, 88 Queensway,
Admiralty
金鐘道 88號太古廣場
www.upperhouse.com

RECOMMENDED RESTAURANTS 餐廳推薦
Café Gray Deluxe 海景軒 ✗✗✗

♦ = $ 4,500-6,000
♦♦ = $4,500-6,000
Suites 套房 = $12,000-17,000
☕ = $250

Rooms 客房 96
Suites 套房 21

Traders
盛貿

HONG KONG 香港

The bedrooms at Traders, which is part of the Shangri-La group and located in a largely residential area, are neat, contemporary and a fair size. Painted in neutral colours, they also offer a good range of facilities for business travellers who can unwind at the day's end in the rooftop pool. The name of the hotel was due to change as we went to print.

座落於港島西住宅區的盛貿酒店將於2014年年底易名。毗鄰市政大樓，令你易於掌握本地生活節奏。以自然色系作主調的客房裝潢時尚，空間寬敞且設備完善，是商務公幹人士的理想選擇。天台游泳池景觀賞心悅目，是放鬆身心的好去處。

TEL. 2974 1234
FAX. 2974 0333
508 Queen's Road West,
Western District
西環皇后大道西 508號
www.tradershotels.com

RECOMMENDED RESTAURANTS 餐廳推薦
Café Malacca 馬來一

♦ = $950-2,050
♦♦ = $950-2,050
Suites 套房 = $2,750-3,700
☕ = $168

Rooms 客房　278
Suites 套房　5

Vibrant Moments

Inspire your senses in this vibrant city
fuelled by lively, energetic festivities and
events throughout year !

TOUCHING MOMENTS
EXPERIENCE

 MACAU GOVERNMENT TOURIST OFFICE
www.macautourism.gov.mo

MACAU
澳門

RESTAURANTS
餐廳

STARRED RESTAURANTS
星級餐廳

Within this selection, we have highlighted a number of restaurants for their particularly good cooking. When awarding one, two or three Michelin Stars there are a number of factors we consider: the quality and compatibility of the ingredients, the technical skill and flair that goes into their preparation, the clarity and combination of flavours, the value for money and above all, the taste. Equally important is the ability to produce excellent cooking not once but time and time again. Our inspectors make as many visits as necessary, so that you can be sure of the quality and consistency.

A two or three star restaurant has to offer something very special that separates it from the rest. Three stars – our highest award – are given to the very best.

Cuisines in any style of restaurant and of any nationality are eligible for a star. The decoration, service and comfort levels have no bearing on the award.

在這系列的選擇裡，我們特意指出菜式上佳的餐廳。給予一、二或三粒米芝蓮星時，我們考慮到以下因素：材料的質素和配搭、烹調技巧和特色、氣味濃度和組合、價錢是否相宜及味道。同樣重要的是能夠持續提供美食。我們的評審員會因應需要而多次到訪，所以讀者可肯定食物品質和一致性。

二或三星餐廳必有獨特之處，比其他餐廳更出眾。最高評級－三星－只會給予最好的餐廳。

不論餐廳的風格如何，供應哪個國家的菜式，都可獲星級。餐廳陳設、服務及舒適程度亦不會影響評級。

Exceptional cuisine, worth a special journey.
出類拔萃的菜餚，值得專程到訪。

One always eats here extremely well, sometimes superbly. Distinctive dishes are precisely executed, using superlative ingredients.

食客可在這裏享用以最高級的材料和細膩的廚藝烹調的獨特菜式，美味的菜餚，偶爾令人讚不絕口。

Robuchon au Dôme 天巢法國餐廳	🟆🟆🟆🟆🟆 French contemporary 時尚法國菜	413
The Eight 8餐廳	🟆🟆🟆 Chinese 中菜	421

Excellent cuisine, worth a detour.
傑出美食，值得繞道前往。

Skilfully and carefully crafted dishes of outstanding quality.
具烹調技巧且用心製作的菜餚，品質優秀。

Golden Flower 京花軒	🟆🟆🟆 Chinese 中菜	393
Zi Yat Heen 紫逸軒	🟆🟆🟆 Cantonese 粵菜	432

A very good restaurant in its category.
同類別中出眾的餐廳。

A place offering cuisine prepared to a consistently high standard.
恆常保持高水準的餐廳。

Jade Dragon 譽瓏軒	🟆🟆🟆 Cantonese 粵菜	400
King 帝皇樓	🟆🟆 Cantonese 粵菜	401
The Golden Peacock 皇雀	🟆🟆 Indian 印度菜	422
The Kitchen 大廚	🟆🟆 Steakhouse 扒房	423
The Tasting Room 御膳房	🟆🟆🟆🟆 French contemporary 時尚法國菜	424
Tim's Kitchen 桃花源小廚	🟆🟆🟆 Cantonese 粵菜	425
Wing Lei 永利軒	🟆🟆🟆 Cantonese 粵菜	428

BIB GOURMAND RESTAURANTS
車胎人美食推介餐廳

This symbol indicates our inspectors' favourites for good value. These restaurants offer quality cooking for \$300 or less (price of a 3 course meal excluding drinks).

這標誌表示評審員認為最超值的餐廳：只需 300 元或以下便可享用優質美食（三道菜式價錢但不包括飲料）。

A Lorcha 船屋	👄	✗	Portuguese 葡國菜	374
Café Leon 利安咖啡屋	NEW	✗	Portuguese 葡國菜	382
Chan Seng Kei 陳勝記		🥢	Cantonese 粵菜	387
Cheong Kei 祥記		🥢	Noodles 麵食	388
Hou Kong Chi Kei 濠江志記美食		🥢	Cantonese 粵菜	396
IFT Educational Restaurant 旅遊學院教學餐廳		✗✗	Macanese 澳門菜	397
Lou Kei (Fai Chi Kei) 老記 (筷子基)		🥢	Cantonese 粵菜	404
Luk Kei Noodle 六記粥麵		🥢	Noodles and Congee 粥麵	405
Manuel Cozinha Portuguesa 阿曼諾葡國餐	👄	✗	Portuguese 葡國菜	407
Noodle & Congee Corner 粥麵莊		🥢	Noodles and Congee 粥麵	412
Square Eight 食·八方		✗	Chinese 中菜	417
Temptations 品味坊	NEW	✗✗	European 歐陸菜	418
Tou Tou Koi 陶陶居		✗	Cantonese 粵菜	426

NEW : New entry in the guide 新增推介
👄 : Restaurant promoted to a Bib Gourmand or Star 評級有所晉升的餐廳

RESTAURANTS BY AREA
餐廳 — 以地區分類

Coloane 路環

Chan Seng Kei 陳勝記	⊕	🍴	Cantonese 粵菜	387
Espaço Lisboa 里斯本地帶		✗	Portuguese 葡國菜	392

Macau 澳門

A Lorcha 船屋	꩜ ⊕	✗	Portuguese 葡國菜	374
Aruna's Maharaja Indian Curry 阿露娜印度皇室咖喱		✗	Indian 印度菜	377
Café Encore 咖啡廷		✗✗	Macanese 澳門菜	381
Carlos 加路		✗	Macanese 澳門菜	384
Chan Kuong Kei (Rua do Dr. Pedro Jose Lobo) 陳光記(羅保博士街)		🍴	Cantonese Roast Meats 燒味	386
Cheong Kei 祥記	⊕	🍴	Noodles 麵食	388
Clube Militar de Macau 澳門陸軍俱樂部		✗✗	Portuguese 葡國菜	389
Don Alfonso 1890 當奧豐素 1890		✗✗✗	Italian 意大利菜	390
Golden Flower 京花軒	❀❀	✗✗✗	Chinese 中菜	393
Guincho a Galera 葡國餐廳		✗✗✗	Portuguese 葡國菜	395
Hou Kong Chi Kei 濠江志記美食	⊕	🍴	Cantonese粵菜	396
IFT Educational Restaurant 旅遊學院教學餐廳	⊕	✗✗	Macanese 澳門菜	397
Il Teatro 帝雅廷		✗✗✗	Italian 意大利菜	398
Imperial Court 金殿堂		✗✗✗	Cantonese 粵菜	399
King 帝皇樓	❀	✗✗	Cantonese 粵菜	401
La Paloma 芭朗瑪		✗✗	Spanish 西班牙菜	402

NEW : New entry in the guide 新增推介
꩜ : Restaurant promoted to a Bib Gourmand or Star 評級有所晉升的餐廳

RESTAURANTS BY CUISINE TYPE
餐廳 — 以菜式分類

Cantonese 粵菜

Canton 喜粵			𝕏𝕏𝕏	Taipa 氹仔	383
Chan Seng Kei 陳勝記		🏮	🍜	Coloane 路環	387
Dynasty 8 朝			𝕏𝕏𝕏	Taipa 氹仔	391
Hou Kong Chi Kei 濠江志記美食		🏮	🍜	Macau 澳門	396
Imperial Court 金殿堂			𝕏𝕏𝕏	Macau 澳門	399
Jade Dragon 譽瓏軒	❀		𝕏𝕏𝕏	Taipa 氹仔	400
King 帝皇樓	❀		𝕏𝕏	Macau 澳門	401
Lei Garden 利苑酒家			𝕏𝕏	Taipa 氹仔	403
Lou Kei (Fai Chi Kei) 老記(筷子基)		🏮	🍜	Macau 澳門	404
Lung Wah Tea House 龍華茶樓			🍜	Macau 澳門	406
San Tou Tou 新陶陶			𝕏	Taipa 氹仔	415
Tim's Kitchen 桃花源小廚	❀		𝕏𝕏𝕏	Macau 澳門	425
Tou Tou Koi 陶陶居		🏮	𝕏	Macau 澳門	426
Wing Lei 永利軒	❀		𝕏𝕏𝕏𝕏	Macau 澳門	428
Ying 帝影樓			𝕏𝕏𝕏	Taipa 氹仔	431
Zi Yat Heen 紫逸軒	❀❀		𝕏𝕏𝕏𝕏	Taipa 氹仔	432

Cantonese Roast Meats 燒味

Chan Kuong Kei (Rua do Dr. Pedro Jose Lobo) 陳光記(羅保博士街)		🍜	Macau 澳門	386

Chinese 中菜

Beijing Kitchen 滿堂彩			𝕏𝕏	Taipa 氹仔	379
Golden Flower 京花軒	❀❀		𝕏𝕏𝕏𝕏	Macau 澳門	393
Square Eight 食 · 八方		🏮	𝕏	Macau 澳門	417
The Eight 8餐廳	❀❀❀		𝕏𝕏𝕏𝕏	Macau 澳門	421

European 歐陸菜

Temptations 品味坊	NEW	🏮	𝕏𝕏	Macau 澳門	418

NEW : New entry in the guide 新增推介

𝒩 : Restaurant promoted to a Bib Gourmand or Star 評級有所晉升的餐廳

RESTAURANTS WITH INTERESTING WINE LISTS
供應優質餐酒的餐廳

NEW : New entry in the guide 新增推介

᠍ᵇ : Restaurant promoted to a Bib Gourmand or Star 評級有所晉升的餐廳

MACAU 澳門

A Lorcha
船屋

🍴   ☎️🍴

Business is booming at this friendly Portuguese restaurant and that's not just because it's close to Barra Temple. The owner's mother still holds the most important role here – as head chef – and she makes sure the quality of the food remains high. A charcoal grill in the kitchen is used for the barbecue and grill dishes and carefully prepared specialities include Ameijoas "Bulhão Pato", Arroz de marisco à Portuguesa and Galinha à Africana.

這家服務親切殷勤的葡國餐廳，位於媽閣廟附近，但地點便利並非其成功的主要因素。餐廳總廚的要職由東主母親擔任，致力保持食品質素和正宗風味。燒烤菜式全部用炭爐烹調。餐廳精選推介包括欖油香蒜炒鮮蜆、葡式燴海鮮飯及非洲辣雞。

TEL. 2831 3193
289 Rua do Almirante Sérigo
河邊新街 289號

■ PRICE 價錢
Lunch 午膳
à la carte 點菜 MOP 200-340
Dinner 晚膳
à la carte 點菜 MOP 200-340

■ OPENING HOURS 營業時間
Lunch 午膳   12:30-15:00 L.O. 14:30
Dinner 晚膳   18:30-23:00 L.O. 22:30

■ ANNUAL AND WEEKLY CLOSING 休息日期
Closed Tuesday 週二休息

A Petisqueira
葡國美食天地

✗

Step through the door and you'll instantly feel as though you've been transported to a cosy little restaurant in the Portuguese countryside. A small bar at the entrance leads you into a simple, rustic dining room where the focus is on classic Portuguese cuisine served in a friendly, unpretentious atmosphere. Authentic dishes include bacalhau prepared in five different ways, and fried clams; look out too for the daily specials.

甫踏進大門，你便會感到仿如置身葡萄牙鄉村中的小餐館內。入口設有小酒吧，緩緩而入便是設計淳樸且帶鄉村風味的餐室；這兒供應的傳統葡國美食做法正宗而不花巧，服務親切友善。推介食物為炒蜆及以五種不同方法烹調的馬介休；每日會提供六至七款是日精選，不妨一試。

TEL. 2882 5354
15 Rua S. Joao, Taipa
氹仔生央街 15號

■ PRICE 價錢
Lunch 午膳
à la carte 點菜 MOP 150-400
Dinner 晚膳
à la carte 點菜 MOP 150-400

■ OPENING HOURS 營業時間
Lunch 午膳　12:30-14:15 (L.O.)
Dinner 晚膳　18:45-22:00 (L.O.)

■ ANNUAL AND WEEKLY CLOSING 休息日期
Closed Monday 週一休息

Antonio
安東尼奧

Antonio now occupies a three storey house, with dining rooms divided between the ground and first floors; it also has a charming little terrace. Wooden floors, Portuguese glazed tiles and leather seats help create a European look, while the paintings add a more contemporary note. The eponymous owner-chef provides friendly service and his specialities include gratinated goat's cheese with honey and olive oil, and seafood stew in a copper pot.

安東尼奧現址在離舊店不遠的一座三層高小屋中，餐室主要在地下和二樓，還附有小陽台。為了營造歐陸風情，店主選用了木地板、葡式瓷磚及皮椅，牆上的油畫替店子添了點現代氣息。店主的好客熱情和餐單卻保持不變，蜜糖橄欖油烤山羊芝士和海鮮雜燴當然仍在餐單上。

TEL. 2899 9998
7 Rua dos Clerigos
氹仔木鐸街 7 號
www.antoniomacau.com

■ PRICE 價錢
à la carte 點菜 MOP 300-840

■ OPENING HOURS 營業時間
12:00-00:00 L.O. 22:30

SPECIALITIES TO PRE-ORDER 預訂食物
Cabidela duck rice 血鴨飯 / Portuguese veal stew 葡萄牙燉牛仔肉

Aruna's Maharaja Indian Curry
阿露娜印度皇室咖喱

Aruna opened one of the first Indian restaurants in Macau, back in 1983; this, her most recent branch, is her biggest. It's spread over two floors and, as the name suggests, there is something palatial about the look, with its marble floors and golden sculptures. The menu is not too big, with northern India providing the most popular specialities, such as samosa chaat and royal lamb curry; be sure to end with gulab jamum.

早於1983年，阿露娜就在澳門開設第一家印度餐廳，而這間店子是她旗下規模最大的分店。樓高兩層，全店鋪上雲石地板並飾以黃金雕塑，裝潢散發着宮庭氣派。其菜牌選擇不多，供應最受歡迎的乳酪咖喱角及皇牌咖喱羊肉等北印度美食，別忘記以甜蜜圓為完美一餐劃上句號。

TEL. 2877 2844
92 Avenida de Marciano Baptista
新口岸畢仕達大馬路 92號

■ PRICE 價錢
Lunch 午膳
à la carte 點菜 MOP 90-180
Dinner 晚膳
à la carte 點菜 MOP 90-180

■ OPENING HOURS 營業時間
Lunch 午膳 11:00-15:30 (L.O.)
Dinner 晚膳 18:00-23:00 (L.O.)

MACAU 澳門

Banza
百姓

🍴　　　　　　　　　　　　　　　　　　　　　　　　　　　　　　　　　　©🕐🍽

The Portuguese owner, whose nickname is Banza, visits local markets each morning to decide on the chef's frequently changing specials; fish dishes tend to be the most popular choice among his many regulars. The restaurant lies in the shadow of a huge apartment complex and comes in tones of green and white, with large paintings and a cosy mezzanine seating about six. Banza can also give you advice on his selection of Portuguese wines.

此店以店主的別名命名，他每天早上都會前往市場，為每日精選尋找靈感和挑選食材。眾多美食中以魚類最受歡迎。餐廳座落於氹仔的大型屋苑內，四周環境寧靜。裝潢以白、綠為主色，掛有大型畫作。暖意洋溢的閣樓約有六個座位。Banza會向你介紹他精選的葡萄牙美酒。

TEL. 2882 1519
Avenida de Kwong Tung, n°s 154A e
154B, Edf. Nam San Garden, Bl. 5, r/c "G"
e "H", Taipa
氹仔廣東大馬路 154A及 154B號
南新花園第 5座地下 G,H座

■ PRICE 價錢
Lunch 午膳
à la carte 點菜 MOP 200-480
Dinner 晚膳
à la carte 點菜 MOP 200-480

■ OPENING HOURS 營業時間
Lunch 午膳　12:00-15:00 (L.O.)
Dinner 晚膳　18:30-22:30 (L.O.)

■ ANNUAL AND WEEKLY CLOSING 休息日期
Closed Monday 週一休息

Beijing Kitchen
滿堂彩

⚙⚒ 🛉 **P** 🍽12 ☎🍴

'Dinner and a show' at Beijing Kitchen means one and the same, as the cooking is divided between four lively show kitchens which will hold your attention. There's a dim sum and noodle area; a duck section with two applewood-fired ovens; a wok station; and a dessert counter whose bounty is well worth leaving room for. Northern China provides many of the specialities. Ask for one of the tables under the birdcages suspended from the ceiling.

這家店子有四個開放式廚房：點心與粉麵區、烤鴨區、明爐小炒區和甜品區；食客在進餐之餘還能欣賞「現場直播」的烹飪表演，稱得上集用膳與娛樂於一身。烤鴨區廚房內懸掛着兩座燃木窯爐，甚具特色，因此絕不能錯過這兒的烤鴨。招牌菜以北方菜為主。建議選擇天花上懸着鳥籠的座位，別有趣味。

TEL. 8868 1930
GF, Grand Hyatt Hotel, Estrado do Istmo, Cotai
路氹連貫公路君悅酒店地下
www.macau.grand.hyatt.com

■ PRICE 價錢
à la carte 點菜 MOP 230-1,150

■ OPENING HOURS 營業時間
11:30-00:00 (L.O.)

MACAU 澳門

Belcanção
鳴詩

🕺 ⚔️　　　　　　　　　　　　　　　　🦽 🏠 🖼️ 🅿️ 🐝

Belcanção is a relaxing buffet restaurant and is ideal for anyone who fancies a quick culinary world tour that's easy on the wallet. Warm, natural colours of brown and beige decorate the elegant room, while chefs from different countries man the open kitchens. There are stations offering Portuguese, Chinese, Indian and international cuisines, along with a selection of mostly French pastries. Brunch at weekends is served from 12-3pm.

鳴詩氣氛閒適輕鬆，價錢實惠，適合喜歡於一頓飯內嘗遍全球美食的食客。餐室以暖色系、感覺自然的棕色和米白色裝飾，來自不同國家的廚師分別掌管各個開放式廚房。店內提供葡萄牙、國際、中國及印度美食和一系列法國糕點。周末早午併餐時間由中午十二時至下午三時。

TEL. 2881 8811
GF, Four Seasons Hotel, Estrada da Baia
de N. Senhora de Esperanca, s/n, The
Cotai Strip, Taipa
氹仔路氹金光大道 -望德聖母灣大馬路
四季酒店地下
www.fourseasons.com/macau/

■ PRICE 價錢
Lunch 午膳
set 套餐 MOP 228-388
Dinner 晚膳
set 套餐 MOP 488

■ OPENING HOURS 營業時間
Lunch 午膳　12:00-14:30 (L.O.)
Dinner 晚膳　18:00-22:30 (L.O.)

Café Encore
咖啡廷

Café Encore is an elegant restaurant on the ground floor of the Encore hotel. The look is that of a classic European café but one with a strong Italian accent. The menu offers a combination of Macanese and Portuguese cuisine, along with a separate menu of Cantonese dishes, but it is in the Macanese specialities that the kitchen particularly excels. Try dishes like curried crab and baked African chicken.

咖啡廷位於萬利酒店地下，格調高雅。餐廳設計以傳統歐洲餐館裝潢作藍本，並滲入大量意大利藝術元素。菜單以澳門菜與葡國菜為主，另設有粵菜菜單。不過這裏最出色的還是地道澳門菜，例如咖喱蟹與非洲雞。

TEL. 8986 3616
GF, Encore Hotel, Rua Cicade de Sintra, Nape
外港新填海區仙德麗街萬利酒店地下
www.wynnmacau.com

■ PRICE 價錢
à la carte 點菜 MOP 250-600

■ OPENING HOURS 營業時間
06:30-03:00 (L.O.)

Café Leon NEW
利安咖啡屋

Many will have fond memories of Café Leon from the years it sat by Sai Van lake. It's now in Taipa and boasts a new and slightly more contemporary look, but what hasn't changed is the food which is prepared by the same kitchen team as before. Signature dishes include grilled Macau sole with butter sauce, braised prime beef rib in red wine, and roasted chicken stuffed with rice.

於1989年開業，座落於西灣湖邊的利安確令不少人留下美好回憶。在2013年遷至現址，環境轉變但美食不變，由原來的廚師團隊繼續為食客炮製一系列美味菜式，包括多道利安名菜如牛油扒金邊龍脷，原條牛肋骨和燒雞釀飯等。

TEL. 2830 1189
Na Taipa Rua Do Regedor No. 79
氹仔地堡街 79號

■ PRICE 價錢
Lunch 午膳
à la carte 點菜 MOP 180-600
Dinner 晚膳
à la carte 點菜 MOP 180-600

■ OPENING HOURS 營業時間
Lunch 午膳 11:30-14:30 (L.O.)
Dinner 晚膳 18:00-22:00 (L.O.)

■ ANNUAL AND WEEKLY CLOSING 休息日期
Closed Wednesday 週三休息

Canton
喜粵

Modern in design and a deep sensual red in colour, Canton is a stylish restaurant with a sophisticated atmosphere, and is hidden in a corner of the world's biggest indoor gaming floor. A Kouan-Chiau (gastronomic) version of Cantonese cooking is on offer, with dishes like braised black cod with scallops in a clay pot, garoupa belly with garlic and ginger, and diced pork loin with chilli. Shanghai steamed dumplings have their own section.

喜粵位於世上最大室內娛樂場的一角，採用誘人的深紅色作主調，裝潢時尚。菜單以廣州粵菜如乾蔥三杯鱈魚煲、蒜子姜蔥斑腩煲及山椒京蔥黑豚粒等為主。此外，店內亦有提供不同款式的上海蒸餃子，讓食客有更多美食選擇。

TEL. 8118 9930
Shop 1018, Casino level, The Venetian Resort, Estrada da Baia de N. Senhora de Esperanca, s/n, The Cotai Strip, Taipa
氹仔路氹金光大道 - 望德聖母灣大馬路
威尼斯人酒店娛樂場地下 1018號舖
www.venetianmacao.com

■ PRICE 價錢
Lunch 午膳
à la carte 點菜 MOP 250-1,200
Dinner 晚膳
à la carte 點菜 MOP 450-1,380

■ OPENING HOURS 營業時間
Lunch 午膳　　11:00-15:00 L.O.14:45
Dinner 晚膳　　18:00-23:00 L.O.22:45

Carlos
加路

A wide choice of reasonably priced Macanese and Portuguese dishes attract plenty of customers to this relaxing, family-style restaurant. The hospitable Carlos is rightly proud of his secret recipe for marinated grilled chicken and bacalhau a bras. He goes to the market each day in search of the freshest seafood and it is always worth ordering the crab in advance; larger parties can also pre-order the whole roasted piglet or leg of lamb.

這家感覺溫馨舒適的家庭式餐廳，供應多款澳門和葡國美食，價格實惠，因此吸引大量食客慕名而來。熱情好客的加路先生，對其加路秘製燒雞及薯絲馬介休深以為傲。他每天會親自到市場搜購新鮮海產、海蟹等食材，嗜蟹者最好預訂海蟹。如人數多，可以考慮預訂原隻燒乳豬或燒羊肫。

TEL. 2875 1838
GF, Rua Cidade de Braga, Ed. Vista
Magnifica, Nape
新口岸填海區柏嘉街帝景苑地下

■ PRICE 價錢
Lunch 午膳
à la carte 點菜 MOP 130-290
Dinner 晚膳
à la carte 點菜 MOP 130-290

■ OPENING HOURS 營業時間
Lunch 午膳 12:00-14:30 (L.O.)
Dinner 晚膳 18:00-22:30 (L.O.)

■ ANNUAL AND WEEKLY CLOSING 休息日期
Closed Public Holidays 公眾假期休息

Castiço

Hidden a few blocks behind the main street of Taipa's old town is this simple, unassuming little place with just five tables. The Portuguese owner-chef, who came to Macau in 2004, treats his many local customers like family and operates from early morning until late evening, preparing home-style dishes in his small open kitchen. Recommended are the stewed pork with clams, oven roasted bacalhau with potatoes and duckling rice.

葡籍東主兼廚師於2004年移居澳門，後開設了這家隱藏於氹仔舊城區大街附近的小店。小店陳設簡約樸實，只有五張餐桌，他就在細小的開放式廚房烹調家庭式美食，待客人如親人。食店營業時間由清早到深夜，收費合理，推介菜有豬肉粒炒蜆、馬介休燴薯仔及鴨飯。

TEL. 2857 6505
65B Rua Direita Carlos Eugénio, Taipa
氹仔施督憲正街 65號 B

■ PRICE 價錢
à la carte 點菜 MOP 125-270

■ OPENING HOURS 營業時間
11:00-22:30 (L.O.)

■ ANNUAL AND WEEKLY CLOSING 休息日期
Closed Thursday 週四休息

MACAU 澳門

Chan Kuong Kei (Rua do Dr. Pedro Jose Lobo)
陳光記(羅保博士街)

Red and yellow are the colours of this very clean shop, as well as the uniforms worn by the team of well-organised ladies who run it. Their barbecue meats and noodles attract an eclectic mix of customers, ensuring that it is always crowded and full of life. The roast goose and the barbecued pork are two of the most popular choices but it is also worth trying the double or triple rice plates.

此店位於澳門中心地點，以紅黃兩種顏色作主調，就是勤快的女店員身上的制服也不例外。這裏的燒味與粉麵吸引了各式各樣的客人，經常門庭若市，整間店子充滿活力。店內供應的食物中以燒鵝和叉燒最受歡迎，雙拼與三拼飯同樣值得一試。

TEL. 2831 4116
19 Rua Do Dr. Pedro Jose Lobo, Centro
羅保博士街 19號

■ PRICE 價錢
à la carte 點菜 MOP 40-200
■ OPENING HOURS 營業時間
10:30-21:30 (L.O.)

Chan Seng Kei
陳勝記

Chan Seng Kei has stood next to the ancient church for over 70 years and is now run by the 3rd generation of the family. It's well known for its traditional Cantonese food, with seafood supplied daily by local fishermen. The signature dish is stewed duck with tangerine peel but, as the cooking process takes more than 10 hours, only a few are available each day. It's a simple, semi open-air restaurant intertwined with several old banyan trees.

座落舊教堂旁的陳勝記開業至今已傳至第三代，向以傳統粵菜和海鮮菜式馳名。新鮮野生海鮮每天直接從漁民處採購；而製作工序繁複，需烹調十個小時的陳皮鴨是其招牌菜，每天限量供應。半開放式餐室非常樸實，當中數棵樹身粗壯的老榕樹，見證着飯店逾七十載的歷史。

TEL. 2888 2021
Rua Caetano No21, Coloane
路環計單奴街 21 號

■ PRICE 價錢
à la carte 點菜 MOP 150-350

■ OPENING HOURS 營業時間
12:00-22:30 (L.O.)

■ ANNUAL AND WEEKLY CLOSING 休息日期
Closed 2 days Lunar New Year
農曆新年休息 2 天

MACAU 澳門

Cheong Kei
祥記

A family business since the '70s, this tiny noodle shop sticks to its roots and its thin, fine noodles are pressed by bamboo shoots in its own little factory nearby. Their soup uses dried prawns and bonito and is cooked for 8 hours. The noodles with dried shrimp roe are great, but also try the wonton and deep-fried fish ball. Although it's handily placed on Rua de Felicidade, you'll need to weave round shoppers and stalls to get here.

這間家族經營的小麵店於七十年代開業，且在鄰近自設小型廠房製造幼細竹昇面。湯底以蝦乾和柴魚熬製八小時；蝦籽撈麵非試不可，雲吞及鯪魚球亦不容錯過。雖然祥記位於福隆新街，位置便利，但食客還是要花一番功夫繞過購物的人潮及攤販才能一嚐麵香。

TEL. 2857 4310
68 Rua de Felicidade
福隆新街 68號

■ PRICE 價錢
Lunch 午膳
à la carte 點菜　MOP 25-50
Dinner 晚膳
à la carte 點菜　MOP 25-50

■ OPENING HOURS 營業時間
11:30-23:30 (L.O.)

■ ANNUAL AND WEEKLY CLOSING 休息日期
Closed 4 days each month 每月休息 4 天

Clube Militar de Macau
澳門陸軍俱樂部

 ♿ ⬜32 ◖◗

Built in 1870 for the benefit of army officers, this striking pink-hued building was renovated in 1995 when its restaurant was opened to the public; but sadly the delightful sitting room and bar are reserved for its club members. The room has a charming colonial feel, thanks largely to the echoing teak floorboards, netted windows and ceiling fans. The kitchen focuses on traditional Portuguese flavours and hosts occasional food festivals.

這座最初為澳門陸軍軍官而設的粉紅色建築物建於1870年，在1995年完成翻新，並將餐廳對外開放，惟俱樂部內的雅致大廳及酒吧則只限會員使用。大廳內的柚木地板，配上窗紗的大窗及天花板上的吊扇，帶有濃厚的殖民地色彩。俱樂部供應傳統葡萄牙菜式，並會偶爾舉辦美食節。

TEL. 2871 4000
975 Avenida da Praia Grande
南灣大馬路 975號
www.clubemilitardemacau.net

■ PRICE 價錢
Lunch 午膳
set 套餐 MOP 153
à la carte 點菜 MOP 260-450
Dinner 晚膳
à la carte 點菜 MOP 260-450

■ OPENING HOURS 營業時間
Lunch 午膳　12:30-15:00 L.O. 14:30
Dinner 晚膳　19:00-23:00 L.O. 22:30

Don Alfonso 1890
當奧豐素 1890

This opulent dining room features dozens of red Murano chandeliers and a huge fresco of the Italian coast divided into five parts. The somewhat dated feel and bright lights can detract a little from the experience but the Italian cuisine uses well-selected ingredients and flavours are clean and sharp. Service can be almost overly attentive. If you're lucky, you'll be here during one of the owner's quarterly visits when he prepares his own tasting menu.

這家豪華餐室的獨特之處是設有許多紅色穆拉諾穆琉璃吊燈，並懸了一幅將意大利海岸分為五個部分的巨型壁畫。古老的風格和明亮的光線配搭令人嚮往，此外，其意大利菜選材不俗，清新味美，服務更是周到得有點超乎常理。如果你運氣不俗，還有機會品嘗店主每季度的特備餐單。

TEL. 8803 7722
3F, Grand Lisboa Hotel, Avenida de Lisboa
葡京路新葡京酒店 3樓
www.grandlisboahotel.com

■ PRICE 價錢
Lunch 午膳
set 套餐 MOP 300-500
à la carte 點菜 MOP 600-1,100
Dinner 晚膳
à la carte 點菜 MOP 600-1,100

■ OPENING HOURS 營業時間
Lunch 午膳　12:00-14:30 (L.O.)
Dinner 晚膳　18:30-22:30 (L.O.)

Dynasty 8
朝

🏋 🏋 🏋　　　　　　　　　　　　　　　　&　🖥️　🍽️20　🕐🍴

Old China is celebrated at this sophisticated and professionally run Chinese restaurant within the Conrad hotel. It takes its name and decorative styling from the eight dynasties of ancient China – Qin, Han, Sui, Tang, Song, Yuan, Ming and Qing – which are also used as the names of the private dining rooms. The traditional Cantonese food includes a varied choice of dim sum at lunch and the restaurant boasts an impressive wine cellar.

朝，顧名思義，其名字和室內裝潢意念源自中國古代八個皇朝：商、秦、漢、唐、宋、元、明、清。雕花木椅、木地板、紅燈籠和中式古典簷篷營造出強烈的中國古風。此店除供應以最新鮮的食材製作的傳統廣東小菜外，午市還有點心供應。店內設有酒窖。

TEL. 8113 8920
Level 1, Conrad Hotel, Estrada da Baia de N. Senhora de Esperanca, s/n, The Cotai Strip, Taipa
氹仔路氹金光大道望德母灣大馬路
康萊德酒店 1樓
www.conradmacao.com

■ PRICE 價錢
Lunch 午膳
à la carte 點菜 MOP 150-1,800
Dinner 晚膳
à la carte 點菜 MOP 250-1,800

■ OPENING HOURS 營業時間
Lunch 午膳　11:00-15:00 (L.O.)
Dinner 晚膳　18:00-23:00 (L.O.)

Espaço Lisboa
里斯本地帶

The owner has created a homely 'Lisbon space' within this two-storey house in this Chinese village. The decorative style comes straight out of Portugal, as do the influences behind many of the home-style dishes. Don't miss the presunto pata negra and if you fancy something a little different then try the African chicken from Mozambique with its coconut flavour. Ask for a table on the veranda when the weather is right.

Espaço意謂「空間」，店主有意在東方這臨海小鎮營造一個充滿葡國情調的空間。不論是鋪地板的石塊、擺設以至烹調用的陶缽，全部從葡國運抵。葡籍廚師用家鄉材料與傳統食譜炮製多款家常菜。源自莫桑比克食譜的非洲雞，啖啖椰汁香，美味無窮；風味絕佳的黑蹄火腿亦不能錯過。

TEL. 2888 2226
Rua das Gaivotas No8, Coloane
路環水鴨街 8 號

SPECIALITIES TO PRE-ORDER 預訂食物
Lobster Rice 龍蝦飯／Suckling pig (whole)
乳豬

■ PRICE 價錢
Lunch 午膳
set套餐 MOP148-1,480　àlacarte點菜 MOP250-1,200
Dinner 晚膳
set套餐 MOP980-1,480　àlacarte點菜 MOP450-1,380

■ OPENING HOURS 營業時間
Lunch 午膳　12:00-15:00 (L.O.)
Dinner 晚膳　18:30-22:00 (L.O.)
Weekends 週末　12:00-22:30 (L.O.)

■ ANNUAL AND WEEKLY CLOSING 休息日期
Closed Wednesday 週三休息

Golden Flower
京花軒

❀❀

Within the Encore hotel is this elegant and sophisticated restaurant, whose kitchen is noted for its dextrous use of superb ingredients in the preparation of three different cuisines: Sichuan, Lu and Tan – along with a few Cantonese dishes. The room is adorned with the colours of gold and orange and the booths are the prized seats, but wherever you sit you'll receive charming service from the strikingly attired ladies, including the 'tea sommelier'.

京花軒座落於澳門萬利酒店內，以金色和橙色裝潢，既典雅又獨特。店內設有圓形白色皮卡座，不管安坐何處，都能享受端莊的女侍應的悉心服務，包括「調茶」服務。廚房最出色之處，除了選料上乘，還能俐落地烹調出川菜、魯菜、譚家菜三款不同菜系的菜式，同時供應少量廣東菜。

TEL. 8986 3689
GF, Encore Hotel, Rua Cicade de Sintra, Nape
外港新填海區仙德麗街萬利酒店地下
www.wynnmacau.com

■ PRICE 價錢
Weekends Lunch 週末午膳
à la carte 點菜 MOP 450-2,100
Dinner 晚膳
à la carte 點菜 MOP 450-2,100
■ OPENING HOURS 營業時間
Weekend Lunch 週末午膳 11:30-14:30 (L.O.)
Dinner 晚膳 18:00-23:00 L.O.22:30

■ ANNUAL AND WEEKLY CLOSING 休息日期
Closed Monday 週一休息

Gosto NEW
葡軒

✗

                             ♿ 🍴 🅿 ⬚12

The cupola ceiling and vintage photographs of old Portugal go some way to imbuing this restaurant within the Galaxy with something of a colonial atmosphere. The kitchen is headed up by a Portuguese chef and you can certainly taste the authenticity in specialities like deep-fried cod fish balls with chickpea salad and the classic Portuguese egg tarts. There are also a number of quality Portuguese wines on offer.

圓拱型的天花及充滿葡萄國風情的掛牆相片，這間在銀河渡假城內的餐館帶着濃厚的舊殖民地色彩。由葡萄牙籍主廚帶領廚房團隊為食客獻上一道道風味正宗的葡國菜。特色菜如炸馬介休球配雞心豆沙及傳統葡國蛋撻尤為滋味。多款葡萄牙餐酒可供選擇。

TEL. 8883 2221
G21, GF East Promenade, Galaxy Hotel,
Estrada da Baia de Nossa Senhora da
Esperença, Cotai
澳門銀河購物大道東地下 G21

■ PRICE 價錢
Lunch 午膳
set 套餐 MOP 148-188
à la carte 點菜 MOP 250-500
Dinner 晚膳
à la carte 點菜 MOP 250-500

■ OPENING HOURS 營業時間
Lunch 午膳　12:00-15:00 (L.O.)
Dinner 晚膳　18:00-23:00 (L.O.)

Guincho a Galera
葡國餐廳

✳✳✳✳   ♿ 🍴12 ☎🍴 &

Portuguese 'fine dining' comes to Macau in the form of this branch of Fortaleza do Guincho restaurant in Cascais, near Lisbon. It occupies the room in the Lisboa hotel that was formerly used by Joël Robuchon. The atmosphere is refined, the decoration vivid and the service attentive. The Portuguese food is refined and classical and is occasionally accompanied by subtle French notes; it is also complemented by a very impressive wine list.

來自鄰近里斯本的卡斯凱什，Fortaleza do Guincho餐廳的分店正式登陸澳門，帶來葡式高級餐飲享受。它位處葡京酒店內，餐廳格調高雅、裝潢精緻，服務亦十分周到。它供應的葡式佳餚製作精美、味道正宗，偶爾亦會滲入些許法國風味。餐廳還提供種類繁多的美酒。

TEL. 8803 7676
3F, Hotel Lisboa, 2-4 Avenida de Lisboa
葡京路 2-4號葡京酒店 3樓
www.hotellisboa.com

■ PRICE 價錢
Lunch 午膳
set 套餐 MOP 280-350
à la carte 點菜 MOP 530-1,500
Dinner 晚膳
set 套餐 MOP 580
à la carte 點菜 MOP 530-1,500

■ OPENING HOURS 營業時間
Lunch 午膳 12:00-14:30 (L.O.)
Dinner 晚膳 18:30-22:30 (L.O.)

MACAU 澳門

Hou Kong Chi Kei
濠江志記美食

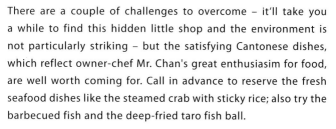

There are a couple of challenges to overcome – it'll take you a while to find this hidden little shop and the environment is not particularly striking – but the satisfying Cantonese dishes, which reflect owner-chef Mr. Chan's great enthusiasim for food, are well worth coming for. Call in advance to reserve the fresh seafood dishes like the steamed crab with sticky rice; also try the barbecued fish and the deep-fried taro fish ball.

要找到這家位置隱蔽的餐廳確是個小小的挑戰，其環境亦非十分出眾；但你所獲得的回報，就是一嘗東主兼廚師陳先生主理的廣式佳餚，並感受他對烹調美食的熱情。個別海鮮美食如蒸糯米蟹飯，需致電預訂；其他推介菜式還有燒魚及香芋炸魚球。

TEL. 2895 3098
GF, Block 3, Lai Hou Gardens, Rua Coelho do Amaral
白鴿巢前地麗豪花園第三座地舖
佳樂園石級上

SPECIALITIES TO PRE-ORDER 預訂食物
Steamed crab on sticky rice 蒸糯米蟹飯／
Grilled fish or prawns 燒魚或蝦

■ PRICE 價錢
Dinner 晚膳
à la carte 點菜 MOP 90-200

■ OPENING HOURS 營業時間
19:00-23:00 (L.O.)

■ ANNUAL AND WEEKLY CLOSING 休息日期
Closed the 15th & 16th of each month
每月 15 及 16 日休息

IFT Educational Restaurant
旅遊學院教學餐廳

🍽🍴   🍽12 🕑🍴

The kitchen is led by a professional chef but his brigade is made up of students, as this restaurant is run by the Institute of Tourism Studies. It offers a good selection of European and Portuguese dishes and uses many herbs, salad leaves and vegetables grown in its own organic garden; look out for African chicken with couscous and IFT seafood rice. This is a good spot for dinner away from the bustle of the casinos.

這家旅遊學院教學餐廳的廚房由專業廚師主理，而團隊則由學生組成，供應多款歐陸及葡國美食，其特色是採用多種自家種植的有機香草、沙律菜和蔬果作食材。推介菜式有非洲雞及學院海鮮飯。遠離澳門喧囂的賭場，這裏是悠閒地享用晚餐的好去處。

TEL. 8598 3077
Colina de Mong-Há, Rampe do Forte de Mong-Há
望廈山
www.ift.edu.mo/pousada

■ PRICE 價錢
Lunch 午膳
set 套餐 MOP 200
à la carte 點菜 MOP 220-420
Dinner 晚膳
set 套餐 MOP 700
à la carte 點菜 MOP 220-420

■ OPENING HOURS 營業時間
Lunch 午膳　12:30-14:30 (L.O.)
Dinner 晚膳　19:00-22:00 (L.O.)

■ ANNUAL AND WEEKLY CLOSING 休息日期
Closed weekends and Public Holidays
週末及公眾假期休息

Il Teatro
帝雅廷

♿ ⟨ 🍷 🅿 🍴14 ☏🍴

To recommend a restaurant whose appeal lies beyond its cooking may be a little odd, but at Il Teatro it seems most diners turn up primarily to watch the stunning fountains; these are in a lake and are musically choreographed to change colour and appearance every few minutes. Ask for a table with a view and don't wear sneakers, or you won't get in. The cuisine is straightforward Italian fare, such as seafood risotto or pasta, served with style and élan.

大多數食客到來是為了觀賞噴泉美景。餐廳七成以上座位面向表演湖噴泉，每數分鐘音樂水柱交替、激光穿梭的震撼，盡收眼簾。因此，記着預訂面向噴泉的座位！此外，穿波鞋者不准內進。菜餚方面，主要提供簡約的意大利菜，如海鮮意大利飯或意大利粉，風味獨特且服務殷勤周到。

TEL. 8986 3663
GF, Wynn Hotel, Rua Cidade de Sintra, Nape
外港填海區區仙德麗街永利酒店地下
www.wynnmacau.com

■ PRICE 價錢
Dinner 晚膳
set 套餐　MOP 868
à la carte 點菜　MOP 350-900

■ OPENING HOURS 營業時間
17:30-23:30 (L.O.)

■ ANNUAL AND WEEKLY CLOSING 休息日期
Closed Monday 週一休息

Imperial Court
金殿堂

XXX   占 ⌂ **P** ⌷36 ஃ

A massive marble pillar with a carved dragon dominates this elegant and contemporary restaurant, which is found on the same floor as the VIP lobby. The kitchen prepares classic Cantonese cuisine, with dishes such as scrambled organic egg whites with sea urchin and crabmeat, topped with caviar; braised frogs' legs with shrimp roe; and Kagoshima Wagyu beef with green chilli peppers. The impressive wine list includes over 1,000 labels.

金殿堂與貴賓大堂位於同一樓層，龐大的雕龍雲石柱是最矚目之處，設計風格高貴優雅中見時尚。餐廳主要供應廣東美食，如海膽鮮蟹肉炒蛋白、蝦籽田雞腿扒柚皮及摩利菌青尖椒爆鹿兒島和牛粒等；餐酒選擇逾千種，令人印象深刻。

TEL. 8802 2361
GF, MGM Hotel, Avenida Dr. Sun Yat Sen, Nape
外港新填海區孫逸仙大馬路美高梅酒店地下
www.mgmmacau.com

■ PRICE 價錢
Lunch 午膳
set 套餐 MOP 188-1,380
à la carte 點菜 MOP 300-2,000
Dinner 晚膳
set 套餐 MOP 1,380
à la carte 點菜 MOP 300-2,000

■ OPENING HOURS 營業時間
Lunch 午膳 11:00-15:00 L.O. 14:30
Dinner 晚膳 18:00-23:00 L.O. 22:30

Jade Dragon
譽瓏軒

Traditional Chinese art, ebony, crystal, gold and silver converge with modern design to form this stunning and eminently comfortable Cantonese restaurant. Equal thought has gone into the details, such as the striking carved jade chopstick holder. The specialities to look out for are goose grilled over lychee wood, and barbecued Ibérico pork. Seafood is also a highlight, along with herbal soups and recipes based on traditional medicine.

譽瓏軒的瑰麗裝潢十分美輪美奐。烏木、金、銀和水晶的運用，揉合了現代設計與中國傳統美學的精髓，透明方柱酒窖、豪華廂房，或是餐桌上的玉雕筷子座，都給人留下深刻印象。食材均是高級用料。按中藥處方熬煮的老火湯和以荔枝柴烤製的燒鵝和黑毛豬叉燒值得一試。

TEL. 8868 2822
Level 2, The Boulevard, City of Dreams
Estrada do Istmo, Cotai
路氹連貫公路新濠天地新濠大道 2樓
www.cityofdreamsmacau.com/restaurant

SPECIALITIES TO PRE-ORDER 預訂食物
Steamed Herbal Chicken Wrap 藥膳紙包雞
／ Whole Supreme Fish Maw 原隻廣肚花膠公

■ PRICE 價錢
Lunch 午膳
à la carte 點菜 MOP 200-1,600
Dinner 晚膳
à la carte 點菜 MOP 300-1,600

■ OPENING HOURS 營業時間
Lunch 午膳　11:00-15:00 (L.O.)
Dinner 晚膳　18:00-23:00 (L.O.)

King
帝皇樓

XX 　　　　　　　　　　　　　P ⊟24 ⏱⏷

Fans of Celebrity Cuisine in Hong Kong will recognise many of Chef Cheng's delicate and sophisticated specialities as he is one of the owners of this elegant and comfortable Cantonese restaurant. These signature dishes include braised abalone with goose web, and baked chicken with Shaoxing wine; the homemade dim sum also comes highly recommended. Being sufficiently removed from the casinos means the atmosphere is comparatively sedate.

香港名廚鄭錦富的擁躉定會覺得帝皇樓的精美菜式似曾相識，因為他正是這家高雅舒適的廣東酒家的東主之一。此酒家的招牌菜有鵝掌扣吉品鮑魚及花雕焗飛天雞，自製點心亦十分值得一試。酒家位置與各大賭場之間有一段距離，氣氛較為寧靜。

TEL. 2875 7218
GF, AIA Tower, 251A-301 Avenida Comercial de Macau
澳門商業大馬路友邦廣場地下

■ PRICE 價錢
Lunch 午膳
à la carte 點菜 MOP 130-1,300
Dinner 晚膳
à la carte 點菜 MOP 230-1,300

■ OPENING HOURS 營業時間
Lunch 午膳　11:30-15:00 (L.O.)
Dinner 晚膳　17:30-23:00 (L.O.)

La Paloma
芭朗瑪

  🍴🍴   🏠 **P** 🍽30 ☎🍷 🎍

Secluded like hidden treasure from the rest of the city, La Paloma is a very appealing restaurant and bar, enhanced by a charming terrace, floor-to-ceiling glass and stone walls which are part of the original 17th century fortress foundations. A bold nouveau riche style of furniture lends it a chic yet casual air; it is wonderfully intimate and romantic at night. The refined Spanish cuisine offers a great assortment of tapas and exquisite paellas.

芭朗瑪餐廳及酒吧，位於一座十七世紀舊城堡改建而成的酒店內，遠離城市的煩囂。迷人的洋台、落地玻璃和古堡原來的石牆，構成獨特風采。傢具陳設時尚高雅，別具氣派且予人舒適感覺，晚上更是浪漫醉人。其西班牙菜精緻優雅，嘗味套餐是不錯的選擇。

TEL. 2896 8686
2F, Pousada de São Tiago Hotel, Avenida da República, Fortaleza de São Tiago da Barra
西灣民國大馬路聖地牙哥古堡酒店 2樓
www.saotiago.com.mo

■ PRICE 價錢
Lunch 午膳
set 套餐 MOP 210-270
à la carte 點菜 MOP 430-900
Dinner 晚膳
à la carte 點菜 MOP 430-900

■ OPENING HOURS 營業時間
Lunch 午膳　12:00-14:30 (L.O.)
Dinner 晚膳　18:30-22:30 (L.O.)

Lei Garden
利苑酒家

🍴✕✕　　　　　　　　　　　　　　🗲 **P** ⇩14 ☎🍴

A smart restaurant set amongst the canals of this vast hotel's third floor – arrive by gondola if you wish…Venetian guests predominate here; gamblers mostly give it a miss as it's too far from the gaming tables. Walls of marble provide the backdrop to a comprehensive range of traditional Cantonese dishes which are delivered by an efficient and well-organised team of servers. The best place to be seated is in one of the cosy booths.

餐廳設於三樓，佔據此大型酒店的運河旁位置，雄據地利，顧客可以乘坐貢朵拉前往這兒。由於離賭場較遠，娛樂場玩家通常會光顧其他餐廳，因此這裏的顧客以酒店住客為主。雲石牆壁與傳統廣東菜互相映襯。服務效率非常高。最好的座位是靠近前門的舒適卡位。

TEL. 2882 8689
Shop 2130, 3F Grand Canal Shoppes, The Venetian Resort, Estrada da Baia de N. Senhora de Esperança, Taipa
氹仔路望德聖母灣大馬路威尼斯人酒店大運河購物中心 3樓 2130號舖
www.venetianmacao.com

■ PRICE 價錢
Lunch 午膳
à la carte 點菜 MOP 200-1,000
Dinner 晚膳
à la carte 點菜 MOP 250-1,000

■ OPENING HOURS 營業時間
Lunch 午膳　11:30-15:00 L.O. 14:30
Dinner 晚膳　18:00-23:00 L.O. 22:15

■ ANNUAL AND WEEKLY CLOSING 休息日期
Closed 3 days Lunar New Year
農曆新年休息 3 天

Lou Kei (Fai Chi Kei)
老記 (筷子基)

If you're looking for a simple, good value supper then Lou Kei may well fit the bill. Granted, it may not be in the centre of town, but every cab driver knows this lively place. It has been renowned for over 20 years for its sizeable selection of tasty noodles, congee and Cantonese dishes; frogs' legs in a clay pot and sea crab congee are both highly recommended. The interior is bright and neat while the service is polite and attentive.

若然你想品嘗價廉物美的美食，老記便是不二之選。儘管餐廳並非位於市中心，但是所有的士司機皆知這間馳名食府的所在地。老記二十多年來提供美味粥品麵食及廣東菜式，其田雞腿煲及水蟹粥更備受食客推崇，店內光猛潔淨，侍應親切有禮。

TEL. 2856 9494
Avenida Da Concórdia N, 12R/C E S/L
Loja H
和樂大馬路 12號宏基大廈第 4座 H及 M鋪

■ PRICE 價錢
à la carte 點菜 MOP 120-250
■ OPENING HOURS 營業時間
18:00-05:00 (L.O.)

MACAU 澳門

Luk Kei Noodle
六記粥麵

The second generation owner-chef insists on making his very popular noodles the traditional way: with a bamboo stick. The small menu provides photos of the specialities which include noodles with dried prawn roe; crunchy deep-fried wontons; crispy fish balls with soft centres served with either oyster or soy sauce; and the filling congee with crab. This is a small and busy shop, found on a lively street next to the pier.

第二代店主兼大廚堅持以傳統手法炮製極受歡迎的竹升麵。小小的餐牌上附有特色食品的照片，包括蝦子撈麵、炸鴛鴦（炸雲吞及米通鯪魚球），還有水蟹粥。這家廣受食客歡迎的小店，就在碼頭旁邊的熱鬧街道上。

TEL. 2855 9627
1-D Travessa da Saudade
沙梨頭仁慕巷 1號 D

■ PRICE 價錢
à la carte 點菜 MOP 40-70

■ OPENING HOURS 營業時間
18:30-02:30 (L.O.)

■ ANNUAL AND WEEKLY CLOSING 休息日期
Closed 4 days Lunar New Year
農曆新年休息 4 天

Lung Wah Tea House
龍華茶樓

Little has changed from when this old-style Cantonese tea house, up a flight of stairs, opened in the 1960s: the large clock still works, the boss still uses an abacus to add the bill and you still have to refill your own pot of tea at the boiler. The owner buys fresh produce, including chicken for their most popular dish, from the market across the road; stir-fried noodles with beef is another speciality. Get here early for the fresh dim sum.

這家有一列樓梯的傳統廣東茶樓自一九六零年代開業以來，變化不大一古老大鐘依然在擺動，老闆依然用算盤算帳單，你依然要自行到熱水器前沖茶。店主從對面街市選購新鮮食材烹調美食，包括茶樓名菜油雞。此外，干炒牛河亦是其招牌菜之一。建議早上前來享用新鮮點心。

TEL. 2857 4456
3 Rua Norte do Mercado Aim-Lacerda
提督市北街 3號

■ PRICE 價錢
à la carte 點菜 MOP 25-140

■ OPENING HOURS 營業時間
07:00-14:00 (L.O.)

■ ANNUAL AND WEEKLY CLOSING 休息日期
Closed 4 days Lunar New Year, 4 days
May and 4 days October 農曆新年、五月
及十月各休息 4 天

Manuel Cozinha Portuguesa
阿曼諾葡國餐

Authenticity and hospitality are what draws customers to this cosy little corner restaurant. Newcomers will find themselves welcomed by the owner-chef just as warmly as if they were regulars. His traditional Portuguese cooking uses quality ingredients and many of the dishes are cooked in the old-fashioned barbecue way. He makes his own cheese and the two specialities of which he is most proud are stewed rabbit, and fried rice with squid ink.

離開氹仔舊城區的熱鬧街道，從施督憲正街向飛能便度街方向走，便會找到路口這家小店。在這兒你能吃到美味正宗的葡國菜。葡籍店東兼主廚親切好客。他堅持選用本地和葡國優質食材，且以碳火燒烤食物，還在店內自製芝士。炆兔肉和墨魚汁炒飯是他最引以為傲的菜式。

TEL. 2882 7571
Rua de Femão Mendes Pinto, Nº 90 R/C, Taipa
氹仔飛能便度街 90號

SPECIALITIES TO PRE-ORDER 預訂食物
Roasted piglet "Manuel style" 原隻阿曼諾燒乳豬 / Baked lobster "Manuel style" 阿曼諾焗龍蝦 /Seafood rice 海鮮飯

■ PRICE 價錢
Lunch 午膳
à la carte 點菜 MOP 130-340
Dinner 晚膳
à la carte 點菜 MOP 130-340

■ OPENING HOURS 營業時間
Lunch 午膳　12:00-15:00 (L.O.)
Dinner 晚膳　18:00-22:00 (L.O.)

■ ANNUAL AND WEEKLY CLOSING 休息日期
Closed Wednesday 週三休息

Mezza9

Mezza9 is ideal for those who can never decide on what nationality of cuisine they fancy but who do like a little theatre with their food. The vast and quite striking interior comes with several show kitchens offering an impressive array of different cuisines: you can choose sushi, chargrilled meats, Cantonese wok dishes, Macanese specialities, South Asian noodles and even Sunday brunch. The vaulted wine cellar is the pick of the private rooms.

如果你是嗜吃一族，又經常無法決定享用哪一國的菜式，Mezza9是你理想之選。餐廳面積非常闊落，設有數個開放式廚房，供應多國菜式，包括壽司、烤肉、廣東小炒、澳門特色菜、南亞麵食等。假日還會提供早午合餐。二人套餐份量不少，且能一次過品嘗多國美食。

TEL. 8868 1920
3F, Grand Hyatt Hotel, City of Dreams,
Estrado do Istmo, Cotai
路氹連貫公路新濠天地君悅酒店 3樓
www.macau.grand.hyatt.com

○PRICE 價錢
à la carte 點菜 MOP 300-1,200

■ OPENING HOURS 營業時間
Dinner 晚膳　17:30-23:00 (L.O.)

Myung Ga NEW
名家

                                                                       ⛴   🍞   🍽8   🕢🍴

Many ingredients are imported from Korea to ensure authenticity at this restaurant specialising in Korean classics and BBQ. If you opt for one of the large booths, instead of the cushioned seating on the floor, you'll get your own grill. The family set menu for up to six people is a popular way to sample dishes like homemade kimchi. Along with the contemporary cocktails, you can also try traditional Korean drinks like milky white makgeolli.

名家供應的食材全都是從韓國搜購回來，確保客人吃到原汁原味的韓國菜。食客除了可以以韓國傳統方式，以墊子墊着坐在地上進餐外，還可選擇坐在擁有獨立燒烤爐的卡座上。家庭套餐和自製泡菜非常受歡迎。餐酒選擇豐富，除了新派雞尾酒外，還提供乳白濁酒之類的傳統韓國餐酒。

TEL. 8883 2221
G27, GF East Promenade, Galaxy Hotel,
Estrada da Baia de Nossa Senhora da
Esperença, Cotai
澳門銀河購物大道東地下 G27
www.galaxymacau.com

■ PRICE 價錢
à la carte 點菜 MOP 300-700

■ OPENING HOURS 營業時間
12:00-23:00 (L.O.)

MACAU 澳門

Ngao Kei Ka Lei Chon
牛記咖喱美食

Set at the corner of a main road and a narrow street full of industrious little shops. The broken neon lights outside may lessen its appeal but this is a friendly, well-run and well-staffed little noodle shop, with regulars popping in and out throughout the day. Bestsellers are the crab noodles and the crab congee but it's also worth trying the clear soup with beef flank and the spicy chicken or beef curry with noodles.

此店位於大街一角的小巷內，四周的小店均其門如市，常客往來不絕。四周老舊的建築物看似減弱了餐廳的吸引力，但小麵店職員的友善態度和管理有序彌補了這個不足，店內服務令人滿意。最暢銷的美食要算是水蟹、蟹黃炆伊麵和蟹粥，清湯牛腩和椰汁咖喱雞、牛筋麵也值得一試。

TEL. 2895 6129
GF, 1 Rua de Cinco de Outubro
十月初五街 1號地下

■ PRICE 價錢
à la carte 點菜 MOP 40-90

■ OPENING HOURS 營業時間
08:00-02:00 (L.O.)

99 Noodles
99麵

✗　　　　　　　　　　　　　　　　　　　♿ ☞ **P** ⛟

Noodle lovers will need a few visits to this stylish pit-stop at the Encore hotel to work their way through the huge choice of Chinese noodles – there's everything from Beijing la mian to Shanxi knife-shaved, tip-ended and one string noodles, all served with various broths and garnishes, along with specialities from Northern China. The colours of the room are vivid; the jumbo chopsticks on the walls are striking; and the atmosphere's buzzy.

細小的餐室以鮮艷的紅色作主調，牆上懸着一雙雙色彩繽紛的巨型筷子，華麗且充滿活力，與四周的賭場環境風格一致。顧名思義，這裏是嘗麵的好地方：北京拉麵、山西刀削麵、轉盤剔尖及一根麵等多款麵食，配以各式湯底和澆頭，令人食指大動。餃子和北方點心當然也不能錯過。

TEL. 8986 3663
GF, Encore Hotel, Rua Cicade de Sintra, Nape
外港新填海區仙德麗街萬利酒店地下
www.wynnmacau.com

■ PRICE 價錢
à la carte 點菜 MOP 150-1,400

■ OPENING HOURS 營業時間
11:00-01:00 (L.O.)

Noodle & Congee Corner
粥麵莊

This simple, good value eatery is located – incongruously – on a gallery that opens onto the casino. It's really a cafeteria, or even 'tea-eria', as one wall is full of teapots. What's special for diners is the view they have of the chefs, who come from different parts of the country, as they prepare noodle specialities from their home region using quality produce. These can be combined with various soups and ingredients: the menus, handily, include photos.

粥麵莊位於娛樂場上層樓上，裝潢樸素、食物價錢合理。店內有一道牆放滿茶壺，營造出「茶檔」感覺。食客在晚膳期間可觀賞來自五湖四海的廚師如何採用新鮮味美的食材炮製家鄉特色麵食的過程！餐廳亦提供多款湯飲和小菜；菜單附有圖片，便於瀏覽。

TEL. 8803 7755
1F, Grand Lisboa Hotel, Avenida de Lisboa
葡京路新葡京酒店 1 樓
www.grandlisboahotel.com

■ PRICE 價錢
à la carte 點菜 MOP 100-200

■ OPENING HOURS 營業時間
Open 24 hours 24 小時營業

Robuchon au Dôme
天巢法國餐廳

✿✿✿

XXXXX

♿ ⟨ 📖 ⌗10 🍽 ⚜

Joël Robuchon's flagship restaurant sits majestically in the dome of the Grand Lisboa hotel, where a striking chandelier competes for your attention with the 360° views of Macau. Impeccable service, immaculate table settings and a superb wine list all complement the superlative contemporary cuisine. Try roast guinea fowl with foie gras or Kagoshima beef with asparagus and black truffles; then order the praline soufflé or something from the dessert trolley.

Joël Robuchon 的旗艦店位於新葡京酒店內。矚目的大型水晶吊燈和令人屏息的360度澳門全景，餐桌亦佈置得十分細緻，實在是賞心悅目。這兒除了供應優質的當代菜式，還提供超過八千種餐酒。服務亦很周到。烤珍珠雞伴鵝肝及和牛露筍伴黑松露都是推介之選。

TEL. 8803 7878
43F, Grand Lisboa Hotel, Avenida de Lisboa
葡京路新葡京酒店 43樓
www.grandlisboahotel.com

■ PRICE 價錢
Lunch 午膳
set 套餐 MOP 458-688
à la carte 點菜 MOP 1,100-2,300
Dinner 晚膳
set 套餐 MOP 1,588-2,288
à la carte 點菜 MOP 1,100-2,300

■ OPENING HOURS 營業時間
Lunch 午膳 12:00-14:30 (L.O.)
Dinner 晚膳 18:30-22:30 (L.O.)

MACAU 澳門

Saffron
尚坊

You'll find this relaxing, impeccably run Thai restaurant in the Banyan Tree, on the same floor as the hotel's lobby. A wide choice of Thai cuisine is served, from traditional, regional specialities to classics from the Royal households; all prepared in a contemporary way while staying true to authentic flavours. Do try the grilled prawn with banana blossom salad or roast peppered pork ribs with ginger, and don't miss the mango sticky rice.

這家位處悅榕莊酒店大堂樓層的泰國餐廳，氣氛柔和閒適。它提供多種泰國美食，由地區傳統特色，到皇家御用經典都包羅其中；所有菜式均以現代方式烹調，同時忠於傳統味道。推介菜式有扒大蝦香蕉花沙律或泰姜黑椒燒豬肋骨，香芒糯米飯也不容錯過。

TEL. 8883 6061
GF, Banyan Tree Hotel, Galaxy Macau,
Avenida Marginal Flor de Lotus, Cotai
路氹城蓮花海濱大馬路澳門銀河渡假城
悅榕莊地下
www.banyantree.com/en/macau

■ PRICE 價錢
Lunch 午膳
à la carte 點菜 MOP 400-600
Dinner 晚膳
à la carte 點菜 MOP 400-600

■ OPENING HOURS 營業時間
Lunch 午膳　07:00-15:00 (L.O.)
Dinner 晚膳　18:00-23:00 (L.O.)

San Tou Tou
新陶陶

Found on a narrow street in the centre of Taipa is this Cantonese restaurant, run by the same family for three generations and now supervised by two brothers. The cooking is very traditional and it is the chicken soup served in very hot clay pots that attracts so many; but there are plenty of other, more affordable, specialities. The restaurant is spread over two floors and the air conditioning is most efficient!

這間家族經營的廣東菜餐廳位於氹仔中心地帶的小巷內，現時由第三代的兩兄弟主理。煮法非常傳統，燉雞湯用砂鍋盛載，吸引大量食客。除此之外，這裏還提供很多價錢相宜的小菜選擇。餐廳雖分為兩層，但空調系統並沒受影響，室內空氣非常流通。

TEL. 2882 7065
26 Rua Correia da Silva, Taipa
氹仔告利雅施利華街 26號

SPECIALITIES TO PRE-ORDER 預訂食物
Salt baked chicken 古法鹽焗雞 / Crispy chicken 脆皮炸子雞

■ PRICE 價錢
Lunch 午膳
à la carte 點菜 MOP 150-550
Dinner 晚膳
à la carte 點菜 MOP 150-550

■ OPENING HOURS 營業時間
Lunch 午膳　11:30-15:00 (L.O.)
Dinner 晚膳　17:30-22:00 (L.O.)

■ ANNUAL AND WEEKLY CLOSING 休息日期
Closed 1 week Lunar New Year, 2 days early May and 2 days early October 農曆新年 7 天、五月初及十月初各休息 2 天

Shanghai Min NEW
上海小南國

✂️✂️　　　　　　　　　　　　　　　　　　🍴24　🕐🍴

This branch differs slightly from the others in the Xiao Nan Guo Restaurant Group by not only serving Shanghainese dishes but by also offering Sichuan and Cantonese classics. So at lunch there are over 30 types of Shanghai dim sum as well as various Canton specialities. This branch is also larger than most and is spread over two floors; the spacious high-ceilinged dining room is on the first level and the five private rooms are located upstairs.

源自上海品牌，此分店於2013年進駐新濠天地，除供應上海菜餚外，還提供少量川粵菜式。與別的小南國不同，此分店午餐時段除了供應超過三十款上海點心和涼菜，還提供廣東點心。餐廳共有兩層，主餐室樓底特高，空間感較強；上層設有五間設備完善的廂房。

TEL. 8868 6661
Level 1, The Boulevard, City of Dreams,
Estrada do Istmo, Cotai
路氹連貫公路新濠天地新濠大道 1樓
www.xiaonanguo.com

■ PRICE 價錢
Lunch 午膳
à la carte 點菜 MOP 120-750
Dinner 晚膳
à la carte 點菜 MOP 200-750

■ OPENING HOURS 營業時間
Lunch 午膳　11:00-15:30 (L.O.)
Weekends & Public Holidays
週末及公眾假期　10:00-16:00 (L.O.)
Dinner 晚膳　18:00-22:30 (L.O.)

Square Eight
食 · 八方

🍴   ♿ 🛎 🅿 🚄

Square Eight's cuisine covers large swathes of China and includes Cantonese noodles, Northern specialities, Shanghainese recipes, Chiu Chow, Macanese rice meals, Hong Kong style noodle dishes and a few offerings from other Asian countries. You're given a large sheet of paper listing all the dishes; simply tick the ones you fancy. It's lively and busy, staff are swift but engaging and the long, open-plan kitchen adds to the bustle.

食 · 八方的餐牌羅列了中國各地菜式：廣東麵類、北方特色菜、上海美食、潮州佳餚、澳門飯餐及港式麵食等，還包羅數款其他亞洲國家的特色美食。食客只需在點菜單上隨意挑選心儀菜式。店子很熱鬧，服務快捷周到，長長的開放式廚房更為餐廳增添一份生氣。

TEL. 8802 2389
GF, MGM Hotel, Avenida Dr. Sun Yat Sen, Nape
外港新填海區孫逸仙大馬路美高梅酒店地下
www.mgmmacau.com

■ PRICE 價錢
Lunch 午膳
à la carte 點菜 MOP 120-350
Dinner 晚膳
à la carte 點菜 MOP 120-350

■ OPENING HOURS 營業時間
Open 24 hours 24 小時營業

MACAU 澳門

Temptations NEW
品味坊

🗝 📞🍴

On the 16th floor atop the StarWorld hotel is a bright, airy restaurant serving a variety of cuisines from a number of European countries – your best bet is to go straight for the Portuguese and Macanese specialities. If you're undecided about dessert, then peek into the kitchen through the window and watch the effort that goes into their creation. This well-run restaurant is ideally suited for those wanting to relax with family or friends.

位於星際酒店16樓的全新餐廳，室內設計以時尚簡約線條配合淺棕色調，淡雅輕鬆的環境氣氛與酒店內其他設施或店舖截然不同，讓人眼前一亮。餐廳主要提供歐陸菜和葡國菜，半自助午餐包含多款前菜與甜品及精選燒烤美食，是不錯的休閒聚餐處。食客可透過開放式廚房的玻璃窗欣賞廚師製作甜品的過程。

TEL. 8290 8688
16F, StarWorld Hotel, Avenida da Amizade
友誼大馬路星際酒店 16樓
www.starworldmacau.com

■ PRICE 價錢
Lunch 午膳
set 套餐 MOP 178
à la carte 點菜 MOP 290-710
Dinner 晚膳
à la carte 點菜 MOP 290-710

■ OPENING HOURS 營業時間
12:00-22:00 (L.O.)

Tenmasa
天政

Taipa's own version of Tenmasa, which opened in Tokyo in 1937 and is still going strong, is a charmingly run restaurant that boasts a sushi bar, a tempura counter and a tatami floor, as well as decked walkways leading across golden pebble ponds to private rooms. Sit and watch the chef at work, as he uses quality ingredients to prepare well-balanced dishes. There are a variety of different menus available at lunch.

天政早於1937年於東京開業，至今仍廣受歡迎。澳門的天政設有壽司吧、天婦羅櫃枱及榻榻米地板，也有鋪板走廊、金石水池和私人餐室。食客可安坐其中，觀看廚師大顯身手，將優質食材炮製成美味菜式。餐廳於午市時代提供多款精選美食。

TEL. 2886 8868
11F, Altira Hotel, Avenida de Kwong
Tung, Taipa
氹仔廣東大馬路新濠鋒酒店 11樓
www.altiramacau.com

■ PRICE 價錢
Lunch 午膳
set 套餐 MOP 288-1,180
à la carte 點菜 MOP 400-1,200
Dinner 晚膳
set 套餐 MOP 488-1,950
à la carte 點菜 MOP 400-1,200

■ OPENING HOURS 營業時間
Lunch 午膳　12:00-14:15 (L.O.)
Dinner 晚膳　18:00-22:15 (L.O.)

■ ANNUAL AND WEEKLY CLOSING 休息日期
Closed Monday 週一休息

MACAU 澳門

Terrazza NEW
庭園

& 🖐 **P** 🍽14 ✻

It is all about relaxation at this large, classically decorated Italian restaurant – thanks largely to the very comfortable chairs and the warm and welcoming service. The menu covers all parts of the country and there's something for everyone, whether you're after a pizza or a more elaborate dish. One thing definitely worth exploring is the wine list. There's a great glass-enclosed private room on the terrace which is surrounded by waterfalls.

古典優雅的設計、柔軟舒適的座椅、友善熱情的服務，讓你身心放鬆。這裏供應的菜式涵蓋意大利全國美食，不論是薄餅或是別的意大利菜，你總能挑選到合心意的美食。最使人驚喜的，是其種類繁多的酒單。露台上的玻璃屋私人廂房給瀑布重重圍着，置身其中猶如身處花果山下的水簾洞，令人嚮往。

TEL. 8883 2221
201, 2F Galaxy Hotel, Estrada da Baia de
Nosssa Senhora da Esperenca, Cotai
路氹望德聖母灣大馬路澳門銀河
銀河酒店 2樓 201號舖
www.galaxymacau.com

■ PRICE 價錢
Dinner 晚膳
set 套餐 MOP 488-1,088
à la carte 點菜 MOP 500-1,500

■ OPENING HOURS 營業時間
18:00-23:00 (L.O.)

■ ANNUAL AND WEEKLY CLOSING 休息日期
Closed Sunday 週日休息

The Eight
8餐廳

P 24

The lavish interior uses the traditional Chinese elements of the goldfish and the number eight to ensure good fortune for all who dine here. The cuisine is a mix of Cantonese and Huaiyang, but the kitchen also adds its own innovative touches to some dishes. Specialities include steamed crab claw with ginger and Chinese wine, and stir-fried lobster with egg, minced pork and black bean. At lunchtime, over 50 kinds of dim sum are served.

豪華的內部裝潢採用了傳統中國元素，如金魚及數目字8，寓意所有到訪的客人都會遇上好運。菜式融合了廣東及淮揚風味，部份美食更滲入了創新點子。推介菜式有薑米酒蒸鮮蟹拑及廣東式炒龍蝦。午餐時段供應逾五十款點心。

TEL. 8803 7788
2F, Grand Lisboa Hotel, Avenida de Lisboa
葡京路新葡京酒店 2樓
www.grandlisboahotel.com

■ PRICE 價錢
Lunch 午膳
à la carte 點菜 MOP 200-1,000
Dinner 晚膳
à la carte 點菜 MOP 400-1,000

■ OPENING HOURS 營業時間
Lunch 午膳 11:30-14:30 (L.O.)
Sunday & Public Holiday lunch
週日及公眾假期
午膳 10:00-15:00 (L.O.)
Dinner 晚膳 18:30-22:30 (L.O.)

The Golden Peacock
皇雀

✗✗   ♿ ⌷·40 ©⫯

The peacock is India's national bird and is used for striking decorative effect at this contemporary Indian restaurant at The Venetian, along with copper, glass, screens and Sadeli mosaics. The chef hails from Kerala but his menu covers all parts of the country making good use of quality ingredients; through the window you can watch his team working with the tandoor oven. At lunch an appealing and good value buffet is provided.

態度嚴謹認真的印度主廚每天以新鮮食材炮製出多道香味俱全的印度美食。除了主餐牌上的菜色，餐廳會在午市時段供應自助餐，價錢相宜。店內以簡約時尚的印度風格為主，並以印度國鳥孔雀作裝飾，帶着濃濃的印度風情。

TEL. 8118 9696
Shop 1037, 1F The Venetian Resort, Estrada de Baia de N. Senhora de Esperanca, Taipa
氹仔路望德聖母灣大馬路威尼斯人酒店
大運河購物中心 1 樓 1037號舖

■ PRICE 價錢
Lunch 午膳
set 套餐 MOP 158
à la carte 點菜 MOP 250-700
Dinner 晚膳
à la carte 點菜 MOP 250-700

■ OPENING HOURS 營業時間
11:00-23:00 (L.O.)

The Kitchen
大廚

There's a handsome, masculine feel to this restaurant on the 3rd floor of the Grand Lisboa. It comes with a sushi bar, a salad counter and a live fish tank but the star of the show is undoubtedly the beef. Prime meat from the US, Japan and Australia is cooked on an open flame and you decide which cut you want and in what size. You're guaranteed to find something to go with your steak from the wine list of over 10,000 labels.

將西式扒房、日式壽司吧及海鮮魚缸融匯一室，這裏的設計確是匠心獨具，閃爍的天花燈飾、金牛形酒吧等，都給人留下深刻印象，更讓人難以忘懷的是其美食!食客可在肉櫃挑選來自美國、澳洲及日本等地的頂級牛肉，並選取不同部位與份量，亦可從魚缸中點選新鮮海產。逾萬款餐酒可供選擇。

TEL. 8803 7777
3F, Grand Lisboa Hotel, Avenida de Lisboa
葡京路新葡京酒店 3樓
www.grandlisboahotel.com

■ PRICE 價錢
Lunch 午膳
set 套餐 MOP 270-460
à la carte 點菜 MOP 480-1,600
Dinner 晚膳
à la carte 點菜 MOP 480-1,600

■ OPENING HOURS 營業時間
Lunch 午膳   12:00-14:30 (L.O.)
Dinner 晚膳   18:30-22:30 (L.O.)

The Tasting Room
御膳房

XXXX　　　　　　　　&. ← ☞ ⌨14 ◎‖ ⅋

Finding respite on the Cotai Strip away from the lively casino vibe can be hard but this relaxing restaurant could help. It's an elegant circular room and offers discreet service. The food is largely French and the Bresse pigeon is the favoured dish of the locals. The chef adds his own unique touches, like onion ice cream to the onion soup. Be sure to have the Chef's Menu.

欲在金光大道賭場上找個地方歇歇，可以到這家氣氛輕鬆的餐廳。圓形的主餐室華麗優雅，侍應服務細心周到。以供應法國菜為主，最著名的是法國乳鴿。大廚喜歡將自己的創意融入菜式中，如洋蔥湯加上洋蔥雪糕。八道菜的總廚精選套餐絕對非試不可。

TEL. 8868 6681
3F, Crown Towers, City of Dreams,
Estrada do Istmo, Cotai
路氹連貫公路新濠天地皇冠度假酒店 3樓
www.cityofdreamsmacau.com/restaurant

■ PRICE 價錢
Lunch 午膳
set 套餐 MOP 388-528
à la carte 點菜 MOP 650-2,150
Dinner 晚膳
set 套餐 MOP 888
à la carte 點菜 MOP 650-2,150

■ OPENING HOURS 營業時間
Lunch 午膳　12:00-14:30 (L.O.)
Dinner 晚膳　18:00-22:30 (L.O.)

Tim's Kitchen
桃花源小廚

🌸

XX X

⌖24 ◐❙ 🕸

Hong Kong foodies make special pilgrimages here and it's easy to see why: the Cantonese dishes may appear quite simple but they are very skilfully prepared. Among the highlights are poached and sliced pork stomach in wasabi sauce, and sweet & sour pork ribs. Do make sure you try the crystal prawn and, during the winter, the tasty snake ragout. The restaurant is decorated with a variety of operatic costumes and photos.

香港食家喜歡專程到此朝聖，原因十分簡單：此食店的廣東菜式看似簡單，卻實在是經過精心巧手炮製。推介菜式包括涼伴爽肚片及京都骨。此外，萬勿錯過玻璃蝦球，而冬天的重點推介則離不開美味的蛇羹。餐廳放滿歌劇照片和戲服裝飾，散發出淡淡的藝術氣息。

TEL. 8803 3682
Shop F25, GF, Hotel Lisboa, East Wing,
2-4 Avenida de Lisboa
葡京路 2-4號葡京酒店東翼地下 F25號舖
www.hotelisboa.com

■ PRICE 價錢
Lunch 午膳
à la carte 點菜 MOP 200-700
Dinner 晚膳
à la carte 點菜 MOP 400-1,300

■ OPENING HOURS 營業時間
Lunch 午膳　12:00-15:00 L.O. 14:30
Dinner 晚膳　18:30-23:00 L.O. 22:30

MACAU 澳門

Tou Tou Koi
陶陶居

🍴   💺24 🕐🍽

As this 80 year old restaurant is always packed, it's vital to book ahead; at the same time why not also pre-order the duck? It's dim sum during the day and Cantonese cuisine at night and among the favourites are deep-fried crab, chicken soup and fish from the tank in the dining room. Service is sufficiently swift to accommodate the non-stop flow of customers. A refurbishment has left the restaurant looking much more contemporary.

有八十多年歷史的陶陶居總是賓客如雲，必須訂座，你亦可順道預訂八寶鴨。日間以點心為主，晚上則提供粵菜，受歡迎菜式包括金錢蟹盒和古法雞煲，還有新鮮烹調的海魚。為了應付絡繹不絕的客人，侍應生的工作效率十分高。酒家翻新後裝潢更見時尚。

TEL. 2857 2629
6-8 Travessa do Mastro
爐石塘巷 6-8號

■ PRICE 價錢
Lunch 午膳
à la carte 點菜 MOP 100-880
Dinner 晚膳
à la carte 點菜 MOP 220-880

■ OPENING HOURS 營業時間
Lunch 午膳   09:00-15:00 (L.O.)
Dinner 晚膳   17:00-00:00 L.O. 23:30

Vida Rica
御苑

♨♨   ♿ ☜ ☞ 🍴24

Dark marble and Asian art combine to create a sophisticated yet relaxing spot here on the second floor of the Mandarin Oriental. The kitchen's plan is to make everyone's life a little richer by covering all bases: the large menu offers international cuisine with a French twist, and also some Cantonese dishes. There's also a simple lunchtime buffet in the bar on the same floor.

座落於文華東方酒店二樓，裝潢結合深色雲石和亞洲藝術的御苑，營造出既豪華又悠閒的氣氣。它的宗旨，是要做到面面俱圓，令所有顧客的生活都更見豐盛。豐富的菜單羅列多國菜式、法式糕點和廣東經典美食。同一樓層的酒吧，更提供簡便的午市自助餐。

TEL. 8805 8918
2F, Mandarin Oriental Hotel, Avenida Dr.
Sun Yat Sen, Nape
外港新填海區孫逸仙大馬路
文華東方酒店 2樓
www.mandarinoriental.com/macau

■ PRICE 價錢
Lunch 午膳
set 套餐 MOP 238-278
à la carte 點菜 MOP 450-1,100
Dinner 晚膳
set 套餐 MOP 798-1,198
à la carte 點菜 MOP 700-1,100

■ OPENING HOURS 營業時間
Lunch 午膳　12:00-14:30 (L.O.)
Dinner 晚膳　18:00-22:30 (L.O.)

Wing Lei
永利軒

✻

XXXX

  ♿ ✐ **P** ⊟12

An opulent, comfortable restaurant in vibrant red, characterised by vast lanterns at the entrance and a striking three-dimensional dragon made of ninety thousand pieces of crystal. As befits such sumptuous surroundings, the service is courteous and attentive. Tourists and a large number of families create a lively ambience as they tuck into the large menu of Cantonese classics.

這家紅彤彤的餐廳入口掛着一些大型燈籠，襯托一條以九萬片水晶製成的立體龍，盡展豪華氣派；舒適的紅色座椅讓人更添好感。餐廳的裝潢實屬一流，服務也親切周到。食客多是一家大小或娛樂場玩家，氣氛非常熱鬧。餐廳供應傳統粵菜，菜式選擇良多。

TEL. 8986 3688
GF, Wynn Hotel, Rua Cidade de Sintra, Nape
外港新填海區仙德麗街永利酒店地下
www.wynnmacau.com

■ PRICE 價錢
Lunch 午膳
à la carte 點菜 MOP 300-2,000
Dinner 晚膳
à la carte 點菜 MOP 300-2,000

■ OPENING HOURS 營業時間
Lunch 午膳　11:30-15:00 (L.O.)
Dinner 晚膳　18:00-23:00 (L.O.)

Wong Kung Sio Kung
皇冠小館

Owner Mr. Cheng, who is native Macanese, has over 30 years of experience when it comes to making noodles using the traditional bamboo pressing method. His shop opened back in 2000 but such was its popularity that he later expanded into next door. A selection of traditional Cantonese dishes is offered but most come here for the sea crab congee and the bamboo noodles with dried shrimp roe (which is also sold in bottles in the shop).

澳門土生土長的東主鄭先生，已有逾三十年以傳統竹竿手打的製作方法製麵的經驗。餐廳早於2000年開業，大受歡迎下擴充至隔鄰鋪位。他的店子提供一系列傳統廣東美食，但慕名而來的食客，通常會點遠近馳名的竹昇蝦子撈麵及海蟹粥。店內亦有出售瓶裝蝦子。

TEL. 2837 2248
308-310A Rua do Campo
水坑尾街 308-310號 A
www.wongkun.com.mo

■ PRICE 價錢
à la carte 點菜 MOP 30-120

■ OPENING HOURS 營業時間
10:00-02:00 (L.O.)
Weekends 週末　09:30-02:00 (L.O.)

■ ANNUAL AND WEEKLY CLOSING 休息日期
Closed 5 days Lunar New Year
農曆新年休息 5 天

MACAU 澳門

Xin

鮮

🍴🍴   ♿

The philosophy behind this restaurant is as simple as its name suggests – it's all about "freshness". On offer are hotpots, seafood and Asian-inspired dishes. You can make up your own hotpot using the superb ingredients from the buffet, along with seven different kinds of broth. There are luxury hotpots too, that include Boston lobster and Wagyu beef. The large contemporary dining room comes with a lively and convivial atmosphere.

此火鍋店以「鮮」為名，意指店內供應的全是最新鮮的食材。除了價格實惠的火鍋自助餐外，喜歡波士頓龍蝦和日本和牛的朋友，可選擇價格較高的精選套餐，且共有七款湯底 供食客選擇。午市時段，還會供應燒味和新派中式點心。

TEL. 8113 1200
L1, Sheraton Hotel, Cotai Central, The
Cotai Strip, Taipa
氹仔路氹金光大道喜來登金城中心酒店 1 樓
www.sheraton.com/macao

■ PRICE 價錢
Lunch 午膳
set 套餐 MOP 228-258
à la carte 點菜 MOP 280-600
Dinner 晚膳
set 套餐 MOP 358-598
à la carte 點菜 MOP 280-600

■ OPENING HOURS 營業時間
Lunch 午膳　11:30-15:00 (L.O.)
Dinner 晚膳　18:00-23:00 (L.O.)

Ying
帝影樓

♿ ⟨ ☞ 🅿 ⊡30 ☎ ⅋

It's not just the breathtaking views looking north to Macau that set this restaurant apart – the beautifully styled interior has been designed with taste and verve; the beaded curtains, which feature gold cranes and crystal trees, are particularly striking. The Cantonese dishes are prepared with contemporary twists and much flair. Try the prawn with herb-scented pear in tangerine paste, and the beef short ribs with red date essence.

帝影樓北望海港及澳門繁華景色，環境宜人。餐廳設計品味獨特，風格絢麗；珠簾上飾有金鶴和水晶樹圖案，使裝潢更添神采。餐廳的粵菜融入了新口味，大廚的烹調技藝精湛。專業的服務態度令人賓至如歸。值得一試的有這裏的柑桔蝦球桂花梨及紅棗炆牛肋骨。

TEL. 2886 8868
11F, Altira Hotel, Avenida de Kwong
Tung, Taipa
氹仔廣東大馬路新濠鋒酒店 11樓
www.altiramacau.com

■ PRICE 價錢
Lunch 午膳
à la carte 點菜 MOP 150-1,700
Dinner 晚膳
à la carte 點菜 MOP 200-1,700

■ OPENING HOURS 營業時間
Lunch 午膳   11:00-15:45 (L.O.)
Dinner 晚膳   18:00-22:30 (L.O.)

Zi Yat Heen
紫逸軒

XXXX 　　　　　　　　　　　　　♿ ☝ P ⏥12 ♬

With a large glass-enclosed wine cellar at its centre, Zi Yat Heen is an elegant yet intimate restaurant, located within the Four Seasons Hotel Macau. By using first rate ingredients and minimal amounts of seasoning, chef Ho prepares a traditional Cantonese menu but one that is lighter and fresher tasting. Interesting creations include the baked lamb chops with coffee sauce, while a more traditional dish would be pigeon with Yunnan ham.

地方寬敞，格調高雅的紫逸軒位於四季酒店一樓，正中位置設有巨型玻璃餐酒庫。大廚何先生烹調傳統菜式時採用最新鮮的食材與最少的調味料，炮製出更鮮味清新的粵菜。有趣創意菜式包括咖啡汁焗羊排，較傳統的選擇有酥香雲腿伴鴿脯。

TEL. 2881 8818
GF, Four Seasons Hotel, Estrada da Baia de N. Senhora de Esperanca, s/n, The Cotai Strip, Taipa
氹仔路氹金光大道 -望德聖母灣大馬路
四季酒店地下
www.fourseasons.com/macau

■ PRICE 價錢
Lunch 午膳
set 套餐 MOP 2,088
à la carte 點菜 MOP 200-1,600
Dinner 晚膳
set 套餐 MOP 2,088
à la carte 點菜 MOP 250-1,600

■ OPENING HOURS 營業時間
Lunch 午膳　11:30-15:00 (L.O.)
Dinner 晚膳　18:00-23:00 (L.O.)

HOTELS
酒店

HOTELS IN ORDER OF COMFORT
酒店 — 以舒適程度分類

Altira
新濠鋒

High quality design, a serene atmosphere and wondrous peninsula views produce something quite spectacular here. Guests arrive at the stylish lobby on the 38th floor and the luxury feel is enhanced by a super lounge and terrace on the same level. Bedrooms face the sea and merge tranquil tones with a contemporary feel. There's also a great spa and a pool-with-a-view.

酒店設計獨特，舒適典雅，位置優越，澳門半島的環迴美景盡入眼簾。38樓的大堂時尚尊貴，同層的「天宮」備有室內酒廊及露天陽台，豪華瑰麗。客房位於較高的樓層，海景一望無際，寧靜的環境與現代設計相互交織，氣派超凡。顧客享用附設的豪華水療設施時可飽覽美景。

TEL. 2886 8888
FAX. 2886 8666
Avenida de Kwong Tung, Taipa
氹仔廣東大馬路
www.altiramacau.com

RECOMMENDED RESTAURANTS 餐廳推薦
Tenmasa 天政　XX
Ying 帝影樓　XXX

♦ = MOP 2,000-5,000
♦♦ = MOP 2,000-5,000
Suites 套房 = MOP 3,500-70,000

Rooms 客房　184
Suites 套房　32

Banyan Tree
悅榕莊

Forming part of Galaxy Macau, this luxurious resort comprises 246 suites, as well as 10 villas which come with their own private gardens and swimming pools. The very comfortable bedrooms all have large baths set by the window and the array of services includes a state-of-the-art spa – the biggest in the group. Guests enjoy full access to all of Galaxy's facilities.

作為路氹城澳門銀河綜合渡假城的一部分及毗鄰澳門國際機場，澳門悅榕莊共有246間套房和10間擁有私人花園和泳池的別墅。所有寬敞套房內均設有私人悅心池，酒店提供一系列貼心服務，當中包括集團最大及最頂級的水療中心。住客更可享用銀河綜合渡假城內所有設施。

TEL. 8883 8833
FAX. 8883 6108
Galaxy Macau, Avenida Marginal Flor de Lotus, Cotai
路氹城蓮花海濱大馬路澳門銀河渡假城
www.banyantree.com/en/macau/

Suites 套房 = MOP 3,100-100,000
Villas 別墅 = MOP 18,000-45,000
☕ = MOP 200

Suites 套房　246
Villas 別墅　10

RECOMMENDED RESTAURANTS 餐廳推薦
Saffron 尚坊　XX

Conrad
康萊德

The largest of all the Conrad hotels is on the Cotai Strip and its guests have access to an abundance of shopping, gaming, dining and entertainment opportunities. The Himalayan and Chinese inspired décor creates a relaxing environment; anyone requiring extra stress reduction should book a restorative session in one of the ten treatment rooms in the luxurious spa.

座落於路氹金光大道上的康萊德，是全球規模最大的酒店，這裏有為數不少的購物、賭博、餐飲及娛樂場所。陳設靈感取材自喜瑪拉雅和中國地區，感覺悠閒舒適。豪華水療中心內設有十間套房，客人可盡情享受水療服務，令壓力和疲勞一掃而空。客房空間寬敞，設計時尚。

TEL. 2882 9000
FAX. 2882 9001
Estrada da Baia de N. Senhora de Esperanca, s/n, The Cotai Strip, Taipa
氹仔路氹金光大道望德聖母灣大馬路
www.conradmacao.com

♦ = MOP 4,000
♦♦ = MOP 6,348
Suites 套房 = MOP 7,098-7,348

Rooms 客房   430
Suites 套房   206

RECOMMENDED RESTAURANTS 餐廳推薦
Dynasty 8 朝 ✕✕

Encore
萬利

For VIPs wanting an even more exclusive resort experience than the Wynn, there is Encore – their luxury brand. The word 'standard' certainly does not apply here as the choice is between suites or villas, all of which are lavishly decorated. You also get an exceptional spa offering bespoke treatments and Bar Cristal: as small as a jewellery box and just as precious.

欲享受比永利更獨特尊貴的服務，可考慮同集團旗下更豪華的萬利。酒店提供豪華套房或渡假別墅，兩者均以紅色與金色裝潢，特顯富麗堂皇。貴賓級水療中心為你提供度身訂造的療程，酒店內的「Bar Cristal」一如其名，像珠寶盒般嬌小高貴。賭場內附設多間貴賓娛樂房。

TEL. 2888 9966
FAX. 2832 9966
Rua Cidade de Sintra, Nape
外港新填海區仙德麗街
www.wynnmacau.com

Suites 套房 = MOP 15,000-22,000
⊊ = MOP 138

Suites 套房 414

RECOMMENDED RESTAURANTS 餐廳推薦
Café Encore 咖啡廷 ХХ
Golden Flower 京花軒 ✿✿ ХхХ
99 Noodles 99 麵 Х

441

MACAU 澳門

Four Seasons
四季

The luxurious Four Seasons fuses East and West by blending Colonial Portuguese style with Chinese traditions. The lobby acts as a living room, with its fireplace, Portuguese lanterns and Chinese lacquer screens. The hotel also has a luxury shopping mall and connects to The Venetian and Plaza Casino. If you want peace, simply escape to the spa or one of the five pools and the charming garden.

2008年開幕的四季酒店融合了東西方元素，將殖民地時代的葡萄牙風格與中國傳統融為一體。大堂設有壁爐、葡國燈籠和中國雕漆屏風，猶如置身家中客廳。酒店設有豪華購物商場，直通威尼斯人酒店及百利沙娛樂場。想離開五光十色稍作喘息，可享用酒店的水療設備和五個泳池，還有迷人的花園。

TEL. 2881 8888
FAX. 2881 8899
Estrada da Baia de N. Senhora de
Esperanca, s/n, The Cotai Strip, Taipa
氹仔路氹金光大道望德聖母灣大馬路
www.fourseasons.com/macau

RECOMMENDED RESTAURANTS 餐廳推薦
Belcanção 鳴詩 ※※
Zi Yat Heen 紫逸軒 ❁❁ ※※※※

☺ = MOP 2,088-10,888
☺☺ = MOP 2,088-10,888
Suites 套房 = MOP 4,400-63,888
🛌 = MOP 238

Rooms 客房 276
Suites 套房 84

Galaxy NEW
銀河

The striking exterior of Galaxy is one of the most recognisable landmarks of Taipa. The guestrooms are very spacious and impressively well equipped. Another of the attractions of the hotel is its 2,000sqm artificial beach and the world's largest wave pool; there also are cinemas and assorted restaurants. It's just a few minutes' walk from the Old Town.

外觀金碧輝煌的銀河渡假城是氹仔的新地標。作為渡假城內三間酒店之一，銀河酒店予人國際化的印象。1500間客房，每間都裝潢時尚、空間寬趟、設備齊全兼現代化。最吸引的設施是佔地2000平方米的人造沙灘及大型衝浪泳池。戲院和餐飲設施一應俱全，與舊城區只有一條馬路之隔，便於觀光購物。

TEL. 2888 0888
FAX. 8883 3988
Estrada da Baia da N. Senhora da Esperanca, s/n, The Cotai Strip, Taipa
路氹望德聖母灣大馬路
www.galaxymacau.com

RECOMMENDED RESTAURANTS 餐廳推薦
Gosto 葡軒 ✗
Myung Ga 名家 ✗
Terrazza 庭園 ✗✗✗

♦ = MOP 1,680
♦♦ = MOP 2,380
Suites 套房 = MOP 7,690
☐ = MOP 138

Rooms 客房   1449
Suites 套房   56

MACAU 澳門

Grand Hyatt
君悅

With its striking 22m ceiling and fabulous artwork, the lobby sets the tone – the droplets appear to be falling from a cloud. The contemporary bedrooms are split between two towers. Along with contemporary and luxurious suites, the Grand Club on the top floor provides a dining service where customers can order any kind of cuisine they choose.

君悅氣店的大堂設計獨特，從22米天花上空墜下的吊飾，配合藝術設計營造出水珠從雲層落下再匯聚一起的壯觀景象。設計時尚的房間分佈在兩棟大樓內。位於頂層，最新開幕的嘉賓軒裝潢高雅，有多間貴賓廂房，按客人喜好提供不同餐飲服務，是與辦私人商務聚會的理想場地。

TEL. 8868 1234
FAX. 8867 1234
City of Dreams, Estrada do Istmo, Cotai
路氹連貫公路新濠天地
www.macau.grand.hyatt.com

RECOMMENDED RESTAURANTS 餐廳推薦
Beijing Kitchen 滿堂彩 ✗✗
Mezza9 ✗✗

♦ = MOP 1,888-3,888
♦♦ = MOP 1,888-3,888
Suites 套房 = MOP 2,300-13,000
⛛ = MOP 228

Rooms 客房 503
Suites 套房 288

Grand Lisboa
新葡京

Impossible to miss, the Grand Lisboa can be seen from miles away with its eye-popping, brightly-lit lotus design atop a shining diamond. Opulent soundproofed bedrooms feature Asian paintings, and offer grand sea or city vistas. If you have a corner room or a suite, you'll get the added bonus of a sauna; if you have neither, you can make use of the sumptuous spa.

2008年12月開幕的新葡京外型像一片耀目的黃蓮葉，座落於一顆閃爍的鑽石之上，遠處可見。客房隔音設備完善，擁有典型的棕色牆壁、紅色扶手椅和亞洲油畫，並坐擁豪華海景或澳門的秀麗風光。角位客房及套房設有桑拿設施，其他客房亦可享用豪華的水療設施。

TEL. 2828 3838
FAX. 2888 2828
Avenida de Lisboa
葡京路
www.grandlisboahotel.com

RECOMMENDED RESTAURANTS 餐廳推薦
Don Alfonso 1890 當奧豐素 1890　✗✗✗✗
Noodle & Congee Corner 粥麵莊　🍴 🍜
Robuchon au Dôme
天巢法國餐廳 ✿✿✿　✗✗✗✗
The Eight 8 餐廳　✿✿✿　✗✗✗
The Kitchen 大廚　✿　✗✗

👤 = MOP 2,600-3,780
👥 = MOP 2,600-3,780
Suites 套房 = MOP 4,480-48,000
🛏 = MOP 150

Rooms 客房　381
Suites 套房　50

Lisboa
葡京

Thanks largely to its 1970s style façade, The Lisboa sports a relatively sober look for Macau, and so stands in stark contrast to the glitzier Grand Lisboa. There are ten types of guestroom available and the decoration is a mix of Chinese and Portuguese styles; it's worth asking for a Tower room, as these are larger and more luxurious than those in the east wing.

仍然保留着七十年代外觀的葡京酒店，帶出澳門較為樸實的一面，與閃閃生輝的新葡京酒店可謂相映成趣。酒店共有十種客房，其陳設融合了中葡兩國的風格與特色；當中尊尚客房比東翼的客房更大更豪華。酒店設有多家餐廳，提供多國菜式。

TEL. 2888 3888
FAX. 2888 3838
2-4 Avenida de Lisboa
葡京路 2-4號
www.hotelisboa.com

RECOMMENDED RESTAURANTS 餐廳推薦
Guincho a Galera 葡國餐廳 XXXX
Tim's Kitchen 桃花源小廚 ✿ XXX

† = MOP 1,480-2,320
†† = MOP 1,480-2,320
Suites 套房 = MOP 3,780-23,880
☕ = MOP 140

Rooms 客房 876
Suites 套房 50

Mandarin Oriental
文華東方

The Mandarin Oriental is a non-gaming hotel but that's not the only reason it stands out – it is also a model of taste and discretion. Local artists' work adds a sense of locale to the bedrooms which come in muted, contemporary tones and offer great views – even from the tub! Those in search of further relaxation can choose between a very serene spa and a slick bar.

於2010年開業的澳門文華東方，除了不經營賭場外，更是品味的典範。本地藝術家的創作，為色調柔和時尚的客房添上韻味，即使在浴室裏也能欣賞醉人景觀。想進一步放鬆身心，可到幽靜的水療中心或雅致的酒吧。此外，服務質素保持極高水準。

TEL. 8805 8888
FAX. 8805 8899
Avenida Dr. Sun Yat Sen, Nape
外港新填海區孫逸仙大馬路
www.mandarinoriental.com/macau

RECOMMENDED RESTAURANTS 餐廳推薦
Vida Rica 御苑 %%

☺ = MOP 4,300-5,900
☺☺ = MOP 4,300-5,900
Suites 套房 = MOP 8,300-63,800
☕ = MOP 299

Rooms 客房　186
Suites 套房　27

MGM
美高梅

Its iconic, wave-like exterior makes MGM one of Macau's more instantly recognisable hotels. The interior is pretty eye-catching too: topped by a vast glass ceiling, the Grande Praça covers over 1,000 square metres and is where you'll find an assortment of bars and restaurants. Spread over 35 floors, bedrooms are suitably luxurious and have glass-walled bathrooms.

標誌性的波浪形建築設計讓美高梅成為澳門最矚目酒店之一。店內設計同樣出色:巨型玻璃天幕下的天幕廣場佔地逾一千平方米,設有多間酒吧和餐廳。如果看膩了浮華的裝潢,不妨前往恬靜的水療中心。酒店有35層,客房華麗得恰到好處,景觀優美,浴室採用玻璃間隔,感覺寬敞。

TEL. 8802 8888
FAX. 8802 3333
Avenida Dr. Sun Yat Sen, Nape
外港新填海區孫逸仙大馬路
www.mgmgrandmacau.com

RECOMMENDED RESTAURANTS 餐廳推薦
Imperial Court 金殿堂 ⅩⅩⅩ
Square Eight 食・八方 ☺ Ⅹ

👤 = MOP 1,788-4,000
👤👤 = MOP 1,788-4,000
Suites 套房 = MOP 4,000-40,000
🍽 = MOP 209

Rooms 客房　471
Suites 套房　111

Okura
大倉

 ♿ ← 👤 ♻ 🚻 🖼 🏊 🏃 Ⓢ

Looking for sanctuary from the outside world? Try this tasteful, discreet and elegant hotel, which is part of Galaxy Macau resort. Charming staff provide excellent service; bedrooms are up-to-the-minute; and all suites have private saunas and steam showers. Dining options include Japanese and international fare and Sakazuki Sake bar has over 90 varieties of sake.

裝修典雅與品味並重的大倉酒店讓賓客感覺如遠離了凡塵的一切。身穿日本和服的服務員服務親切貼心，時尚的酒店客房寬敞舒適，套房內設有私人桑拿及蒸氣浴。酒店內設有供應日式及世界美食的餐廳，其「清酒盃」酒吧提供九十多種清酒予賓客享用。

TEL. 8883 8883
FAX. 8883 2345
Galaxy, Avenida Marginal Flor de Lotus, Cotai
路氹城蓮花海濱大馬路澳門銀河渡假城
www.hotelokuramacau.com

♂ = MOP 1,788-5,000
♂♂ = MOP 1,788-5,000
Suites 套房 = MOP 3,288-30,000

Rooms 客房 429
Suites 套房 59

Pousada de Mong-Há
望廈迎賓館

A very good value hotel with a distinct difference – it is run by the Institute for Tourism Studies, so you will be welcomed at the desk by students learning their trade. The hotel benefits from a very peaceful position, away from the casinos and surrounded by a lovely garden. Its bedrooms may not be big but they are quiet and come with some nice Asian touches.

這家與眾不同的超值賓館由旅遊學院營運，因此全部服務員由學院的學生擔任，為你悉心服務。它位處寧靜的望廈山半山腰，遠離娛樂場的煩囂，更給可愛的花園重重圍繞。客房地方不算大，不過環境寧靜，設計帶有亞洲風格。教學餐廳是品嘗澳門美食的好去處。

TEL. 2851 5222
FAX. 2855 6925
Rua Cidade de Sintra, Nape
外港新填海區仙德麗街
www.ift.edu.mo/pousada

RECOMMENDED RESTAURANTS 餐廳推薦
IFT Educational Restaurant
旅遊學院教學餐廳 ⊕ ℵℵ

♦ = MOP 700-1,300
♦♦ = MOP 700-1,300
Suites 套房 = MOP 1,300-1,800

Rooms 客房 16
Suites 套房 4

Pousada de São Tiago
聖地牙哥古堡

An exquisite boutique hotel, built into the hillside on the foundations of a 17th century fort alongside traditional Portuguese villas. Ancient steps lead up to reception; by contrast, the interior is modern and stylish, with subdued taste the key feature. Guestrooms boast cool marble floors and rich colours and fabrics – all look onto the Straits of Macau.

這家座落於山腰的精品酒店，由一座十七世紀的城堡改建而成，毗鄰傳統葡式住宅。古樸的石階別具風情，拾級而上可經入口到達接待處。內部設計十分現代時尚，獨樹一格而不浮誇。客房採用大理石地板、鮮明的顏色和布料；每間客房都坐擁澳門內港景色。陽台設有戶外泳池。

TEL. 2837 8111
FAX. 2855 2170
Avenida da República, Fortaleza de São Tiago da Barra
西灣民國大馬路聖地牙哥大炮台
www.saotiago.com.mo

Suites 套房 = MOP 3,000-5,400
☕ = MOP 126

Suites 套房　12

RECOMMENDED RESTAURANTS 餐廳推薦
La Paloma 芭朗瑪 ✕✕

Rocks
萊斯

This seaside hotel's ambience is inspired by the Victorian era and, as part of Fisherman's Wharf, is a good choice for those who prefer the quieter side of Macau. It has a lobby full of Victorian-style décor and furnishings including a fireplace and paintings, as well as a big marble staircase. A terrace overlooks the bay, while bedrooms have balconies and sea views.

酒店座落於澳門漁人碼頭，設計採用維多利亞時期風格。酒店大堂佈滿維多利亞時期的裝飾及傢俱:火爐、掛畫及大型白色雲石樓梯。舒適怡人的花園盡收海灣醉人景色，設有海景露台的臥室讓你盡情放鬆身心。這裏不設賭場，專為嚮往澳門寧靜一面的遊客而設。

TEL. 2878 2782
FAX. 2870 8800
Macau Fisherman's Wharf
澳門漁人碼頭
www.rockshotel.com.mo

♦ = MOP 1,650-2,530
♦♦ = MOP 1,650-2,530
Suites 套房 = MOP 3,600-5,500
☕ = MOP 130

Rooms 客房　66
Suites 套房　6

Sheraton
喜來登

Currently the biggest hotel in Macau, Sheraton Macau forms part of the resort complex of Sands Cotai Central and is connected to a huge shopping mall. Needless to say, the facilities are comprehensive and include a varied choice of restaurant, three outdoor pools with private cabanas and an impressive spa. There are Family suites and special amenities for children.

作為全澳門最大規模、位於金沙城中心的喜來登酒店,連接大型購物商場,便於閒逛購物。酒店內設備亦相當完善:設有數間餐館、三個戶外泳池及舒適的水療設施,吃喝玩樂與休憩,一網打盡。酒店還設有家庭套房和兒童遊樂設施,適合一家大小住宿。

TEL. 2880 2000
FAX. 2880 2111
Estrada da Baia de N. Senhora de
Esperanca, s/n, The Cotai Strip, Taipa
氹仔路氹金光大道望德聖母灣大馬路
www.sheraton.com/macao

RECOMMENDED RESTAURANTS 餐廳推薦
Xin 鮮 ✕✕

 = MOP 1,388-5,088
 = MOP1,388-5,088
Suites 套房 = MOP 5,988-20,838
 = MOP 188

Rooms 客房　3603
Suites 套房　260

StarWorld
星際

Opened in 2006, StarWorld Macau is a comfortable, well-managed hotel in a good location. Its bedrooms are bright and contemporary and the bathrooms are smart and well-equipped. Along with various restaurants and assorted gaming, the hotel also offers comprehensive entertainment and leisure facilities and these include a bar with live music every night.

在2006年開業的星際酒店地點便利之餘，亦是一間管理完善的酒店。光猛的房間設計風格前衛，時髦的浴室設施相當完備。除了各式餐館和娛樂場所外，酒店內還附設各種休閒設施，例如每天晚上都有現場音樂演奏的酒吧 。

TEL. 2838 3838
FAX. 2838 3888
Avenida da Amizade
友誼大馬路
www.starworldmacau.com

RECOMMENDED RESTAURANTS 餐廳推薦
Temptations 品味坊 ⊞ 𝖷𝖷

⚊ = MOP 2,500-2,800
⚊⚊ = MOP 2,500-2,800
Suites 套房 = MOP 4,800-7,800
⚏ = MOP 138

Rooms 客房 465
Suites 套房 42

The Venetian
威尼斯人

One thing you'll need at Asia's largest integrated resort is a map to find your way around. Expect vast shopping malls and even canals with singing gondoliers; there are frescoes, colonnades and sculptures everywhere – it's easy to get caught up in the sheer scale and exuberance of it all. Identikit luxury is assured in a towering bedroom skyscraper with 3,000 rooms.

你需要一張地圖才能環遊這間全亞洲最大型綜合渡假酒店！在這裏你會找到大型購物商場，更有貢多拉船夫一邊掌舵一邊唱歌。遍佈各處的壁畫、柱廊和雕塑裝飾，具規模且色彩繽紛，令人目不暇給。高聳的摩天大樓設有三千間客房，全部房間都很寬敞。

TEL. 2882 8888
FAX. 2882 8889
Estrada da Baia de N. Senhora de
Esperanca, s/n, The Cotai Strip, Taipa
氹仔路氹金光大道望德聖母灣大馬路
www.venetianmacao.com

RECOMMENDED RESTAURANTS 餐廳推薦
Canton 喜粵　✗✗✗
Lei Garden 利苑酒家　✗✗
The Golden Peacock 皇雀 ✿ ✗✗

🧍 = MOP 5,500
🧍🧍 = MOP 5,500
Suites 套房 = MOP 8,000
☕ = MOP 200

Rooms 客房　2900
Suites 套房　100

Wynn
永利

The Wynn's easy-on-the-eye curving glass façade is enhanced with a lake and dancing fountains, while the classically luxurious interior includes Murano glass chandeliers, plush carpets and much marble. An attractively landscaped oasis pool forms the centrepiece to corridors lined with famous retail names. Comfortable bedrooms display a considerable degree of taste.

弧形的玻璃外牆十分奪目，更設有表演湖及噴池。酒店內部散發著古典豪華氣息：穆拉諾穆玻璃吊燈、豪華的地毯，觸目所及皆是大理石。走廊中心設有一個造型迷人的綠洲池，而兩旁滿是名店。客房融合了傳統與現代兩種設計風格，盡顯卓越品味。其吉祥樹同樣令你印象深刻。

TEL. 2888 9966
FAX. 2832 9966
Rua Cidade de Sintra, Nape
外港新填海區仙德麗街
www.wynnmacau.com

RECOMMENDED RESTAURANTS 餐廳推薦
Il Teatro 帝雅廷 ХхХ
Wing Lei 永利軒 ✿ ХхХ

♦ = MOP 3,500-4,300
♦♦ = MOP 3,500-4,300
Suites 套房 = MOP 16,500-41,000
☕ = MOP 185

Rooms 客房　460
Suites 套房　140

MAPS
地圖

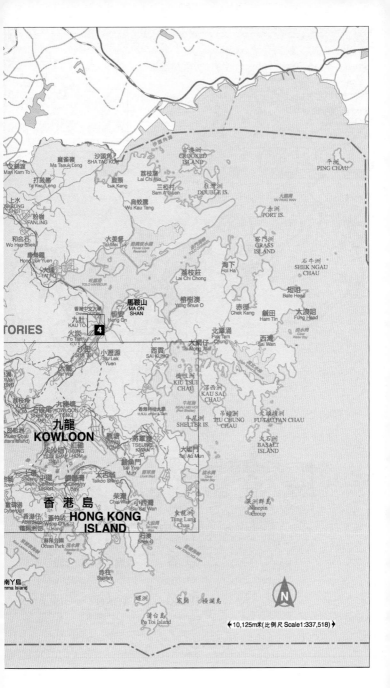

文錦渡
Man Kam To

沙頭角
SHA TAU KOK

香澳洲
CROOKED
ISLAND

平洲
PING CHAU

廟雀嶺
Ma Tseuk Leng

打鼓嶺
Ta Kwu Leng

荔枝窩
Lai Chi Wo

簕竹排
Luk Keng

三椏村
Sam A Tsuen

往灣洲
DOUBLE IS.

大鵬灣
TAI PANG WAN

上水
SHEUNG
SHUI

粉嶺
FANLING

烏蛟騰
Wu Kau Tang

赤洲
PORT IS.

和合石
Wo Hop Shek

大美督
Tai Mei Tuk

鶴藪接水塘
Flower Cove
Reservoir

葛洲
GRASS
ISLAND

石牛洲
SHEK NGAU
CHAU

康樂園
Hong Lok Yuen

大埔
TAI PO

吐露港
TOLO HARBOUR

滘枝角
Lai Chi Chong

海下
Hoi Ha

榕樹澳
Yung Shue O

赤徑
Chek Keng

鹹田
Ham Tin

短咀
Bate Head

大滘阻
Fung Head

TORIES

馬鞍山
MA ON
SHAN

香港中文大學
Chinese University of H.K.

九肚
KAU TO

恒安
Heng On

4

火炭
Fo Tan

小瀝源
Siu Lek
Yuen

西貢
SAI KUNG

大網仔
Tai Mong Tsai

北潭涌
Pak Tam
Chung

西灣
Sai Wan

沙田
SHA TIN

大圍
Tai Wai

滘涌灣
Clear
Water Bay

橋咀洲
KIU TSUI
CHAU

滘西洲
KAU SAI
CHAU

吊鐘洲
TIU CHUNG
CHAU

伏狼牌洲
FU TAU FAN CHAU

荔枝角
LAI CHI KOK

九龍塘
KOWLOON
TONG

石硤尾
SHEK KIP
MEI

牛尾海
Port Shelter

香港科技大學
H.K.U. of Sci. & Tech.

牛尾洲
SHELTER IS.

昂船洲
Stonecutters Island

九龍
KOWLOON

觀塘
KWUN
TONG

將軍澳
TSEUNG
KWAN
O

大廟阿
Tai Miu Wan

火石洲
BASALT
ISLAND

尖沙咀
TSIM SHA TSUI

藍田
LAM TIN

鯉魚門
Lei Yue
Mun

調景嶺
Tiu Keng Leng

大圍
清水灣
Clear
Water Bay

上環
SHEUNG
WAN

中環
CENTRAL
District

太古城
Taikoo Shing

柴灣
Chai Wan

小西灣
Siu Sai Wan

東龍洲
Tung Lung
Chau

萊洲群島
Ninepin
Group

香港島
HONG KONG
ISLAND

香港仔
Aberdeen

黃竹坑
Wong Chuk
Hang

鰂魚涌
Quarry Bay

大浪
Tai Long

石澳
Shek O

清水灣郊野公園
CLEAR WATER BAY PARK

數碼港
Cyberport

香港仔
Aberdeen

海洋公園
Ocean Park

深水灣
Deep Water
Bay

南丫島
Lamma Island

赤柱
Stanley

蒲台島
Po Toi Island

螺洲

宋崗

橫瀾島

10,125m米(比例尺 Scale1:337,518)

N

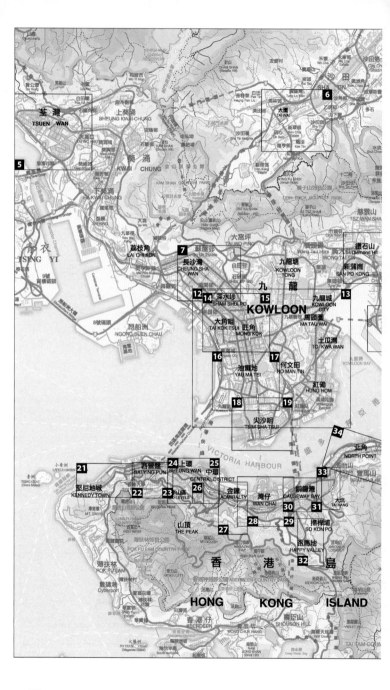

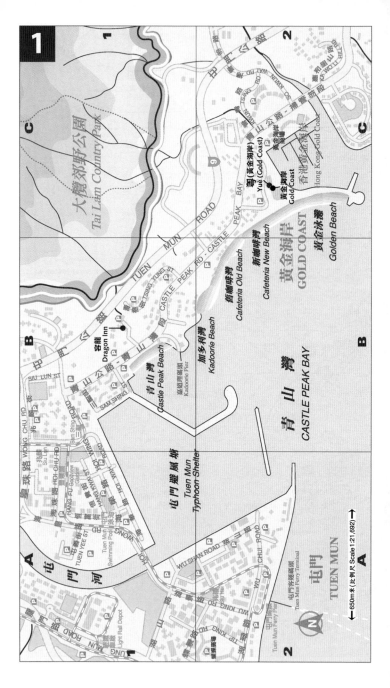

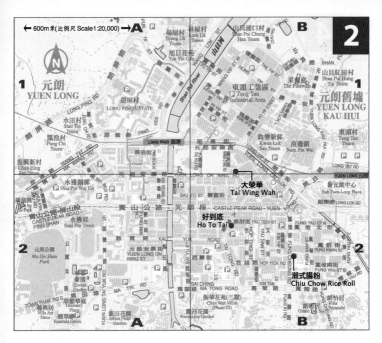

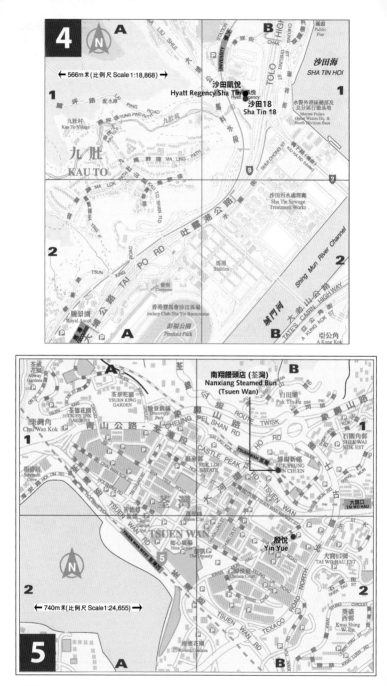

4

A

B

← 566m米(比例尺 Scale 1:18,868) →

沙田海
SHA TIN HOI

歌頭
Public Pier

沙田凱悅
Hyatt Regency Sha Tin

沙田18
Sha Tin 18

水警外港區總部及
北分區行動基地
Marine Police Outer
Waters Hq. & North
Division Base

九肚村
Kam To Village

九肚
KAU TO

沙田河水處理廠
Sha Tin Sewage
Treatment Works

馬房
Stables

城門河
Shing Mun River Channel

會所
Clubhouse

大老山公路
TATES CAIRN HIGHWAY

廣景園
Royal Ascot

香港賽馬會沙田馬場
Jockey Club Sha Tin Racecourse

彭福公園
Penfold Park

亞公角
A Kung Kok

5

A

B

茶威花園
Allway
Gardens

南翔饅頭店 (荃灣)
Nanxiang Steamed Bun
(Tsuen Wan)

白田壩
Pak Tin Pa

石圍角邨
SHEK WAI
KOK EST

柴灣角
Chai Wan Kok

茶景花園
TSUEN KING
GARDEN

荃德花園
TSUEN TAK
GARDENS

愉景新城
Discovery
Park

象鼻山路
PEL SHAN RD

青山公路-荃灣段
CASTLE PEAK

福來邨
FUK LOI
ESTATE

綠楊新邨
LUK YEUNG
SUN CHUEN

大窩口
TAI WO HAU

荃灣
TSUEN WAN

祈德尊新邨
Clague
Garden
Est.

愉景新城
Vision City

如心廣場
Nina Tower

殷悅
Yin Yue

大窩口邨
TAI WO HAU EST

悅海
The Dynasty

荃景圍
Chelsea Court

葵盛西邨
Kwai Shing
W. Est.

N

← 740m米(比例尺 Scale1:24,655) →

荃灣西約
TSUEN WAN WEST

麗城花園
Riviera Gardens

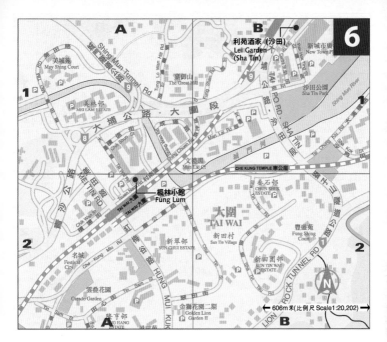

6

利苑酒家 (沙田)
Lei Garden
(Sha Tin)

楓林小館
Fung Lum

大圍
TAI WAI

← 606m米(比例尺 Scale1:20,202) →

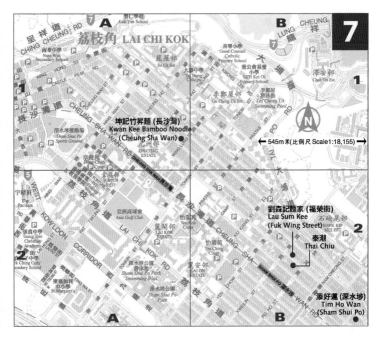

7

荔枝角 LAI CHI KOK

坤記竹昇麵 (長沙灣)
Kwan Kee Bamboo Noodle
(Cheung Sha Wan)

← 545m米(比例尺 Scale1:18,155) →

劉森記麵家 (福榮街)
Lau Sum Kee
(Fuk Wing Street)

泰潮
Thai Chiu

添好運 (深水埗)
Tim Ho Wan
(Sham Shui Po)

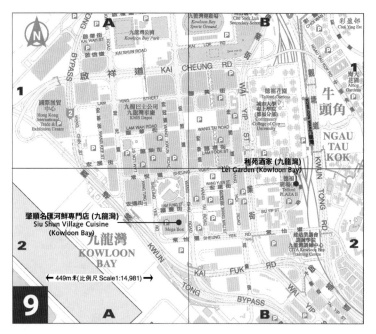

468

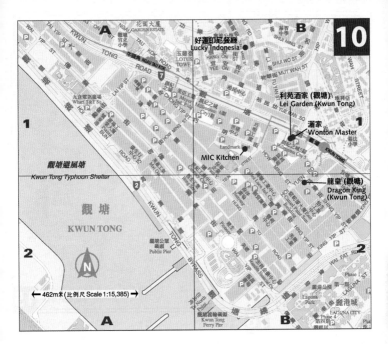

好運印尼餐廳
Lucky Indonesia

利苑酒家 (觀塘)
Lei Garden (Kwun Tong)

灘家
Wonton Master

MIC Kitchen

龍皇 (觀塘)
Dragon King (Kwun Tong)

觀塘避風塘
Kwun Tong Typhoon Shelter

觀塘
KWUN TONG

觀塘公眾碼頭
Public Pier

← 462m米 (比例尺 Scale 1:15,385) →

龍翔流輪碼頭
Kwun Tong Ferry Pier

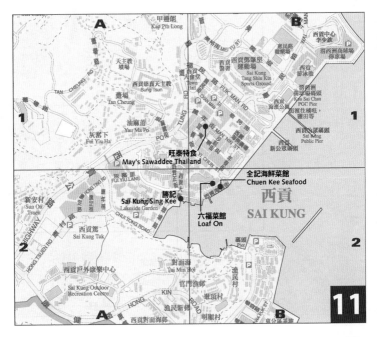

甲遍朗
Kap Pin Long

西貢崇真天主教
Sung Tsun

油麻蒲
Yau Ma Po

灰窰下
Fui Yiu Ha

西貢鄧肇堅運動場
Sai Kung Tang Shiu Kin Sports Ground

旺泰特食
May's Sawaddee Thailand

西貢公眾碼頭
Sai Kung Public Pier

全記海鮮菜館
Chuen Kee Seafood

灰窰
Fui Yiu Lane

勝記
Sai Kung Sing Kee

西貢
SAI KUNG

六福菜館
Loaf On

新安村
Sun On Tsuen

西貢篤
Sai Kung Tuk

西貢戶外康樂中心
Sai Kung Outdoor Recreation Centre

對面海
Tui Min Hoi

官門漁港
漁民村

西貢對面海邨

明廊村

469

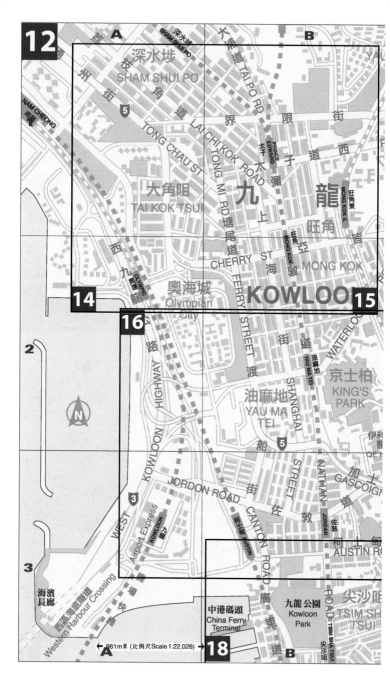

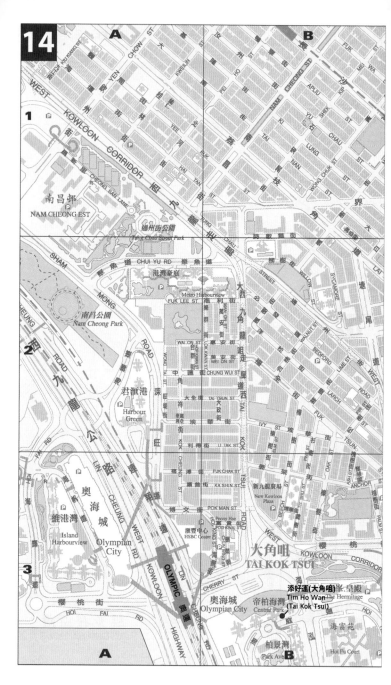

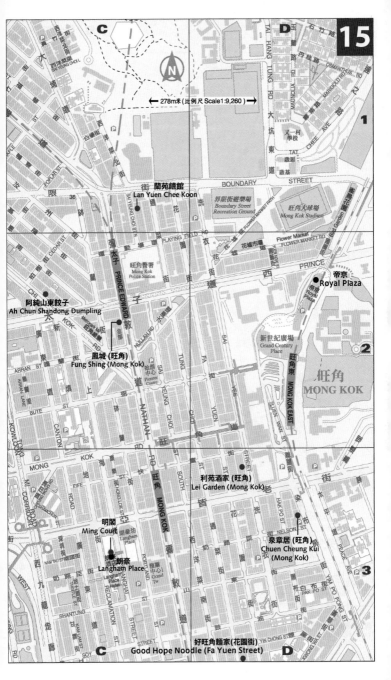

←278m米 (比例尺 Scale 1:9,260) →

街 蘭苑饡館
Lan Yuen Chee Koon

界限街遊樂場
Boundary Street
Recreation Ground

旺角大球場
Mong Kok Stadium

BOUNDARY STREET

花墟市道
FLOWER MARKET RD.

花墟公園
Flower Market

旺角警署
Mong Kok
Police Station

PRINCE EDWARD

PRINCE

帝京
Royal Plaza

帝京
Royal Plaza

阿純山東餃子
Ah Chun Shandong Dumpling

鳳城 (旺角)
Fung Shing (Mong Kok)

新世紀廣場
Grand Century
Place

旺角東
MONG KOK EAST

旺角
MONG KOK

ABRAN ST

BUTE ST

CANTON RD

NATHAN RD.

MONG KOK

KOWLOON

FIFE ST

MONG KOK RD

利苑酒家 (旺角)
Lei Garden (Mong Kok)

明閣
Ming Court

朗豪
Langham Place

泉章居 (旺角)
Chuen Cheung Kui
(Mong Kok)

PAK PO ST

NELSON ST

SHANTUNG

好旺角麵家(花園街)
Good Hope Noodle (Fa Yuen Street)

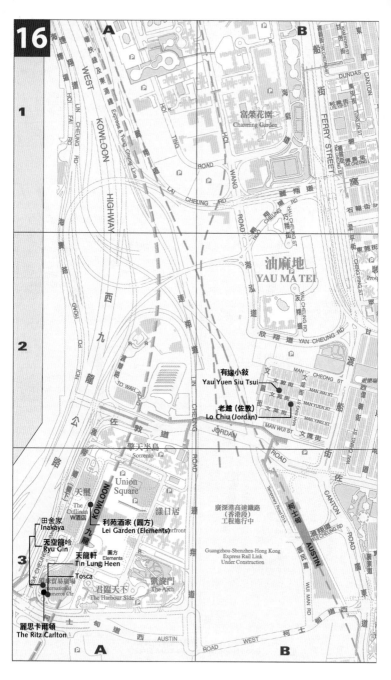

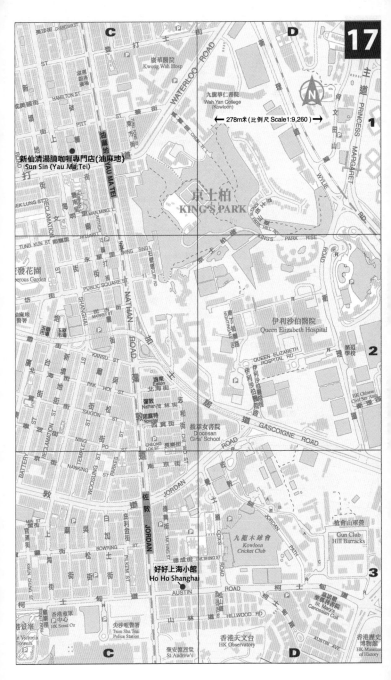

主
道
PRINCESS

CHANGSHA ST

廣華醫院
Kwong Wah Hosp

WATERLOO ROAD

九龍華仁書院
Wah Yan College
(Kowloon)

HAMILTON ST

PITT

新仙清湯腩咖喱專門店(油麻地)
Sun Sin (Yau Ma Tei)

油麻地
YAU MA TEI

NATHAN ROAD

RECLAMATION ST

京士柏
KING'S PARK

← 278m米(比例尺 Scale 1:9,260) →

WYLIE ROAD

KING'S PARK RISE

1

TUNG KUN ST

WING SING

PUBLIC SQUARE ST

SHANGHAI

MARKET ST

KANSU ST

發花園
Prosperous Garden

油麻地
警署

NATHAN ROAD

PAK HOI
ST

廣東
SAIGON

逸東
Eaton
北海街

諾富特
Nathan茂 林街
Novotel
西貢街

NING PO

伊利沙伯醫院
Queen Elizabeth Hospital

NIGHTINGALE

QUEEN ELIZABETH
HOSPITAL RD

拔萃女書院
Diocesan
Girls' School

CHEONG
LOK ST

GASCOIGNE ROAD

ROAD

理學院

新邊
HK Chinese
Civil Ser. Inst.
衛理道

2

BATTERY

RECLAMATION ST

TEMPLE

NANKING

WOOSUNG ST

南京街

JORDAN ROAD

佐敦
JORDAN

TAK HING ST

九龍木球會
Kowloon
Cricket Club

JORDAN ROAD

COX'S

PATH

ROAD

檳會山軍營
Gun Club
Hill Barracks

3

MAIN ST

KWUN CHUNG

BOWRING

吳松街

PILKEM ST

好好上海小館
Ho Ho Shanghai

德成街
TAK SHING ST

AUSTIN ROAD

柯士甸道

HILLWOOD RD

AUSTIN

西鐵嘉諾撒書院
St. Mary's
Canossian Coll

香港歷史
博物館
HK Museum
of History

he Victoria
Towers

香港童軍
中心
HK Scout Ctr

尖沙咀警署
Tsim Sha Tsui
Police Station

聖安德烈堂
St. Andrew's

香港天文台
HK Observatory

AUSTIN AVE

C · **D**

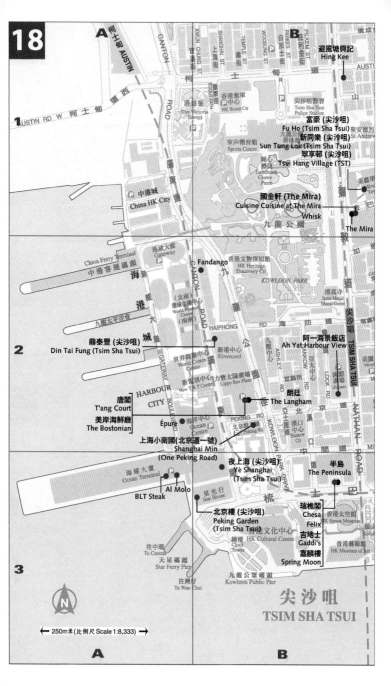

避風塘興記
Hing Kee

尖沙咀警署
Tsim Sha Tsui
Police Station

富豪 (尖沙咀)
Fu Ho (Tsim Sha Tsui)
新同樂 (尖沙咀)
Sun Tung Lok (Tsim Sha Tsui)
翠享邨 (尖沙咀)
Tsui Hang Village (TST)

中港城
China HK City

國金軒 (The Mira)
Cuisine Cuisine at The Mira
Whisk

The Mira

China Ferry Terminal
中港客運碼頭

Fandango

香港文物探知館
HK Heritage
Discovery Ctr

KOWLOON PARK

港 威 大

鼎泰豐 (尖沙咀)
Din Tai Fung (Tsim Sha Tsui)

城 道

阿一海景飯店
Ah Yat Harbour View

朗廷
The Langham

HARBOUR
CITY

唐閣
T'ang Court
美岸海鮮廳
The Bostonian

Épure

上海小南國(北京道一號)
Shanghai Min
(One Peking Road)

夜上海 (尖沙咀)
Yè Shanghai
(Tsim Sha Tsui)

半島
The Peninsula

海運大廈
Ocean Terminal

Al Molo

BLT Steak

北京樓 (尖沙咀)
Peking Garden
(Tsim Sha Tsui)

HK Cultural Centre
港文化中心

鐘樓
Clock
Tower

往中環
To Central
天星碼頭
Star Ferry Pier

往灣仔
To Wan Chai

九龍公眾碼頭
Kowloon Public Pier

瑞樵閣
Chesa
Felix
吉地士
Gaddi's
嘉麟樓
Spring Moon

香港太空館
HK Space Museum

香港藝術館
HK Museum of Art

尖沙咀
TSIM SHA TSUI

N

← 250m米 (比例尺 Scale 1:8,333) →

A   B

九龍草地滾球會
Kowloon
Cricket Club

Kowloon Bowling
Green Club

香港理工大學
The Hong Kong
Polytechnic University

HONG KONG

1

CHEONG WAN ROAD

香港天文台
HK Observatory

福臨門 (尖沙咀)
Fook Lam Moon
(Tsim Sha Tsui)

唯港薈
Icon

天外天
Above & Beyond

莊園
Chang Won

千禧新世界
New World Millennium

阿利水 (尖沙咀)
Arisu (Tsim Sha Tsui)

La Saison

錦
Nishiki

海景嘉福
Intercontinental
Grand Stanford

金燕島
Come-Into
Chiu Chow

瑞士餐廳
The Swiss Chalet

帝苑
The Royal
Garden

尖沙咀凱悅
Hyatt Regency
Tsim Sha Tsui

利苑酒家 (尖沙咀)
Lei Garden (Tsim Sha Tsui)

麗景
Panorama

九龍香格里拉
Kowloon Shangri-La

2

希戈
Hugo's
Steik World Meats

東來順
Dong Lai Shun

Le Soleil

SALISBURY

香宮
Shang Palace

EAST TSIM SHA TSUI

尖東道

面譜京川料理
Mask of Sichuen & Beijing

New World Centre

喜來登
Sheraton

洲際
Intercontinental

Avenue of Stars

維多利亞港
VICTORIA HARBOUR

3

天寶閣
Celestial Court

Nobu
Spoon by Alain Ducasse
The Steak House Wine bar + grill

欣圖軒
Yan Toh Heen

C

D

477

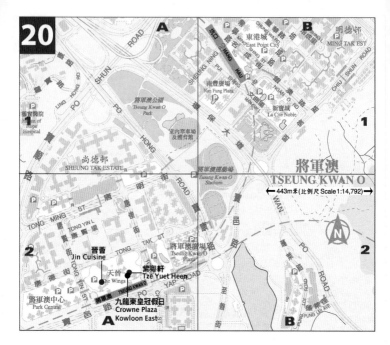

A

B

ROAD

SHUN

LING HONG RD

廣賢路

寶林路

PO

HONG

SHUN

PO

博寶醫院
Hospital of
Hope

尚德邨
SHEUNG TAK ESTATE

將軍澳公園
Tseung Kwan O
Park

室內車場
及體育館

SHEUNG NING

尚寧路

寶邑路

PUI

尚富

NING

將軍澳

東港城
East Point City

明德邨
MING TAK EST

CHIU SHUN ROAD

昭信路

南豐廣場
Nan Fung Plaza

新寶城
La Cité Noble

CHUI LING RD

翠嶺

NGAN PO

將軍澳
TSEUNG KWAN O

◄── 443m米(比例尺 Scale 1:14,792) ──►

將軍澳運動場
Tseung Kwan O
Stadium

N

TONG MING ST

唐明街

TONG YIN L

唐賢里

寶寧路

TAK ST

唐德街

Jin Cuisine
晉薈

TONG

將軍澳廣場路
Tseung Kwan O
Plaza

WAN

PO

蓬萊路

ROAD

2

TONG YIN ST

唐賢街

天晉
The Wings

紫玥軒
Tze Yuet Heen

将軍澳

TSEUNG KWAN O

PO

YAP

至善街

將軍澳中心
Park Central

寶邑路

九龍東皇冠假日
Crowne Plaza
Kowloon East

ROAD

蓬萊路
PUNG LOI RD

A

B

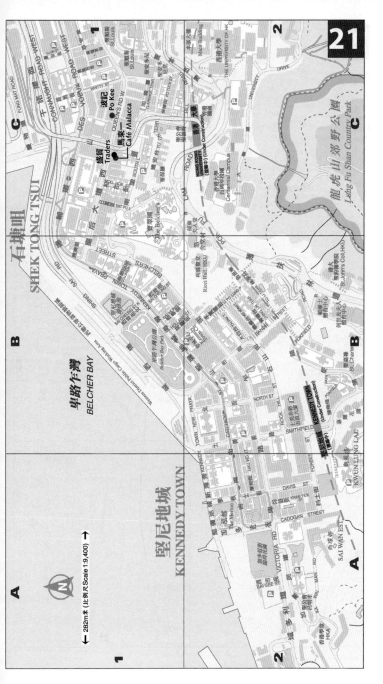

石塘咀
SHEK TONG TSUI

堅尼地城
KENNEDY TOWN

卑路乍灣
BELCHER BAY

龍虎山郊野公園
Lung Fu Shan Country Park

Po Kee
渡記

Café Malacca
馬來

Traders
盛貿

Main Building
本部大樓

THE UNIVERSITY OF HK
香港大學

KENNEDY TOWN
(Under Construction)

← 282m米 (比例尺Scale 1:9,400) →

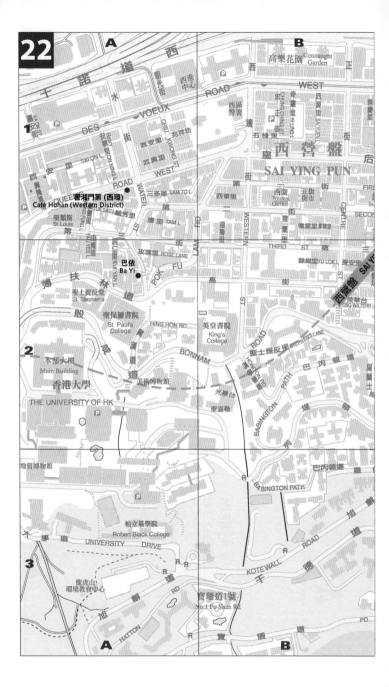

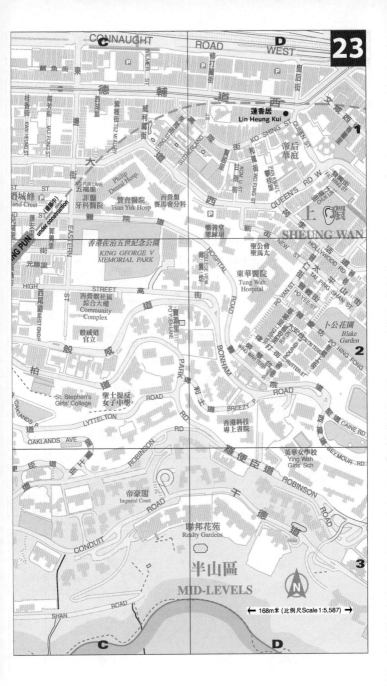

CONNAUGHT ROAD WEST

德 輔 道 西

蓮香居
Lin Heung Kui

上環
SHEUNG WAN

五福里
Philip Dental Hosp.
菲臘牙科醫院

贊育醫院
西營盤賽馬會分科
'Isan Yuk Hosp
樂善堂梁銶琚

香港佐治五世紀念公園
KING GEORGE V
MEMORIAL PARK

聖公會聖馬大

東華醫院
Tung Wah
Hospital

卜公花園
Blake
Garden

西環西醫中醫聯合大樓
Community
Complex
般咸道官立

St. Stephen's
Girls' College
聖士提反女子中學

香港科技專上書院

英華女學校
Ying Wah
Girls' Sch

帝豪閣
Imperial Court

聯邦花苑
Realty Gardens

半山區
MID-LEVELS

ROBINSON ROAD

CONDUIT ROAD

SHAN ROAD

under construction

瀚城峰
land Crest

← 168m米 (比例尺Scale 1:5,587) →

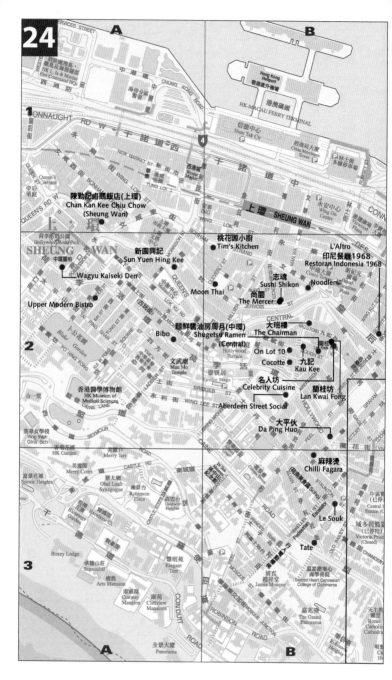

24

A

B

SERVICES STREET

中港道 CHUNG KONG ROAD

海傍公園

西消防

Hong Kong
香港港升降台

港澳碼頭
HK-MACAU FERRY TERMINAL

信德中心
Shun Tak Ctr

招商局東樓
China Merchants Tower

1

CONNAUGHT RD W — 干諾道西

NEW MARKET ST 新街市街

西港城
Western Market

永安中心 Wing On Centre

Queen's Terrace

陳勤記鹵鵝飯店(上環)
Chan Kan Kee Chiu Chow
(Sheung Wan)

上環 SHEUNG WAN

SHEUNG WAN 上環

桃花源小廚
● Tim's Kitchen

新園興記
Sun Yuen Hing Kee

L'Altro
印尼餐廳1968
Restoran Indonesia 1968

Wagyu Kaiseki Den

志魂
Sushi Shikon

Noodlemi

Upper Modern Bistro

Moon Thai

尚園
The Mercer

大班樓
The Chairman

麵鮮醬油房周月(中環)
Shugetsu Ramen
(Central)

Bibo

On Lot 10

九記
Kau Kee

文武廟
Man Mo Temple

Cocotte

香港醫學博物館
HK Museum of
Medical Sciences

名人坊
Celebrity Cuisine

蘭桂坊
Lan Kwai Fong

英華女學校
Ying Wah
Girls' Sch

Aberdeen Street Social

大平伙
Da Ping Huo

2

HK Garden

Merry Terr

Merry Court

Obel Leah
Synagogue

麻辣燙
Chilli Fagara

Robinson
Place

Goldwin
Heights

富景花園
Scenic Heights

Bickerton
Gardens

Excelsior Ct

Le Souk

Central
Station

Buxey Lodge

Elegant
Terr

Tate

Victoria Prison
(Closed)

3

Arts Mansion

Conway
Mansion

Cliffview
Mansions

Jamia Mosque

嘉諾撒聖心
商學書院
Sacred Heart Canossian
College of Commerce

全景大廈
Panorama

ROBINSON ROAD

The Grand
Panorama

A

B

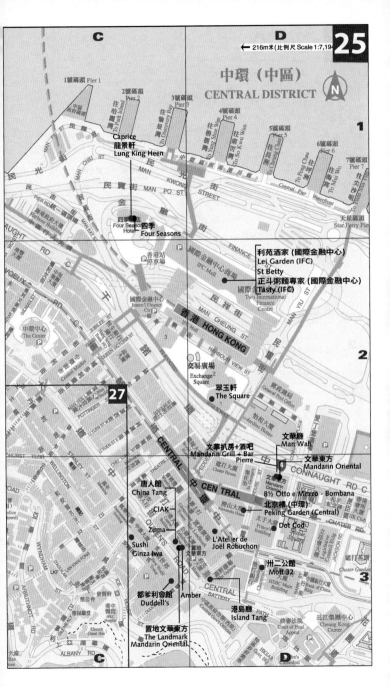

1號碼頭 Pier 1
2號碼頭 Pier 2
3號碼頭 Pier 3
4號碼頭 Pier 4
5號碼頭 Pier 5
6號碼頭 Pier 6
7號碼頭 Pier 7

往坪洲 To Peng Chau
往梅窩 To Mui Wo
往愉景灣 To Discovery Bay
往榕樹灣 To Yung Shue Wan
往索罟灣 To So Kwu Wan
往長洲 To Cheung Chau

中區民航村碼頭
Central Pier Waterfront

天星碼頭
Star Ferry Pier

Caprice
龍景軒
Lung King Heen

PIER RD 干諾道
港外線碼頭一號停車場
Harbour Building

四季酒店
Four Seasons Hotel
四季
Four Seasons

香港站停車場

國際金融中心商場
IFC Mall

利苑酒家 (國際金融中心)
Lei Garden (IFC)
St Betty
正斗粥麵專家 (國際金融中心)
Tasty (IFC)

國際金融中心一期
Intern'l Finance Ctr 一期

中環中心
The Center

國際金融中心二期
Two International Finance Centre

香港 HONG KONG

郵政總局
General Post Office

交易廣場
Exchange Square

翠玉軒
The Square

27

文華扒房+酒吧
Mandarin Grill + Bar
Pierre

文華廳
Man Wah

文華東方
Mandarin Oriental

8½ Otto e Mezzo - Bombana

唐人館
China Tang
CIAK
Zuma
Sushi
Ginza Iwa

北京樓(中環)
Peking Garden (Central)
Dot Cod

L'Atelier de
Joël Robuchon

卅二公館
Mott 32

都爹利會館
Duddell's
Amber

CENTRAL
BATTERY

港島廳
Island Tang

置地文華東方
The Landmark
Mandarin Oriental

長江集團中心
Cheung Kong
Center

483

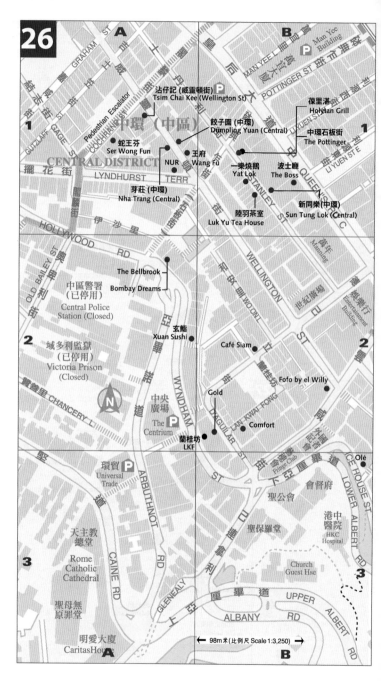

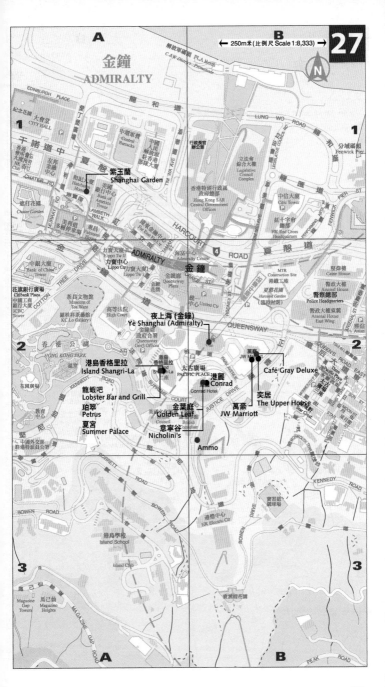

金鐘
ADMIRALTY

解放軍碼頭
C./.W. District
PLA Berth
Promenade

EDINBURGH PLACE

紀念花園
大會堂
CITY HALL

簡 和 道 LUNG WO ROAD

分域碼頭
Fenwick Pier

中国人民解放军驻香港部队
Central Barracks

行政長官
辦公室

立法會
綜合大樓
Legislative
Council
Complex

香港特別行政區政府總部
Hong Kong SAR
Central Government
Offices

中信大廈
Citic Tower

紅十字會
總會
HK Red Cross
Headquarters

紫玉蘭
Shanghai Garden

HARCOURT

金鐘 ADMIRALTY

力寶天樓
Lippo Tw II
力寶中心 力寶大廈
Lippo Ctr Lippo Tw I

海富中心
Admiralty Centre

金鐘站
Admiralty

MTR
Construction Site
港鐵工地

警察總部
Police Headquarters

夏慤花園
Harcourt Garden
(臨時性質)

堅偉樓
Caine House

茶具文物館
Museum of
Tea Ware

高等法院
High Court

夜上海 (金鐘)
Yè Shanghai (Admiralty)

QUEENSWAY

警政大樓
東翼
Arsenal House
East Wing

金鐘廊
Queensway
Plaza

UNITED CTR

羅桂祥茶藝館
K.C. Lo Gallery

金鐘道
政府合署
Queensway
Gov't Offices

香 港 公 園
HONG KONG PARK

港島香格里拉
Island Shangri-La

太古廣場
PACIFIC PLACE

港麗
Conrad
Conrad Hotel

Café Gray Deluxe

龍蝦吧
Lobster Bar and Grill

珀翠
Petrus

夏宮
Summer Palace

JW萬豪
JW Marriott

奕居
The Upper House

金葉庭
Golden Leaf

萬豪
JW Marriott

意寧谷
Nicholini's

英國領事館
British
Consulate

Ammo

港燈中心
HK Electric Ctr

KENNEDY

港島學校
Island School

Island Club

馬己仙峽
Magazine
Gap
Towers

馬己仙
Magazine
Heights

寶雲道運動場

實雲纈花園

PEAK ROAD

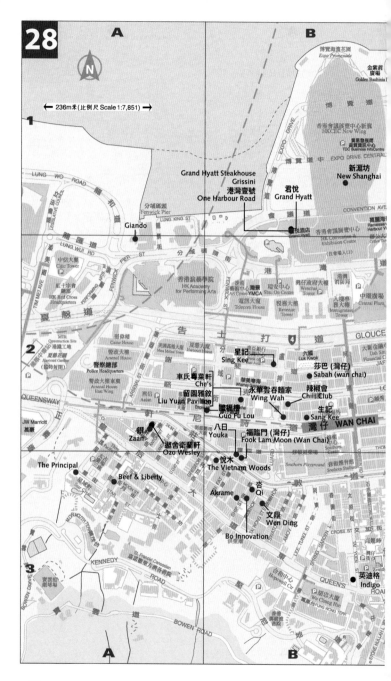

A　　　　　　　　B

N

← 236m米 (比例尺 Scale 1:7,851) →

1

博覽海濱花園
Expo Promenade

金紫荊廣場
Golden Bauhinia

LUNG WO ROAD 龍和道

EXPO DRIVE 博覽道

香港會議展覽中心新翼
HKCEC New Wing

貿易發展局
TDC Business InfoCentre

EXPO DRIVE CENTRAL 博覽道中

Grand Hyatt Steakhouse
Grissini
港灣壹號
One Harbour Road

君悅
Grand Hyatt

新滬坊
New Shanghai

分域碼頭
Fenwick Pier

LUNG KING ST 龍景街

CONVENTION AVE 會議道

Giando

LUNG WUI RD 龍匯道

分域碼頭街

香港會議展覽中心
HK Convention &
Exhibition Centre
(冀灣入口)

Renaissance
Harbour Vi

萬麗海景

悅酒店
Grand Hyatt

中信大廈
Citic Tower

TIM MEI AVE 添美道

PERFORMING ARTS 演藝

FENWICK 分域

ARSENAL ST 軍器廠街

香港演藝學院
HK Academy
for Performing Arts

灣景
演藝
Arts Centre

YMCA

Shiu On Centre

瑞安中心

P

灣仔政府大樓
Wanchai
Tower

稅務大樓
Revenue
Tower

入境事
務大樓
Immigration
Tower

中區廣場
Central Plaza

香港紅十字會
HK Red Cross
Headquarters

紅十字會

電訊大廈
Telecom House

GLOUCE

告

士

打

道

2

MTR
Construction Site
港鐵工地

堅偉樓
Caine House

夏慤花園
(臨時開放)
Harcourt Garden
(Temporarily Open)

夏慤道
Harcourt Road

QUEENSWAY 金鐘道

警察總部
Police Headquarters

警察大樓東翼
Arsenal House
East Wing

堅偉樓
Caine House

夏愨大樓
Harcourt House

星記
Sing Kee

六國
Luk Kwok

永安銀行

莎巴 (灣仔)
Sabah (wan chai)

大新金融中心
Dah Sing
Financial Cen

JAF

車氏嘟菜軒
Che's

留園雅敘
Liu Yuan Pavilion

裕福樓
Guo Fu Lou

華發集華

永華雲吞麵家
Wing Wah

辣椒會
Chili Club

生記
Sang Kee

灣仔 WAN CHAI

JW Marriott
萬豪

饌
Zaan

邀舍衛蘭軒
Ozo Wesley

八日
Youka

福臨門 (灣仔)
Fook Lam Moon (Wan Chai)

The Principal

Beef & Liberty

STAR 星

悅木
The Vietnam Woods

Southorn Playground
修頓遊樂場

Southorn Stadium
修頓室內場

Akrame

杏
Qi

3

KENNEDY

ROAD

BOWEN ROAD

聖芳濟書院
St Francis' Carpenian

文鼎
Wen Ding

Bo Innovation

合和中心
Hopewell Ctr

胡忠大廈
Wu Chung Hse

We Chung Ho

QUEEN'S

英迪格
Indigo

BOWEN 道

A　　　　　　　　B

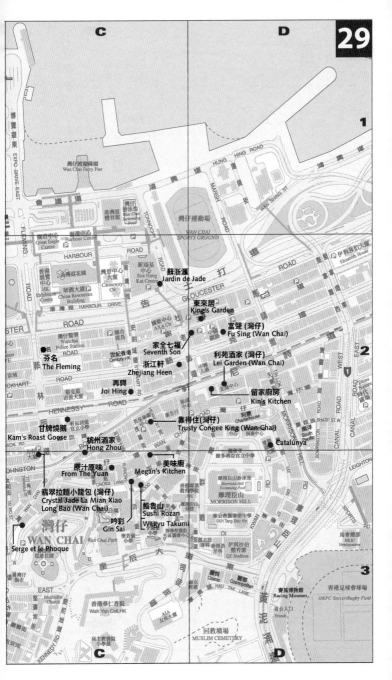

蘇浙滙
Jardin de Jade

東來居
Kin's Garden

富聲 (灣仔)
Fu Sing (Wan Chai)

家全七福
Seventh Son

利苑酒家 (灣仔)
Lei Garden (Wan Chai)

浙江軒
Zhejiang Heen

芬名
The Fleming

再興
Joi Hing

留家廚房
Kin's Kitchen

甘牌燒鵝
Kam's Roast Goose

靠得住(灣仔)
Trusty Congee King (Wan Chai)

杭州酒家
Hong Zhou

Catalunya

原汁原味
From The Yuan

美味廚
Megan's Kitchen

翡翠拉麵小龍包 (灣仔)
Crystal Jade La Mian Xiao
Long Bao (Wan Chai)

吟彩
Gin Sai

鮨魯山
Sushi Rozan
Wagyu Takumi

灣仔
WAN CHAI

Serge et le Phoque

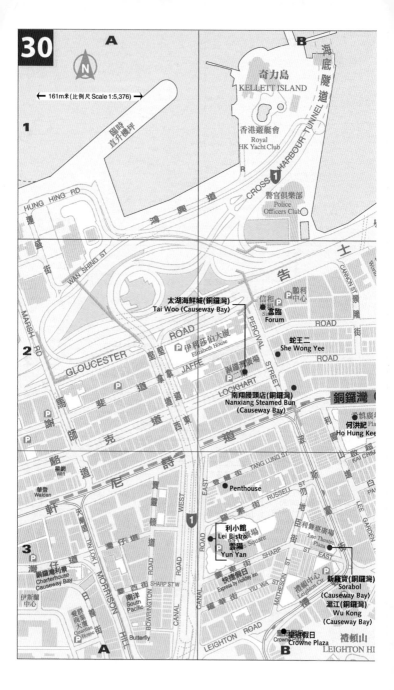

30

A   B

← 161m米(比例尺 Scale 1:5,376) →

1

奇力島
KELLETT ISLAND

海底隧道

香港遊艇會
Royal
HK Yacht Club

HUNG HING RD
鴻興道
連盈街

CROSS HARBOUR TUNNEL

警官俱樂部
Police
Officers Club

WAN SHING ST
堅尼

太湖海鮮城(銅鑼灣)
Tai Woo (Causeway Bay)

CANNON ST

告

信利
大廈

富臨
Forum

富臨
中心

蛇王二
She Wong Yee

ROAD

2

GLOUCESTER
JAFFE
ROAD

伊利莎伯大廈
Elizabeth House

PERCIVAL
STREET

LOCKHART

銅鑼灣廣場

南翔饅頭店(銅鑼灣)
Nanxiang Steamed Bun
(Causeway Bay)

銅鑼灣

MARSH RD

謝師道

馬克
克道

西道

羅素

何洪記
Ho Hung Kee

星期Wifi

華登
Walden

軒尼詩道

WEST

賓賓

YANG LUNG ST

● Penthouse

RUSSELL ST
勿
地

利舞臺廣場
Lee Theatre
Plaza

3

灣仔道
Charterhouse
Causeway Bay

銅鑼灣利景
商業大廈

EAST
ROAD

利小館
Lei Bistro
雲陽
Yun Yan

Square

SHARP

ST EAST

新羅寶(銅鑼灣)
Sorabol
(Causeway Bay)
滬江(銅鑼灣)
Wu Kong
(Causeway Bay)

BOWRINGTON

CANAL

ROAD

南洋
South Pacific

快捷假日
Express by Holiday inn

禮頓中心
Leighton Ctr

YIU WA ST

MATHESON

LEIGHTON

ROAD

皇冠假日
Crowne Plaza

禮頓山
LEIGHTON HI

伊斯蘭
中心

怡群
商業
大廈

Butterfly

TIN LOK LN

SHARP ST W

MORRISON HILL

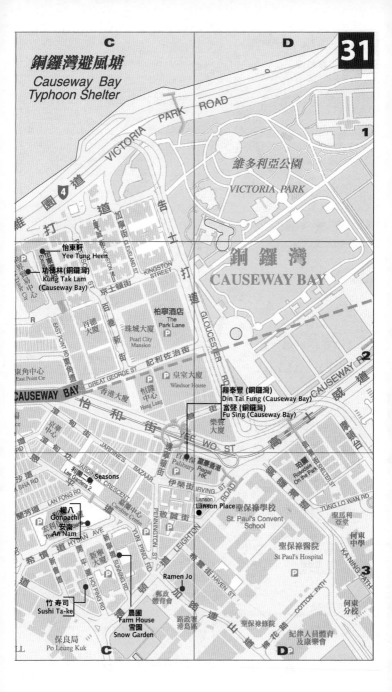

銅鑼灣避風塘
**Causeway Bay
Typhoon Shelter**

維多利亞公園
VICTORIA PARK

銅鑼灣
CAUSEWAY BAY

怡東軒
Yee Tung Heen

功德林 (銅鑼灣)
Kung Tak Lam
(Causeway Bay)

柏寧酒店
The Park Lane

珠城大廈
Pearl City Mansion

鼎泰豐 (銅鑼灣)
Din Tai Fung (Causeway Bay)

富聲 (銅鑼灣)
Fu Sing (Causeway Bay)

富豪香港
Regal HK

Seasons

Lanson Place

櫻八
Gonpachi

安南
An Nam

聖保祿學校
St. Paul's Convent School

聖保祿醫院
St Paul's Hospital

Ramen Jo

竹 寿司
Sushi Ta-ke

農園
Farm House
雪園
Snow Garden

保良局
Po Leung Kuk

何東
分校

32

禮頓山 Leighton Hill

保良局歷史博物館

連道 LINK ROAD

禮頓山道 LEIGHTON HILL ROAD

CAROLINE HILL ROAD 加路連山道

CAROLINE HILL 加路連山

SO KON PO RECREATION GROUND 掃桿埔遊樂場

SOUTH CHINA ATHLETIC ASSN STADIUM 南華體育會運動場

南華體育會

東院道

BROADWOOD RD 布律活道

HAPPY VIEW TERRACE 樂景台

聖瑪加利教堂 St Margaret's

樂活道

印度遊樂會

EASTERN HOSPITAL ROAD 東院道

WONG NAI CHUNG RD 黃泥涌道

比華利山 Beverly Hill

孔聖堂 Confucius Hall

奧運大樓 Olympic House

聖保祿大主教

聖保祿中學

樂翠台 Villa Rocha

香港大球場 HONG KONG STADIUM

HAPPY VALLEY RECREATION GROUND Horse Race Track

香港三育中學

掃桿埔 SO KON PO

樂陶苑 Villa Lotto

← 234m米 (比例尺 Scale 1:7,463) →

VENTRIS ROAD 黃泥涌道

跑馬地 HAPPY VALLEY

源公廟

BROADWOOD ROAD

養和醫院 H.K. Sanatorium & Hospital

彭慶記 Pang's Kitchen

奕蔭街 YIK YAM ST

景光街 KING KWONG ST

BLUE POOL ROAD 藍塘道

Valley View Terr 駿景台

英皇駿景園

毓秀街

YUK SAU ST

RD 山村 VILLAGE

TSUI MAN ST 聚文街

SING WOO ROAD 成和道

駿景軒 Golden Valley

山光道 SHAN KWONG RD

東蓮覺苑

JEWISH CEMETERY 猶太墳場

跑馬地警署

KWAN KONG RD

HAWTHORN RD 桃李道

永安新廈

SING WOO

STUBBS ROAD 司徒拔道

賽馬會體育綜合大樓

賽馬會會所 Jockey Club Clubhouse

HOLLY RD 冬青道

藍塘別墅

GREEN LANE 黃泥坊

玫瑰新邨 Villa Monte Rosa

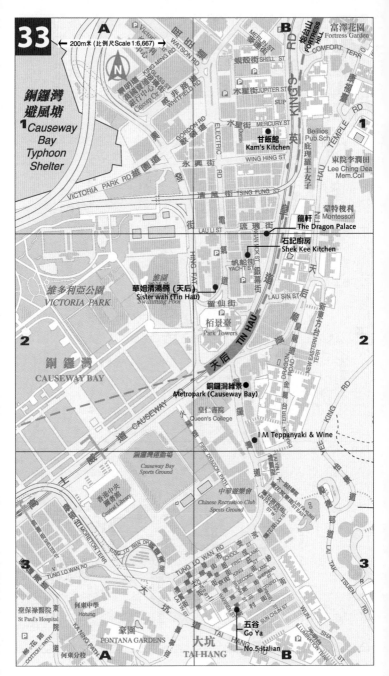

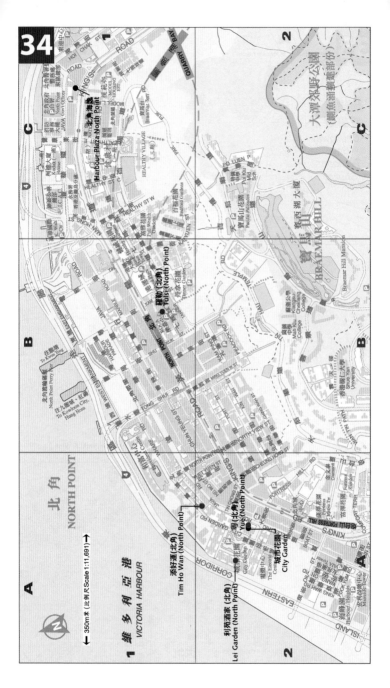

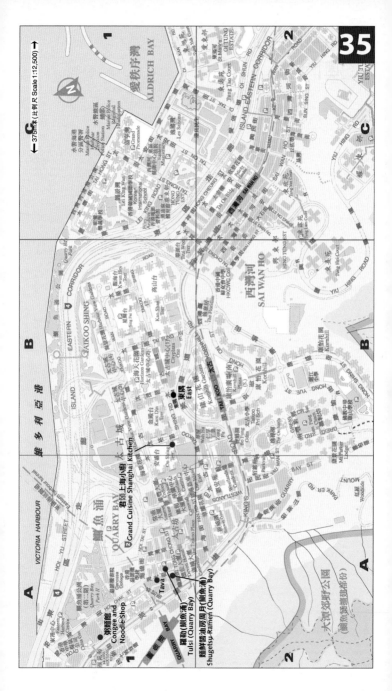

1

ALDRICH BAY
愛秩序灣

C

ISLAND EASTERN CORRIDOR

2

YIU TUNG ESTATE
耀東邨

VICTORIA HARBOUR
維多利亞港

HOI YU STREET
海裕街

QUARRY BAY
鰂魚涌

EASTERN ISLAND CORRIDOR

GAIKOO SHING
太古城

SHING RD
城
RD

TAI TUNG AV
太東
街

SAI WAN HO
西灣河

B

A

QUARRY BAY
鰂魚涌

KING'S
英皇道

TONG CHONG ST
糖廠街

QUARRY
鰂魚涌

WESTLANDS
華蘭路

BAY ST

MOUNT
柏
架
PARK

A

C

B

粥麵館
Congee and
Noodle Shop

Tava 印

羅勤(鰂魚涌)
Tulsi (Quarry Bay)

顏鮮醬油房月(鰂魚浦)
Shugetsu Ramen (Quarry Bay)

君品上海小廚 太古城
Grand Cuisine Shanghai Kitchen

東隅
East

SAI WAN HO
西灣河

大潭郊野公園
(鰂魚涌擴建部份)

N

← 375m米 (比例尺 Scale 1:12,500) →

493

MACAU
澳門

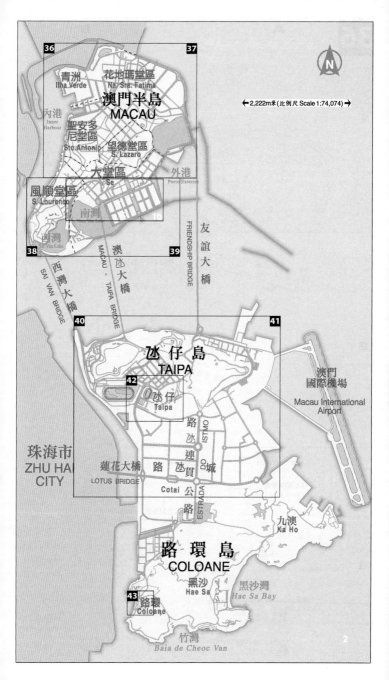

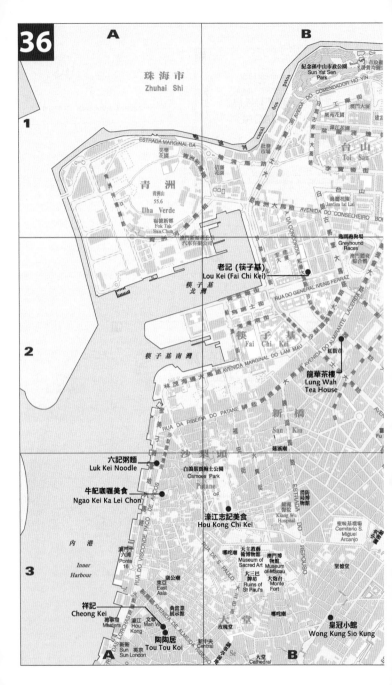

珠海市
Zhuhai Shi

A

B

紀念孫中山市政公園
Sun Yat Sen Park

市政綠廊

1

AVENIDA DO COMENDADOR HO YIN

威斯大馬路

台山
Toi San

ESTRADA MARGINAL DA

青洲
青洲山
55.6
Ilha Verde

福德新邨
Fok Tak Sun Chun

AVENIDA DO CONSELHEIRO BO

Jardim Iat Lai

澳門賽狗場
Greyhound Races

澳門體育綜合體

AVENIDA DA CONCORDIA

老記 (筷子基)
Lou Kei (Fai Chi Kei)

筷子基北灣

RUA DO GENERAL IVENS FERRAZ

2

筷子基
Fai Chi Kei

AVENIDA DO ALMIRANTE LACERDA

筷子基南灣

紅街市

AVENIDA MARGINAL DO LAM MAU

龍華茶樓
Lung Wah Tea House

RUA DA RIBEIRA DO PATANE

新橋
San Kiu

沙梨頭

六記粥麵
Luk Kei Noodle

白鴿巢賈梅士公園
Camoes Park
Patane

ESTRADA DO REPOUSO

牛記咖喱美食
Ngao Kei Ka Lei Chon

RUA DO VISCONDE PACO DE ARCOS

濠江志記美食
Hou Kong Chi Kei

鏡湖醫院
Kung Wu Hospital

聖彌基墳場
Cemiterio S. Miguel Arcanjo

星臨堂

3

內港
Inner Harbour

澳門十六浦
Ponte 16

康公廟

East Asia

天主教藝術博物館
Museum of Sacred Art

澳門博物館
Museum of Macau

大三巴牌坊
Ruins of St Paul's

大炮台
Monte Fort

哪吒廟

祥記
Cheong Kei

AVENIDA DE ALMEIDA RIBEIRO

文化會館
Man Va

玫瑰堂

皇冠小館
Wong Kung Sio Kung

陶陶居
Tou Tou Koi

Sun London

新中央
Central

大堂
Se

大堂
Cathedral

A

B

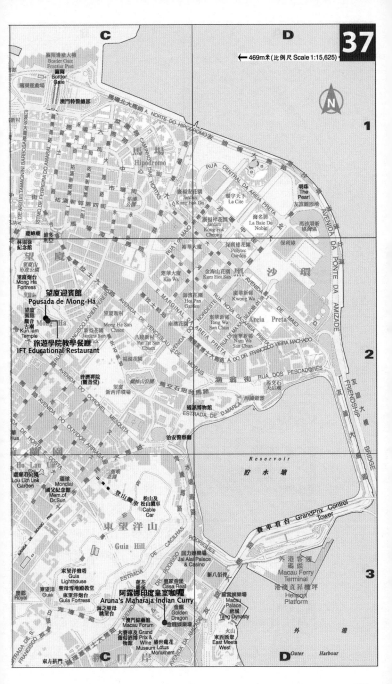

←469m米 (比例尺 Scale 1:15,625) →

N

關閘邊檢大樓
Border Gate
Frontier Post
關閘
Border
Gate
關閘邊檢廣場

澳門特警總部

馬場北大馬路 A. NORTE DO HIPODROMO

RUA CENTRAL DA AREIA PRETA

1

明珠
The Pearl
友誼圓形廣場

馬場
Hipodromo

廣福安花園
Jardim
Kong Fok On

瑾宇天下
La Cité

海名居
La Baie Du
Noble

黑沙環新填海區

CAMINHO DAS HORTAS

ISTMO DE FERREIRA DO AMARAL

廣福祥花園
Jardim
Kong Fok
Cheong

AVENIDA DA PONTE DA AMIZADE

蓮峰廟
維多
利亞

ISTMO DE FERR. TAMAGNINI BARBOSA

保利達花園
Polytec
Garden

林茂塘
紀念碑

AVENIDA MARGINAL DO LAM MAU

望廈烟台
市政公園
Mong Ha
Fortress

金海山花園
Kam Hoi San

沙　環

嘉華大廈
Kin Wa

望廈迎賓館
Pousada de Mong-Há

AVENIDA XAVIER PEREIRA

E MARGINAL DA AREIA PRETA

嶺南新村
Kwong Wa

AVENIDA DE VENCESLAU

南濱花園

海濱花園
Hoi Pan
Garden

Areia　Preta

望廈村古迹
Mong Ha
觀音古廟
Kun Iam
Temple

Mong Ha San
Chuen

望廈新村

RUA NOVA DA AREIA PRETA

SEQUEIRA

東華新村
Tong Wa
San Chun

南華新村
Nam Wa
San Chun

旅遊學院教學餐廳
IFT Educational Restaurant

AVENIDA DE

Mong Ha Sun
Chuen

八晚廟祠堂
Pat Tat San
Chuen

AVENIDA DO DR. FRANCISCO VIEIRA MACHADO

2

AVENIDA DO OUVIDOR ARRIAGA

福慶花園

普濟禪院
(觀音堂)

RUA DOS PESCADORES

馬交石
天后廟

AVENIDA DO CORONEL MESQUITA

新西洋墳場

鏡湖山公園

螺絲山公園

沙梨頭水坑尾街

沙梨頭望海觀音

ESTRADA DE D. MARIA II

通訊博物館

治安警察廳

FRIENDSHIP

BRIDGE

友誼大橋

蓮峰球場

AVENIDA DO COSTA

鷹喇叭士街

Ho Lan

盧廉若公園
Lou Lim Iok
Garden

國父紀念館
Mem.of
Dr.Sun

Reservoir

貯　水　塘

松山及
松山纜車
Cable
Car

蒙地卡羅
二龍喉
公園

蒙地卡羅
花園
Mondial

東望洋山

AVENIDA DE SIDONIO PAIS

松山
東望洋烟台
Guia Hill

ESTRADA DE CACILHAS

RODRIGUES

澳車看台 GrandPrix Control
Tower

外港客運
碼頭
Macau Ferry
Terminal

3

東望洋燈塔
Guia
Lighthouse

聖母雪地殿教堂
Guia
東望洋
Guia
Fortress

花地瑪堂
ESTRADA

回力娛樂場
Jai Alai Palace
& Casino

新八佰伴

港澳音昇機坪
Helisport
Platform

廬
Royal

ESTRADA DE S. FRANCISCO

海之藍母
峨湖看台

RODRIGUES

皇宮金星
Casa Real

金星娛樂場
Macau
Palace
唐朝
Tang Dynasty

澳門綜藝館
Macau Forum

阿露娜印度皇室咖喱
Aruna's Maharaja Indian Curry

金龍
Golden
Dragon
金龍娛樂場

東望洋新村

火山

東方拱門

大賽車及
葡萄酒博
物館

Grand
Prix &
Wine
Museum

蓮世雞花
Lotus
Monument

AVENIDA DA AMIZADE

東亞運圓場
East Meets
West

D Outer　Harbour

外　　港

497

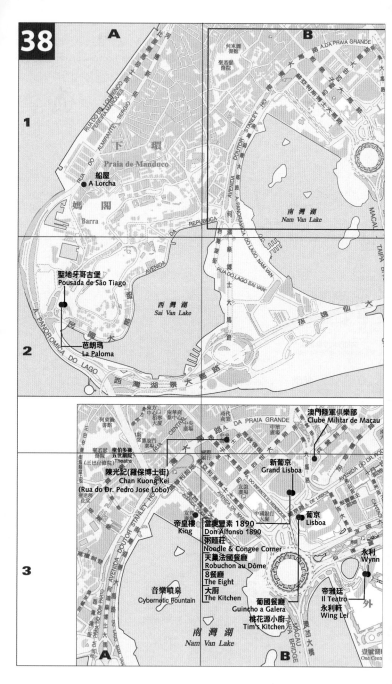

38

1

RUA DO ALMIRANTE SÉRGIO
RUA DO ALMIRANTE, SÉRGIO, PEREIRA MARQUES

何東區
御府

聖若瑟
修院

A DA PRAIA GRANDE

船屋
A Lorcha

Praia de Manduco

媽 閣
Barra

RUA DO PRAIA GRANDE

南 灣 湖
Nam Van Lake

MACAU

2

聖地牙哥古堡
Pousada de São Tiago

芭朗瑪
La Paloma

A PANORÂMICA DO LAGO

西 灣 湖
Sai Van Lake

RUA DO LAGO SAI VAN

孫 逸 仙 大

西 灣 湖 景 大 馬 路

TAIPA DO

3

何東圖
書館

中央
廣場

時代
廣場

A DA PRAIA GRANDE

CENTRAL

澳門陸軍俱樂部
Clube Militar de Macau

聖若瑟 聖伯多祿
五世歸館
(三世仔修院)
Theatre

陳光記(羅保博士街)
Chan Kuong Kei
(Rua do Dr. Pedro Jose Lobo)

帝皇樓
King

當奧豐素 1890
Don Alfonso 1890
粥麵莊
Noodle & Congee Corner
天巢法國餐廳
Robuchon au Dôme
8餐廳
The Eight
大廚
The Kitchen

DOUTOR STANLEY HO

音樂噴泉
Cybernetic Fountain

AVENIDA DOUTOR STANLEY HO

DO BOM PARTO

南 灣 湖
Nam Van Lake

新葡京
Grand Lisboa

AVENIDA DO INFANTE D HENRIQUE

中國銀行
大廈

友誼
廣場

AVENIDA DA PRAIA GRANDE

葡京
Lisboa

永利
Wynn

葡國餐廳
Guincho a Galera

桃花源小廚
Tim's Kitchen

帝雅廷
Il Teatro
永利軒
Wing Lei

外

MACAU BRIDGE

澳氹大橋

A

B

南灣湖
One Central

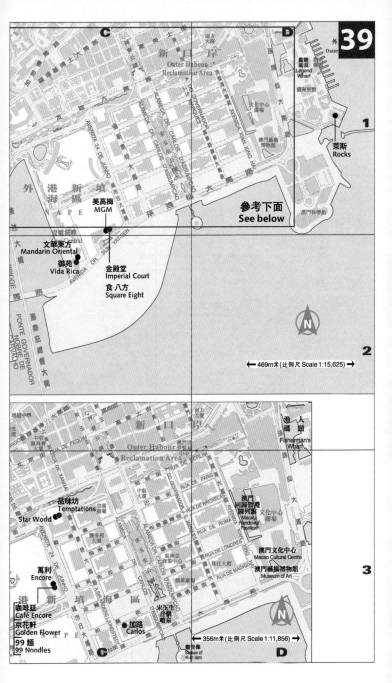

外港
Outer

新口岸
Outer Habour
Reclamation Area

隄觀碼頭
Legend Wharf

過渡警館

外 港 新 填 區
NAPE

萊斯
Rocks

文化中心
廣場

澳門藝術
博物館

美高梅
MGM

參考下面
See below

澳門科學館

孝臘湖畔
Central

文華東方
Mandarin Oriental

御苑
Vida Rica

金殿堂
Imperial Court

食 八方
Square Eight

AVENIDA DR. SUN YAT-SEN

N

←469m米 (比例尺 Scale 1:15,625) →

PONTE GOVERNADOR NOBRE DE CARVALHO

新口岸
Outer Habour
Reclamation Area

漁人碼頭
Fisherman's
Wharf

RUA DE PEQUIM

RUA DE BERLIM

中航
大廈

RUA DE PARIS

RUA DE BRUXELAS

澳門
回歸寶物
陳列館
Macau
Handover
Pavilion

品味坊
Temptations

Star World

RUA DE ROMA

RUA DE LONDRES

澳門文化中心
Macao Cultural Centre

萬利
Encore

RUA DE MADRID

AVENIDA DE ALMEIDA RIBEIRO

AVENIDA DR. CARLOS D'ASSUMPÇÃO

澳門藝術博物館
Museum of Art

咖啡廷
Café Encore

京花軒
Golden Flower

99 麵
99 Noodles

宋玉生
公園
廣場

加路士
Carlos

N

觀音像
Statue of
Kun Iam

←356m米 (比例尺 Scale 1:11,856) →

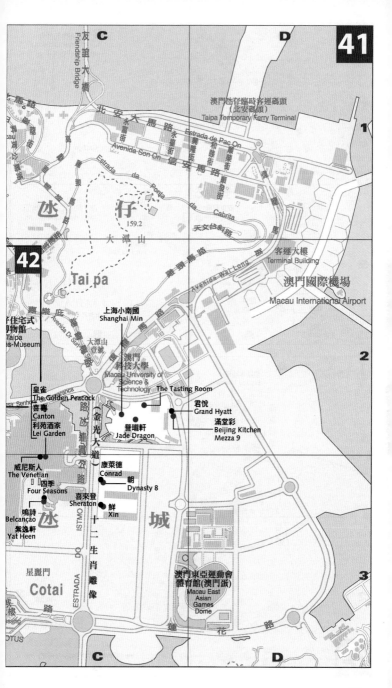

友誼大橋
Friendship Bridge

澳門氹仔臨時客運碼頭
（北安碼頭）
Taipa Temporary Ferry Terminal

北安大馬路
永福街
Estrada de Pac On
Avenida Son On
信安馬路
Avenida Son On

氹仔
Estrada da Ponta da Cabrita
天文台斜路

159.2
大潭山

客運大樓
Terminal Building

42

Tai pa

澳門國際機場
Macau International Airport

嘉樂庇
Avenida Dr Sun Yat
大潭山登山

上海小南國
Shanghai Min

澳門科技大學
Macau University of
Science &
Technology

子住宅式
物館
Taipa
s-Museum

皇雀
The Golden Peacock

喜粵
Canton

利苑酒家
Lei Garden

The Tasting Room

君悅
Grand Hyatt

譽瓏軒
Jade Dragon

滿堂彩
Beijing Kitchen
Mezza 9

威尼斯人
The Venetian

四季
Four Seasons

鳴詩
Belcanção

紫逸軒
Yat Heen

康萊德
Conrad

朝
Dynasty 8

喜來登
Sheraton

鮮
Xin

氹城

十二生肖雕像

星麗門
Cotai

澳門東亞運動會
體育館(澳門蛋)
Macau East
Asian
Games
Dome

A **B**

阿曼諾葡國餐
Manuel Cozinha
Portuguesa

1

市政于禮街
RUA DE TAI LIN
RUA DE EVORA
RUA DE NAM KENG
ESTRADA GOVERNADOR NOBRE DE CARVALHO

布拉架街

AVENIDA DE GUIMARAES
大連街
RUA DE BRAGANÇA
埃武拉街
RUA OLIMPICA
AVENIDA OLIMPICA
RUA DE COIMBRA

奧林匹克馬路

澳門
賽馬場
Macau
Jockey Club

澳門
運動場
Eetadio
De Macau

RUA DE BENG TOU

PONTE DA
NEGRA

RUA DO DOGO

RUA DIRETA

RUA DE ELGENIO

Castiço

1

葡國美食天地
A Petisqueira

安東尼奧
Antonio

迷仔住宅式博物館
Taipa Houses-Museum

奧林匹克
游泳館
Piscina
Olimpica
De Macau

AVENIDA DO ESTADIO
RUA DO DESPORTO
體育路

RUA CORREIA DA SILVA

RUA DA CUNHA

新陶陶
San Tou Tou

2

澳門
三育
Escola
Secundaria
Sam Yuk

RUA DO REGEDOR

吉利雅施利華街

迷仔市區
TAIPA TOWN

蓮花海濱大馬路
AVENIDA MARGINAL FLE DE LOTUS

望德聖母灣大馬路

利安
Café Leon

←325m米 (比例尺 Scale 1:10,850)→

葡軒
Gosto

名家
Myung Ga

庭園
Terrazza

銀河
Galaxy

ESTRADA DA BAIA DE NOSSA SENHORA DA ESPERANCA

A **B**

A **B**

里斯本地帶
Espaço Lisboa

1

船人街
RUA DOS NAVEGANTES

馬場前地

石街
迷仔圍
里斯緣新街

ESTRADA DO CAMPO

ESTRADA DE CHEOC VAN

竹灣馬路

RUA DA CORDOARIA

田畔街

1

鹹蝦巷

十月初五

客商街
中
街
打纜街

2

客商街

打纜前地

陳勝記
Chan Seng Kei

MEIO
大街

水泉
公地
情人街

A DE CINCO DE OUTUBRO

新利街

船舶前地

民國馬路

LARGO DA CORDOARIA

打纜前地

2

天后廟
前地

菜園巷

路環市區
COLOANE TOWN

←157m米 (比例尺 Scale 1:5,220)→

A **B**

PICTURE COPYRIGHT
圖片版權

64 - Aberdeen Street Social,   65 - Above & Beyond, 66 - Michelin, 67 - Ah Yat Harbour View, 68 - Akrame, 69 - Al Molo, 70 - Amber / Michelin, 71 - Ammo, 72 - An Nam, 73 - Arisu, 74 - Ba Yi, 75 - Beef & Liberty, 76 - Bibo, 77 - BLT Steak, 78 - Michelin, 79 - Bombay Dreams, 80 - Café Gray Deluxe, 81 - Michelin, 82 - Café Malacca, 83 - Café Siam, 84 - Caprice, 85 - Catalunya, 86 - Celebrity Cuisine, 87 - Celestial Court, 88, 90 - Michelin, 91 - Chesa, 92 - Michelin, 93 - Chilli Fagara, 94 - China Tang, 95 - 97 - Michelin, 98 - CIAK - In The Kitchen, 99 - Cocotte, 100 - Michelin / Come-Into Chiu Chow, 101 - Comfort, 102 - Congee and Noodle Shop / Michelin, 103 - Crystal Jade La Mian Xiao Long Bao , 104 - Cuisine Cuisine at The Mira, 105, 106 - Michelin, 107 - Din Tai Fung, 108 - Din Tai Fung / Michelin, 109 - Dong Lai Shun, 110 - Dot Cod, 111 - Michelin, 112 - Dragon King, 113 - Duddell's, 114 - Michelin, 115 - Epure, 116 - Fandango, 117 - Michelin, 118 - Felix, 119 - Fofo by el Willy, 120 - Fook Lam Moon, 121 - Fook Lam Moon , 122 - Forum, 123 - 125 - Michelin, 126 - Fu Sing / Michelin, 127, 128 - Michelin, 129 - Gaddi's, 130 - Michelin, 131 - Giando, 132 - Gin Sai, 133 - Go Ya, 134 - Gold, 135 - Golden Leaf, 136 - Michelin / Golden Valley, 137 - Gonpachi, 138, 139 - Michelin, 140 - Grand Hyatt Steakhouse, 141 - Grissini, 142 - Guo Fu Lou, 143, 144 - Michelin, 145 - Ho Hung Kee, 146 - Michelin, 147 - Holytan Grill, 148 - Michelin, 149 - Hugo's, 150 - IM Teppanyaki & Wine, 151 - Inakaya, 152 - Island Tang, 153 - Jardin de Jade, 154 - Jin Cuisine, 155 - Inakaya, 156 - Michelin, 157 - Kam's Roast Goose, 158 - Michelin, 159 - Kazuo Okada, 160 - Michelin, 161 - Michelin / Kin's Kitchen, 162 - Michelin, 163 - Kwan Kee Bamboo Noodle, 164 - La Saison, 165 - L'Altro, 166 - Michelin, 167 - L'Atelier de Joël Robuchon, 168 - Michelin, 169 - Le Soleil, 170 - Le Souk / Michelin, 171 - Lei Bistro, 172 - 180 - Lei Garden , 181 - 184 - Michelin, 185 - Lobster Bar and Grill, 186, 187 - Michelin, 188 - Lung King Heen / Michelin, 189 - Man Wah, 190 - Michelin / Mandarin Grill + Bar, 191 - Mask of Sichuen & Beijing, 192 - Michelin, 193 - Megan's Kitchen, 194 - MIC Kitchen, 195 - Ming Court, 196 - Moon Thai, 197 - Mott 32, 198, 199 - Nanxiang Steamed Bun, 200 - New Shanghai, 201 - Michelin, 202 - Nicholinis, 204 - No.5 Italian (Tai Hang), 205 - Nobu, 206 - Noodlemi, 207 - NUR, 208 - Olé, 209 - On Lot 10, 210 - One Harbour Road, 211 - Michelin/8½ Otto e Mezzo - Bombana, 212 - Michelin, 213, 214 - Peking Garden, 215 - Penthouse, 216 - Petrus, 217 - Pierre / Michelin, 218 - Michelin, 219 - Qi, 220 - Ramen Jo, 221 - Restoran Indonesia 1968, 222 - Ryu Gin, 223 - Sabah (Wan Chai), 224, 225 - Michelin, 226 - Seasons, 227 - Michelin, 228 - Serge et le Phoque, 229 - Seventh Son, 230 - Sha Tin 18, 231 - Shang Palace, 232 - Shanghai Garden, 233 - Shanghai Min , 234, 235 - Michelin, 236, 237 - Shugetsu Ramen, 238 - Sing Kee, 239 - 241 - Michelin, 242 - Sorabol, 243 - Spoon by Alain Ducasse/Michelin, 244 - Spring Moon, 245 - St Betty, 246 - Steik World Meats, 247 - Summer Palace, 248 - Michelin, 249, 250 - Sun Tung Lok, 251 - Michelin, 252 - Michelin / Sushi Ginza Iwa, 253 - Sushi Rozan, 254 - Sushi Shikon/Michelin, 255 - Sushi Ta-ke, 256 - Michelin, 257 - Tai Woo, 258 - Michelin, 259 - T'ang Court, 260 - Tasty , 261 - Tate, 262,

NOTES
備註

NOTES
備註

NOTES
備註